Priorities for the Conservation of Mammalian Diversity
Has the Panda had its day?

Recent analyses have shown that about a quarter of all mammal species are threatened with extinction. At the same time, the conservation movement is moving rapidly away from a traditional 'protectionist' approach to nature to a more integrated view of wildlife and landscape conservation, within the context of human use. This volume provides the first review of modern conservation approaches as they relate to mammals. Bringing together both researchers and conservation managers, it presents perspectives on issues relating to the role of mammals within the conservation movement, how priorities should be set and funds allocated within mammalian conservation and which techniques and approaches are likely to be most successful in conserving mammals in the twenty-first century. The focus on mammals allows issues of broader conservation relevance to be highlighted, including the integration of species- and biodiversity-approaches to conservation, the role of 'flagship species' and the need to develop holistic conservation models that relate to the broader context of society and government.

ABIGAIL ENTWISTLE is Senior Scientist at Fauna & Flora International, where she has worked on a broad range of conservation issues from biological surveys to the development of National Biodiversity Strategies and Action Plans. Her particular interest is in the integration of conservation biology research into policy development and project management.

NIGEL DUNSTONE is Lecturer in Zoology at the Centre for Tropical Ecology, Department of Biological Sciences in the University of Durham. He is a member of the Cat Specialist group of the IUCN Species Survival Commission, and a consultant on the impact of introduced species of mammals and on ecotourism development. He is author of *The Mink* (1993), and co-editor of *Mammals as Predators* (1993) with M. L. Gorman, *The Exploitation of Mammal Populations* (1996) with V. J. Taylor, and *Behaviour and Ecology of Riparian Mammals* (1999) with M. L. Gorman.

Conservation Biology series

Conservation biology is a flourishing field, but there is still enormous potential for making further use of the science that underpins it. This new series aims to present internationally significant biology. It will focus on topics where basic theory is strong and where there are pressing problems for practical conservation. The series will include both single authored and edited volumes and will adopt a direct and accessible style targeted at interested undergraduates, postgraduates, researchers and university teachers. Books and chapters will be rounded, authoritative accounts of particular areas, with the emphasis on review rather than on original data papers. The series is the result of a collaboration between the Zoological Society of London and Cambridge University Press. The series editor is Professor Morris Gosling, of the University of Newcastle. We hold the common belief that there are unexploited areas of basic science that can help define conservation biology and bring a radical new agenda to the solution of pressing conservation problems.

Published Titles

1. *Conservation in a Changing World*, edited by Georgina M. Mace, Andrew Balmford & Joshua R. Ginsberg 0 521 63270 6 (hardback), 0 521 63445 8 (paperback).

2. *Behaviour and Conservation*, edited by L. M. Gosling & William J. Sutherland 0 521 66230 3 (hardback), 0 521 66539 6 (paperback).

Priorities for the Conservation of Mammalian Diversity
Has the Panda had its day?

Edited by
ABIGAIL ENTWISTLE
Flora & Fauna International
and
NIGEL DUNSTONE
University of Durham

CAMBRIDGE
UNIVERSITY PRESS

PUBLISHED BY THE PRESS SYNDICATE OF THE UNIVERSITY OF CAMBRIDGE
The Pitt Building, Trumpington Street, Cambridge, United Kingdom

CAMBRIDGE UNIVERSITY PRESS
The Edinburgh Building, Cambridge CB2 2RU, UK   http://www.cup.cam.ac.uk
40 West 20th Street, New York, NY 10011–4211, USA   http://www.cup.org
10 Stamford Road, Oakleigh, Melbourne 3166, Australia
Ruiz de Alarcón 13, 28014 Madrid, Spain

First published 2000

Printed in the United Kingdom at the University Press, Cambridge

Typeset in FF Scala 9.75/13 pt [VN]

A catalogue record for this book is available from the British Library

Library of Congress Cataloguing in Publication data

Priorities for the conservation of mammalian diversity: has the panda had its day? /
Abigail Entwistle and Nigel Dunstone
    p. cm.   (Conservation biology ; 3)
    Includes bibliographical references (p.).
    ISBN 0 521 77279 6 (hardback)   ISBN 0 521 77536 1 (paperback)
    1. Mammals.   2. Wildlife conservation.   3. Biological diversity.   I. Entwistle, Abigail,
1970–   II. Dunstone, N. (Nigel)   III. Conservation biology series (Cambridge, England) ; 3.
QL703.P75   2000
33.95'416–dc21   99–053250

ISBN 0 521 77279 6 hardback
ISBN 0 521 77536 1 paperback

Contents

Contributors

ELLEN ANDRESEN
Department of Zoology, University of
Florida, Gainesville, FL 32611, USA

ANDREW BALMFORD
Department of Zoology, University of
Cambridge, Downing Street,
Cambridge CB2 3EJ, UK

RICHARD E. BODMER
Department of Wildlife Ecology and
Conservation and Center for Latin
American Studies, University of
Florida, Gainesville, FL 32611, USA

PAUL W. BRIGHT
School of Biological Sciences, Royal
Holloway, University of London,
Egham, Surrey TW20 0EX, UK

NEIL BURGESS
Danish Centre for Tropical Biodiversity,
University of Copenhagen, DK-2100,
Copenhagen Ø, Denmark

TIM M. CARO
Department of Wildlife, Fish and
Conservation Biology, University of
California, Davis, CA 95616 USA

HOLLY T. DUBLIN
WWF Africa and Madagascar
Programme, P. O. Box 62440, Nairobi,
Kenya

NIGEL DUNSTONE
Department of Biological Sciences,
University of Durham, South Road,
Durham DHI 3LE, UK

ABIGAIL C. ENTWISTLE
Fauna & Flora International, Great
Eastern House, Tenison Road,
Cambridge CB1 2DT, UK

ANNA T. C. FEISTNER
Durrell Wildlife Conservation Trust,
Les Augrès Manor, Jersey JE3 5BP
Channel Islands, UK

HAROLD J. GOODWIN
Tourism, Conservation & Sustainable
Development,
School of Earth & Environmental
Sciences,
University of Greenwich,
Pembroke, Kent ME4 4TB, UK

JOHN HANKS
Peace Parks Foundation, PO Box 227,
Somerset West 7129, South Africa

STEPHEN HARRIS
School of Biological Sciences,
University of Bristol, Woodland Road,
Bristol BS8 1UG, UK

ANNETTE LANJOUW
African Wildlife Foundation, PO Box
48177, Nairobi, Kenya

NIGEL LEADER-WILLIAMS
Durrell Institute of Conservation and
Ecology, Department of Anthropology,
University of Kent at Canterbury,
Canterbury, Kent CT2 7NS, UK

LU ZHI
Wildlife Research Center, Peking
University, Beijing 100871, China

DAVID W. MACDONALD
Wildlife Conservation Research Group,
Department of Zoology, South Parks
Road, Oxford OX1 3PS, UK

GEORGINA M. MACE
Institute of Zoology, Zoological Society
of London, Regent's Park, London
NW1 4RY, UK

KATHY MACKINNON
Global Environment Division, The
World Bank, Washington DC 20433,
USA

JEREMY J. C. MALLINSON
Durrell Wildlife Conservation Trust,
Les Augrès Manor, Jersey JE3 5BP,
Channel Islands, UK

GRAEME MCLAREN
School of Biological Sciences,
University of Bristol, Woodland Road,
Bristol BS8 1UG, UK

JEFFREY A. MCNEELY
IUCN – The World Conservation
Union, Rue Mauverney 28, CH-1196
Gland, Switzerland

SIMON MICKLEBURGH
Fauna & Flora International, Great
Eastern House, Tenison Road,
Cambridge CB1 2DT, UK

MARY MORRIS
School of Biological Sciences, Royal
Holloway, University of London,
Egham, Surrey TW20 0EX, UK

PATRICK A. MORRIS
School of Biological Sciences, Royal
Holloway, University of London,
Egham, Surrey TW20 0EX, UK

CYNTHIA MOSS
African Wildlife Foundation, PO Box
48177, Nairobi, Kenya

PHILIP MURUTHI
African Wildlife Foundation, PO Box
48177, Nairobi, Kenya

PAN WENSHI
Wildlife Research Center, Peking
University, Beijing 100871, China

NEIL PELKEY
Department of Environmental Science
and Policy, University of California,
Davis, CA 95616, USA

PAUL A. RACEY
Department of Zoology, University of
Aberdeen, Tillydrone Avenue, Aberdeen
AB24 2TZ, UK

CARSTEN RAHBEK
Zoological Museum,
University of Copenhagen, DK-2100,
Copenhagen Ø, Denmark

MARCEL REJMÁNEK
Section of Evolution and Ecology,
University of California, Davis, CA
95616, USA

STEVE RUSHTON
Centre for Land Use and Water
Resources Research, University of
Newcastle, Newcastle upon Tyne
NE1 7RU, UK

PRITPAL SOORAE
African Wildlife Foundation, PO Box
48177, Nairobi, Kenya

MARK STANLEY PRICE
African Wildlife Foundation, PO Box
48177, Nairobi, Kenya

PETER J. STEPHENSON
Africa & Madagascar
Programme, WWF International,
CH-1196 Gland, Switzerland

WANG DAJUN
Wildlife Research Center, Peking
University, Beijing 100871, China

WANG HAO
Wildlife Research Center, Peking
University, Beijing 100871, China

PAUL H. WILLIAMS
Biogeography and Conservation
Laboratory, The Natural History
Museum, London SW7 5BD, UK

DEREK YALDEN
School of Biological Sciences,
University of Manchester, Manchester
M13 9PT, UK

ZHU XIAOJIAN
Wildlife Research Center, Peking
University, Beijing 100871, China

Foreword

At the end of the twentieth century, nature conservation as an activity, and as a set of personal and organisational beliefs, is more widely endorsed by the public (and supported by many administrations) than ever before. But the pace and scale of environmental change have accelerated, in too many instances biological resources are deteriorating as a consequence of the actions of people or their governments. By their visibility, vulnerability, and biological importance in ecological systems, mammals have attracted a major share of interest, and significant resources have been dedicated to their conservation. However, not all this effort has met with success and, by its provocative title, this book justifiably challenges the prominence of this group of animals.

In the history of nature conservation, important external initiatives have influenced public policy for the conservation of wildlife. Dominant among these have been the advice of research scientists working in the field and laboratory round the world, and the pressure of informed voluntary conservation organisations. Over the same time, in all legislation, there has been a progressive transition from local or national issues to international conventions (and, in Europe, Community legislation) as the dominant target setters. These influences form recurrent themes in this volume.

Government conservation agencies need the ultimate backing of legal sanction, but the operation of law has shown itself to be an insufficient tool. These chapters remind us that legislation has not halted the deterioration of habitats nor prevented many of the losses documented in this book. In many cases, the causes are attributable to legitimate activities such as the development of natural habitats for agriculture, plantation or other land-uses, drainage and water abstraction, and overstocking of pasture ranges. Worldwide, there has been a failure to control pervasive pollution, including atmospheric acidification.

For successful conservation, it is clear that nations need the convergence of dedicated research scientists, able and willing to tackle the complexity of the issues, informing confident voluntary conservation movements, in turn able to influence committed politicians. These last must understand and then integrate biological, social and economic issues into enforceable regulations. International initiatives can force the pace, but concerned citizens must find routes to influence the policy setters in their own national, regional or local administrations. Contemporary policies place biodiversity firmly in the context of sustainable development. I commend this volume to all who strive to safeguard this precious nature conservation resource for the benefit of those to come. The final message is not without hope.

Earl of Cranbrook
President of Fauna & Flora International

Preface

This volume represents the outcome of a collaboration between two organisations, Fauna & Flora International and The Mammal Society, both of which have a long history of mammalian conservation. The Mammal Society has led research into, and protection of, mammals in Britain for nearly 50 years, and has been actively involved in survey and monitoring over this time. Fauna & Flora International (FFI) has a long record of involvement in various mammalian conservation programmes, dating back to its original foundation in 1903. Over the years, FFI has been involved with a wide range of mammal projects, including the reintroduction of the Arabian oryx into Oman, conservation of mountain gorillas, and the development of some of the first bat conservation campaigns. In planning for this volume, both organisations recognised the need to reevaluate approaches to mammalian conservation, and to challenge some of the assumptions underlying today's conservation programmes. This book represents the outcome of consultation with some of the key leaders in the field of mammalian conservation as to the past, present and future of this discipline.

Many of the ideas in this book were first expressed at a symposium organised by Fauna & Flora International and The Mammal Society in November 1997. At that time the interest in the topic of mammalian conservation was clear not just from the full auditorium and range of opinions expressed therein, but also by the significant media attention the symposium received. This book was developed on the basis of the symposium, but other contributions have since been sought to ensure a well-balanced and synthetic volume.

The ideas expressed within this volume have revealed important principles for the future of the conservation movement, not just for mammals, but also for other taxonomic groups. Many of the ideas expressed here have already been incorporated into conservation programmes, and will help to guide the development of new conservation priorities. The opportunity to reflect on the values we place on mammals, and how these affect our approach to conservation, has in turn helped to determine future directions in the sphere of mammalian conservation.

Of particular interest has been the opportunity to compare approaches at a national level, with international approaches to mammalian conservation, reflecting the involvement of the two organisations with their differing regional interests. It is clear that one of the future priorities for mammalian conservation will be increased cooperation between different sectors and interest-groups, and between NGOs with different remits. This book demonstrates the opportunities offered by such collaboration, not just between the two organisations, but across all the individual contributors and the institutions which they represent.

Mark Rose,
Director,
Fauna & Flora International

Professor Stephen Harris,
Chairman,
The Mammal Society

Acknowledgements

A wide range of people have contributed to the development of this book, and have smoothed the editorial process. In particular we would like to thank Simon Mickleburgh of Fauna & Flora International, for his guidance and direct assistance during the sub-editing and Dorothy Entwistle who copy-edited the volume. Tracey Sanderson at Cambridge University Press gave invaluable advice on the mechanics of preparing this volume for publication. We would like to thank all the contributors for their co-operation, and a group of anonymous referees for review of the manuscripts. This book evolved from a joint FFI/Mammal Society symposium, and we would like to thank all those who helped in the organisation of that meeting, including Fran Tattersall, Kirstie Sawyer, Hugh Baynes, Stephanie Pendry and Evan Bowen-Jones. We would also like to thank all the speakers and those who attended the symposium and helped to make it such a success. Finally we would like to thank Mark Rose of FFI and Steve Harris of The Mammal Society for their support throughout the development of this volume.

Mammal conservation: current contexts and opportunities

ABIGAIL C. ENTWISTLE, SIMON MICKLEBURGH
AND NIGEL DUNSTONE

INTRODUCTION

This volume offers an opportunity to reflect on, and reconsider, the role of mammals within the conservation movement. In doing so we hope to identify future directions and priorities within this discipline, and to explore the relationship between single species approaches and conservation of biodiversity (including mammalian diversity). In this we will attempt to answer the question in the subtitle of this book ('Has the panda had its day?'), in which the panda implicitly represents traditional species-focused conservation approaches. In developing this volume we considered the current status of mammalian conservation, and identified a series of issues and questions which are outlined in this chapter. These in turn served as the framework for the subsequent development of the rest of this volume.

It would seem to many people that mammals receive a disproportionate amount of attention within conservation, and in books about conservation. This relatively small class comprising around 4500 species (many fewer compared, for instance, to insects or fish), has long been the focus, and often the catalyst, for conservation efforts. Why then produce a book focused specifically upon the conservation of mammals, especially when many other, less charismatic, taxa appear to receive so little attention? Historically the conservation movement developed in response to perceived declines in mammal populations, particularly those of large species, such as carnivores, elephants and rhinos (Fitter and Scott, 1978). Since then, mammals have continued to be the focus for a broad range of conservation programmes, and have often provided the models for management approaches then applied to other groups. However, it is not clear how successful mammalian conservation has actually been. Despite the long history of mammalian conservation and the willingness to take action to protect these species, recent reviews indicate that over 25% of mammal species face some risk of extinction (IUCN, 1996). If we cannot conserve mammals – with their strong inherent appeal – the question must be, what can we conserve? If conservation of mammals is failing, then the reasons why and the ways forward need to be identified, not just for the benefit of mammals, but also to provide information relevant to other taxonomic groups. There is clearly a need for all involved in conservation to reassess on a regular basis their criteria for action. Only by questioning and re-examining progress can we identify new perspectives and directions for the conservation work that we undertake.

VALUES PLACED ON MAMMALS

People care about mammals. In general the risk of extinction faced by gorillas or whales appears to have a greater emotional impact for the general public than loss of rainforest habitat or degradation of the coral reefs. Many species of mammals have assumed important cultural significance in some human societies, and have been idolised in various cultures such as the Ancient Egyptians and native Americans. In many countries, including Britain, mammals have important symbolism (consider, for example, the lion rampant as a symbol of strength and of royalty). Certain mammals release a strong emotional response in a broad range of people, as is well demonstrated by our desire to eat livestock, yet disgust at the utilisation of many other species (such as large African ungulates, cats or dogs) as a resource exploited by local communities elsewhere in the world.

The emotional appeal of mammals affects their conservation in many positive and negative ways. On the one hand, the appeal of these animals has been harnessed for fundraising, and 'flagship species' of mammals are often used as symbols promoting conservation (consider the use of the giant panda by WWF, the oryx by FFI and even the humble hedgehog by The Mammal Society). However, the emotional appeal of mammals often makes decisions about their management contentious. In many cases judgements about mammal conservation, based on recommendations from quantitative approaches and scientific analysis may be difficult to reconcile, particularly when emotional feelings about mammals run high. Strong views are frequently expressed, and differing opinions and standpoints often appear irreconcilable. As we write, the debate about the lifting of the ban on the ivory trade has once again emerged, with the first sale of ivory by three African countries in 10 years having just commenced (Trent,

1999). Similar issues are raised by the bushmeat trade, when the ethical and emotional impacts of hunting of primates, including great apes, are contrasted with the needs of local populations to provide for themselves (Redmond, 1995). Thus the issue of mammalian conservation can become mired in confusion and conflict between emotional and scientific evaluations, values and judgements, as well as differing attitudes between Western donors and local communities. This is well illustrated when we consider mammals as a resource, and the need for their conservation in terms of not just their potential attractiveness (e.g., for tourists), but also as a source of food and other materials (see Taylor and Dunstone, 1996). If we are aiming to develop more integrated and defensible approaches to mammalian conservation, how do we reconcile disparate emotional and scientific judgements about mammals? Who are we conserving mammals for and why? Ultimately, who should make decisions about the future of mammalian conservation?

BIODIVERSITY AND MAMMALIAN CONSERVATION

With a shift towards a 'systems' and integrated 'biodiversity' approach to conservation (e.g., Heywood, 1995), there is an increasing question regarding the role of single-species programmes within conservation. This is particularly relevant to mammals, where much of the conservation effort has seen a species (or species assemblage) focus. Obviously a single-species approach is particularly important where valued taxa are at particular risk of extinction, and can only be saved by targeted intervention, and action planning should reflect the value which we place on certain species. The question 'Has the panda had its day?' examines how far such single-species intervention can now go, given an increased global emphasis on the conservation of integrated systems. The relationship between single-species conservation and biodiversity has been made through the use of flagship species and through 'umbrella species', by which focus on one species serves to protect the ecosystem it inhabits, and consequentially other sympatric species. However, the underlying assumptions for this argument have rarely been assessed, and the true worth of single-species approaches for biodiversity conservation may vary dramatically from species to species, and project to project. We need to consider the role of species-driven conservation programmes in achieving truly effective protection of biodiversity and ecosystems. If we are to use flagship species, how can we ensure they will be most effective in achieving broader biodiversity goals?

Similar issues are raised specifically concerning the conservation of maximal mammalian diversity. Relatively few mammal species receive direct conservation attention, and the question of protecting mammalian diversity rather than individual species is rarely considered. Although, some mammalian assemblages (such as savannah ungulates) are managed as a group, in general the need to maximise mammalian diversity is rarely considered in conservation planning. However, if our ultimate aim is to protect ecosystem integrity and function, this may need to be addressed. It is not clear to what extent existing protection of particular flagship mammal species actually also protects the overall species richness of mammals as well. Given that 25 % of mammal species are now considered at risk (IUCN, 1996), there is a danger that a quarter of our mammalian diversity could be lost in coming years unless this issue is addressed, and single-species approaches are likely to be insufficient to achieve broader mammalian conservation. We need to consider how we should conserve mammals – should they be targeted as a separate group or within a larger system? Is a biodiversity approach sufficient to protect all mammals, or do some species have special needs?

MAMMALIAN 'FLAGSHIPS' AND CONSERVATION

The conservation of mammals is frequently carried out in the public eye and often attracts considerable media attention. For this reason it cannot be a closed discipline, but is instead open to external pressures, interest and controversy. The issue of public interest and concern frequently lies at the heart of how conservation is funded – not only for mammal projects – but for a broader 'biodiversity' approach as well. The promotional potential of mammals makes them important fundraising tools. The sight of a distressed mammal often provides a greater incentive for charitable funding than do pictures of habitat loss, even though the latter represents the ultimate threat to these species

However, the use of flagship species for conservation campaigns may create an unrealistic perspective of what conservation actually entails. Such expectations may be at odds with the reality of biodiversity conservation – often dealing with problems and creating solutions far removed from target species or their habitats. In most cases such approaches can be reconciled with a species-focused funding mechanism, however there are other instances where there appears to be a risk of 'public feeling' itself driving the conservation initiative. In such cases it must be asked whether the use of flagship species is setting its own conservation agenda. Does public interest in particular mammals and species-focused fundraising affect the way in which conservation programmes are developed? Can the use of mammals as fundraising tools be reconciled with the need for objectivity in setting priorities for conservation?

GLOBAL PERSPECTIVES AND NATIONAL CONSERVATION ISSUES

As many countries develop and extend policies on biodiversity, in response to the Convention on Biological Diversity, there is an increased recognition of the global links within conservation. This provides an opportunity for sharing and comparing the different approaches and activities implemented in countries with very different conditions and contexts for biodiversity conservation. Given the involvement of two organisations in the development of this book (one focused on UK and the other on international conservation), this provides a specific opportunity to compare the situation and needs for mammalian conservation in the UK with that elsewhere in the world.

UK conservation has its roots in the gentlemen naturalists of the eighteenth and nineteenth centuries (e.g., Thomas Bewick and others), and since then we have seen major impacts on our wildlife, including the decline and extinction of a number of mammal species. While scarcely a role model for effective mammalian conservation, the UK serves as an example of conservation of mammal populations in intensively managed agricultural landscapes. Mammalian conservation in the UK is in many ways a last ditch stand against further loss, and there are many lessons to be learnt for effective conservation under increasing human pressure on a small land area.

However, a national conservation movement also has much to gain from experiences in other countries. There is often a perceived gap between the issues of conservation elsewhere (e.g., the false glamour of conservation of the charismatic African megafauna) and grassroots conservation in our own backyard. Given the recent losses of Sites of Special Scientific Interest (SSSIs) in the UK it can be argued that we have much to learn from the evolving conservation movement in developing countries.

The attitudes of people in the West towards mammals and their relationships with humans often differ dramatically from those expressed by people whose backyards are frequently invaded by elephants and other potentially dangerous (but glamorous) large mammals (Stephenson and Entwistle, in preparation). Similar divisions also exist in our own countries between conservationists and land owners, including farmers, who wish to mitigate the constraints imposed by a system of protected areas. We need to consider what elements of conservation approaches elsewhere in the world have a direct bearing on how we approach conservation closer to home, wherever that may be.

REVIEWING MAMMALIAN CONSERVATION – FUTURE PRIORITIES FOR THE CONSERVATION OF MAMMALIAN DIVERSITY

This book aims to examine the current success of and approaches to mammalian conservation, and to ultimately decide how this discipline could be strengthened and further evolve in future years. A number of questions about mammalian conservation have already been posed, and many of these points are addressed by the various contributors to this volume.

In order to organise and focus the thoughts of authors and readers alike, the book has been divided into three sections – although many of the same themes recur throughout. An attempt is made to synthesise these themes and identify overall conclusions in the final chapter.

The first section addresses the question of 'why we should conserve mammals?' – this provides some justifications for the specific reasons why mammals might continue to remain high on the conservation agenda. These range from ecological justifications (such as their role in ecosystems, exemplified by their role as seed dispersers; Andresen, chapter 2), through examination of actual conservation status (Mace and Balmford, chapter 3), to more pragmatic approaches – including a review of the use of mammals as flagship and umbrella species (Leader-Williams and Dublin, chapter 4). This section aims to provide a brief introduction to what the priorities might be for conservation of mammals in a more general context, and why continued focus on mammals is likely to be of importance within conservation.

The second section of the book examines 'what to protect?' – how different mammal species are prioritised, and how assessment of priority might be made. This ranges from how key sites for mammals can be selected (Williams *et al.*, chapter 5) to possible revisions of how assessment of threat should be made (Harris *et al.*, chapter 6). In addition, two chapters consider from different perspectives the relative priorities that might be put on smaller mammals (Entwistle and Stephenson, chapter 7) and particularly on rarer species (Bright and Morris, chapter 8).

The third section of the book is the largest, and examines previous and future approaches to mammalian conservation. Within this section are contained reviews of the success of different mechanisms for mammalian conservation – including research and legislation (Racey, chapter 9), monitoring and enhancement (Macdonald *et al.*, chapter 10), protected areas (Caro *et al.*, chapter 12; Muruthi *et al.*, chapter 11) and international (transboundary) cooperation over protected areas (Hanks, chapter 13). This section also reviews opportunities for exploitation of mammals in different ways – both as subsistence food or bushmeat (Bodmer, chapter 15) and as a source of ecotourism revenue (Goodwin and Leader-Williams, chapter 14). The role of *ex situ* conservation for different types of mammals is examined (Balmford, chapter 16), while holistic approaches based on successful partnerships are examined as a means for effective conservation (Feistner and Mallinson, chapter 17). In particular, the case of the giant panda – as a high profile flagship – is considered, and the changes in conservation approaches on the basis of new research and new opinions is examined (Lu *et al.*, chapter 18). As well as these reviews and indications for future directions in mammal conservation, some further chapters provide specific viewpoints on the future of mammalian conservation, including chapters examining the global requirements for integrating mammals within biodiversity management systems and for gaining high level political support (MacKinnon, chapter 19; McNeely, chapter 20).

Overall, the organisation of the chapters is an attempt to rationalise our approaches to mammalian conservation, within the broader context of biodiversity. Although each chapter represents an important contribution in its own right, it is hoped that recurring generalities and the breadth of issues covered by the different contributors will increase our collective understanding of what mammalian conservation may require over the coming decades.

PART 1

Justifying the conservation of mammals

The chapters in this section consider some of the reasons why mammals remain so high on the conservation agenda, compared to other groups. Although it is not comprehensive, this section presents a number of key issues which may justify the conservation of mammals. These include:

- The ecological roles of mammals (illustrated here through a single example – that of seed dispersal – a role more typically associated with avifauna).
- The conservation status of mammals, in relation to other groups, and in regard to trends and patterns in the level of threat between different orders of mammals.
- More pragmatic arguments linked to the use of mammalian species as flagships, and the appeal that many mammals have for the general public.

Other important justifications for conserving mammals, beyond the scope of this section – but touched on elsewhere in this volume, include the economic importance of mammals (particularly their direct value through hunting), and the varied cultural associations for mammals held by different societies across the world.

In this section we attempt to examine how the reasons why we protect mammals can be applied to both species level conservation, and to broader issues relating to the protection of mammalian diversity. However, the challenge over future years may be to integrate the different justifications for mammalian conservation, and harness the emotional appeal of mammals so that conservation programmes focused on single species also serve to meet the scientific justifications for the protection of mammalian diversity overall.

Ecological roles of mammals: the case of seed dispersal

ELLEN ANDRESEN

INTRODUCTION

Mammals account for a substantial proportion of the animal biomass in most terrestrial habitats. Terrestrial mammals display an enormous variation in body size, utilise many types of food, and occupy almost all trophic levels. It is therefore not surprising that mammals can have a great impact on their environments. Through their activity, mammals directly or indirectly affect the populations of other animals and plants, influencing the structure and composition of biotic communities. In some grassland ecosystems, for example, herbivorous mammals have been shown to stimulate grass productivity which in turn favours other animals (McNaughton, 1979). In other ecosystems several mammal species affect the nutrient dynamics of soil, indirectly affecting the functioning of plant communities. Some mammal species have even been identified as 'keystone species' because changes in their populations cause many changes in the community. Prairie dogs (*Cynomys* spp.), for example, are thought to act as a keystone species in some North American grassland ecosystems. Prairie dogs favour the survival of many animals that depend on their extensive burrow systems, and they also seem to be important in maintaining grasslands by preventing woody plants from establishing or attaining dominance (Weltzin *et al.*, 1997).

A group of mammals that has a large direct influence on plant populations, and on plant community structure and composition, is that which disperses the seeds of plants. Seed dispersal is an essential process in plant reproduction, and is a crucial life history phase. Most of the mortality in a plant's life occurs during the early seed and seedling stages. Therefore, any process, such as seed dispersal, that conveys a higher chance of survival to plant propagules can have a significant effect on the fitness of those plant species.

Most commonly, mammals disperse seeds when feeding on fruits. Eight families of mammals, containing approximately 460 species, have primarily frugivorous diets (Fleming and Sosa, 1994), and 19 additional mammalian families have species that are at least partially frugivorous and that disperse viable seeds after swallowing them (Howe, 1986). Additionally, several families of rodents include species that store seeds for future consumption. These rodents also act as effective dispersers for the stored seeds that they fail to recover. Finally, mammals also disperse seeds that attach to their fur, or that are accidentally ingested as part of other food items.

Traditionally, most studies on seed dispersing vertebrates focused on the role played by frugivorous birds and to some extent bats. In the last decade, however, the role that non-flying mammal species play in plant regeneration through seed dispersal has been given increasing attention. Although much of the information comes from studies focusing on the diets of mammals, recent studies have also addressed the consequences of mammal seed dispersal from the plant's perspective, bridging the gap between animal feeding ecology and plant demography. Thus, it is now possible to better assess the role that seed dispersing mammals play on the regeneration of plant species, and ultimately on plant community structure and composition.

In this chapter I will review the current knowledge on seed dispersal by fruit- and seed-eating mammals, focusing particularly on those fruit–frugivore systems in tropical forests that appear to play a crucial role in plant recruitment and/or community structure and composition. In order to better understand the importance of the role that seed-dispersing mammals can play in plant communities, I will start by briefly describing why seed dispersal is important for plant reproduction, and how plants accomplish it. Then, I will address the specific case of seed dispersal by fruit/seed-eating mammals: the fruit–frugivore mutualism, focusing on mammal seed dispersal in tropical forests. Finally, I will stress the interdependence of fruit-bearing plants and their mammal consumers in tropical forests, pointing out the risks involved in the loss of fruiting plants and seed-dispersing animals.

THE WHY AND HOW OF SEED DISPERSAL

Advantages of seed dispersal

Plants started evolving structures and mechanisms for seed dispersal at least 300 million years ago (Tiffney, 1986). Since then, seed dispersal adaptations have appeared independently many times in plants of diverse origins (Mack, 1993). It is thus reasonable to assume that the dispersal of seeds away from parent plants must be advantageous for many plant species. Howe and Smallwood (1982) recognised three main advantages of seed dispersal from the plant's perspective.

(1)   Escape from detrimental conditions in the vicinity of the parent plant. The rationale behind this hypothesis is that seed/seedling predators and pathogens will be more active where their resources are more common. Most seeds fall directly under the crown of the parent plant, and their density decreases with increasing distance from the parent. This hypothesis predicts that seeds/seedlings dispersed some distance away from the parent tree have a much higher chance of survival than do those that are close to the parent.

(2)   Colonisation of scattered favourable sites. According to this hypothesis, the habitat where a plant grows is continually changing. As a consequence, favourable sites for seed/seedling survival are unpredictable in both space and time. The strategy of the parent plant in such a situation should be to disperse as many seeds as possible, as widely as possible, so that some will encounter a favourable spot, or lie dormant until such conditions arrive.

(3)   Directed dispersal to predictable favourable sites. According to this hypothesis, the dispersal agents take seeds that require specific conditions for survival and/or seedling growth to non-random places, where survival of seeds/seedlings will predictably be better than in random sites.

These three advantages are not exclusive and may act simultaneously. The relative importance of each dispersal advantage depends on the plant species, and may even vary among plant populations of the same species.

How are seeds dispersed?

The ways in which plants can disperse their seeds can be classified into three general groups: (1) self-dispersal, which is present in plants that disperse their seeds themselves, through explosive or creeping fruits; (2) abiotic dispersal, which includes fruits/seeds adapted for wind and water dispersal; and (3) biotic dispersal, which is accomplished by animals.

Biotic dispersal can be subdivided into four types, according to the way the animals acquire the fruit/seed.

(1) Passive-external, when the fruit/seed, through the presence of sticky substances or hooks, adheres to the external surface of animals and becomes dislodged again after the animal has moved a variable distance.

(2) Passive-internal, when fruits/seeds are accidentally ingested as part of some other food. For example, when grazing mammals ingest small seeds whilst foraging on grasses, or when carnivores ingest seeds present in their prey's guts.

(3) Active-external, occurs under two scenarios. When animals with food-hoarding behaviour (mostly ants, rodents, and some bird species) fail to eat the seeds/fruits that they had hoarded for future consumption, or when they lose them during transportation. It also occurs when animals that feed on other parts of the fruit (pulp, aril, elaiosome) discard the seed instead of ingesting it.

(4) Active-internal, occurs when seeds are actively ingested as part of the fruit, and later discarded through defecation. This type of dispersal is accomplished mostly by frugivorous birds and mammals, although in certain habitats or for certain plant species, reptiles, amphibians and fishes can also be important seed dispersers.

Only the last two forms of biotic dispersal can be viewed as mutualistic relationships between plants and animals. Animals may depend as much on the fruits/seeds they eat, as the plants depend on their animal consumers to attain effective seed dispersal. It is on these types of animal dispersal that I will focus the rest of the chapter.

Fruits and frugivores

In most ecosystems, a large proportion of plants disperse their seeds through frugivorous animals, mostly producing fleshy fruits to attract the frugivores. The percentage of all seed plants that have fleshy fruits is highest in forest ecosystems (48 %), lower in shrublands (20 %), and grasslands (13 %), and very low in alpine communities (6 %) and deserts (2 %). Among forest communities, tropical rain forests have the highest percentages of fleshy fruits (77 %), this percentage is lower in more seasonal tropical forests (66 %), and lowest in montane tropical forests (41 %) and temperate forests (36 %) (Willson et al., 1989). When distinctions are made between different plant growth forms, the highest percentage of plants with fleshy fruits is found among trees in tropical forests (78–98 %), whereas it is found among shrubs and vines in temperate forests (85–100 %) (Howe and Smallwood, 1982). Regarding the relative frequencies of birds and mammals as dispersal agents, birds are the most important dispersers for temperate forests and shrublands habitats (Willson, 1986), while both birds and mammals are probably equally important in many tropical forests (Terborgh, 1986a).

Although these are broad generalisations, and great variability exists both between and within geographic regions and ecosystem types, active seed dispersal by animals seems to be most important in tropical forests. Because of this, and because it is in these ecosystems that fruit-eating mammals play their most conspicuous role as seed dispersers, I will focus the next sections of this chapter on fruit-eating mammals in tropical forests.

FRUGIVORY AND SEED DISPERSAL BY MAMMALS IN TROPICAL FORESTS

In tropical forests, most mammal species have at least partially frugivorous diets, and frugivores often make up the largest proportion of the mammalian biomass (Terborgh, 1986a). The importance of fruits for mammalian frugivores has been clearly shown by studies that document behavioural shifts in response to periods of fruit scarcity. Some mammals have been shown to reproduce only when fruit availability is high while others exploit less preferred food items when fruit is scarce. Still other species have a flexible social system that allows them to forage in smaller groups during times of low fruit production and some even engage in long-distance migrations in search of fruit.

In spite of the obviously mutualistic nature of the fruit–frugivore relationship, great variability characterises this plant–animal interaction. From the animal's perspective, there is not only the seasonal variability associated with the phenological cycles of plants, but there is also variability in terms of number of fruiting species and trees in a given year, fruit crop sizes, and number of competing frugivores. From the plant's perspective, there is variability in the number and identity of the frugivores dispersing its fruits in a given year, number of seeds dispersed by each species, and treatment of the seeds by frugivores.

Because of this variability, frugivores do not depend on a single fruit species as food source and most plants do not depend on a single frugivore species for the dispersal of its seeds. Sometimes the disperser assemblage of a plant species is extensive, encompassing many species of birds and mammals. Other times a plant species relies on a smaller number of frugivores, which may be restricted to a taxonomic group (e.g., birds, bats, rodents, primates), or an ecological group (e.g., flying frugivores, arboreal mammals, terrestrial mammals). Only on rare occasions are plant species dispersed by one or a few animal species.

Since mammals encompass such a broad array of body sizes and inhabit all layers in a tropical forest (from ground to canopy), most plants that are dispersed by other animals are generally also dispersed by some mammal species. What is important from the plant's perspective, however, is the effectiveness of a given disperser species, which is defined by the quantity of seeds dispersed, and the quality of dispersal. Animals can easily be compared in terms of dispersal quantity, but the quality of dispersal is difficult to assess since it depends on the post-dispersal fate of seeds. Thus, it is often not known if mammals are more effective dispersers for a plant species than other groups of animals. Many cases exist, however, in which mammals play a crucial role in a plant's reproduction, either because they are the only consumers, or because they convey a clear survival advantage to the seeds they disperse, compared to seeds dispersed by other groups of animals. Seed dispersing mammals are not only important in assisting a plant species in its reproduction, but they can also play a role in determining the patterns of spatial distribution of plants, affecting forest structure and composition.

In the next sections I will describe in more detail some of the examples in which mammal seed dispersers play an important role in plant reproduction and/or forest structure, focusing on four groups of mammalian seed dispersers in tropical forests: primates; bats; rodents; and large terrestrial mammals.

Primates

Primate communities can be very diverse in tropical forests, consisting of up to 14 different species in some neotropical and African forests, and constituting a very high proportion of the vertebrate frugivore biomass (Terborgh, 1983; Fleming et al., 1987). Most primates in tropical forests include a large amount of fruits in their diets (Chapman, 1995). Aside from a few species that prey on seeds, primates disperse a high proportion of viable seeds for the majority of plant species whose fruits they consume.

The treatment of seeds passing through primates' gut is generally benign and most studies report no effect, or a positive effect on germination.

Primates often include many different fruit species in their diets, and lists of over 50 plants dispersed by single species are common in the literature. Additionally, due to their average large size when compared to other arboreal mammals and birds, primates can ingest large quantities of fruits in each feeding bout. Consequently, not only the number of species but also the number of seeds dispersed by monkeys can be very high. On average, primates also have longer gut passage times than smaller frugivores, and seeds can potentially be dispersed very long distances.

A possible negative consequence of both the large quantity of fruits ingested each day, and the long gut retention times, is that large primates may disperse many seeds in a clumped distribution pattern (Howe, 1980). Seeds dispersed in this manner may suffer, similarly to seeds that fall under the parent tree, from intense sibling competition and/or high predator/pathogen attack. However, most of the tropical forest primates are arboreal, and as they defecate from the trees, the seed/dung clumps hit several layers of vegetation before reaching the ground, thus producing a more scattered seed rain pattern. Additionally, secondary seed dispersers often move the seeds dispersed by primates, thus changing the initial distribution of dispersed seeds. Dung beetles, for example, play an important role as secondary dispersers of seeds dispersed through primate defecation in the Amazon forest, burying a large proportion of the seeds and enhancing their survival probability (Andresen, 1999).

Many primates also disperse seeds through spitting them after removing the pulp or aril. This mode of seed dispersal is most common in Old World monkeys that have cheek pouches. Primate seed dispersal, either through defecation or spitting, is probably crucial for many plant species that have large seeds and/or fruits with hard husks. Since the ability to swallow a seed depends on fruit/seed size relative to the size of the frugivore, the seeds of many tropical forest trees cannot be swallowed by even the largest avian frugivores, and are only dispersed by mammals. Similarly, other plant species produce fruits that cannot be consumed by seed-dispersing birds because they have a hard protective husk that requires manipulative and biting abilities to reach the pulp. Therefore, primates, together with other arboreal mammals, may be the most important seed dispersers of these plant species.

Many studies have reported the presence of such fruits in the diets of primates. For example, in parts of Amazonia, howler monkeys (*Alouatta* spp.) are the main dispersers of tree species in the Sapotaceae family, which have fruits with hard coats and/or large seeds that most birds and small mammals cannot ingest (Julliot, 1996). In the forests of French

Guiana, howler monkeys ate the fruits of 21 Sapotaceae species (Julliot, 1996), and in Brazil, the seeds of over 35 species of Sapotaceae were found in the faeces of this primate (E. Andresen, unpublished data). In Brazil, Spironello (unpublished data) studied the assemblage of animals feeding on the fruits of nine Sapotaceae species. He found that the seeds of only one of the species were occasionally dispersed by toucans, and that all other seed dispersal was accomplished by arboreal mammals, most importantly howler and capuchin monkeys (*Cebus* spp.). Similarly, in a forest in Surinam, van Roosmalen (1985) found that spider monkeys (*Ateles* spp.) were probably the only dispersal agent for several large-seeded tree species that were not dispersed by large birds or smaller arboreal mammals.

Another example in which one primate species may be the most important dispersal agent in terms of plant fitness, is the case of lowland gorillas *Gorilla gorilla gorilla* in Gabon, and two of the large-seeded species they disperse. For one of the species, *Ganophyllum giganteum*, gorillas remove most of the total fruit crop, while for *Cola lizae*, gorillas are the only species to swallow the seeds (Rogers *et al.*, 1998). Additionally, seedling survival and growth is highest in some gorilla nest sites.

Seed dispersal by gorillas is not only important for the reproduction of plants, but through their feeding and ranging behaviour, these primates are also affecting the spatial distribution of plants. A few other studies have also suggested that the seed dispersal and foraging activities of primates can cause the patchy distribution of the plant species they disperse. Julliot (1997), for example, found that howler monkeys in French Guiana deposit about 40 % of their defecations under sleeping trees. Sleeping trees are often used repetitively over time, and this behaviour is probably responsible for the fact that densities of seedlings of six plant species were four times higher under sleeping trees than in other places.

Finally, primate frugivores probably play crucial roles as seed dispersers in areas where other frugivores are absent or have disappeared. For example, in Singapore and the montane forests of Madagascar, where many large frugivores are absent, the dispersal of some large-seeded plants may be dependents on macaques (*Macaca* spp.) and lemurs, respectively (Corlett and Lucas, 1990; Dew and Wright, 1998). Similarly, some primate species are able to survive long-term in the small isolated forest fragments that often remain after deforestation. In forest fragments most other large frugivores disappear, and many large-seeded plant species probably depend on the surviving populations of primates for reproduction. Howler monkeys, for example, have been reported to survive in fragments of 10 ha or less in Mexico, the Brazilian Amazon, and the Brazilian Atlantic forest

(Neves and Rylands, 1991; Ferrari and Diego, 1995; Estrada and Coates-Estrada, 1996). This suggests that howler monkeys may be the main disperser of many plant species in these disturbed habitats.

Bats

Phyllostomid bats in the New World and pteropodid bats in the Old World include many highly frugivorous species that are important seed dispersers of numerous plant species in tropical forests. In the neotropics at least 96 plant genera are dispersed by at least 96 bat species, while in the palaeotropics 145 plant genera are dispersed by at least 26 bat species in Africa and 66 bat species in southeast Asia (Fleming, 1986; Fleming et al., 1987).

Bats can disperse both small and large seeds. In the case of small seeds, these can be dispersed through defecation when bats swallow whole fruits, or through spitting when bats press the fruit against the palate, squeezing out the juice and spitting out the pulp and seeds. Large seeds can be dropped while flying or after gnawing off the pulp, or, in the case of Old World bats, they can also be ingested and defecated. Some bat species can disperse hundreds of seeds every night. Dispersal distances can be very large, and seed treatment by the bats can even have a positive effect on seed germination.

Diets of frugivorous bats have been found to be quite distinct from those of other frugivorous animals (both birds and mammals), and low dietary overlap between bats and other frugivores exists both in the neotropics and the palaeotropics. This suggests that for many plant species bats may be the only or the most efficient group of seed-dispersing animals. This may be the case of the tree *Cecropia obtusa* in French Guiana, which disperses about 80 % of its fruit crop through bats (Charles-Dominique, 1986). Like *Cecropia*, many other pioneer plant species in tropical forests are dispersed mainly by bats and birds. Birds however, commonly defecate seeds from branches in the edges of forest gaps, while bats often defecate seeds while flying over gaps. Therefore, bats are more likely than birds to deposit the seeds in the more illuminated sites within treefall gaps (Charles-Dominique, 1986). Thus, bats play an important role in the reproduction of these plants, as well as in the successional dynamics of forest gaps and other successional habitats.

Due to the ongoing deforestation and fragmentation of tropical forests, bats may become increasingly important as seed dispersers. In a study in Mexico, Estrada et al. (1993) found that several bat species moved between forest fragments, and also between forest fragments and agricultural habitats. Bats moved up to 8 km between areas, and when captured they defecated or were carrying the seeds of both pioneer and mature forest plant species.

Rodents

Rodents eat seeds, but their interaction with plants is not a simple one, since they also de-husk, move, and store seeds which they may subsequently fail to eat. Consequently, they not only change initial seed numbers, but also their spatial distributions and survival probabilities (Price and Jenkins, 1986). When rodents store seeds for later consumption they act as potential seed dispersers. Seeds hoarded by terrestrial rodents are usually buried under the soil surface or stored under leaf litter. This behaviour may allow seeds to escape consumption by other predators/pathogens, may prevent desiccation, and may accelerate germination (Forget, 1990). Additionally, rodents sometimes take seeds to habitats where conditions for establishment and growth are more suitable (Vander Wall, 1993).

Rodents act as secondary seed dispersers when they move the seeds deposited on the ground by another dispersal agent, thus altering the seed shadow produced by primary dispersal. Alternatively, rodents act as primary dispersers when they remove fruits from the tree crown or fruits/seeds fallen under the trees. For some plant species, rodents may even be the only seed dispersers (e.g., Hallwachs, 1986).

Hoarding behaviour is common in seasonal or unpredictable environments such as temperate forests and deserts, but seed-hoarding rodents are also found in tropical forests. Numerous examples exist for temperate areas in which rodents clearly favour plant reproduction and/or are responsible for observed plant distributions (Price and Jenkins, 1986, and references therein). In some instances seed dispersal by rodents even affects succession rates between habitats (Jensen and Nielsen, 1986).

In tropical forests many species of rodents can coexist, and they act as seed dispersers and predators of numerous plant species. However, due to the difficulty of finding seeds stored by rodents in tropical forests, few studies have attempted to follow the fate of seeds removed by these mammals. Thus, it is likely that the overall role of rodents as seed dispersers in tropical forests has been greatly underestimated. In the last decade, however, several studies have shown the important role that rodents can play in plant recruitment in neotropical forests. In French Guiana the tree *Voucapoua americana* has no arboreal seed disperser, and most of the seeds that fall on the ground are removed by rodents, which hoard almost 70 % of the seeds (Forget, 1990). Seeds are buried individually up to 22 m from the parent tree, and between 15 to 60 % of buried seeds are not eaten by the rodents.

These seeds have a much better chance of establishment than unburied seeds, which are attacked by insects and/or lose their ability to germinate. Similarly, in the same forest, seeds of *Astrocaryum paramaca* and *Carapa procera* are also actively hoarded by rodents, and some seeds survive and establish as seedlings (Forget, 1991, 1996).

Most studies on rodent seed dispersal in tropical forests have focused on large neotropical terrestrial rodents (agoutis *Dasyprocta* spp. and acouchis *Myoprocta* spp.) as dispersers of large-seeded plant species, and little is known about the role of smaller rodents, and the hoarding of small seeds. This is an interesting topic for future research in the seed dispersal ecology of tropical forests.

Large terrestrial mammals

Large terrestrial mammals ingest very large quantities of seeds. Like rodents, these mammals act often as seed predators, and many seeds are destroyed by chewing or by digestion in the gut. However, seeds can escape destruction under several circumstances. Seed size, relative to mammal size, can largely determine whether chewing kills a seed, whether it is swallowed intact, or whether it is spat out. Seeds that are small relative to their consumer, often escape being chewed. Because of this, very small seeds are probably dispersed by all terrestrial mammals that ingest them, while large seeds avoid being destroyed only when ingested by the largest mammals in the community. Additionally, seeds that are large relative to the size of their consumer, or that are very hard, are often spat out during mastication or rumination (Gautier-Hion *et al.*, 1985). Sometimes, seeds ingested or spat out by large terrestrial mammals benefit from enhanced germination probabilities when compared to uningested seeds, and in some instances the digestive fluids kill eggs and larvae of insect predators present in the consumed fruit/seed (Miller, 1995).

Dispersal by large terrestrial mammals may also be crucial for the reproduction of some plant species. For example, plant species with very large fruits/seeds may primarily depend on very large mammals for dispersal. Such is the case of *Balanites wilsoniana* in Uganda, a tree species which has its 88 mm long seeds only dispersed by elephants (Chapman *et al.*, 1992). Another example is that of the shade-intolerant tree *Trewia nudiflora* in southern Asia (Dinerstein and Wemmer, 1988). The fruits of this species are large and hard, are unattractive to birds, bats and primates, and are only dispersed by large terrestrial mammals. In the Royal Chitwan National Park in Nepal, the main seed disperser of this species is the Indian rhinoceros *Rhinoceros unicornis*. In other areas, where the rhinoceros is not present, *Trewia* is either a rare tree, or it is dispersed by other species of wild or domestic large terrestrial herbivores. Rhinoceroses deposit *Trewia* seeds in the forest as well as in grasslands. It is in the latter habitat that this light-demanding species establishes best, thus colonising successional habitats that were previously major river courses. Therefore, not only do rhinoceroses ensure the reproduction of *Trewia* in Chitwan, but they also seem to be affecting the rate of succession in riverine floodplains.

In neotropical forests, tapirs (*Tapirus* spp.) are the main seed dispersers among large terrestrial mammals (Bodmer, 1991). While deer and peccaries kill most of the seeds they ingest, a large percentage of seeds swallowed by tapirs are deposited in a viable state in forest latrines. Both in Costa Rica and Perú, tapir latrines have only been found in inundated or seasonally inundated areas. This behaviour may only facilitate establishment of the few plant species that are adapted for such environments, while killing many other seed species through exposure to excessive moisture (Janzen, 1982; Bodmer, 1991). In the northern Brazilian Amazon, however, 74 % of tapir latrines were found in forests that are never subject to flooding (Fragoso, 1997). In these forests, tapirs are responsible for the spatial distribution of a common palm species, *Maximiliana maripa*. While other animals disperse seeds of this species very short distances, depositing them close to the parent crown where 77 % are killed by bruchid beetles, tapirs disperse them up to 2 km away from the parent tree and only 0.7 % of these seeds are killed by beetles. Tapirs deposit large number of seeds in latrines that are used by them repeatedly over long periods of time, and rodents are then responsible for the secondary dispersal of these clumped seeds. Together, tapirs and rodents affect forest structure by creating patches that have very high densities of *Maximiliana* palms.

THE LOSS OF FRUITS AND MAMMALIAN FRUGIVORES IN TROPICAL FORESTS

It is clear that many mammal species in tropical forests depend at least partially on fruits as a food source, dispersing large numbers of seeds. It is clear too, that many species of plants produce fruits adapted for animal consumption, and depend on their consumers to attain successful reproduction. Many ecologists, conservationists and forest managers agree that frugivorous animals are of critical importance for the natural regeneration of tropical forests and even for the maintenance of biodiversity. In turn, the existence of certain plant species is crucial in determining the biomass and diversity of frugivores that a forest can sustain.

From the plants' perspective, we have seen that most species in tropical forests have their fruits dispersed by more than one species, and thus it will probably be uncommon that plant species will suffer extinction due to the disappearance of a single frugivore species. However, those cases in which high specificity exists between a plant and a mammal species should be identified and given particular attention. Such plants are at the highest risk of local extinction should their main dispersal agent disappear. On the other hand, it is not uncommon for plant species to rely on a group of mammals for their dispersal (e.g., primates, terrestrial frugivores). Unfortunately, ample evidence exists now showing that mammalian frugivores, in particular the large species, are highly sensitive to various forms of forest disturbance, including hunting, selective logging, extraction of forest fruits and forest fragmentation (Johns and Skorupa, 1987; Symington, 1988; Redford, 1992; Estrada et al., 1994; Bodmer et al., 1997a). Thus, the threat of local extinction of plant species may become increasingly imminent, as whole disperser assemblages disappear from the forests. In a study of 25 tree species in Kibale National Park in Uganda, Chapman and Chapman (1995) concluded that up to 60 % of the tree species may be lost if their animal seed dispersers disappeared.

Even if plant species do not disappear from a forest community, their densities and spatial distributions will most likely be affected by the loss of all or some disperser species, thus altering forest diversity and structure. Patterns of plant recruitment and diversity are known to be affected in tropical forests that have altered communities of herbivorous and seed-eating mammals (Dirzo and Miranda, 1991; Asquith et al., 1997). It is likely that changes in the communities of seed-dispersing mammals will have similar effects. In Uganda, Chapman and Onderdonk (1998) found that forest fragments which had reduced populations of primate seed dispersers, also had lower seedling densities and diversities than the intact forest. Additionally, more than 80 % of the seedlings in areas without primates were from small-seeded species that could also be dispersed by small frugivores, while less than 25 % were small-seeded species in the intact forest.

From the animals' perspective, few mammals are completely frugivorous, and those species that rely heavily on fruits feed on many different species. Evidence exists, however, indicating that some plant species may be of critical importance for the maintenance of the frugivorous community. These plants have been called 'keystone species', and it is believed that their abundance plays an important role in determining how many frugivorous species and individuals can be supported by a forest area

(Leighton and Leighton, 1983; Howe, 1984; Terborgh, 1986b). Through selective logging and exploitation of forest fruits for human consumption, the abundance of these keystone plant species can be heavily reduced. In Borneo, for example, several species of climber and strangler figs provide many frugivores with a relatively continuous availability of fruit (Leighton and Leighton, 1983). The trees on which these figs grow, however, are often large dipterocarps, which are the most important timber trees in Borneo, suggesting that logging may have indirect negative effects on the frugivore community.

In areas where keystone plant species are not present or abundant, highly frugivorous mammals that do not rely on alternative food resources (e.g., leaves) during the times of fruit scarcity, have very large home ranges to exploit the patchily distributed fruit crops, or migrate to other areas. In either case the result is that many large frugivores require enormous areas of protected forests to ensure their long-term survival. Fragmentation of tropical forests is rapidly increasing worldwide, constituting the largest current threat to global biodiversity. Most forest fragments and even protected forest areas are of inadequate size to maintain populations of large mammals, including large mammalian seed dispersers (Redford and Robinson, 1991). Thus, it is likely that in these fragmented forests, species of large mammalian frugivores will disappear, endangering also the long-term survival of the plants they disperse, and of other animal species that feed on these plants.

CONCLUDING REMARKS

The relationship between fruit-eating mammals and the plants that produce fruits adapted to animal dispersal is one of dynamic mutualism. This plant–animal interaction is geographically widespread, and is predominantly represented in tropical forests. While in most cases this mutualism involves a large number of fruits in the frugivore's diet, and a large number of frugivores as the plant's dispersers, for some plant and mammal species, the relationship is more specialised. These are the systems that deserve most of our attention, since it is these plants and animals that will be more prone to disappearance in disturbed habitats. Such may be the case of many tropical trees with large seeds that are not dispersed by small-bodied vertebrates. These trees probably depend for their long-term survival on large frugivorous mammals, which in turn is one of the groups of rainforest vertebrates that is most susceptible to forest disturbances.

Thus, while the fruit–frugivore interaction can be addressed from the plant's as well as the animal's perspective, to ensure the long-term survival of both components, it is necessary to recognise their interdependencies and to address them as a mutualistic system. One cannot strive to conserve species of frugivorous mammals without keeping healthy populations of their fruit plants, and vice versa. A crucial difference in both components exists however, and it is one that, when ignored, endangers their long-term conservation. Plants, in particular woody species, have very long generation times compared to their animal consumers. Consequently, trees may remain in forests where large animals have been decimated by human activities, creating what Redford (1992) has called 'the empty forest'. Such forests give the false impression that an intact ecosystem is being conserved, but in the long term many plant species will disappear just like their seed dispersers disappeared in the short term. If we keep this in mind, and strive to conserve the diversity of ecological interactions rather than individual components, the priorities and justification for conservation efforts will become clear.

3

Patterns and processes in contemporary mammalian extinction*

GEORGINA M. MACE AND ANDREW BALMFORD

INTRODUCTION

The publication of the *1996 IUCN Red List of Threatened Animals* (IUCN, 1996) marked an important watershed in our knowledge of the conservation status of the world's mammals. For the first time in a global list, all mammals (rather than just the better known species) were considered, and all assessments were based on the new quantitative criteria introduced by IUCN in 1994 (IUCN, 1994). The result was a much more comprehensive and systematic description of the degree to which the entire class of mammals is threatened than had hitherto been available. In this chapter, we combine data from the *1996 IUCN Red List* with other recently available information to summarise what is known about the overall extent of threat to mammals, and to explore how threat levels and threatening processes vary taxonomically and geographically.

After a brief overview of global levels of threat across all mammals, we examine how the level of threat varies across orders and families. Previous perceptions that certain, generally larger-bodied, groups were more threatened than others (see discussion by Cole *et al.*, 1994) can now be investigated systematically with new information. Here we look at all mammalian groups together, including those previously incompletely assessed, and specifically identify those orders and families with significantly more or less threatened species than one would expect, given the global level of threat to mammals. We also test whether these groups are indeed generally large-bodied, and whether they tend to be relatively species-poor (see Russell *et al.*, 1998). Next, we examine the use of the different quantitative criteria set out by IUCN (IUCN, 1994), before analysing data drawn from

---

*This chapter is dedicated to Émile Lefebvre (1971–1998).

the IUCN Action Plans (Gimenez-Dixon and Stuart, 1993) to identify the main processes which threaten mammals. This assessment provides a picture of how the relative importance of these processes varies across different mammalian groups. Finally, by combining threat data with distribution at the country level, we look at spatial variation in the degree to which mammals are threatened, and in particular examine how threat levels compare between the Old and New Worlds, and between species found on islands and on continental landmasses.

METHODS

We adopted the mammal classification of Wilson and Reeder (1993) with minor additions and amendments used by IUCN (1996). These changes largely affect the primates and mostly involve the addition of South American species, as recommended by Rylands *et al.* (1995). All mammal species are included in our analysis, giving a total of 4761 species (see Table 3.1).

The category of threat – threat level

We assembled data on the conservation status of all mammal species from the *1996 IUCN Red List of Threatened Animals* (IUCN, 1996). The IUCN categories measure the severity of threat faced by each species (IUCN, 1994). The categories for threatened species are Extinct, Extinct in the Wild, Critically Endangered, Endangered, and Vulnerable (the lowest category for threatened species). Lower Risk is used for species that do not qualify for threatened status and has three subcategories – species are either close to qualifying ('near threatened'), only fail to qualify because of continuing specific conservation actions that protect them ('conservation dependent'), or are considered not at risk ('least concern'). These subcategories are included in the analysis. There are also two categories for species that fall outside the threat classification: Data Deficient is used for species for which there is insufficient information to assess the level of threat; and Not Evaluated is for species for which no evaluation has yet been made. Since all mammals have been assessed, there were no species in this last category.

Taxonomic spread of threat

After quantifying the level of threat to mammals as a whole, we explored variation in the severity of threat among different mammal groups. We identified those orders and families with significantly fewer or more threatened species than expected by chance by testing observed frequencies of threat against a binomial distribution, given the number of species in the group, and the overall frequency of threat across all mammals. We also analysed how the degree of threat to different families compared with their species richness. Our last analysis on the taxonomic spread of threat examined the relationship between extinction risk and body size among families and orders. The mean body size for these groups was calculated from body size information generously provided by A. Purvis (personal communication).

Criteria for listing

We recorded information on the way in which species qualify for threatened status under the IUCN criteria. The IUCN classification system is based around five criteria that determine whether species qualify for one of three threatened categories (Critically Endangered, Endangered and Vulnerable). The Extinct and Extinct in the Wild categories do not use such criteria. A species has only to meet one of the five criteria, which have different quantitative threshold values. The five criteria essentially measure different ways in which a species may be perceived as being at risk of extinction (IUCN, 1994; Mace, 1994). Some criteria reflect species at risk from continuing declines in range or abundance while others detect those at risk from small population size; these two paradigms affect both the dynamics of the extinction process and the measures that can be taken to reverse the situation (Caughley, 1994). Species that have shown, or are expected to show, marked declines in population size are listed under criterion A. Criterion B allows species to qualify if they have a restricted distribution, either in total or in terms of the particular habitat that they use, and are declining, fragmented or showing wide fluctuations in abundance. Criteria C and D reflect small total population size. Criterion C covers species in continuing decline where the population is also fragmented, isolated or fluctuating widely. Criterion D does not require evidence of continuing decline but allows species to qualify if they are restricted to a very tiny area or if the number of breeding individuals is very small. Criterion E requires evidence from a quantitative analysis (such as a model, including Population Viability Analysis) that the extinction risk faced by the species meets the critical thresholds for each of the threat categories.

The threatening processes – threat type

More specific information about the nature of the threatening processes was collected from IUCN Action Plans (Gimenez-Dixon and Stuart, 1993; see Table 3.1). These publications review the status of species within

Table 3.1
The orders of mammals included in the analysis and sources of information on threatening processes

Order	Species	Number species	Source of threat information
Monotremata	echidnas, platypuses	3	Kennedy, 1992
Didelphimorphia	American opossums	66	—
Paucituberculata	shrew and rat opossums	5	—
Microbiotheria	colocolos	1	—
Dasyuromorphia	Australian marsupial carnivores	68	Kennedy, 1992
Peramelemorphia	bandicoots and bilbies	21	Kennedy, 1992
Notoryctemorphia	marsupial mole	2	Kennedy, 1992
Diprotodontia	cuscus, gliders, possums, kangaroos	132	Kennedy, 1992
Xenarthra	sloths, anteaters, armadillos	29	—
Insectivora	solenodons, tenrecs, hedgehogs, shrews, moles	433	Soricidae – Stone, 1995
Scandentia	tree shrews	19	—
Dermoptera	flying lemurs	2	—
Chiroptera	bats	986	Pteropodidae – Mickleburgh et al., 1992
Primates	monkeys and apes	266	Cheirogaleidae, Lemuridae, Megaladapidae, Indridae, Daubentoniidae – Mittermeier et al., 1993; Loridae, Galagonidae, Cercopithecidae, Hominidae – Oates, 1986, 1996; Hylobatidae, Hominidae – Eudey, 1987
Carnivora	dogs, cats, mongooses, weasels, otters, seals, bears, civets, genets	274	Canidae – Ginsberg and Macdonald, 1990; Felidae – Nowell and Jackson, 1996; Herpestidae – Schreiber et al., 1989; Mustelidae – Schreiber et al., 1989, Foster-Turley et al., 1990; Procyonidae – Glatson, 1994; Ursidae – Glatson, 1994; Servheen et al., 1999; Viverridae – Schreiber et al., 1989; Otariidae – Reijnders et al., 1993; Phocidae – Reijnders et al., 1993

Order	Examples	No.	References
Cetacea	whales, dolphins, porpoises	80	Delphinidae, Phocoenidae, Platanistidae – Reeves and Leatherwood, 1994
Sirenia	dugongs, manatees	5	—
Proboscidea	elephants	2	Cumming *et al.*, 1990; Santiapillai and Jackson, 1990
Perissodactyla	horses, rhinos, tapirs	17	Equidae – Duncan, 1992; Rhinoceratidae – Cumming, *et al.*, 1990, Foose and van Strien, 1997; Tapiridae – Brooks *et al.*, 1997
Hyracoidea	hyrax	7	—
Tubulidentata	aardvark	1	—
Artiodactyla	pigs, peccaries, hippos, camels, deer, giraffe, antelope, cattle, sheep, goats	220	Suidae, Tayassuidae, Hippopotamidae – Oliver, 1993; Tragulidae, Moschidae, Cervidae – Wemmer, 1998; Bovidae – East, 1988, 1989, MacKinnon and Stuart, 1989, East, 1990; Shackleton, 1997
Pholidota	pangolins	7	—
Rodentia	squirrels, gophers, mice, rats, porcupines, cavies, mole rats	2020	—
Lagomorpha	rabbits, hares, pikas	81	Ochotonidae, Leporidae – Chapman and Flux, 1990
Macroscelidea	elephant shrews	14	—

Table 3.2
The major threatening processes. Classification of threat types, and the percentage of threats within each classification level which are of each type

Major process	% occurrence	Threat types	% occurrence	Further breakdown of threat types	% occurrence
Habitat loss	46.6	1a. Habitat cleared	61.1		
		1b. Habitat not entirely cleared	38.9		
Overexploitation	33.9	2a. Local exploitation	65.8	2ai. Utilitarian, incl. medicines, food, skins, horn, fibres	88.7
				2aii. Ornamental, incl. pets, trophies, collections	11.3
		2b. Commercial exploitation	20.7	2bi. Utilitarian, incl. medicines, food, skins, horn, fibres	93.7
				2bii. Ornamental, incl. pets, trophies, collections	6.3
		2c. Incidental and by-catch	5.3		
		2d. Persecution and hunting as a pest	8.2		
Introductions	12.7	3a. Predation incl. herbivory, disturbance	30.9		
		3b. Disease including parasitism	26.3		
		3c. Competition	34.9		
		3d. Hybridisation	8.0		
Chains of extinction	0.7				
Rarity	6.0				

taxonomic groups according to a relatively standard format, and provide details on the status of particular populations as well as the threats they face. Using these data, we classified threat types into five major classes, the first four being familiar as Diamond's 'evil quartet' (Diamond, 1984a): (1) habitat loss, including habitat degradation and pollution; (2) overkill, including persecution as well as direct overexploitation; (3) the effects of introduced species, including domestic species; (4) chains of extinction, where a combination of different threat processes interact; and (5) natural rarity, where the species has long been characterised by a very small but apparently stable distribution. These major threat types were further subdivided as shown in Table 3.2.

We could not gather information on threatening processes for all mammal groups. In particular, there was no information for most of the small mammals such as rodents, bats (other than fruit bats) and insectivores. Table 3.1 gives details on the families for which threat type information was collected as well as the source for each family.

Species commonly experienced more than one threat type. This poses a slight problem for assessing the relative importance of different threatening processes, either overall, or across different groups. One approach is to weight each species equally. This has the obvious disadvantage of giving less weight to each individual threat recorded for species facing multiple threats. Therefore here, we take the alternative approach of treating each recorded threat (rather than each species) equally, so that when calculating its overall importance, a single major threat is given equal weight whether it is the only threat to the species in question or one of many. In practice, however, our conclusions are unaffected by the weighting method used.

Biogeographical spread of threat

Using a variety of sources (Meester and Setzer, 1975; Corbet, 1978; Eisenberg, 1989; Skinner and Smithers, 1990; Corbet and Hill, 1991; Strahan, 1991; Redford and Eisenberg, 1992; Wilson and Reeder, 1993; Flannery, 1995a, b) we recorded the biogeographic regions in which species were found, as summarised in Figure 3.1. For present purposes, we ignored species that ranged over two or more of these zones. For those species endemic to a single biogeographical region, we also recorded whether they were island or continental forms, with island species defined here (to reflect a long period of evolution in relative isolation) as those endemic to an island country with greater than 10 % of its mammals listed as endemics (Groombridge, 1992), or to islands in the West Indies or the Indian, Atlantic or Pacific Oceans. Note that under this definition, Madagascar, Borneo and

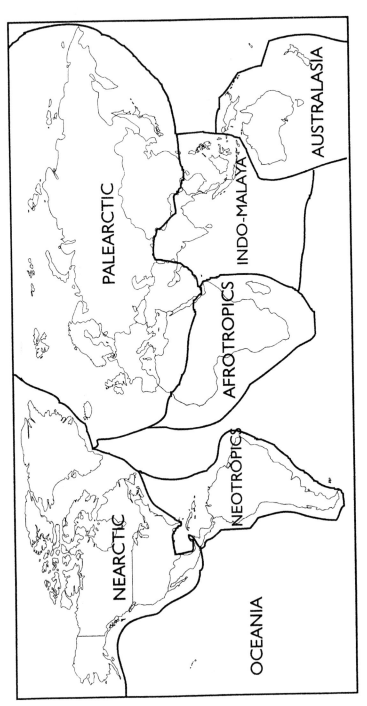

Figure 3.1 Biogeographical regions used in this analysis.

Australia are all considered islands. We defined all other species as continental, including those whose ranges extended (but were not restricted) to islands.

RESULTS

Threat level

Of the 4761 species in the data set, 1097 (23.0%) were recorded as threatened, of which 169 were classified as Critically Endangered, 314 as Endangered, and 614 as Vulnerable. This is a lower percentage than stated by IUCN (1996) because of an error in their number of non-threatened species. However, the 23.0% figure may itself also be misleading, in that of the 4761 species, 208 were recorded as Data Deficient and were therefore not assessed for threat, while 94 species that were Extinct or Extinct in the Wild were not included in the total of 1097 threatened species. Thus two more correct estimates are 24.6% excluding Data Deficient and Extinct species from the total and 26.2% including the Extinct species as threatened but excluding the Data Deficient ones. We use the latter method to calculate percentages of threatened species in the rest of this chapter.

In addition to those mammals classified as threatened, 596 species were classified as Lower Risk: near threatened. This classification has no specific criteria, and is used for species that come close to meeting the qualifying thresholds for Vulnerable. The vast majority of near threatened mammals are bats and rodents (210 and 242 species respectively). The other subcategory of Lower Risk species is conservation dependent. This was rather rarely used for mammals – altogether there were 67 species in this category, 43 of which were artiodactyls.

Taxonomic spread

We found marked differences in percentages of threatened species in particular orders. Table 3.3 gives these numbers for each order and also shows the corresponding probability of obtaining them under a binomial distribution, given the average mammalian threat frequency of 0.262. Only the rodents are less threatened than expected under a binomial distribution, while five orders contain significantly more threatened species than expected – the Artiodactyla, Insectivora, Primates, Perissodactyla and Sirenia. Apart from the order Sirenia, which has four threatened and one extinct species, there are three other orders that have all their species listed as threatened, although it is not possible to obtain a significant binomial test

Table 3.3

Orders of mammals, ranked by the percentage of all assessed species that are recorded as extinct or threatened by IUCN (i.e. classified as EX, EW, CR, EN or VU). The first block lists orders that contain less than the average percentage of threatened species, and the lower block contains the orders with more than the average number.

All proportions are tested against the binomial expectation with $P = 0.2616$ (see text), and the asterisks indicate those orders where the proportion is significantly different from the expected (*** indicates $P < 0.001$, ** indicates $P < 0.01$ and * indicates $P < 0.05$)

Order	Total number of species	Data Deficient (DD)	Extinct (EX) or Extinct in the Wild (EW)	Lower Risk (LR)	Threatened (CR, EN, VU)	Threatened and Extinct Total	Total species assessed	% threatened	Binomial probability	Probability
Tubulidentata	1	0	0	1	0	0	1	0.0	1	
Pholidota	7	0	0	7	0	0	7	0.0	0.2014	
Rodentia	2020	32	45	1614	329	374	1988	18.8	0	***
Paucituberculata	5	0	0	4	1	1	5	20.0	1	
Lagomorpha	81	3	1	61	16	17	78	21.8	0.4404	
Chiroptera	986	43	13	699	231	244	943	25.9	0.8532	
Carnivora	274	19	4	186	65	69	255	27.1	0.7757	
Dasyuromorphia	68	10	1	41	16	17	58	29.3	0.6539	
Scandentia	19	0	0	13	6	6	19	31.6	0.6039	
Diprotodontia	132	11	6	81	34	40	121	33.1	0.0973	
Monotremata	3	0	0	2	1	1	3	33.3	1	
Cetacea	80	38	0	28	14	14	42	33.3	0.2941	
Didelphimorphia	66	5	0	40	21	21	61	34.4	0.1889	
Xenarthra	29	6	0	15	8	8	23	34.8	0.3469	
Artiodactyla	220	6	8	134	72	80	214	37.4	0.0003	***
Insectivora	433	6	10	265	152	162	427	37.9	0	***
Primates	266	22	0	148	96	96	244	39.3	0	***
Hyracoidea	7	0	0	4	3	3	7	42.9	0.3877	
Peramelemorphia	21	7	3	7	4	7	14	50.0	0.0625	

Dermoptera	2	0	0	1	1	1	2	50.0	0.4548
Macroscelidea	14	0	0	7	7	7	14	50.0	0.0625
Perissodactyla	17	0	2	4	11	13	17	76.5	0 ***
Microbiotheria	1	0	0	0	1	1	1	100.0	0.2616
Notoryctemorphia	2	0	0	0	2	2	2	100.0	0.0684
Sirenia	5	0	1	0	4	5	5	100.0	0.0012 **
Proboscidea	2	0	0	0	2	2	2	100.0	0.0684
Total	4761	208	94	3362	1097	1191	4553		

result for these as they each have fewer than five species. These are the marsupial moles (Notoryctemorphia), the colocolos (Microbiotheria) and the elephants (Proboscidea). There were also clear differences across orders in the relative degree of threat to species. Considering only orders with more than 10 species, the bats (Chiroptera) and opossums (Didelphimorphia) have over 70 % of threatened species listed as Vulnerable, while at the other extreme, the Perissodactyla have almost 40 % of species listed in the most seriously threatened category of Critically Endangered.

Moving on to families, we again found striking variation in the percentages of species which were threatened (Table 3.4). The rodent families Bathyergidae, Ctenomyidae, Caviidae, Sciuridae, Echimyidae and Muridae, and the primate family Galagonidae have a significantly lower than expected number of threatened species according to a binomial test. Several of the very highly threatened families are those with large numbers of extinct species, such as the Antillean insectivores and rodents belonging to the families Solenodontidae, Nesophontidae and Heptaxodontidae. Highly threatened families with more species still extant are the hutias (Capromyidae), indris and lemurs (Indridae and Lemuridae), and the equids, rhinoceroses and tapirs (Equidae, Rhinocerotidae and Tapiridae).

When we explored potential correlates of the variation in the degree of threat across higher taxa, we found no clear cut relationships between the percentage of species in a group which was threatened and either its species richness or its average body mass. There was no straightforward correlation between degree of threat and species richness among families; instead, the plot was characterised by a large amount of scatter (Figure 3.2; Spearman rank correlation: $r_s = -0.07$, $N = 123$ families, N.S.). The families with highest species richness tend to have a relatively small proportion of threatened species. Many of the most threatened families are species-poor, but some species-poor families exhibit very low threat.

Figure 3.3 compares threat levels across mammalian orders ranked by increasing mean body mass; treating each order as statistically independent suggests there is no correlation between threat rates and body size ($r_s = -0.06$, $N = 26$ orders, N.S.). This is because although there are a number of small-bodied orders with a low frequency of threatened species, such as the bats and rodents, there are also some small-bodied but highly threatened orders, most notably the insectivores and elephant shrews (Macroscelidea). The most threatened order, the Perissodactyla, is large-bodied, but there are also large-bodied orders with a relatively low proportion of threatened species, such as the Carnivora and Cetacea. Even when the analysis was done after weighting the orders by their species richness, the correlation was not significant (Pearson correlation: $r = -0.06$, $N = 26$, N.S.).

Criteria for listing

Mammals qualified for the categories of threat by all the different criteria (Table 3.5), although criterion E, the quantitative analysis, was never used alone. Most species qualified by meeting only one of the five criteria (920 species), but 152 met two and 25 species met three. Criterion B, concerning small range, was the most common way in which species qualified, although criterion A, concerning decline, was more commonly seen with other criteria.

Threat type

We were able to gather data about the nature of the threatening processes for 600 species from those families listed in Table 3.1. This total included species classified as Lower Risk: near threatened and conservation dependent, as well as those in the threatened categories. Altogether, we recorded a total of 1102 major threats to these species.

The most common major threatening process was habitat loss (Table 3.2). Where information was available on the nature of the habitat loss, we were able to distinguish wholesale habitat clearance from habitat degradation, fragmentation and pollution. In our sample, most of the species threatened by habitat loss were threatened by the more serious form, i.e., clearance (Table 3.2). The second most common threat type was overkill of some kind. Here, further analysis of the nature of the threat reveals that most overkill is to supply local markets, and is for utilitarian (rather than ornamental) use. Threats from introduced species were also prevalent. When examined in more detail, we found that species threatened by introductions were affected by predation, disease and competition in almost equal measure; the problem of interspecific hybridisation was less common (Table 3.2). There were very few species in the category of chains of extinction, and natural rarity was the least common causal factor listed.

Among orders, we found marked variation in the frequency with which species face the various major threat processes (Table 3.6). Habitat loss is most common in all orders assessed, except the Artiodactyla, where overkill affects more species. Overkill is also very important for the other ungulate groups, for fruit bats (frequently harvested for food), and for the Carnivora (which are frequently persecuted, as well as hunted for traditional medicines and skins). Of all the groups, habitat loss is most prevalent among primates; over 70 % of the primates in our sample suffered directly from

Table 3.4

Families of mammals which are significantly more or less threatened than expected by chance (at $P < 0.01$), are entirely threatened or are entirely non-threatened. Families are ranked by the proportion of all assessed species that are recorded as extinct or threatened by IUCN, i.e., classified as EX, EW, CR, EN or VU. The first block lists families that contain less than the average percentage of threatened species, and the lower block contains the families with more than the average number.

All proportions are tested against the binomial expectation with $P = 0.2616$ (see text), and the asterisks indicate probability values as in Table 3.2

Order	Total number of species	Data Deficient (DD)	Extinct (EX) or Extinct in the Wild (EW)	Lower Risk (LR)	Threatened (CR. EN. VU)	Number EX, EW and threatened	Total assessed species	% threatened	Binomial probability	Probability
Megalonychidae	2	2	0	0	0	0	0	0		
Antilocapridae	1	0	0	1	0	0	1	0.0	1	
Aplodontidae	1	0	0	1	0	0	1	0.0	1	
Eschrichtiidae	1	0	0	1	0	0	1	0.0	1	
Hydrochaeridae	1	0	0	1	0	0	1	0.0	1	
Myocastoridae	1	0	0	1	0	0	1	0.0	1	
Neobalaenidae	1	0	0	1	0	0	1	0.0	1	
Odobenidae	1	0	0	1	0	0	1	0.0	1	
Ornithorhynchidae	1	0	0	1	0	0	1	0.0	1	
Orycteropodidae	1	0	0	1	0	0	1	0.0	1	
Petromuridae	1	0	0	1	0	0	1	0.0	1	
Phascolarctidae	1	0	0	1	0	0	1	0.0	1	
Tarsipedidae	1	0	0	1	0	0	1	0.0	1	
Acrobatidae	2	0	0	2	0	0	2	0.0	1	
Agoutidae	2	0	0	2	0	0	2	0.0	1	
Castoridae	2	0	0	2	0	0	2	0.0	1	
Giraffidae	2	0	0	2	0	0	2	0.0	1	
Noctilionidae	2	0	0	2	0	0	2	0.0	1	
Tarsiidae	7	5	0	2	0	0	2	0.0	1	

Thryonomyidae	2	0	0	2	0	0	2	0.0	1	
Hyaenidae	4	0	0	4	0	0	4	0.0	0.5747	
Peroryctidae	11	7	0	4	0	0	4	0.0	0.5747	
Tragulidae	4	0	0	4	0	0	4	0.0	0.5747	
Ziphiidae	19	15	0	4	0	0	4	0.0	0.5747	
Anomaluridae	7	0	0	7	0	0	7	0.0	0.2014	
Manidae	7	0	0	7	0	0	7	0.0	0.2014	
Bathyergidae	12	0	0	12	0	0	12	0.0	0.0446	*
Galagonidae	16	4	0	12	0	0	12	0.0	0.0446	*
Caviidae	13	0	0	13	0	0	13	0.0	0.027	*
Ctenomyidae	38	0	0	38	0	0	38	0.0	0	***
Delphinidae	33	17	0	15	1	1	16	6.3	0.0873	
Hystricidae	11	0	0	10	1	1	11	9.1	0.3084	
Heteromyidae	58	0	0	51	7	7	58	12.1	0.0113	*
Mormoopidae	8	0	0	7	1	1	8	12.5	0.4693	
Sciuridae	271	1	1	234	35	36	270	13.3	0	***
Echimyidae	79	4	7	63	5	12	75	16.0	0.0483	*
Erethizontidae	12	0	1	10	1	2	12	16.7	0.5381	
Geomyidae	35	0	0	29	6	6	35	17.1	0.2547	
Dipodidae	50	4	4	38	4	8	46	17.4	0.1857	
Muridae	1330	21	22	1051	236	258	1309	19.7	0	***
Bovidae	141	0	4	84	53	57	141	40.4	0.0002	***
Pteropodidae	169	2	8	98	61	69	167	41.3	0	***
Potoroidae	12	0	2	6	4	6	12	50.0	0.0926	
Macroscelididae	14	0	0	7	7	7	14	50.0	0.0625	
Chrysochloridae	18	0	0	7	11	11	18	61.1	0.0019	**
Phocoenidae	6	3	0	1	2	2	3	66.7	0.0496	*
Balaenopteridae	7	1	0	2	4	4	6	66.7	0.0441	*
Peramelidae	10	0	3	3	4	7	10	70.0	0.0046	**
Ursidae	8	1	0	2	5	5	7	71.4	0.0158	*
Hippopotamidae	4	0	2	1	1	3	4	75.0	0.0576	
Tapiridae	4	0	0	1	3	3	4	75.0	0.0576	
Equidae	8	0	2	2	4	6	8	75.0	0.0054	**

Table 3.4 (*cont.*)

Order	Total number of species	Data Deficient (DD)	Extinct (EX) or Extinct in the Wild (EW)	Lower Risk (LR)	Threatened (CR, EN, VU)	Number EX, EW and threatened	Total assessed species	% threatened	Binomial probability	Probability
Rhinocerotidae	5	0	0	1	4	4	5	80.0	0.0185	*
Lemuridae	10	0	0	2	8	8	10	80.0	0.0006	***
Indridae	6	0	0	1	5	5	6	83.3	0.0057	**
Capromyidae	24	0	10	4	10	20	24	83.3	0	***
Thylacinidae	1	0	1	0	0	1	1	100.0	0.2616	
Craseonycteridae	1	0	0	0	1	1	1	100.0	0.2616	
Daubentoniidae	1	0	0	0	1	1	1	100.0	0.2616	
Dinomyidae	1	0	0	0	1	1	1	100.0	0.2616	
Microbiotheriidae	1	0	0	0	1	1	1	100.0	0.2616	
Monodontidae	2	1	0	0	1	1	1	100.0	0.2616	
Myrmecobiidae	1	0	0	0	1	1	1	100.0	0.2616	
Myzopodidae	1	0	0	0	1	1	1	100.0	0.2616	
Pedetidae	1	0	0	0	1	1	1	100.0	0.2616	
Dugongidae	2	0	1	0	1	2	2	100.0	0.0684	
Mystacinidae	2	0	1	0	1	2	2	100.0	0.0684	
Elephantidae	2	0	0	0	2	2	2	100.0	0.0684	
Notoryctidae	2	0	0	0	2	2	2	100.0	0.0684	
Solenodontidae	3	0	1	0	2	3	3	100.0	0.0179	*
Trichechidae	3	0	0	0	3	3	3	100.0	0.0179	*
Hominidae	4	0	0	0	4	4	4	100.0	0.0047	**
Platanistidae	5	1	0	0	4	4	4	100.0	0.0047	**
Heptaxodontidae	5	0	5	0	0	5	5	100.0	0.0012	**
Nesophontidae	9	0	9	0	0	9	9	100.0	0	***

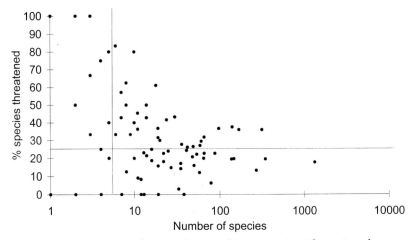

Figure 3.2 Percentage of species threatened versus species richness (on a log₁₀ scale) for each mammal family. Lines illustrate the mean percentage of all species which are threatened, and mean family size.

loss of habitat, and this was commonly their only cause of threat. Threats from introduced species were most common for the three orders of marsupials examined, where Australasian forms were suffering from multiple introductions of non-native predators and competitors, and for ungulates which frequently faced competition with domestic livestock.

Biogeographical spread

Most mammal species (4059 out of 4761) are restricted in distribution to just one of the eight biogeographic regions shown in Figure 3.1 (see Table 3.7). Of these, the Afrotropical region contains the most species, closely followed by the other tropical regions – the neotropical and Indomalayan. Temperate zones, represented by the palearctic and nearctic, have only about half the endemic species of their tropical counterparts. Island endemics are most numerous in the Australasian and Indomalayan regions. In Oceania, all species are island endemics, whereas there are no island endemics in the nearctic region.

Threat levels vary consistently among regions, and between island and continental species (Figure 3.4). Species found on continents are consistently less threatened than those restricted to islands. The region with the highest level of threat is Oceania. Intriguingly, the Australasian region (including Australia, which one could argue could be classified as either a continent or an island) has a frequency of threatened endemics that is intermediate between that of island and continental regions.

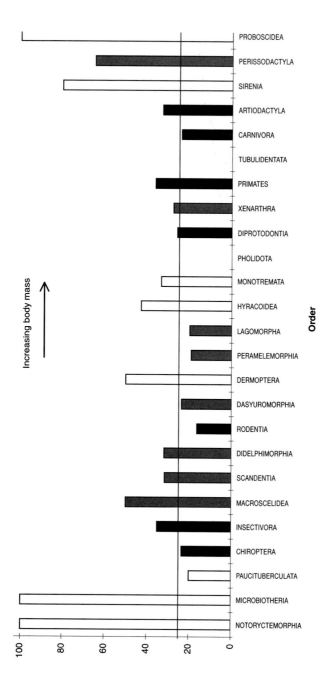

Figure 3.3 Percentage of species threatened in each mammal order. The mean body mass of the orders' members increases from left to right. The horizontal line gives the average figure for all mammals. Open bars indicate orders with fewer than 10 species, grey bars those with 11–100 species, and black bars those with > 100 species.

Besides this difference in threat levels between species on continents and those restricted to islands, there is also a consistent difference in the frequency of threat experienced by mammals from different regions (Figure 3.4). For both island and continental species, those restricted to the New World regions of the nearctic and neotropical are less threatened than those from the Old World regions of Indomalayan, palearctic and Afrotropical.

DISCUSSION

Threat level

One of the most striking findings of the *1996 IUCN Red List of Threatened Animals* (IUCN, 1996) was that about a quarter of all mammal species were recorded as being threatened. This appeared to be a dramatic increase from the estimate of 11 % in the previous edition of the same publication (IUCN, 1993a). However, until 1996 there had been no comprehensive survey of the mammals, and in fact only about 2400 species had been assessed. In particular, there was no consideration of large numbers of species in some poorly known groups such as the rodents, bats and insectivores. In 1994, there were 741 mammalian species listed as threatened, which is about 30 % of those that were assessed. The addition of new taxa in 1996 brought this percentage down to between 24 and 26 % (depending on the inclusion of recent extinctions) because the previously unassessed groups have a lower than average degree of threat. The apparent increase in degree of threat between 1994 and 1996 is thus largely due to a marked increase in coverage, rather than either a real change in status or the adoption of new criteria for the threatened categories.

Nevertheless, between 24 and 26 % is a high level of threat, especially compared to birds, for which complete assessment using the same criteria gives a figure of 11 % (Collar *et al.*, 1994). There are reasons to expect mammals to be more threatened than birds. They tend to have smaller home ranges and geographical ranges, both of which probably increase their vulnerability to extinction (Lawton, 1994; Pimm, 1998). They are also more likely to be targeted by hunting or persecution – overkill accounts for only 10.2 % of threats to birds (Collar *et al.*, 1994), compared to 33.9 % of threats to mammals (Table 3.2). An alternative view – that the difference is due to the IUCN criteria overestimating mammal threats relative to birds – seems unlikely, since a comparable analysis of United States species, carried out by The Nature Conservancy (TNC) using different criteria gives a similar

Table 3.5
Use of the different criteria (A to E) that qualify species for listing in categories
of threat

Criteria	Total number of species	Alone	With other criteria
Criterion A – declining population	430	304	126
Criterion B – small range and evidence of decline	526	430	96
Criterion C – small population and evidence of decline	189	92	97
Criterion D – very small population	145	94	51
Criterion E – unfavourable analysis	9	0	9

Table 3.6
Variation in the major threatening processes across orders

Order	% major threats recorded for species in each order					Total number of threats recorded
	Habitat loss	Overkill	Introduced species	Chains of extinction	Rarity	
Monotremata	0	100.0	0	0	0	1
Dasyuromorphia	57.1	0	25.0	0	17.9	28
Peramelemorphia	31.6	15.8	26.3	0	26.3	19
Diprotodontia	49.3	22.5	18.3	0	9.9	71
Chiroptera	52.3	34.8	2.3	0.8	9.9	132
Primates	70.6	26.2	2.4	0	0.8	126
Carnivora	44.7	37.3	10.2	2.4	5.4	295
Proboscidea	40.0	40.0	20.0	0	0	5
Perissodactyla	37.5	37.5	22.5	0	2.5	40
Artiodactyla	36.5	40.4	19.6	0	3.6	337
Lagomorpha	54.7	26.4	7.6	0	11.3	53
Total	46.6	33.9	12.7	0.73	6.0	1102

result (TNC, 1997). TNC lists about 15% of United States birds as threatened; their corresponding figure for mammals, just over 17%, is lower than IUCN's global estimate, but higher than their own estimate for birds.

Moreover, taking a wider view of the TNC list (which represents the biggest analysis to date providing complete assessment for groups other than mammals and birds), mammals are probably less threatened than

Table 3.7
The diversity of mammals in the eight biogeographic
regions. The table shows the total number of species
endemic to each region, and the number of these species
which are island or continental forms

Region	Number of endemic species		
	Island	Continent	Total
Afrotropical	102	910	1012
Antarctic	1	5	6
Australasian	419	5	424
Indomalayan	394	295	689
Nearctic	0	443	443
Neotropical	74	863	937
Oceania	49	0	49
Palearctic	41	458	499

many other groups. The Nature Conservancy estimates that in the United
States 18 % of reptiles, 26 % of gymnosperms, and 33 % angiosperms are
threatened (TNC, 1997). Figures for freshwater organisms are higher still,
at 39 % for freshwater fish, 41 % for amphibians, 51 % for crayfish, and
68 % for freshwater mussels. These data clearly reflect the serious vulnerability and degradation of inland water habitats worldwide. Mammals are
not the most threatened of the world's species.

Taxonomic spread

Our survey of different mammalian groups confirms some general perceptions about the most threatened mammals (see Cole *et al.*, 1994; IUCN,
1996). The Rodentia are the only order with a significantly smaller number
of threatened species than would be expected from the mammalian average. However, the great species richness of this order means that it still
dominates the *IUCN Red List* numerically, with 329 threatened and 45 extinct species. Furthermore, given that many threatened rodents are members of small but evolutionarily divergent lineages, such as the golden
moles of sub-Saharan Africa (Chrysochloridae) and the hutias of the West
Indies (Capromyidae), any impression that the rodents are relatively secure
would be premature.

Among the orders with a very high degree of threat, the Perissodactyla
(equids, rhinos and tapirs) contains only 17 species, of which 11 are
threatened and 2 extinct or extinct in the wild. One other species, the white
rhino, *Ceratotherium simum*, is classified as Lower Risk: conservation

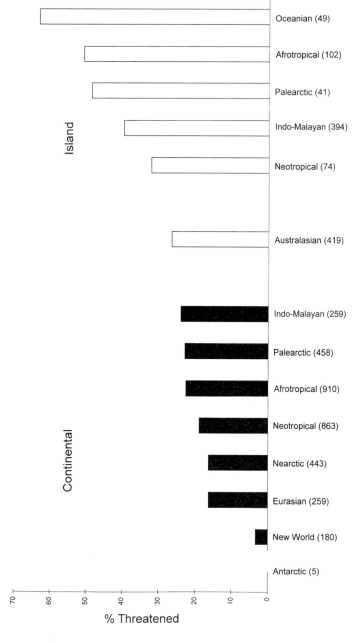

Figure 3.4 Percentage of those species restricted to single biogeographical regions which are threatened; species are further split according to whether they are endemic to islands, or occur on continents.

dependent, reflecting its recovery from near extinction at the beginning of this century. The Perissodactyla clearly present a major challenge to conservationists. The second major ungulate group, the Artiodactyla, is also highly threatened, through direct exploitation for food, skins and horn, habitat loss, and interference and competition from domestic livestock. Two other large orders of particular concern are the Primates, threatened very largely by rapid land use changes in the tropics, and the Insectivora.

In general across the mammals, many of the most threatened orders (Table 3.3) and families (Table 3.4, Figure 3.2) are species poor. A similar result has previously been reported across genera for both mammals and birds (Russell et al., 1998). Coupled with observations for birds and plants that more threatened higher taxa also tend to be of greater evolutionary age and by implication, evolutionary distinctiveness (McDowall, 1969; Hodgson, 1986; Gaston and Blackburn, 1997), this distribution of threat across groups is alarming. It strongly suggests that impending extinctions will lead to a disproportionate loss of evolutionary novelty (see discussions by Bennett and Owens, 1997; McKinney, 1998; Russell et al., 1998). Null models of the decline in evolutionary history that assume extinction is randomly distributed across the phylogeny (Nee and May, 1997) may be overoptimistic.

In contrast to the situation in birds (Gaston and Blackburn, 1995a; Bennett and Owens, 1997), levels of threat in different mammalian groups are not positively correlated with body size in any simple way. A more detailed analysis is required to investigate the nature of the relationship between threat and body size in mammals. However, we suspect that even if a positive correlation does exist, it may well be caused by a life history trait such as reproductive rate, that is linked to both size and a species' resilience (see Bennett and Owens, 1997). Moreover, such a relationship may not be very strong because some threatening processes (such as interspecific hybridisation, and wholesale habitat clearance) will nowadays drive species to extinction whatever their life history. While extinctions in the fossil record might be clearly linked to life history patterns, the broader suite of threat types facing biodiversity today may result in more complex patterns, requiring more detailed analyses to disentangle causes and constraints.

Criteria for listing

Analysis of the criteria used to classify the species into threatened categories reveals that most are listed due to observed serious declines in population size or declines associated with small ranges. Most mammalian species are apparently at risk from continuing deterministic threats.

Caughley (1994) distinguished between the intrinsic risks to small populations, that will ultimately lead to their extinction, and extrinsic processes that, unless controlled, will either lead to extinction directly or will result in population sizes so small that the intrinsic factors again come in to play. He emphasised that the appropriate actions to reduce the effects of declining populations will involve analyses of causes and then efforts to control these processes. While small populations may persist with appropriate, albeit difficult and expensive, interventions, declining populations inevitably eventually go extinct. The fact that so many mammal species qualify for inclusion in the *IUCN Red List of Threatened Animals* as a result of ongoing declines is indicative of the widespread, persistent threats that require analysis and treatment, before the situation can be improved.

Threat type

Habitat loss has previously been demonstrated to be the most common threat to both birds and mammals (Groombridge, 1992; Collar *et al.*, 1994). Here we show that for mammals, the more serious form of habitat loss – clearance as opposed to degradation or fragmentation – is also the more common. Almost two-thirds of species facing habitat loss are affected by clearance. This seems to us to be the most serious and least reversible of all threats documented to date. However, a large number of species face threats that are potentially less serious and are, at least in theory, more readily reversed.

Most forms of overkill, which affects about a third of species, could be remedied, sometimes quite quickly. Most easily tackled is hunting for sport, but other forms of overkill, including local, utilitarian use of species for food and body parts, can be addressed by effective analysis and by the implementation of management programmes to provide alternative resources or to place offtake on a sustainable basis. Ornamental uses and commercial exploitation, apparently the less prevalent forms of overexploitation, can also be addressed by effective controls and legislation at national and international levels. In all these cases conservation action needs to be associated with effective information and education programmes.

Introduced species clearly present a serious problem, especially on islands and in other areas where species have for a long time evolved in relative isolation. In some cases, especially where interspecific hybridisation is under way, these are very difficult threats to address successfully. Invasive species typically have characteristics, such as high vagility and reproductive rate, that make them very difficult to eradicate, and even when this is done, further invasions are often difficult to halt (see review by Godfray and Crawley, 1998). Nevertheless, there are some cases where effective habitat management can protect native forms, and this is certainly possible in cases where domestic animals are part of the problem. A careful analysis of the species threatened by introduced predators and competitors would be useful to identify the kinds of actions that are most likely to reverse current trends.

Taking an overview of the challenges posed by the different threatening processes, the threats due to habitat clearance and by some invasive species appear the most intractable. But the majority of species facing overkill and some of those threatened by habitat degradation and by introduced species could have their status improved where there is sufficient will and resources to do so. Putting the threat type information together with data on how threat types are distributed across the orders of mammals gives us a new way of looking into the future of different major taxa. Once again, primates emerge as the group for whom the situation is most serious. They have a large number of threatened species, mostly experiencing habitat loss, much of which is wholesale clearance. In contrast, the artiodactyls and perissodactyls, though also highly threatened, are frequently more affected by overkill of various forms, for which restorative action could be successful in the short to medium term.

Biogeographical spread

Two final points that emerge from our analyses involve the global distribution of threatened mammals. First, species restricted to islands, wherever they are, have a higher level of threat than continental species endemic to the same biogeographic region. That island species are generally more vulnerable to contemporary extinction has been widely noted before (see Groombridge, 1992; Magin et al., 1994; Pimm et al., 1995), but the consistency seen here across different clusters of islands is remarkable. Second, there are equally consistent differences in the threat levels of species from different biogeographic regions. For both island endemics and continental species, threat levels are higher in the Old World than in the New World.

The greater vulnerability of island mammals is readily understood. In general, island species will have smaller geographic ranges than their continental counterparts, and hence be more likely to be driven to extinction by any spatially-restricted threat (Pimm, 1998). This effect is presumably compounded by the fact that island species have evolved in relative isolation, and many islands have only relatively recently been colonised by people: hence island biotas are less likely than continental biotas to have been purged of their more vulnerable species or to have evolved resilience to exotic competitors, predators and pathogens (Magin et al., 1994). These twin effects, of small range size and naivety, presumably outweigh any greater resilience that island forms might be expected to exhibit to the effects of anthropogenically-induced population smallness (Lawton, 1994; Manne et al., 1999).

Explanations for the contrast between the New and Old Worlds are less obvious. However, the pattern has been noted before, both in a subset of mammals (Cole et al., 1994), and in a comparison of Neotropical versus other birds (Collar et al., 1997). One possible explanation is historical. Across tropical countries, human populations first showed rapid increases in size rather earlier in Central and South America than in Asia or Africa (data from McEvedy and Jones, 1978). This may mean that neotropical mammal faunas were purged of some of their more vulnerable species before extensive biological collection began (see Balmford, 1996 for a synthesis of similar cases). Perhaps a more convincing explanation comes from the scanty data on recent habitat losses. For the best documented habitats, tropical forests, there is good evidence that the percentage of original cover still remaining is higher for the neotropics than for either the Indomalayan region or Africa (Sayer and Collins, 1991; Sayer, 1992, 1996). This pattern is reiterated in global analyses of disturbance of all habitat types (Hannah et al., 1995), which indicate that of the tropical regions, the neotropics are the least disturbed, while the nearctic is less disturbed than the palearctic. Whether the greater level of threat of Old World mammals is driven by historical or contemporary factors (or indeed by some combination of the two), our results suggest a pattern which, if general to other groups, may be of considerable interest to policy-makers and funding agencies concerned with stemming the ongoing loss of mammalian diversity.

ACKNOWLEDGEMENTS

The data sets on which these analyses are based were compiled by the late Émile Lefebvre, with additional input from Andy Purvis, Nathalie Walker and Nick Isaac. We are grateful to Jonathan Baillie and Brian Groombridge for access to the IUCN Red List information, Nigel Collar for helpful comments, and the editors of this volume for their patience. This research was funded by a Small Grant from NERC; GMM is grateful to NERC for support.

4

Charismatic megafauna as 'flagship species'

NIGEL LEADER-WILLIAMS AND HOLLY T. DUBLIN

INTRODUCTION

Species are the fundamental building blocks of nature and ecology. Without the continued survival of many of their number, the goals of ecosystem and biosphere management are unattainable. Species are also the fundamental units of the evolutionary process, and their increasing loss due to anthropogenic causes represents an irreversible depletion of genetic material upon which evolutionary potential can work in future. Hence, extinctions arising from man's influence are the events that the conservation movement aims to prevent (Diamond, 1989). Equally, there has been considerable debate among academic conservation biologists and practising conservationists about whether conservation goals are best achieved by promoting single-species management as opposed to management of whole ecosystems. Hence, a recent review asked the question 'is single-species management passé in the landscape era?', and came to the conclusion that ecosystem management, usually at a landscape scale, was a possible solution to the problems of single-species management (Simberloff, 1998b).

A number of different concepts lie at the heart of the single-species management approach. The term 'flagship species' receives wide currency, and many throw-away sentences among practising conservationists, but what exactly does it mean? Is it simply jargon, a glib expression that rolls easily off the tongue, or does the term have a well-defined, useful or potential role in real world conservation? Furthermore, other terms such as 'keystone', 'indicator' and 'umbrella' species also appear in the scientific literature and, less commonly, among the jargon used by practising conservationists. To what extent are these terms used inter-changeably with 'flagship', and to what extent do they and should they actually differ?

The term 'flagship' is often used with respect to mammals, the subject of this volume, and most often to large charismatic species of mammal. Hence, this chapter aims to explore the role of large mammals as flagship species, with the ultimate aim of determining the extent to which this distorts priorities away from more broadly-based biodiversity conservation or ecosystem management. The chapter first aims to clarify the origin, definition and use of the term 'flagship species', and of related terms in single-species conservation, based on a survey of existing literature across all groups of species. The chapter next seeks to explore the role of large mammals as flagship species, from the perspectives of different stakeholders in conservation, including those living among large mammals in developing countries, those from whom money is raised for conservation in developed countries, and those conservation organisations who support conservation action in the field. Finally, we summarise our conclusions that use of mammals as flagship species has a clear strategic purpose and need not deflect from wider conservation goals.

ORIGIN, DEFINITION AND USE OF 'FLAGSHIP SPECIES' AND RELATED TERMS

The focus of flagship species

The Oxford Dictionary defines *Flagship* as 'a ship bearing the admiral's flag'. In other words, this ship acts as a focus, rallying point and command centre for other ships in the fleet. This sense of focus, rallying and command has given rise to the linked concept of flagship species, which first appears to have been used by conservationists in the mid-1980s in connection with the successful programme to restore the status of golden lion tamarins *Leontopithecus rosalia* in Brazil (Mittermeier, 1986), and to highlight the plight of African elephants *Loxodonta africana*, and of black and white rhinos (*Diceros bicornis* and *Ceratotherium simum*), throughout Africa (Western, 1987).

The initial use of 'flagship species' also recognised that charismatic megavertebrates might be the best vehicles for conveying the entire issue of conservation to the public (Mittermeier, 1986, 1988; Western, 1987). Primates, in particular, were considered the best flagships for tropical forest conservation, and have been subjects of major public awareness campaigns. Thus, primates became the flagship species for entire regions, and the campaigns using them as symbols are excellent examples of the way in which key groups of animals can be used to sell the whole issue of conservation, both in tropical countries and in the developed world. Thus, there is a strategic, rather than an ecological or biological, sense to the original use of flagship species (Mittermeier, 1986, 1988).

Later authors also believed that the term 'flagship species' described an animal that stands for or promotes conservation in a general or regional sense. Elephants and rhinos, as the world's largest terrestrial mammals, took on special significance as conservation flagships, and also served as flagships for the sanctuaries set up to preserve Africa's wildlife (Western, 1987). Dietz *et al.* (1994) considered that 'the giant panda used in the logo of the World Wide Fund for Nature to be a flagship species for nature conservation efforts worldwide, particularly for securing financial support. From a practical stand-point, the image helps to focus attention on a single species, rather than on the fuzzy concept of species richness, or fuzzier concept of genetic diversity. Flagship species, then, are those that when conserved *in situ* result in the conservation of a significant number of other species across a wide array of taxonomic groups, and in functioning natural systems.' Equally, the last part of this statement of Dietz *et al.* (1994) illustrates some of the dilemmas that this chapter aims to clarify. Their last sentence could also be construed as encompassing some biological or ecological role for flagship species, that in turn stray into the concepts encompassed within the definitions of other terms in common use in single-species management, namely 'keystone', 'indicator' and 'umbrella' species. Accordingly, the next section explores the extent to which there is separation or overlap between the use of, and definitions for, these terms.

Textbook search for use and definitions of terms in single-species management

A search was undertaken of the indexes and contents of 25 conservation and biodiversity textbooks published between 1986 (when the term 'flagship species' was first used) and 1998 to determine how widely reference was made to terms currently used in single-species management. These books encompassed both single author and edited volumes (in some cases the latter also contained chapters that are cited in the case studies below). This survey showed that in textbooks, 'keystone species' appears more commonly, while the terms 'indicator', 'flagship' and 'umbrella' species appear less commonly (Figure 4.1). Hence, academic conservation biologists who author or edit textbooks appear to feel more comfortable with the idea of 'keystone species', and feel less comfortable with, or see less value in using, the other terms, including 'flagship species'.

To determine if there is separation and/or overlap in the definitions between terms, we compared textbooks where all terms are defined in the same volume. While all four terms are shown in a table in Spellerberg (1996), only 'keystone' and 'umbrella' are defined. Hence, our comparison relies on Heywood (1995), and Meffe and Carroll (1997), together with

Box 4.1 Definitions of common terms in single-species conservation taken from the same source, based on (a) Heywood (1995), (b) Meffe and Carroll (1997) and (c) Simberloff (1998b)

Flagship species

(a) Popular, charismatic species that serve as symbols and rallying points to stimulate conservation awareness and action. At the larger scale these include animals such as condors, pandas, rhinos, large cats and large primates, while at the smaller scale they include orchids, cacti and invertebrates such as large butterflies and stick insects. Flagship species may serve as both indicators and/or umbrella species and also provide a highly visible reminder of the progress of a particular conservation management plan (p. 491).

(b) The focus on species in conservation has largely centred on vertebrates, especially birds and large mammals. They are visible, dominant parts of our natural environments, and, for better or for worse, extract more sympathy from the public than do most plants or insects. These flagship or 'charismatic' species draw financial support more easily..., and by doing so serve to protect habitat and other species under the 'umbrella' of their large habitat requirements (p. 80).

(c) A species that has become a symbol and leading element of an entire conservation campaign (p. 250).

Keystone species

(a) A species whose impacts on its community or ecosystem are large and would be greater than would be expected from its relative abundance. This definition is unconstrained by a species trophic status, mode of impact, or nature of community or ecosystem response. Keystone species are usually detected when they are removed or disappear from the ecosystem (p. 290).

(b) A species whose impact on its community or ecosystem is large, and disproportionately large relative to its abundance (p. 238).

(c) A species having impacts on many others, often far beyond what might have been expected from a consideration of their biomass or abundance (p. 254).

Indicator species

(a) Species that reflect the quality and changes in environmental conditions as well as aspects of community composition. Species of amphibians, molluscs, birds, chirnomid flies, fungi, corals and other marine invertebrates may all be useful indicators. Changes in distributions, abundances and demographic characteristics of such species may indicate impending adverse changes in the ecosystem as a whole. However, indicator species are often chosen for monitoring simply because they represent a particular use, ecosystem or management concern, or are easily sampled, sorted and identified (p. 487).

Box 4.1 *continued*

(b) Species that act as surrogates for the larger community. This strategy requires providing suitable habitat for species that are known to be sensitive to habitat fragmentation, pollution, or other stresses that degrade biodiversity, and monitoring their populations (p. 395).

(c) Species whose presence and fluctuations are believed (or hoped) to reflect either those of other species in the community or chemical and/or physical changes in the environment (p. 248).

Umbrella species

(a) Those whose area of occupancy or home range are large enough and whole habitat requirements are wide enough that, if they are given a sufficiently large area for their protection will bring other species under their protection (p. 490).

(b) Species requiring large blocks of relatively natural or unaltered habitat to maintain viable populations (p. 69).

(c) A species with such demanding habitat requirements and large area requirements that saving it will automatically save many other species (p. 249).

Simberloff (1998b). These definitions generally achieve good internal agreement and consistency (Box 4.1). This is perhaps not surprising for the term most used and valued by academic conservation biologists, who have already put considerable effort into reaching a consensus definition for 'keystone species' (Paine, 1995; Power and Mills, 1995; Power *et al.*, 1996), which largely appears to have been incorporated in textbooks without alteration. That the definitions for the less used terms of 'flagship' and 'umbrella' species also achieve some internal consistency (Box 4.1) is both perhaps more surprising, but nevertheless pleasing. Of all the terms, the definitions for indicator species perhaps achieve the least internal consistency (Box 4.1). Equally, indicator species appear to encompass two different roles or purposes, given that they are expected both to reflect changes in the environment and to reflect community composition (see also Simberloff, 1998b).

A number of conclusions may be drawn from this comparison (Table 4.1).

- Definitions for 'keystone' and 'umbrella' species encompass different but purely ecological roles for particular species, as follows:
'keystone' species have a disproportionate effect on their ecosystem, due to their size or activity, and any change in their population will have

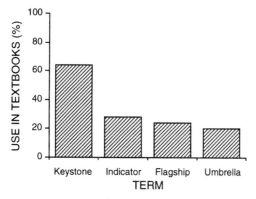

Figure 4.1 Use of common terms in single-species management by authors and editors of conservation and biodiversity textbooks published since 1986 (based on Norton, 1986; Soulé, 1986; Jones, 1987; McNeely, 1988; Wilson, 1988; Western and Pearl, 1989; McNeely *et al.*, 1990; Fiedler and Jain, 1992; Groombridge, 1992; Primack, 1993; Huston, 1994; Olney *et al.*, 1994; Heywood, 1995; Primack, 1995; Caughley and Gunn, 1996; Dobson, 1996; Gaston, 1996a; Hunter, 1996; Spellerberg, 1996; Jeffries, 1997; Meffe and Carroll, 1997; Perlman and Adelson, 1997; Reaka-Kudla *et al.*, 1997; Milner-Gulland and Mace, 1998; Sutherland, 1998). The difference between the use of keystone and other terms is significant ($G = 13.31$, $df = 3$, $P < 0.01$).

correspondingly large effects on their ecosystem; and, 'umbrella' species have such demanding habitat and/or area requirements that, by maintaining minimum areas needed for viable populations, sufficient areas should also be maintained to ensure the viability of smaller and more abundant species.

- In contrast, definitions for 'flagship' species encompass purely strategic objectives in single-species conservation (see also Table 3.2 of Spellerberg, 1996), as follows: 'flagship' species are chosen to raise public awareness or financial support for conservation action.

- In further contrast, definitions for 'indicator' species encompass both ecological and strategic roles, largely depending on whether they are intended to reflect community composition or environmental change (Table 4.1). In the latter situation, the definitions (Box 4.1) imply that indicator species must both respond to the particular environmental change of concern, and be chosen because they are amenable to an appropriate form of monitoring that demonstrates that change.

- One species may fulfil the definitions for one or more of these terms, depending on the situation or context in which the term is used. However, the terms 'keystone' and 'umbrella' are likely to remain more of a fixed characteristic or property of that species. In contrast, the term

Table 4.1
Definitions of common terms in single-species conservation

Term	Role		
	Ecological	Ecological and Strategic	Strategic
Keystone species	Vital role in ecosystem		
Umbrella species	Shelter other species		
Indicator species (i)	Reflect community composition		
Indicator species (ii)		Chosen to reflect environmental change	
Flagship species			Chosen to raise public awareness, action and funding

'flagship' and, possibly to a lesser extent, 'indicator' may be more context-specific.

This analysis appears to have shown that there is clear separation of the definitions and different roles for terms used in single-species conservation, with almost no overlap (Box 4.1 and Table 4.1). Hence, the next section will explore how the term 'flagship species' may have been used or misused in the literature.

Examples of the use and misuse of the term 'flagship species' in case studies
A BIDS (Bibliographical Databases) search of flagship species was conducted to determine the different ways in which the term has been used in the literature from 1986 to 1998. This search aimed to cover the widest possible use of the term and capture examples from species outside our own experience. The search produced 14 journal articles, and a further four book chapters incorporating case studies from textbooks were also included in this analysis (Table 4.2). The term 'flagship species' appears to have been used in a much wider context than the current definitions allow (Box 4.1 and Table 4.1).

Correct use of 'flagship species'
The coining of the term 'flagship species' and its subsequent use for various primates in biodiversity hotspots (Mittermeier, 1986, 1988) has already been discussed. Primates, especially golden lion tamarins, lemurs and

Table 4.2

The context and species or group in which the term 'flagship species' is used in the literature

Species or issue	Group	Context	Reference
Golden lion tamarin (*Leontopithecus rosalia*) Murqui (*Brachyteles arachnoides*)	Mammal: Primate	Habitat and regional conservation of Atlantic forest, Brazil	Mittermeier (1986, 1988)
African elephant (*Loxodonta africana*) Black and white rhinoceros (*Diceros bicornis, Ceratotherium simum*)	Mammal: Proboscid Perissodactyl	Africa's declining populations of large mammals	Western (1987)
Wild maize (*Zea diploperennis*)	Plant	Biodiversity and species conservation in Mexico's mountains, including mammals	Iltis (1988)
Lemurs	Mammal: Primate	Malagasy fauna, flora and habitat	Mittermeier (1988)
Lion-tailed macaque (*Macaca silenus*)	Mammal: Primate	Rain forest habitat protection in India	Karanth (1992)
Kakapo (*Strigops habroptilus*)	Bird	Species as conservation units, with habitat restoration as complementary to species conservation	Towns and Williams (1993)
Lion tamarin spp. (*Leontopithecus* spp.)	Mammal: Primate	Captive breeding for reintroduction in support of species and habitat conservation of Atlantic forest, Brazil	Dietz *et al.* (1994) Kleiman and Mallinson (1998)
Asian elephant (*Elephas maximus*)	Mammal: Proboscid	Elephant reserves as areas covering larger tracts of land than tiger reserves in India	Johnsingh and Joshua (1994)
Butterflies	Invertebrate	Focus for global efforts to conserve invertebrates through sound management of species and habitat protection	New *et al.* (1995)

Species	Taxonomic group	Description	Reference
British upland birds	Birds	Focus for habitat restoration of upland communities in Britain	Thompson *et al.* (1995)
Species held in captivity	—	Captive breeding to excite public attention in support of protecting habitat and other taxa	Hutchins *et al.* (1995)
Mountain tapir (*Tapirus pinchaque*)	Mammal: Perissodactyl	Focus for conservation of national park and high northern Andes	Downer (1996)
Endemic freshwater algae	Algae	Distinctive or novel endemic species in support of less distinguished species in Australia	Tyler (1996)
Eurasian otter (*Lutra lutra*) European water vole (*Arvicola terrestris*)	Mammal: Carnivore Rodent	Economic valuation of willingness to pay for species conservation programmes	White *et al.* (1997)
Puku (*Kobus vardoni*)	Mammal: Artiodactyl	Focus for conservation of national park in Zambia	Goldspink *et al.* (1998)
Arabian oryx (*Oryx leucoryx*)	Mammal: Artiodactyl	Captive breeding for reintroduction in support of species conservation and creating protected areas in Saudi Arabia	Ostrowski *et al.* (1998)
Single species management *in situ*	—	Single-species management no longer appears as appropriate as landscape management	Simberloff (1998b)

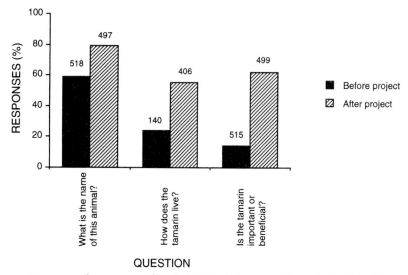

Figure 4.2 The response of local adults to different questions about golden lion tamarins before and after two years of project activities (from Dietz *et al.*, 1994). More local people could identify the name and correct social organisation of tamarins, and more people thought they were important or beneficial after the project. All differences are highly significant (G = 155.05, 43.01, and 236.52, respectively, df = 1, *P* < 0.001).

macaques, have served to raise public awareness for rain forest as well as their own conservation in Brazil and Madagascar (Mittermeier, 1986, 1988) and India (Karanth, 1992), and for captive breeding programmes designed to help reinforce *in situ* populations through introduction (Dietz *et al.*, 1994). Indeed, questionnaire data from before and after the golden lion tamarin programme has shown heightened awareness of some key issues in the conservation of tamarins (Figure 4.2) and of other species in the rain forest (Dietz *et al.*, 1994). Equally, to have more conclusively proven the point about the value of flagship species, the questionnaires could have included more questions about rain forest conservation. Nevertheless, the earliest use of primates as flagship species for rain forest conservation fully corresponds to the strategic role outlined in current definitions (Box 4.1 and Table 4.1).

The willingness of the public to pay for the conservation of two aquatic British mammals, the Eurasian otter *Lutra lutra* and the water vole *Arvicola terrestris*, living in similar riparian habitats and facing similar threats of habitat change, habitat fragmentation and pollution, was tested in North Yorkshire (Table 4.2). The otter is a well known charismatic species seen in advertisements to raise funds for conservation (see Figure 4.3), with bodies

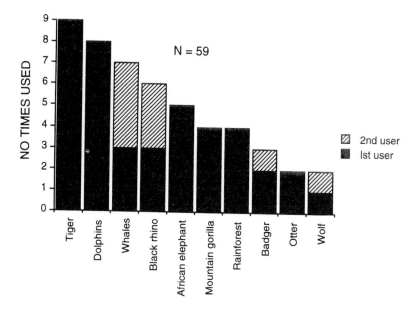

Figure 4.3 The number of times that advertisements appeared in *BBC Wildlife* magazine during January to November 1997. In some cases (e.g., whales and black rhino), the same taxa were used by different organisations hoping to raise funds. Advertisements that appeared only once for orangutan, cheetah, bear, hippo, fisheries, British birds, ducks and fisheries, and a general advertisement for WWF's work that appeared twice, are not shown in the figure.

such as the International Otter Survival Fund dedicated to ensuring its survival in the UK. In contrast, the water vole is less well known to the general public, despite the enduring popularity of Kenneth Grahame's *Wind in the Willows*. The study found that on average a member of the public was willing to pay significantly more for the otter than the water vole, and indeed more for the otter alone than for the otter and water vole combined (Figure 4.4). Hence, the public perceived the two species and indeed both species combined quite differently, suggesting that the more simple and the more charismatic the message, the more money could be raised for conservation. Furthermore, aggregated over the whole North Yorkshire population, these results equated to considerably more than the sums allocated for the whole country in the United Kingdom Action Plans for otters and water voles. Hence, charismatic species can be used to raise more money than is provided through planned government expenditure (White *et al.*, 1997). While willingness to pay techniques are only hypothetical surrogates that cannot be equated with actual money put in a collection box, a

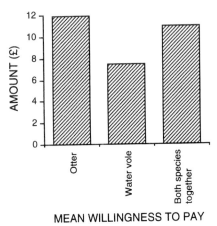

MEAN WILLINGNESS TO PAY

Figure 4.4 The mean willingness to pay for the conservation of two threatened aquatic mammals by the people of North Yorkshire, shown as willingness to pay for the otter and water vole alone and for both species combined (from White et al., 1997).

clear value was demonstrated for flagship species, which has been used correctly in the strategic context of raising funds for conservation.

The discovery of a new species of virus-resistant wild maize, with its possible utilitarian value for human food production, high in Mexico's mountains highlighted their importance as areas for biodiversity (Table 4.2). This increase in local public awareness led to the establishment of the 1350 km² Sierra de la Manantlan Biosphere Reserve that was dedicated by Mexico's President and that also serves to provide protection for parrots and jaguars *Panthera onca*, orchids and ocelots *Leopardus pardalis*, crested guans *Penelope purpurascens* and giant magnolias, among a list of 10 000 other species (Iltis, 1988). Hence, describing this species of wild maize as a flagship species in this particular strategic context of raising public awareness and stimulating support for conservation action is fully justified. Indeed, this context-specific example is interesting for two reasons. First, species other than charismatic megafauna can serve as flagships for wider action in a local context, as shown here by the uncharismatic, but possibly utilitarian, species of maize working for the benefit of the charismatic and all other biodiversity! Second, it serves to reinforce the importance of the specific strategic context in which the term 'flagship species' is used.

The captive breeding and reintroduction community also use the concept of flagship species (Table 4.2). In broad terms, there are two schools of thought on how captive breeding and reintroduction can maximise its value to *in situ* conservation. One school of thought believes that selecting taxa for captive breeding solely on the possibility of a future reintroduction provides too narrow a focus. Instead, serious consideration should be given to the ability of a species to contribute to more immediate conservation goals, including public education, fund-raising to support field conservation and scientific research. Because zoos have limited resources, they could focus their long-term breeding programmes on flagship species that can excite public attention and help protect habitat and other taxa, rather than on the broad array of species that are currently endangered (Hutchins *et al.*, 1995). Another school of thought believes that taxa for captive breeding should be selected on the basis that they can be most successfully and most economically returned to the wild (Balmford *et al.*, 1996). Probably the best example of a captive bred species that has been returned to the wild is the Arabian oryx *Oryx leucoryx*, which has served as a focus for the conservation of other species and for the establishment of protected areas (Ostrowski *et al.*, 1998). Whatever one believes is the most appropriate direction for the captive breeding community to follow, the use of the term flagship species in the context of both papers (Table 4.2) appears correct.

Flagship species can be misapplied or fulfil the definitions for other terms

The use of flagship species to describe African elephants and rhinos (Western, 1987) has been discussed already. These species have certainly been used to raise public awareness and funding for conservation (Figure 4.3). However, much discussion in this paper centres around declines in rhino and elephant numbers, and the failure of protected areas in their intended purpose of securing populations of wildlife (Western, 1987). Hence, in the context of this paper, elephants and rhinos also take on a largely strategic role as indicators that reflect change in status of large mammal populations, in this case through overhunting by man, rather than the role of flagships.

Asian elephants *Elaphas maximus* have also been described as conforming to the role of flagship species (Table 4.2). Asian elephants are a highly revered and glamorous species through which to gain public support for conservation in India (Johnsingh and Joshua, 1994). They are also a species that needs large and well-managed units for their conservation. This would also provide excellent habitat for the conservation of other species, which fulfils the definition and ecological role for 'umbrella species'. Most of this paper dealt with habitat restoration to ensure this umbrella role, rather than with how to raise public awareness or funds for elephant conservation (Johnsingh and Joshua, 1994). Clearly Asian elephants can fulfil both the ecological role of umbrella and the strategic role of flagship species.

However, the term 'umbrella species' was not applied to Asian elephants, rather the term 'flagship species' was enlarged to encompass the role of a second term, and therefore used out of context.

Mountain tapirs *Tapirus pinchaque* were also described as a flagship species for the high Andes (Table 4.2). They are critically endangered and face threats from deforestation, encroachment from livestock and humans, hunting and lack of public awareness of their plight (Downer, 1996). This paper made a plea for conservation action in Sangay National Park, Ecuador that is a vital stronghold for mountain tapir. Measures suggested included education of local people and various forms of benefit sharing through contractual agreements and ecotourism. If the mountain tapir were used as the strategic focus for raising public awareness and/or funding for conservation action, then it would clearly fulfil the role of a flagship species. However, much of this paper discusses the mountain tapir as a seed disperser, browse modifier and as prey for other species, also suggesting its clear ecological role as a possible keystone species (Downer, 1996). In addition, decreases in home range size of mountain tapirs reflected increasing cattle densities, also suggesting a possible role for tapirs as indicator species for increasing livestock densities.

Heather moorland is a declining habitat, virtually confined to Great Britain, that contains important assemblages of plants, insects and birds, with less impressive assemblages of mammals, reptiles and amphibians (Thompson *et al.*, 1995). Since 1940 20 % of heather moorland has been lost as a result of afforestation, agricultural reclamation, high grazing pressure by sheep and bracken invasion. Further areas of moorland are under threat. National and regional targets for heather moorland regeneration have been set. Furthermore, six species of birds dependant on heather moorland (red grouse *Lagopus lagopus*, black grouse *Tetrao tetrix*, hen harrier *Circus cyneus*, merlin *Falco columbarius*, golden eagle *Aquila chrysaetos* and golden plover *Pluvialis apricaria*) were selected as flagships, of which it was aimed to extend or enhance their breeding distributions (Table 4.2). These flagships were selected 'on the basis of their international importance, declining status, capacity to colonise, or economic value... Owners and managers can readily adjudge the changing status of these species, which also generate strong public interest' (Thompson *et al.*, 1995). This choice of criteria also included an explicit role for birds as indicators and possibly an implicit umbrella role. Furthermore, it was not made clear how the most perceived conservation need of a new system of countrywide incentives for farmers, tied closely to meeting nature conservation objectives, would be achieved through focusing on the proposed flagship species.

An African antelope, the puku *Kobus vardoni*, was described as a flagship species for Kasanka National Park, Zambia (Table 4.2). The park had become run down and the puku population depleted as a result of uncontrolled burning and poaching. The private Kasanka Trust was established in an attempt to arrest and reverse these changes. The puku, and other antelopes such as the sitatunga *Tragelaphus spekii* were seen as the main attraction for tourists, who in turn were likely to be the main source of revenue for the foreseeable future, therefore justifying the label of flagship species and the straightforward scientific study of status that formed the focus of this paper (Goldspink *et al.*, 1998). This would appear a rather passive and therefore inappropriate use of the term 'flagship species', through a species attracting tourists, that in turn provide revenue for a private trust to rehabilitate the park. There is no sense here of rallying public awareness around puku or using a 'Save the Puku Trust' to raise funds for conserving Kasanka.

Butterflies act as flagships for a growing global interest in invertebrate conservation (Table 4.2). Recent developments emphasise species and habitat management based on a sound understanding of ecology. Single species form a clear focus for efforts to conserve butterflies in temperate zones in developed countries, through management and recovery plans. In contrast, butterfly faunas are more diverse in many tropical zones, assemblages may be poorly known, and resources for practical conservation may be restricted. Hence the major emphasis here must be on habitat protection, and on conservation measures that benefit local people, rather than on single species management (New *et al.*, 1995). The sense of this paper centres around the laudable wish of respected invertebrate scientists to see invertebrates conserved. However, the term 'flagship species' was not used in the sense of rallying for the wider public to their objectives, and its use in this context therefore also appears weak.

Some new and endemic genera of freshwater Australian algae were of such distinctive appearance or novelty as to be regarded as flagship taxa, and their existence increases the probability of less distinguished species also being endemic (Table 4.2). In this case, the distinctive endemics were indicating the likely presence of other endemic species (Tyler, 1996). Hence, in this context the use of indicator species for the purpose of reflecting community structure would have been most appropriate. If ways can be found in future to use the distinctive endemic algae in a strategic sense to raise public awareness or funds for algal, and freshwater, conservation in Australia, then they would also become flagship species in this context.

Conclusions on use of 'flagship species' and related terms

Our analysis based on surveys of textbooks and scientific literature show mostly clear distinctions in the definitions and roles of terms used in single-species conservation (Table 4.1). There is an obvious split between the relatively ecological roles of keystone and umbrella species, and the highly strategic role in choosing flagship species to raise public awareness, action and funding. However, some confusion still remains in the dual roles and definitions for indicator species, which is not of direct concern to this consideration of flagship species.

Equally, our survey shows that several authors have misapplied or misused the term 'flagship species' (Table 4.2), with the following areas of confusion:

- One species may fulfil the definitions for one or more terms commonly used in single-species conservation, depending on the situation or context in which the term is used.
- The term 'flagship' should only be used in very strategic, and possibly more context-specific, sense (Table 4.1).

Our literature survey has confirmed that those academic conservation biologists and practising conservationists who have (correctly) used the term 'flagship species' usually apply it to mammals (Table 4.2). Therefore, the next section examines for whom large mammals may be charismatic and the extent to which large mammals may be marketed and promoted.

MAMMALS AS FLAGSHIP SPECIES

Much early interest in wildlife conservation grew out of a desire to save some of the world's most spectacular species (Fitter and Scott, 1978), and in some situations conservationists still wish to see refined approaches to single-species management as the basis for their conservation actions (Towns and Williams, 1993). As noted already, many practising conservationists believe that charismatic megavertebrates still remain the best and most used vehicles to communicate the entire issue of conservation to the public (Mittermeier, 1988). As discussed elsewhere in this volume, large mammals have been used as the basis for promoting:

- The establishment of individual protected areas as a focus both for conservation and tourism, although this has led to many ad hoc reservations (e.g., Leader-Williams et al., 1990b; Pressey, 1994).

- The monitoring of success of conservation action, although this may not provide any clear picture of how successfully less visible and easily countable species are being conserved (e.g., Western, 1987; Downer, 1996).
- The establishment of captive breeding and reintroduction programmes (Hutchins et al., 1995; Balmford et al., 1996).

Equally, others note that basing conservation objectives on single-species management poses problems (reviewed in Simberloff, 1998b). Therefore, before considering whether large mammals have a valuable role as flagship species, it is also pertinent to ask two important and somewhat inter-related questions, 'What makes these species charismatic?' and 'To whom are they charismatic?'.

Dissonance in attitudes towards mammals

It must be recognised that many species of large mammals, for example wolf *Canis lupus*, bison *Bison bison*, tiger *Panthera tigris* and rhino, have been lost from areas inhabited by high density populations of Caucasians and Asians, including those areas to which they have emigrated elsewhere in the developing world. Furthermore, consumption patterns of Caucasians and Asians have contributed to habitat loss in the developing world, for example through rubber, oil palm and tea plantations and through logging. In addition, Caucasians have introduced many other species around the world, either by accident or to meet their needs. In other words, it is largely Caucasian and Asian actions in causing mammalian (and avian) extinctions since the 1600s that allowed definition of the 'evil quartet' (Diamond, 1989). Yet it is now largely Caucasians who are setting the conservation agenda in other parts of the world, such as Latin America, Africa and tropical Asia, causing people in those regions to face the same dilemmas as Caucasians once did many years ago.

Hence there may be considerable dissonance in what is perceived 'charismatic' by different people, depending on their background and socio-economic grouping (Dublin, 1994, 1996). In extreme terms, there are groups of people, living in isolation from wild species and yet attributing high aesthetic values to wild species and wild areas. Such people have considerable freedom of choice with regard to wildlife, and while their commitment to conservation of species may be high, their actual experience of conservation is low. They may choose to spend their discretionary disposable income to pay for an opportunity to buy an experience with wild animals, either close to home in zoos, or far away on a safari to Africa. At the

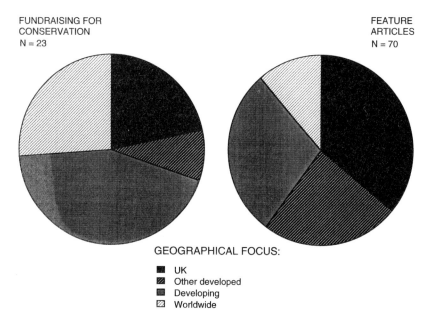

FUNDRAISING FOR
CONSERVATION
N = 23

FEATURE
ARTICLES
N = 70

GEOGRAPHICAL FOCUS:
- UK
- Other developed
- Developing
- Worldwide

Figure 4.5 A comparison of the geographical focus of feature articles and of advertisements seeking funding for conservation that appeared in BBC *Wildlife* magazine during January to November 1997. The difference tends to significance $(G = 6.77, df = 3, P < 0.10)$.

opposite extreme, there are groups of people who live amongst wild species in remote areas, lacking the basic necessities of life, often competing with wildlife over limited resources and which may threaten their lives or livelihoods. Such people usually lack choice about sharing their time with wildlife, to which they may be overtly hostile. Hence conservation of wildlife may be a low priority relative to the survival of family members. This dissonance can be highlighted by data from developed countries.

The magazine *BBC Wildlife* is published in the UK, a country that has lost many of its large mammals, and which hotly debates the circumstances, if any, under which large carnivores like wolves may be introduced to former range on these islands (Yalden, 1986). A year's issue of *BBC Wildlife* was surveyed to determine if attempts to raise funds for conservation in advertisements differed from feature articles aimed to inform. This survey produced 70 feature articles and 23 different advertisements, some of which were used several times throughout the year. In terms of the geographical focus, feature articles tended to concentrate on the UK and other developed countries more than advertisements seeking funds, which tended to concentrate more heavily on developing countries and issues

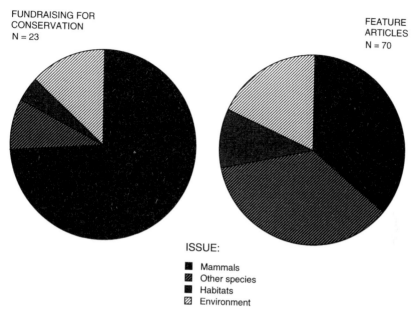

FUNDRAISING FOR
CONSERVATION
N = 23

FEATURE
ARTICLES
N = 70

ISSUE:

■ Mammals
▨ Other species
■ Habitats
▨ Environment

Figure 4.6 A comparison of the issues raised in feature articles and in advertisements seeking funding for conservation that appeared in *BBC Wildlife* magazine during January to November 1997. The difference is significant ($G = 11.62$, $df = 3$, $P < 0.05$).

worldwide (Figure 4.5). More strikingly, feature articles covered relatively equally a broad range of issues including mammals, other species, habitats and wider environmental issues such as pollution, as befits a broadly titled magazine. In contrast, advertisements aimed at raising funds for conservation concentrated very heavily on mammals (Figure 4.6).

A further analysis of the 59 times that fund-raising advertisements used particular species or issues, including in some cases by a second advertiser, shows the preponderance of large charismatic mammals (Figure 4.3). The featured terrestrial mammals came from both overseas (tiger, black rhino, African elephant, mountain gorilla *Gorilla gorilla beringei*, wolf, orang utan *Pongo pygmaeus*, cheetah *Acinonyx jubatus*, bear and hippo *Hippopotamus amphibius*) and the UK (badgers *Meles meles* and otters), while dolphins and whales also featured strongly. Many of the advertisements were placed by organisations carrying emotive names (e.g., Care for the Wild, Wildlife Aid) or names directly associated with the species in question (e.g., Whale and Dolphin Conservation Society, Dian Fossey Gorilla Fund). Pandas, however, did not feature directly in the advertisements, except in the context of the WWF logo (see comments above by Dietz *et al.*, 1994).

These *BBC Wildlife* data therefore show that very different tactics are used to inform an affluent readership that mostly lives remotely from wildlife, and to raise money from that same readership in support of conservation. When aiming to raise money, there is a definite dumbing down to charismatic single-species and a tendency to move away from home. However, how does this perceived charisma among an affluent western readership parting with money tally with other interest groups? The tiger, featured most heavily among the *BBC Wildlife* advertisements (Figure 4.3), will serve as an example. This species is endangered, largely as a result of habitat loss and poaching pressure (IUCN, 1996; Nowell and Jackson, 1996), and has immense national and cultural significance in India. Tigers have also recently been shown by a group of conservation biologists to serve as a useful focus for a landscape-based approach to conservation (Wikramanayake *et al.*, 1998). In seeking measures to further protect the tiger, calls are frequently made for the identification of high priority populations, better legislation, reduction of habitat loss and prey base decline, control of trade in tiger parts, and support for tigers among people living near them (Nowell and Jackson, 1996). However, a less voiced concern is how to respond to problem tigers, those that kill or injure humans and livestock (Tilson and Nyhus, 1998). Such attacks are one of the most basic causes of local animosity towards tiger conservation (Saberwal, 1997), and local farmers may be the most important 'illegal' killers of tigers in some areas (Plowden and Bowles, 1997). Yet there is a dissonance, as it seems hard for those in distant lands to understand that others do not share their enthusiasm for tigers as a purely charismatic flagship species, though not wishing to entertain large predators in their own backyard! Nevertheless, it is clear that conservation organisations with their funding bases in more affluent societies will continue to use charismatic species to promote conservation both at home and abroad, and we now examine how two such organisations use and/or are influenced by the concept of flagship species.

The strategic use of mammals as flagships by conservation organisations

The historic focus of conservation organisations on species conservation provides communicators and fund-raisers with two very significant benefits. First it is easy to communicate and promote such an organisation as a coherent focused institution, comprehensible to the large public of potential supporters in a competitive environment. Second, it provides few intellectual impediments to the scope of appropriate fund-raising activities, as already shown in *BBC Wildlife* (Figures 4.3, 4.5, 4.6). This section examines how two international conservation organisations, Fauna & Flora International and the World Wide Fund for Nature (WWF), use species, and particularly charismatic mammals, as part of their strategies to promote conservation.

Fauna & Flora International 100 % Fund

Fauna & Flora International (FFI) is the oldest international conservation organisation in the world, having been founded in 1903. The organisation still remains relatively small compared with those founded more recently, and has embraced a clear mission to focus on projects, taxonomic groups and geographical areas where its relatively small funding base can make a difference and by seeking projects that do not attract the attention of other larger conservation organisations. In 1971, FFI launched its 100 % Fund, which aimed to make funding available to catalytic projects without any loss of administrative overheads. It should be noted that the 100 % Fund is only reactive to the applications it receives, rather than proactive in designing projects that FFI believes are needed. Nevertheless, data from the 100 % Fund are interesting in relation to the issue of flagship species because of the assumption that FFI tends to support projects missed by other organisations.

From 1971 to 1996, the 100 % Fund has provided funding to 584 projects, which have recently been compiled on a single database (Mickleburgh, 1997). Of these projects, 79 % could be assigned to particular taxonomic groups (Figure 4.7). The preponderance of these taxonomically-based projects provided funding for projects concerning mammals (49 %) and birds (21 %). Relatively few projects have been funded that concern less charismatic taxonomic groups, such as reptiles (12 %), amphibians (1.3 %), fishes (2.4 %), invertebrates (5.2 %) and plants (8.2 %). Even among the mammal projects supported by the 100 % Fund, there is somewhat of a bias towards the larger-bodied and more charismatic groups (Figure 4.7), mainly primates (26 %), even-toed ungulates (22 %) and carnivores (20 %). Relatively few projects have supported the smaller-bodied and less charismatic groups, including insectivores (2.2 %), lagomorphs (0.4 %) and rodents (1.3 %). Equally, the very largest and, to many, most charismatic mammalian groups did not feature very highly in 100 % Fund support, including whales and dolphins (2.2 %), elephants (1.8 %), and odd-toed ungulates (5.2 %). In contrast, although relatively small-bodied and, to many, uncharismatic, the bats featured strongly in 100 % Fund support (13 %).

The conclusion that can be drawn from the FFI 100 % Fund data is that mammals and birds feature strongly in the projects supported. Furthermore, with certain exceptions in both directions, the 100 % Fund still tends

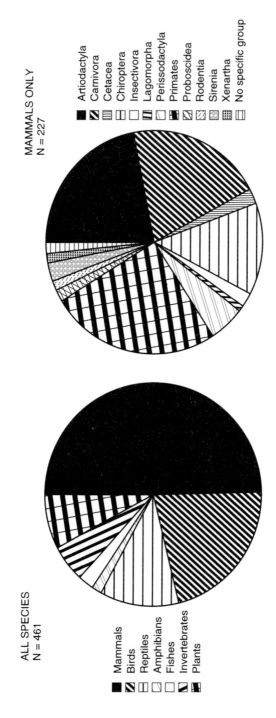

ALL SPECIES
N = 461

■ Mammals
◪ Birds
▨ Reptiles
□ Amphibians
□ Fishes
◪ Invertebrates
▰ Plants

MAMMALS ONLY
N = 227

■ Artiodactyla
◪ Carnivora
▤ Cetacea
▯ Chiroptera
□ Insectivora
◫ Lagomorpha
◩ Perissodactyla
◪ Primates
◪ Proboscidea
▨ Rodentia
▒ Sirenia
▦ Xenartha
▯ No specific group

Figure 4.7 The focus projects supported by the FFI 100% Fund from 1971 to 1996, shown as the order for all projects that could be assigned a species focus, and for the subset of mammal projects (data from Mickleburgh, 1997). Read pie charts clockwise for key categories.

to support the larger-bodied and charismatic mammal groups (Figure 4.7), despite FFI's stated mission to support projects and species that are 'missed' by others.

World Wide Fund for Nature project support

WWF was founded in 1961 and is now the most widely supported conservation organisation in the world. Its well known panda logo has been described as a flagship species for nature conservation efforts worldwide, particularly for securing financial support (Dietz et al., 1994). WWF has grappled with the need for both the single-species conservation approach it adopted in its earliest days as the World Wildlife Fund, and for the wider needs of people, habitats and ecosystem management, plus the increasing range of tools, techniques and strategies now employed to achieve wider conservation objectives as the World Wide Fund for Nature. Furthermore, with today's increasingly complex programmes, WWF has recognised the major challenge of communicating its work in a simple and compelling way. Hence, WWF has defined Species of Special Concern as including any animal or plant whose protection advances the cause of conservation by safeguarding biological diversity and ecological processes as a whole. The list is not just restricted to taxa like the panda *Ailuoropoda melanoleuca* in immediate danger of extinction. However, all Species of Special Concern face some degree of threat to their survival, either directly or through habitat loss. Some species are included because they are biologically and scientifically important, others for their strategic importance to broader-based habitat conservation initiatives. Flagship species are included among the strategic considerations, and are defined in a manner and with a role that is consistent with definitions from textbooks (Tables 4.1 and 4.2), as follows: 'A species for which protection serves as a catalyst for broader conservation efforts, or which serves as a tool for achieving a specific conservation objective. Difficulties faced by certain species may be representative of a larger conservation problem. In such cases, it should be possible to scale up from a species protection campaign to a broader conservation agenda: e.g., Javan rhino and Ujung Kulon reserve; bluefin tuna and marine fisheries conservation; jaguar and Cockscomb reserve; golden lion tamarin and Atlantic forest.'

WWF produces an annual list of all their existing projects for the current and the next two years. These projects are listed according to several classifications, including:

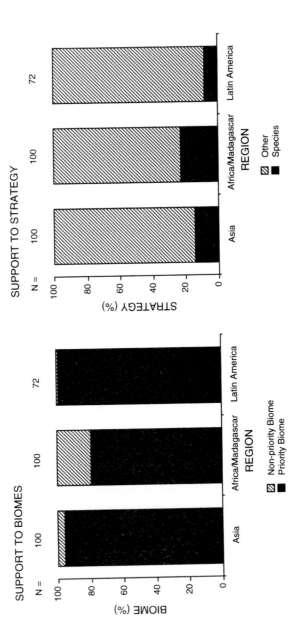

Figure 4.8 WWF support to biomes and to strategy in three regions during 1996. Support to biomes is classified according to whether the biome supported is priority or non-priority (non-biome specific projects are excluded from this figure). The difference between the support to biomes across regions is significant (G = 11.59, df = 2, P < 0.01). Support to strategy is classified according to whether the strategy supported is species or other, e.g., protected areas, capacity building, etc. The difference between the support to strategy across regions is also significant (G = 9.02, df = 2, P < 0.05).

- Biome, whether Priority (forests, freshwater, and marine and coasts), Non-Priority, or Non-Biome Specific, by per cent.
- Strategy, whether Species or one of six others, e.g., protected areas, capacity building, treaties and legislation, by per cent.
- When species are involved, lists those species at which project targeted.

The 272 WWF projects in the Asian, Africa/Madagascar and Latin American regions during 1996 were examined to determine how much single-species conservation, and charismatic large mammals in particular, influenced the projects that WWF supported. A particular question that could be asked of these data (and that could not be asked of the FFI data) was whether species conservation goals deflected from wider biodiversity conservation objectives, along the lines argued by Simberloff (1998b).

WWF support to biomes showed that most projects focused on a priority biome, although more projects in the Africa/Madagascar region supported a non-priority biome than projects in Asia and Latin America (Figure 4.8). Similarly, WWF support to strategy showed that most projects focused on wider issues than single species, although projects in the Africa/Madagascar region provided more support to species than did projects in Asia and Latin America (Figure 4.8). Furthermore, there was a very marked difference in the support noted to species between regions (Figure 4.9). In Latin America, most support to species went to projects that supported wide assemblages spanning different taxonomic orders, while fewer projects supported more general mammalian assemblages alone, and fewer still supported single species (pampas deer *Ozotoceros bezoarticus*, a species of bird and a species of tree). In Asia, there was still some project support for wide species assemblages and for more general mammalian assemblages. However, more project support for the large charismatic species is evident in Asia than in Latin America, including for the giant panda, elephants and rhinos and tigers. However, support for the large charismatic species was most evident in projects for Africa/Madagascar, with considerable emphasis on elephants and rhinos, and large apes. Nevertheless, there was still some project support in Africa/Madagascar for wide species assemblages and for more general mammalian assemblages (Figure 4.9). Of those projects where species were named as a component, most projects took place in priority biomes in all three regions. However, there were more projects in non-priority biomes in Africa/Madagascar than in other regions (Figure 4.9), due largely to support for elephant and rhinos projects in savannah and woodland habitats.

Several conclusions can be drawn from these data. WWF, having based

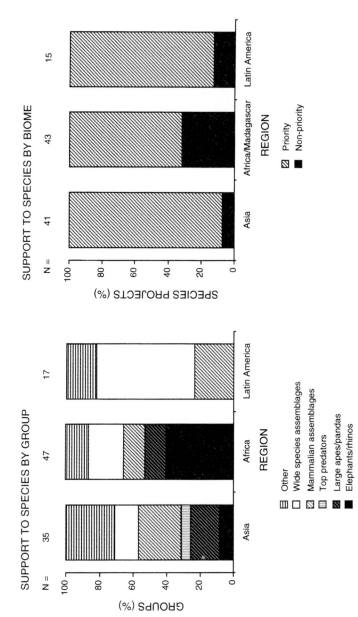

Figure 4.9 WWF support to species by different groups and to species by different biomes during 1996, where it was possible to assign that support to named species or groups from the full number of projects shown in Figure 4.8. The difference between the support to different species groups across regions is significant ($\chi^2 = 24.21$, df $= 6$, $P < 0.001$, with elephants and rhinos, large apes and top predators combined as a single charismatic megafauna category to fulfil the requirements of the chi-square test). Projects that support species classified according to whether the biome supported is priority or non-priority (non-biome specific projects are excluded from this figure). The difference between regions is significant ($C = 0.21$, df = 3, $P < 0.001$).

its image initially on single-species conservation and particularly through its widely recognised and highly distinctive panda logo, has now considerably broadened its support to projects that take a wider approach to biodiversity and ecosystem conservation. Nevertheless, WWF still finds it useful and appropriate to include single species management in its portfolio, including the adoption of definitions for terms such as 'flagship species' and identifying target flagships to focus their attention. Indeed, WWF has launched the Living Plant Campaign which has as one of its central themes Flagship Species. The first phase focused on action planning for tigers, pandas and African rhinos, and the second phase will bring in Asian rhinos and Asian elephants. Further species are under consideration for subsequent phases.

CONCLUDING DISCUSSION

This chapter has presented varied evidence showing that flagship species, and in particular large charismatic mammals, have had a strategic role in raising public awareness and providing funding for conservation action, including:

- The improved awareness of conservation issues two years after a project on golden lion tamarins had begun (Figure 4.2).
- The marketing of large mammals and far away issues by those seeking to raise funds in the developed world for conservation in the developing world (Figure 4.3).
- The willingness of people to pay more for conserving the more charismatic otter than the water vole (Figure 4.4).
- The use of various flagship species, usually but not invariably mammals, to achieve various forms of conservation action (Table 4.2).
- The support provided to large mammal conservation by two conservation organisations (Figures 4.7 and 4.9), without evidence in the case of one organisation of detracting from achieving parallel goals in mammalian and in biodiversity conservation (Figure 4.8).

Equally, not everybody may believe that large mammals provide a rallying call as flagship species, including:

- Academic conservation biologists, who use the term much less than another closely related term with a biological role, that of keystone species (Figure 4.1). Equally, academics are usually not at the sharp end

Arabian oryx, *Oryx leucoryx*, Oman. Photograph: Marie Matthews.

in terms of implementation and tend to be more interested in theory and their own publication record.

• People living among wildlife may not see a large mammal as charismatic if it causes them loss of life and livelihood, in turn creating some dissonance between themselves and those from distant lands who provide financial support to fund conservation of charismatic species. Indeed, a utilitarian and very uncharismatic species can equally well act as a flagship species for conservation action among local people (Table 4.2), as a charismatic mammal might to a Westerner (Figure 4.3)!

A number of other issues have also been examined about the use and definitions of the term 'flagship species', including:

• The definition and role of the term 'flagship species' appears clear in and of itself, and in relation to other closely related terms in single-species conservation (Box 4.1 and Table 4.1).
• However, in certain contexts the term has not always been used clearly and this, rather than its definition, has given rise to understandable confusion about what the term means (Table 4.2).

Some key questions remain. Despite their past role and success, should flagship species, as one of the icons among the somewhat passé concept of single-species management, continue to feature in our armoury of conservation tools? Simberloff (1998b) has proposed that only keystone species have a meaningful linkage to the real need for effective habitat and ecosystem conservation in the landscape era. Although this might well be correct from a theoretical and biological perspective, it does not necessarily take full account of how to raise awareness or funds for conservation action among a public that may not have a full grasp of the complex issues involved in the conservation of natural ecosystems. Hence, those who market (in its widest sense) conservation will most probably still continue to use single species of charismatic megafauna as flagship species (Figure 4.3) because they bring extra funding and awareness into conservation (Figures 4.2 and 4.4) that cannot be achieved by marketing landscapes or ecosystems, or even two species of mammal at one time (Figure 4.4). Therefore, future approaches should seek flagships that are also good keystone (or umbrella and indicator) species (see Heywood, 1995) or that act as surrogates for landscapes (Wikramanayake et al., 1998). In this way, conservation organisations can increasingly support more parallel efforts and investments in biodiversity and single-species conservation (Figure 4.8), and give added value based on additional awareness and funds raised through charismatic species. But even if this proves impossible, who will be the judge of the importance or otherwise of saving rhinos and elephants in non-priority habitats such as African savannahs? In part, the answer may well lie with those who are prepared or not to pay for the charisma!

PART 2

Setting priorities for mammalian conservation

In this section means for identifying conservation priorities among mammals are examined, and relative conservation priorities are reinterpreted. A number of factors underlying prioritisation within conservation are examined: including species richness and co-occurrence, relative threat, rarity and 'importance' and current protection afforded to different groups. Priority setting is considered across a range of levels – from the identification of key areas, to determination of focal species or main forms of threats. Many such approaches reflect the wide variation in the values we place upon different mammalian groups in terms of their conservation. The setting of priorities also relates to arguments about rationalising single-species and biodiversity-driven approaches to conservation. Many questions are raised about how we choose what to protect, in a climate of limited resources for conservation. We need to consider whether we need to conserve the common or only the rare, and whether the investment focused on those species on the brink of extinction (and possibly biologically unrecoverable) can be justified.

5

Assessing large 'flagship species' for representing the diversity of sub-Saharan mammals

PAUL H. WILLIAMS, NEIL BURGESS AND CARSTEN RAHBEK

INTRODUCTION

Priority areas for biodiversity have been chosen by one of three quantitative methods when a rigorous and explicit treatment is needed to make the process accountable: (1) hotspots of total richness; (2) hotspots of endemism; or (3) hotspots of complementary richness. Since the 'Rio Earth Summit' on biodiversity in 1992 (ISCBD, 1994), all three methods have been advocated by different groups. We compare these methods by looking at their consequences when applied to two questions for the conservation of African mammals that have been raised in other chapters in this volume: (1) which areas can represent the greatest diversity of sub-Saharan mammals?; and (2) how well do areas chosen for large 'flagship' mammals represent the diversity of all mammals?

Priorities are unavoidable in conservation practice because of competition for resources. The idea of priorities can be applied not just to individual species, but also to areas, based on an assessment of the assemblages of species that occur there. Priority areas may then be used to decide the 'where first?' of *in situ* conservation, rather than the 'how?'. Of course, choosing priorities does not mean that other areas have no value, rather it is that in relation to a particular conservation goal, action for the other areas is less urgent. These areas might still be high priorities for other goals.

Accountability and flexibility within the process of selecting priority areas are, we believe, principles of supreme importance, because they allow people to see whether their values are being applied faithfully by conservationists when developing strategies for environmental management. A first step towards accountability is to make the various factors influencing decisions explicit, quantitative and consistent. One common approach has been to score the different kinds of value and then to combine them. The problem is that the component scores for the different kinds of value (such as biodiversity, and numbers of rare or threatened species) are not inter-convertible, which makes the inevitable trade-offs from combining scores arbitrary, inconsistent, and so reduces accountability (Williams, 1998). This problem can be overcome in two ways. First, by identifying as precisely as possible the primary underlying value as the single currency to be maximised, such as the number of persisting species. Second, by separating the different questions to be asked, such as which areas would be needed to represent the valued species, and which of these representative areas would be the most urgent priorities for action to manage known threats?

Part of this study is about questions of how good one group of species is for choosing areas to represent the diversity of another group. At least three variations on this question have been asked in the past. First, is the overall distribution of species richness similar between groups? (Pomeroy, 1993; Gaston, 1996c; Williams and Gaston, 1998). Second, to what extent do priority areas identified for the two different groups coincide? (Pomeroy, 1993; Prendergast *et al.*, 1993; Lombard, 1995). Third, do the priority areas chosen for one group represent many of the species of the other groups? (Ryti, 1992; Lombard, 1995). The third form of the question seems to us particularly important, because it is closest to the problem faced by many conservationists, who with limited resources, may be asked to choose priority areas for representing broader biodiversity when armed with information for only relatively few groups.

AREA-SELECTION GOALS

A major difficulty for assessing priorities is that the same values and goals are not shared by all people. If we value biodiversity, then we might choose a goal of seeking to represent as many species as possible within a set of conservation areas. Seeking full or maximum *representation* of a group of species can be used to approach conservation 'proactively', as opposed to 'fire-fighting' (reactively) as and when particular species become endangered (Groves, 1992). Much of today's conservation effort is reactive, addressing the increasing threats to particular species and habitats (e.g., through Red Data Books and Species Action Plans), although the proactive approach would be more desirable if more strategic plans for conservation actions are to be developed. With the proactive approach, resources for priority action may still be deployed in relation to perceptions of imminent threat. However, representativeness in this sense implies monitoring all species, not just those that are currently most threatened.

For the sake of illustration, let us assume that we wish to represent as much of the diversity of sub-Saharan mammals as possible, and let us also assume that initially we are only able to influence the management of up to 5 % of the land area for this purpose (an arbitrary figure). Technically this is described as a 'maximal covering location problem' (Church et al., 1996) (or 'maximum coverage problem'). So which areas do we choose?

DATA FOR SUB-SAHARAN MAMMALS

For practical implementation, we recognise that an analysis of priorities is likely to require consideration of data at a detailed local scale (e.g., Freitag et al., 1996). It would also require a consideration of local viabilities of species and of threats to their survival, as well as other social and land use factors affecting suitability of priority areas for selection, information that is not available to us at present. Nonetheless, we can begin to discern some patterns of biological value from available data for the broad-scale distribution of mammals across sub-Saharan Africa.

Distribution data for 937 mammal species (species list follows Wilson and Reeder, 1993; data for six species of small mammals are not yet available) have been compiled on a one-degree grid across mainland sub-Saharan Africa (1966 cells, each measuring approximately 105×105 km) by the Zoological Museum, University of Copenhagen in collaboration with an international network of mammalogists. For the larger and better-known species, the data are an estimate of potential distributions at the middle of the twentieth century. For smaller and less well-known species, expected distribution ranges have been interpolated by assuming a continuous distribution between confirmed records within relatively uniform habitat, using available information on species' habitat associations, and taking into account specialist opinion, especially concerning any known gaps in distribution (discussed by Williams et al., 1996b). For the least well-known species, records are plotted without interpolation. Even though these data are not estimates of species' current distributions, they are useful for drawing inferences about the relative merits of different methods, and should give an indication of priorities at a continental scale.

METHOD A: HOTSPOTS OF (TOTAL) RICHNESS

The simplest and perhaps most obvious method for choosing areas to represent biodiversity is to choose the most species-rich areas. The term 'hotspots' was used by Myers (1988, 1990) for regions of the world that combine particularly high species richness, endemism and threat. However, 'hotspots' has often been used in the sense of areas of highest total species richness, and often at the scale of continents or countries (Prendergast *et al.*, 1993).

To apply hotspots of richness as an area-selection method, we select the most species-rich areas (Scott *et al.*, 1987; Prendergast *et al.*, 1993; Mittermeier *et al.*, 1994a, 1998). As an example, we rank the grid cells by their species richness scores for mammals and then map the 50 grid cells with the highest scores (Figure 5.1a).

METHOD B: HOTSPOTS OF (NARROW) ENDEMISM

Alternatively, some people consider the species with the more restricted distribution ranges to be most important. Terborgh and Winter (1983) working with South American birds, and Bibby *et al.* (1992) working with birds worldwide, have identified priority areas from hotspots of richness, but measured using just the more narrowly distributed species, which they defined as those with range sizes of less than 50 000 km². The species identified by Bibby *et al.* (1992) as fulfilling this arbitrary criterion correspond, by chance, to the quartile (approximately) of bird species that have the narrowest distribution ranges (i.e. the narrow endemics).

To apply hotspots of narrow endemism as an area-selection method comparable to the Endemic Bird Areas method of Bibby *et al.* (1992), but for use at any spatial scale, we identify the 25% of species with the most restricted ranges (the 'rare quartile' approach; Gaston, 1994), map the richness in these species and then select the richest areas (Williams *et al.*, 1996a). As an example, we rank the grid cells by their richness in the rarest 25% of mammal species and then map the 50 grid cells with the highest richness scores as hotspots of endemism (or 'endemic mammal areas') within sub-Saharan Africa (Figure 5.1b).

METHOD C: HOTSPOTS OF COMPLEMENTARY RICHNESS

If our goal is to represent as many species as possible in our priority areas, then the most direct approach is to search for a combination of areas that add to one another as many different species as possible. This uses the idea of complementarity, which in this context refers to the degree to which an area contributes otherwise unrepresented species to a set of areas (Vane-Wright *et al.*, 1991). It differs from the other methods in that it deals explicitly and directly with differences in species identities between areas. Complementarity has often been used in seeking sets of areas to represent diversity (Kirkpatrick, 1983; Ackery and Vane-Wright, 1984; Pressey *et al.*, 1993; Scott *et al.*, 1993). Dobson *et al.* (1997) have recently used the term 'hotspots' when referring to areas chosen using complementarity.

Applying complementarity as an area-selection method to maximise the representation of diversity is not entirely straightforward. Fortunately, simple rules for selecting areas often give good results (Csuti *et al.*, 1997; Pressey *et al.*, 1997). The procedure used here is based on the area-selection rules introduced by Margules *et al.* (1988) to find near-minimum-area sets. However, we add two important steps to the Margules *et al.* algorithm (Table 5.1): (1) a test to reject any areas that in hindsight are redundant to the representation goal; and (2) a final reordering of areas by complementary richness. The second step is an innovation to address the kind of 'maximum-coverage' problem faced here, even when the number of areas exceeds the number required for a minimum-area set. Different criteria for reordering near-minimum-area sets were discussed by Williams *et al.* (1996b). A trial of an earlier version of this procedure with reordering has shown that it is equal to the most area-efficient of the other approximate procedures available for finding near-minimum sets, but is better than the others when seeking smaller 'maximum-coverage' solutions (see 'algorithm 8' in Csuti *et al.*, 1997). As an example, we use the procedure in Table 5.1 to map a 'near-maximum-coverage' set of 50 areas for mammals (Figure 5.1c). Any flexibility among areas for selection at each step was not investigated for this study.

TESTING THE METHODS

In order to assess how well the three area-selection methods perform, we need to know how their results compare with the consequences of choosing areas at random. It may be argued that areas are never really chosen at random, but area-selection methods that take no account of biodiversity information could, in effect, be doing something very similar.

We simulate choosing areas at random (without replacement) from among those grid cells in which species have been recorded. This is repeated 1000 times to estimate the median number of species that would be

a: 50 hotspots of richness

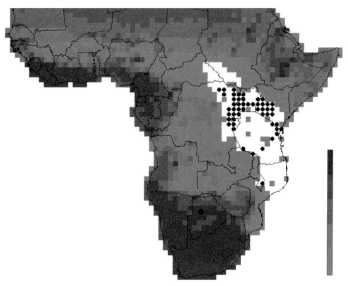

b: 50 hotspots of endemism

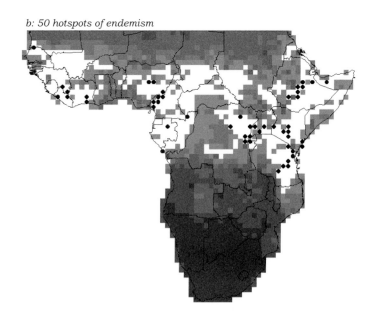

c: 50 hotspots of complementary richness

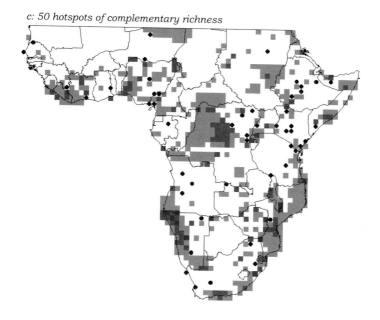

Figure 5.1 Three quantitative methods of selecting 50 priority areas for representing the diversity of mammal species. Map (*a*) shows 50 hotspots of richness (as black spots) together with richness in those species that remain unrepresented (435 species). Map (*b*) shows 50 hotspots of endemism (as black spots) together with richness in those species (irrespective of range size) that remain unrepresented (252 species). Map (*c*) shows 50 hotspots of complementary richness (as black spots) together with richness in those species that remain unrepresented (106 species). In each case, species richness counts are divided into five grey-scale classes of approximately equal size by numbers of grid cells, with maximum richness shown in dark grey and minimum richness in light grey, with white for zero counts. For this grey scale (right of map *a*), each class represents a consistent part (20 %) of the frequency distribution of richness counts for each map, despite the maximum number of unrepresented species differing among maps.

expected by chance. Furthermore, from the top 5 % of scores for numbers of species represented among these 1000 trials, we have a guide to the maximum number of species we would expect by chance (19 times out of 20), so that any larger numbers would be significantly larger than expected (this is an improvement over earlier tests, which made additional assumptions about the expected distribution of representation scores, e.g., Williams and Humphries, 1994: figure 19.2). This test can be used to judge the performance of the three methods.

Table 5.1

The set of rules for selecting a given number (*n*) of hotspots of complementary richness in order to provide a near-maximum coverage of species. In this context, the rarest species is taken to be the one with the fewest grid-cell records. This procedure can also be used to complement an existing set of protected areas, as a form of 'gap' analysis

Step	Procedure
1	Select all areas with species that have single records
2	The following rules are applied repeatedly until all species are represented – (a) select areas with the greatest complementary richness in just the rarest species (ignoring less rare species), if there are ties, then: (b) select areas among ties with the greatest complementary richness in the next-rarest species and so on, if there are persistent ties, then: (c) select areas among persistent ties with the lowest grid-cell number (this is an arbitrary rule, used rather than random choice among ties in order to ensure repeatability in tests; other criteria, such as proximity to previously selected cells, or number of records in surrounding cells, can be substituted) (repeat steps a–c until all species are represented).
3	Identify and reject any areas that in hindsight are unnecessary to represent all species.
4	Repeat steps 1–3 for representing every species at least once, twice and so on, until the required number of areas, *n*, is attained or exceeded, disregarding all areas selected in one iteration before moving to the next
5	Reorder areas by complementary richness. If before all areas are reordered the complementary richness reaches all species, or if the maximum complementary richness increment declines to zero, continue to resequence areas by resetting the cumulative richness to zero (ignoring previously reordered areas, species more restricted than a particular multiple representation target, and species that are already represented the required number of times within smaller sets), and starting again with scoring complementary richness from the current position on the area list, repeating this resetting as often as necessary to reorder all areas.
6	Choose the first *n* areas from the reordered area list.

All of the procedures described here have been automated within the WORLDMAP software for personal computers (Williams, 1996), which is a simple, specialised geographic information system (GIS). This allows the analysis in this chapter to be completed in a few minutes, using facilities available in all countries of the world. Speed is important, because it means that many variations on a question can be explored easily and the results can be reassessed routinely as new data become available from new surveys and monitoring programmes.

QUESTION 1: WHICH AREAS CAN REPRESENT THE GREATEST DIVERSITY OF SUB-SAHARAN MAMMALS?

The results of selecting 50 priority areas in Table 5.2 (row 1) show that hotspots of richness are least successful, representing only 54 % of all 937 mammal species, hotspots of endemism are more successful with 73 % of mammals, and hotspots of complementary richness are most successful with 89 % of mammals. Figure 5.1a shows that the 50 hotspots of species richness for sub-Saharan mammals are narrowly grouped, predominantly in the mountains around Lake Victoria. Figure 5.1b shows that the 50 hotspots of endemism for sub-Saharan mammals cover a broader scatter of geographical areas, although they still omit arid areas of the southern Sahara, and of southern Africa. Figure 5.1c shows that 50 hotspots of complementary richness for sub-Saharan mammals cover the broadest scatter of geographical areas.

The simulated selection of 50 areas at random shows that hotspots of endemism and of complementary richness both represent significantly more species than expected by chance, whereas the hotspots of richness do no better than expected by chance (Table 5.2 row 1: 54 % is close to the median and so very similar to the result expected from choosing areas at random). This poor performance by hotspots of richness may appear counter-intuitive, though it is by no means unique to choosing 50 areas, as shown by Figure 5.2a. The geographical clumping of the hotspots of richness (Figure 5.1a) leads to the same species being, to a large extent, represented repeatedly. Despite the range of habitats within these areas in the mountains around Lake Victoria (for example, at different altitudes), they still represent a relatively narrow range of the total habitat and faunal variation within sub-Saharan Africa. Consequently, many species from other faunas in other parts of Africa are unrepresented in these 50 hotspots (which is apparent from the broad distribution of richness in the 435 residual, unrepresented species shown in Figure 5.1a, cf. Figure 5.1b, c).

The relative performance of the three methods for representing the greatest diversity of sub-Saharan mammals (Table 5.2 row 1, Figure 5.2a) agrees in its rank ordering with the results of a similar comparison using data at a finer spatial scale for birds in Britain by Williams *et al.* (1996a).

Table 5.2

Three quantitative methods of selecting 50 priority areas for representing species applied to two questions in sub-Saharan biodiversity conservation and assessed against the consequences of choosing 50 areas at random.
Random draws of 50 areas are simulated 1000 times to calculate the median percentage of species expected to be represented by chance. The percentage threshold score to the top 5 % of randomly drawn scores (single-tailed, shown in parenthesis) shows the maximum that would be expected by chance (significantly higher results in the same row indicated with*)

Question	Assessment	Method used			Random
		Method A Hotspots of richness	Method B Hotspots of endemism	Method C Hotspots of complementary richness	Median, estimated from 1000 random draws (with estimated threshold to the 5 % upper tail of the random distribution)
Question 1 *Which areas can represent the greatest diversity of sub-Saharan mammals?*	% all 937 mammal species represented in 50 priority grid cells selected using all mammals	54	73*	89*	55 (60)
Question 2 *How well do areas chosen for large mammals represent the diversity of all mammals?*	% all 937 mammal species represented in 50 priority grid cells selected using 228 large mammal species	50	54	69*	55 (60)

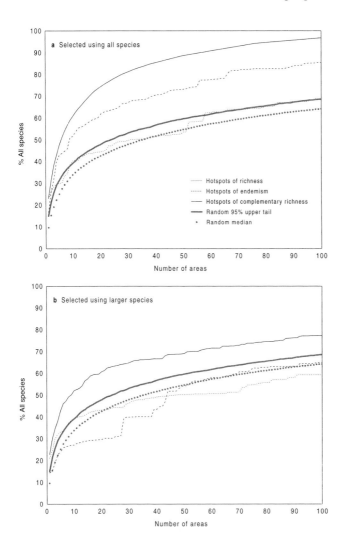

Figure 5.2 Three quantitative methods of selecting priority areas for representing species applied to two questions in sub-Saharan biodiversity conservation and assessed against the consequences of choosing areas at random. Graph (*a*) shows the percentage of all mammal species represented within between 1 and 100 areas selected by the three methods when these are applied to data for all 937 mammal species. Graph (*b*) shows the percentage of all mammal species represented within between 1 and 100 areas, selected by the three methods when these are applied to data for the 228 large mammal species alone. Hotspots of richness are shown by dotted lines, hotspots of endemism by dashed lines, and hotspots of complementary richness by continuous black lines. Scores below the grey line are within the range expected when choosing areas at random (the percentage threshold score to the top 5 % within 1000 randomly drawn scores).

QUESTION 2: HOW WELL DO AREAS CHOSEN FOR LARGE FLAGSHIP MAMMALS REPRESENT THE DIVERSITY OF ALL MAMMALS?

This question has been asked by Entwistle and Stephenson (chapter 7, this volume) and others. One interpretation of flagship mammals is that they are the larger species (Leader-Williams and Dublin, chapter 4, this volume). One reason why they might perform well in this role would be if they have particularly large home ranges, so that they encompass the habitats of many other organisms (Simberloff, 1998b). For a preliminary analysis, the large mammals can be defined by membership of particular taxonomic groups (following A. Entwistle, personal communication). For our purposes, the large mammals consist of the orders Primates, Carnivora, Proboscidea, Perissodactyla and Artiodactyla.

The results of selecting 50 priority areas in Table 5.2 (row 2) show that hotspots of richness and endemism using large mammals are least successful, representing only 50 % and 54 % of all mammal species, whereas hotspots of complementary richness for large mammals are more successful in representing 69 % of all mammals. Figure 5.2b shows that hotspots of complementary richness are consistently better than the other methods. The simulation test (Table 5.2 row 2, Figure 5.2b) shows that only the hotspots of complementary richness perform significantly better than random choices, except when selecting very small numbers of areas (Figure 5.2b).

Selecting up to 5 % of areas using large mammals is apparently no better for representing all mammals than choosing areas at random, unless we use hotspots of complementary richness. However, the results could be different for other continents or at other spatial scales.

PUTTING QUANTITATIVE AREA SELECTION INTO PRACTICE

Our analysis is designed to make comparisons of three of the more popular and accountable methods for selecting areas to represent the diversity of species within sub-Saharan Africa. The advantage of using hotspots of richness over other area-selection methods is that we do not need to know the identities of the species in any area to make it work, we need only know how many species there are. The advantage of hotspots of endemism over the other methods is that there is no need to know the details of every species distribution in order to make it work: we need only know the distributions of the most narrowly distributed species, assuming we know which ones they are. Nevertheless, the best results for representing diversity should always be obtained by applying hotspots of complementary richness (Williams, 1998). This method does need more information about species differences among areas than the other methods, although the difficulties this presents are often overemphasised.

Indeed, before any of these area-selection methods could be applied for prescribing practical priority areas for conservation, a great deal more detailed information would be needed (Howard *et al.*, 1997). This information would allow us to gain more realistic answers to questions of the form: which areas should we choose if we are to conserve the most biodiversity for X pounds or dollars? Three principal aspects would need further consideration.

First, an appropriate spatial scale would have to be chosen for the analysis. In practice, more realistic land management units might be of very different shapes and sizes. This is not a problem, because the methods are already fully capable of optimising species representation among dissimilar land ownership units by maximising diversity against land area or against cost when this information is available. In fact, the three methods are essentially scale-independent, although in contrast, the results of applying them may be highly dependent on spatial scale. For example, Stoms (1994) has shown how apparent patterns of species richness can change when measured on grids of different sizes. This effect has inevitable consequences, not only for the distribution of hotspots of richness, but also for the selection of areas by other methods, because all three depend on the patterns of coincidence among species within area units.

Second, the degree to which distribution data are representative of species' true distributions is a question that hangs over all area-selection exercises. The danger is that many of the rarest species in the data may be recorded only in those areas that have been sampled most intensively (Nelson *et al.*, 1990). This problem cannot be overcome entirely by habitat-based distribution modelling, particularly if available data represent a biased sample of the habitat associations for these species. The consequence for area selection could be that the areas chosen will be simply those that have been most intensively sampled. It is particularly easy to see how this will affect hotspots of 'endemism', but all three area-selection methods are affected strongly by the distribution of the rarer species. In practice, we are constrained to use the best information available to us, which at the scale of one-degree grid cells is expected to be at least as reliable as using any of the less direct surrogates, e.g., ecoregions or vegetation classes, and to look forward to more rigorous sampling programmes and data modelling procedures in the future. Among our data, while large mammals, insectivores and bats are better known, the data for rodents, although the best available, may be far from truly representative.

Third, we have ignored differences among areas in species viability and threat, and in the political willingness to conserve mammals. To some extent this might be accommodated from the flexibility that usually exists for many area choices. Considering these factors would be essential to establishing any real conservation priorities. There are already possibilities for taking into account many of these differences within the methods used here when the information becomes available (reviewed by Williams, 1998).

CONCLUSIONS

The most general conclusion we can draw is that for both of the questions we have tackled, using hotspots of complementary richness is consistently the most successful method for maximising the number of species that can be represented for conserving biodiversity. The basic requirement of this method is knowledge of the identities of the species present in each area, or at least knowledge of some pattern that can be used to predict the complementarity among these faunas. Apart from its ability to represent the most diversity, some of the great strengths of the complementary areas method are its abilities to identify precisely which species justify the choice of each area in a priority set (enhancing accountability of the process, and possibly aiding difficult management choices), and from this information, to identify which other areas might be fully flexible alternatives.

We look forward to improving quantitative priority-areas analyses as information becomes available on local variation in important factors such as viability, threat and cost. There is a growing wealth of information on some of these factors, some of which should be available for integration in the future. Above all, we need to work collaboratively, to identify and address the most pressing questions.

ACKNOWLEDGEMENTS

We thank Andrew Balmford, Abigail Entwistle, Kevin Gaston, Helen de Klerk and Paul Toyne for comments. Neil Burgess and Carsten Rahbek were funded by the Zoological Museum, University of Copenhagen (ZMUC) (Grant No. 11–0390 from the Danish Natural Science Research Council). The ZMUC acknowledges the assistance of the following taxonomists in the compilation of the provisional data for mammals: Dieter

Kock and Jakob Fahr (Senckenberg Museum, Frankfurt), Paula Jenkins (Natural History Museum, London), Rainer Hutterer (Alexander Koenig Museum, Bonn), Simon Stuart and the IUCN Species Survival Commission chairmen for the different mammal groups, Peter Taylor (Durban Natural Science Museum, South Africa) and Gary Bronner (Transvaal Museum, Pretoria). Many other mammal taxonomists and ecologists have provided further sources of mammal distribution data and we thank them all. Louis Hansen, Line Sørensen, Thomas Lehmberg, Steffan Galser and Jesper Larsen (ZMUC) helped to prepare the databases used here.

6

Abundance/mass relationships as a quantified basis for establishing mammal conservation priorities

STEPHEN HARRIS, GRAEME McLAREN, MARY MORRIS,
PATRICK A. MORRIS AND DEREK YALDEN

INTRODUCTION

When trying to identify conservation priorities, the two key criteria used in Britain, and often in other countries, are rarity and/or recent population declines. Thus, two of the fundamental criteria used to select species for Action Plans in the UK's response to the Rio Convention were species whose numbers or range had declined by more than 25 % in five years, and species found in fewer than 15 10–km squares in the UK (Anon., 1995a). Yet data on population declines or distribution of British mammals are often lacking (Harris et al., 1995), and so applying these criteria objectively can be difficult. For British mammals, they may not necessarily be complementary measures for deciding conservation priorities or assessing the risk of extinction or further population declines. For instance, of the species of bat in Britain, the two rarest (grey long-eared bat *Plecotus austriacus* and Bechstein's bat *Myotis bechsteini*) appear to have stable populations (Harris et al., 1995). The former has no Species Action Plan and the second only received one in 1998. However, the commonest species of bat (pipistrelle *Pipistrellus pipistrellus*) has a Species Action Plan, on the premise that its numbers are declining, although the basis for estimating population changes for the pipistrelle is questionable (Harris et al., 1995).

In addition, there is the difficulty of standardising the present criteria. Populations can be recorded as rare or declining, but when establishing conservation priorities, a standardised method must be sought to allow for the current population status of different species to be compared directly. The brown hare, *Lepus europaeus*, provides a good example of the problems with the current criteria. This species was introduced and reached very high densities in areas of game management until the early 1960s, when the population rapidly declined (Hutchings and Harris, 1996). At present, we have no reliable criteria to determine how abundant this species should be, yet the Species Action Plan aims to double the present population by 2010 (Anon., 1995b).

Deciding objective criteria to determine conservation priorities is particularly important for mammals, since changes in mammal populations can be influential in driving large changes in biodiversity. The decline of rabbits *Oryctolagus cuniculus* following the introduction of myxomatosis in 1953, led to widespread ecological changes, culminating in the loss of the large blue butterfly *Maculinea arion* (Sumption and Flowerdew, 1985). Changes in the number of field voles *Microtus agrestis* have a large impact on the breeding success of predators such as kestrels *Falco tinnunculus* (Snow, 1968), and weasels *Mustela nivalis* (Tapper, 1992), and the decline in the number and/or availability of field voles has been a major factor leading to the widespread decline in the number of barn owls *Tyto alba* in Britain (Shawyer, 1987). Within guilds of predators, larger species can have significant impacts on the population density of smaller species, at least locally (Mulder, 1990).

It is clearly important to use objective criteria to identify conservation priorities for British mammals, and in particular to assess the ecological consequences of any changes in population size. Yet deciding on appropriate criteria is further complicated because mammals are relatively abundant compared to some other vertebrate taxa. Greenwood *et al.* (1996) showed that species of non-flying mammals are more abundant than comparable sized species of resident birds, migrant birds and bats by approximately 45, 300 and 200 times respectively. Thus, whilst we should expect terrestrial mammals to be more common than at least some other vertebrate taxa, their apparent abundance poses a problem when trying to rank conservation priorities, especially between taxa. The relationships identified by Greenwood *et al.* (1996) suggest that, since terrestrial mammals occur at densities 45 times greater than those for resident birds of the same biomass, absolute population size, especially when compared to other taxa, may not be a useful measure for setting conservation priorities for terrestrial mammals.

At present, it is unclear why terrestrial mammals occur at such high densities (Greenwood *et al.*, 1996). Nor is it clear whether terrestrial mammals can withstand significant population declines without population fragmentation becoming a serious cause for concern. Although Bright

(1993) used life history traits to identify those species most at risk of habitat fragmentation, there are no criteria to assess the level of population decline at which population fragmentation becomes a conservation issue.

In this chapter we use the abundance/mass relationships identified by Greenwood *et al.* (1996) to identify those species and/or taxa that are particularly abundant or rare, and explore the use of these relationships as an aid to identifying conservation priorities, both in Britain as a whole and separately in England, Scotland and Wales. We then compare these results with the species currently identified as being 'most at risk' in the UK's response to the Rio Convention (Anon., 1994a). Five species of terrestrial mammal originally qualified for Species Action Plans, all on the basis of perceived past population declines: they were brown hare, red squirrel *Sciurus vulgaris*, water vole *Arvicola terrestris*, dormouse *Muscardinus avellanarius* and otter *Lutra lutra* (Anon., 1995a). We then explore the problems associated with focusing on species conservation rather than trying to maintain, or re-establish, a faunal balance.

SOURCES OF DATA

Because of the difference in relative abundance between volant and terrestrial mammals (Greenwood *et al.*, 1996), we have confined these analyses to the terrestrial mammal fauna. The data we used are from two sources. First, population estimates for Britain as a whole, and for each of the three constituent countries, are taken from Harris *et al.* (1995). These authors detail the methods used to estimate the population size for each species of mammal, and also provide a quality assessment to indicate the reliability of each population estimate. Generally, the estimates were produced by using known densities in different habitat types scaled up to take account of the area of suitable habitat within a species' range. For a few larger species with limited ranges much of the population had been counted. These population estimates are for the pre-breeding adult population, and so generally represent the minimum population size for each species. For some species, such as badgers *Meles meles*, the population has changed in recent years (Wilson *et al.*, 1997). However, new data are only available for a minority of species. Since this is intended as an exploratory analysis, for uniformity we have used the population estimates given by Harris *et al.* (1995) throughout.

Second, estimates of biomass are based on individual weights given in Corbet and Harris (1991). Where there are significant differences between the sexes, an average figure was used for these calculations, since the population estimates are for all adults, and for many species there are no reliable data on the contribution of each sex to the adult population. Thus, we have assumed that the sex ratio is parity for all species.

ORIGINS OF THE BRITISH TERRESTRIAL MAMMAL FAUNA

Of the terrestrial species listed in Harris *et al.* (1995), 56 % are native, 34 % introduced and 10 % feral. The high proportion of non-native species further complicates attempts to identify conservation priorities in Britain; one of the five species with a Species Action Plan, brown hare, is probably introduced. The limited number of native species is a consequence of Britain's early separation from continental Europe around 9500 years before present (Yalden, 1991) and the subsequent extinction of the larger species of mammal. The high proportion of introduced species in part reflects the vogue for acclimatisation in the 19th century (Lever, 1992).

When comparing the contribution of the native and introduced species to the total mammal biomass, only 41 % of the biomass is from native species; 56 % is from introduced species and 3 % from feral species. Considering herbivores and carnivores separately, 54 % of the carnivore biomass is from native species, compared to only 37 % for the herbivores. This reflects the overriding contribution of deer and rabbits to the total wild mammal biomass in Britain. Hence, whilst there are introduced species within all orders of terrestrial mammals, the introduced herbivores make the most significant contribution to the structure of the terrestrial mammal fauna. However, all species of wild mammal constitute only 3 % of the non-human mammal biomass in the British countryside; domestic stock constitute the other 97 %, and hence dominate productivity (Yalden, 1999).

COMPARING THE ABUNDANCE OF DIFFERENT SPECIES OF MAMMAL

A previous analysis comparing the abundance and biomass of British birds and mammals (Greenwood *et al.*, 1996) showed that for each group abundance declines as body mass increases, with an exponent close to the value of −0.75, as is predicted by the energetic equivalence rule. This relationship has subsequently been confirmed by Silva *et al.* (1997).

For all species, log abundance = −0.59 $\log_{10}$ body weight + 7.4. A few very rare introduced species were omitted from this analysis (e.g., edible dormouse *Glis glis*); this accounts for the slight difference between the values presented here and in Greenwood *et al.* (1996). The slope of the relationship is shallower than predicted by the energetic equivalence rule because the heavier mammals are more abundant than predicted, when compared to the smaller mammals. This may in part be due to the absence of any predators of the larger herbivores in Britain; three large predators (brown bear *Ursus arctos*, wolf *Canis lupus* and lynx *Lynx lynx*) were exterminated by humans (Yalden, 1999). The situation is likely to have been further complicated by the recent introduction of several species of large herbivore.

To check that the abundance/biomass relationship was not in part due to the limited range of some of the species, we also examined the maximum density achieved by each species/biomass relationship; the slope of the line was little different (log density $= -0.62 \log_{10}$ body weight $+ 1.6$), nor was the relative position of each species. However, the skew in the relationship was in large part due to the introduced species; when looking at just the introduced mammals, log abundance $= -0.50 \log_{10}$ body weight $+ 7.2$. When considering just the insectivores, lagomorphs (excluding the highly abundant rabbit), rodents and carnivores, the relationship is exactly as predicted by the energetic equivalence rule (log abundance $= -0.75 \log_{10}$ body weight $+ 7.7$). The same is true for population density; excluding the riparian carnivores (mink *Mustela vison* and otter), whose densities are likely to be much lower as a result of the linearity of their habitat, and deer, log density $= -0.73 \log_{10}$ body weight $+ 2.2$.

Clearly, the abundance and biomass relationship for the British terrestrial mammal fauna is close to that predicted by the energetic equivalence rule, and the relationship is particularly close when just considering the native species. Therefore, we feel justified in exploring this relationship further. In particular, we look at the residuals of this relationship to see which species, and orders, are more or less abundant than expected.

IDENTIFYING SPECIES OF CONSERVATION CONCERN

In all the analyses in this section, we used the relationship derived from the insectivores, lagomorphs (excluding the rabbit), rodents and carnivores i.e., log abundance $= -0.75 \log_{10}$ body weight $+ 7.7$. This relationship has exactly the same exponent as the theoretical relationship predicted by the energetic equivalence rule. The estimate of the constant, 7.7, was similar to thatfound when all British mammals were included in the relationship (7.4) and so is unlikely to be a major source of error. We used the theoretical relationship in the analysis because we wished to determine which species deviated significantly from the energetic equivalence rule. We aimed to determine if the difference between the observed and the theoretical abundance could provide a directly comparable, quantified assessment of the conservation status of Britain's terrestrial mammal fauna.

For each species the theoretical abundance was calculated as -0.75 $\log_{10}$ body weight $+ 7.7$. This value was then subtracted from the real log abundance value, giving the residual value. The residuals had a normal distribution, as regression theory predicts, a mean near to zero (0.19), and a standard deviation of 1.03. Residuals with a value close to zero identify species which have a population size close to that predicted by the energetic equivalence rule, those with a high positive residual have a population size greater than that predicted, while those with a high negative value have a lower population size than predicted. When we examined the pattern of these residuals, we looked not only for extreme values but also attempted to examine the overall distribution of residuals, to determine if there were any effects of species type on residual value.

Because the residuals were scaled to body weight, they were directly comparable between species, regardless of the expected species abundance. For example, the house mouse *Mus musculus* residual is very low, 0.02, and the actual population difference between the estimate based on body size and that calculated by Harris *et al.* (1995) was $270\,802$ individuals, a small difference when compared to the overall population estimate of $5\,398\,000$. However, the pine marten *Martes martes* had a large residual of -1.77, and the difference in population size between the estimate based on body size and that calculated by Harris *et al.* (1995) was $209\,935$, which is substantially greater than the calculated population size of 3650. Thus, residuals can be compared directly between species and, more importantly, can be used to determine the relative imbalance of species population sizes.

First, we examined the data for biases. Harris *et al.* (1995) provided a quality rating for each of their population estimates. We used these ratings to determine whether there was any trend for larger residuals to occur for those species with lower quality population estimates. There was no such trend (Kruskal–Wallis test, $\chi^2 = 0.71$ for 4 df, N.S.); the size of the residuals was not related to the quality of the population estimate. The only trend we could detect was the vulnerability of species to habitat fragmentation. Bright (1993) used life history traits to allocate mammals to one of four groups (1, $2a$, $2b$, 3), these indicating a declining vulnerability to the effects of habitat fragmentation. When we compared the residuals of these four groups, group 1 was significantly different from the other three groups (Kruskal–Wallis, $\chi^2 = 9.54$ for 3 df, $P < 0.05$ for all groups; $\chi^2 = 0.40$ for 2 df, N.S. for groups $2a$, $2b$ and 3). Group 1 had significantly more negative residuals i.e., mammals thought to be particularly at risk from the effects of habitat fragmentation were less common than predicted from abundance/ mass relationships.

No other trends in life history traits (productivity, home range size) were detected. This could have implications for the interpretation of the residuals, in that some species or taxa may naturally have negative or positive residual values. For instance, carnivores might be expected to be rarer than herbivores. Whilst this may be true for some species, positive and negative residuals occurred across orders.

Since there appeared to be no bias towards particular taxa or life history traits, we then plotted the residuals from the abundance/mass relationship (Figure 6.1). For this, we separated the species into three groups: those that were less common than predicted (negative residual greater than 0.75), those that were more common than predicted (positive residual greater than 0.75), and those that were roughly as abundant as expected (residuals between 0.75 and −0.75). Although a residual greater or less than 0.75 might appear to be a low value on which to describe species as being too common or too rare, it actually represents a large overall difference between the calculated and predicted abundance. We found that for species with a residual greater than 0.75, their calculated abundance was at least 80 % greater than the theoretical abundance; for those with a residual below −0.75, the calculated abundance was at least 600 % below the theoretical abundance. This imbalance reflects the fact that there are ecological constraints on how abundant a species can become, but there are no restrictions on the severity of population declines.

In choosing a residual of 0.75, we had to balance statistical considerations with the considerations of conservation biology. Whilst a range of residuals is to be expected, those species which had residuals greater or less than 0.75 had a residual which was unlikely to be caused by the inaccuracy of the estimate of the constant in the abundance/mass relationship, and the slope of 0.75 is assumed to be the absolute theoretical value. Thus, we considered species with residuals exceeding plus or minus 0.75 to be of critical conservation importance. Whilst it is possible that there are species which naturally occur at densities where the residuals are outside the 0.75 limit we used here, this approach provided a standardised, directly comparable technique to compare population abundance between species.

When comparing the pattern of residuals across Britain as a whole (Figure 6.1), most carnivores had negative residuals (i.e., were less common than expected), and the group with particularly large negative residuals comprised mainly carnivores. Only three species of carnivore (red fox *Vulpes vulpes*, badger and feral cat *Felis catus*) had positive residuals, all less than 0.75. Of these three species, red fox and feral cat are generalist predators, and the badger is a specialist predator of non-mammalian prey

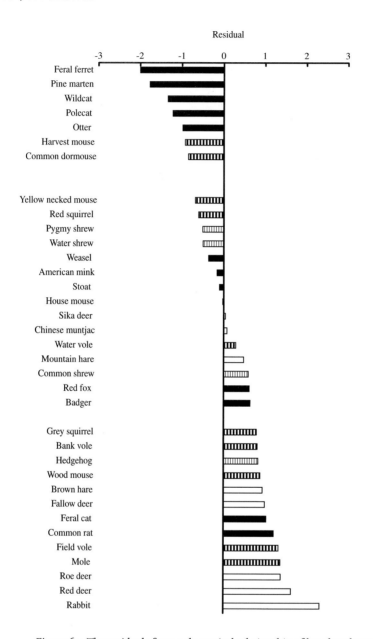

Figure 6.1 The residuals from a theoretical relationship of log abundance $= -0.75 \log_{10}$ body weight $+ 7.7$, for the main species of terrestrial British mammal. Carnivores are represented by black bars, herbivores by clear bars, rodents by heavy striped bars and insectivores by light striped bars. The break between the bars denotes those species which have a residual value of greater than 0.75 or less than -0.75.

(Roper, 1994); the significance of this is discussed when we consider food webs.

Of the species with positive residuals greater than 0.75, three (rabbit, roe deer *Capreolus capreolus*, red deer *Cervus elaphus*) are herbivores, and the only herbivores with negative residuals are two introduced species (sika deer *Cervus nippon* and Chinese muntjac *Muntiacus reevesi*) with ranges that are currently limited but rapidly expanding (Harris *et al.*, 1995). The other species that are particularly abundant (mole *Talpa europaea*, bank vole *Clethrionomys glareolus*, field vole, wood mouse *Apodemus sylvaticus* and common rat *Rattus norvegicus*) are all widespread and exploit a diversity of habitats. Of the five species with Action Plans to aid their recovery, three (red squirrel, common dormouse and otter) had negative residuals greater than 0.75, or nearly so. Of the other two, despite a dramatic population decline, water voles are still about as abundant as might be expected, and brown hares have a large positive residual (0.94). However, a recent survey has shown that water vole numbers have declined substantially since that estimate was produced (D. J. Jefferies, personal communication). Of the eight species with negative residuals greater than 0.75, one (ferret *Mustela furo*) is feral; the other four (harvest mouse *Micromys minutus*, pine marten, polecat *Mustela putorius* and wildcat *Felis silvestris*) have no Action Plan. Whether harvest mouse, probably a long-standing accidental introduction, should be considered for positive conservation action is debatable. Since brown hare, which is probably a deliberate introduction, has an Action Plan to aid its recovery, presumably harvest mouse is also eligible.

We repeated the analysis for England, Scotland and Wales separately. The formula used again assumed an exponent of -0.75, and the constant was based on the observed relationship in each case. For England, log abundance $= -0.75 \log_{10}$ body weight $+ 7.3$, for Scotland log abundance $= -0.75 \log_{10}$ body weight $+ 7.1$, and for Wales log abundance $= -0.75 \log_{10}$ body weight $+ 6.7$. The pattern of residuals was similar for all three countries, although there were some differences, such as the relative scarcity of deer in Wales. Otherwise, there are no major regional differences in the pattern of relative abundance between species and orders.

Based on these analyses and current patterns of population change (Harris *et al.*, 1995), we then prepared a list of species of conservation concern, for native and long-standing accidental introductions (Table 6.1) and recent deliberately introduced species (Table 6.2). In these tables, the terms 'too few' and 'common' are used to describe species with negative and positive residuals respectively exceeding 0.75, and the term 'right number' to describe species with residuals between 0.75 and -0.75. For native species,

Table 6.1

Conservation priorities for native terrestrial mammals and long-standing accidental introductions suggested by abundance/mass relationships and current population trends in Harris et al. (1995)

	Species of high conservation concern	Species of medium conservation concern	Species of potential conservation concern	Species of no conservation concern	Overabundant species
		Too few; stable/ slow increase	Too few but increasing	Common/right number and stable or slow increase	Too many and increasing
	Too few and declining	Right number but declining Limited range	Common/right number but declining		
Native species	Red squirrel Yellow-necked mouse Dormouse	Pygmy shrew Water shrew Mountain hare Skomer vole Water vole Pine marten Stoat Weasel Polecat Wildcat	Hedgehog Field vole Otter	Mole Common shrew Bank vole Wood mouse Red fox Badger	Red deer Roe deer
Long-standing accidental introductions	Harvest mouse	Scilly shrew Orkney vole			

Table 6.2

Conservation priorities for recently introduced terrestrial mammals suggested by abundance/mass relationships, current population trends in Harris *et al.* (1995) and the international importance of the British population

Species of high conservation concern	Species of medium conservation concern	Species of potential conservation concern	Species of no conservation concern	Overabundant species
Limited wild range and of international importance	A significant proportion of the world population	Limited range but expanding	Declining and not of world importance Limited range and stable	Right number but increasing Too many and stable/declining
Water deer Feral goat Feral sheep		Fat dormouse	Bennett's wallaby Brown hare Ship rat Feral ferret Reindeer	Rabbit Grey squirrel House mouse Common rat American mink Feral cat Sika deer Fallow deer Chinese muntjac

these assessments are based solely on their status in Britain; their status in Europe is discussed by Harris *et al.* (1995). Whilst Britain has important populations of species such as badger and otter, none of our native species is of international conservation concern.

For the recently introduced species, however, three with relatively small populations are of international conservation importance (Harris *et al.*, 1995). Two (feral goat *Capra hircus* and feral sheep *Ovis ammon*) are ancient breeds. The third is Chinese water deer *Hydropotes inermis*, whose British population is limited in distribution and probably numbers less than 1000 adults, but constitutes about 10 % of the entire world population of the Chinese subspecies (Cooke and Farrell, 1998). Thus, three introduced species are of greater international conservation concern than any of our native species.

However, looking at species in isolation is of limited conservation benefit, since it is also important to consider species interactions when setting conservation goals. We used an energetic analysis to investigate this further.

ENERGETIC RELATIONSHIPS

We undertook a preliminary analysis of the food web involving mammalian carnivores and their main mammalian prey items, and those avian predators for which mammals form the majority of their prey; the species are listed in Table 6.3. We excluded piscivorous predators such as otters, and carnivores such as badgers, whose prey includes only a small proportion of mammals. We also excluded the ungulates from these analyses, since no mammalian or avian predator hunts adult ungulates, although new-born young are taken occasionally and scavenging from carcasses can be an important source of food for some species. All these analyses were based on the pre-breeding population estimates; the abundance of avian predators came from Gibbons *et al.* (1993).

The energy available from each of the prey species was calculated by assuming 6.41 kJ/g and that they were 90 % digestible (Saunders *et al.*, 1993). The energetic requirements (field metabolic rates) of the mammalian and avian predators were based on Nagy (1987); the total energetic requirement of each predator was based on the abundance of each species and its field metabolic rate. The total digestible energy of the standing crop of mammalian prey was $4.29E + 11$ kJ, and the total energy requirements of the predators $3.29E + 9$ kJ/day, or $1.43E + 12$ kJ/year. Of this, 1.9 % is the energy requirement of avian predators; the rest is the energy requirement

Table 6.3
Species included in the energetic analyses

Prey species	Digestible energy of prey (kJ)	Percent of total prey energy	Total potential productivity per annum	Mammalian carnivores	Birds of prey
Hedgehog	9.85E+9	2.3	5	Red fox	Hen harrier
Mole	1.96E+10	4.6	3.5	Pine marten	Buzzard
Common shrew	1.68E+9	0.4	12	Stoat	Golden eagle
Pygmy shrew	9.91E+7	<0.1	10	Weasel	Kestrel
Water shrew	1.64E+8	<0.1	12	Polecat	Barn owl
Rabbit	3.24E+11	75.6	15	Feral ferret	Little owl
Brown hare	1.67E+10	3.9	9	American mink	Tawny owl
Mountain hare	5.45E+9	1.3	9	Wildcat	Long-eared owl
Red squirrel	2.59E+8	0.1	4	Feral cat	Short-eared owl
Grey squirrel	7.48E+9	1.7	8		
Bank vole	3.97E+9	0.9	15		
Field vole	1.30E+10	3.0	15		
Water vole	2.09E+9	0.5	18		
Wood mouse	4.16E+9	1.0	35		
Yellow-necked mouse	1.25E+8	<0.1	35		
Harvest mouse	4.92E+7	<0.1	15		
House mouse	4.97E+8	0.1	25		
Common rat	1.96E+10	4.6	96		
Common dormouse	8.64E+7	<0.1	8		

of the terrestrial carnivores. Rabbits account for over 75 % of the total energy available to predators (Table 6.3); most other prey species contribute less than 2 %. Thus, the vast majority of the energy available to carnivores is from an introduced species that only became widespread in the countryside within the last two centuries (Harris *et al.*, 1995).

Calculating the increase in prey biomass that is available to predators due to the recruitment of young is difficult to quantify accurately, since it is unclear at what stage most young will be taken by predators. If it is assumed that, on average, the offspring are eaten at half adult weight, this would give a total digestible energy available in a year of 2.33E + 12 kJ, roughly 1.5 times as high as the basic energy requirements of the predators. Assuming the energy needs of predators for reproduction (gestation, lactation and rearing the young) is roughly three times basic energy requirements (Gittleman and Thompson, 1988), and half the predator population is female, this would suggest that the extra energy requirements of the predators for reproduction is close to the extra energy available through the productivity of the prey base.

Whilst these are only intended to be approximate estimates of the energy available in the mammalian food web in Britain, it is clear that the energy available to predators is limited and probably close to the limit that can sustain the current predator population. Further evidence for this is seen in the calculations provided by Dyczkowski and Yalden (1998).

STRUCTURE OF THE FOOD WEB

The limited food base for predators, and the heavy reliance on one species of prey, suggests an imbalance to the food web. There are 19 prey species supporting 18 species of predator (1 prey to 0.95 predators). Other food webs show a much larger prey base; in the Ythan Estuary, for instance, Hall and Raffaelli (1991) recorded 1 prey species to 0.41 predators, and they concluded that this was similar to that recorded in other studies. Thus, whilst at least some of the predators listed in the present analysis will take other prey items (birds, amphibians, fish, invertebrates, fruit), at least at some times of the year, there would appear to be a heavy reliance on few prey items. Even compared to continental Europe, the mammalian food web in Britain is heavily skewed, with few prey species per predator. In continental Europe there are 89 prey species (17 insectivores, three lagomorphs, 50 rodents and 19 large herbivores), 23 mammalian carnivores (excluding polar bear *Ursus maritimus*) and 30 birds of prey (three buzzards, eight eagles, three kestrels, four harriers and 12 owls), a ratio of 1 prey species: 0.60 predators. This is much closer to that typical of food webs.

The problem faced in Britain is that, having been isolated from the continental land mass, a disproportionately high number of mammalian predators colonised (both naturally and following introductions), probably because of their greater mobility/larger home ranges. Hence, we have an almost equal number of species of predators and prey, and many of the potential prey species are either not eaten by mammalian predators (mole, the shrews) or rarely eaten by either mammalian and/or avian predators (bank vole, house mouse, common dormouse). Out of the total of 59 species of mammalian predators in Europe, Britain has 20 (34 %), but only 24 out of 89 mammalian prey species (27 %). Furthermore, of the prey species that are available to predators, just two (rabbit and field vole) predominate in the diet of most predators, although archaeological evidence suggests that the water vole was a much more important food item for many predators prior to the introduction of rabbits (Yalden, 1999). The absence of voles common in arable farmland in continental Europe (pine vole *Microtus subterraneus* and common vole *Microtus arvalis*) is particularly significant in reducing the prey base in Britain.

CONCLUSIONS

Setting conservation priorities for mammals is not easy. So far, there are few data comparable to those for birds to monitor population trends, and significant declines can go unrecorded for long periods e.g., the water vole (Jefferies et al., 1989). It was only possible to quantify the dramatic decline in the number of water voles in Britain because there were good baseline data from the nineteenth century. Comparable baseline data are not available for most other species.

Yet even data such as those for the water vole cannot be used to quantify the magnitude of the population decline, only the loss of known populations. There are few monitoring systems currently in place that can measure changes in British mammal populations (Macdonald et al., 1998a). For most species, there are not even tested census methods, and so it is not possible for most mammals to fulfil the current criteria for Species Action Plans. In this analysis, we have tried to demonstrate that the rationale underpinning the selection criteria for those species of mammals with Action Plans should be broadened, and that a number of mammals without Action Plans may give greater cause for concern than at least some of the Action Plan species. We argue, therefore, that a variety of criteria should be used to identify mammal conservation priorities.

A species focus based on few assessment criteria also fails to take account of the importance of any interrelations with other species of mammals. Competition effects are ignored, as is the importance of the food base. The preliminary analysis presented here suggests that many terrestrial carnivores, especially the specialised predators of smaller mammals, may be limited in abundance because the food base is not there to support them. Two species (rabbit and short-tailed field vole) are of particular importance in supporting a high proportion of the mammalian and avian predators in Britain. Whilst these are two of the commonest species of mammal in Britain (Harris *et al.*, 1995), the field vole seems to have undergone a dramatic population decline since last century, when vole plagues were frequently recorded (Elton, 1942). The magnitude of this decline, particularly in lowland areas of Britain (Harris *et al.*, 1995), has been implicated as a key factor leading to the decline of predators such as the barn owl, and an increase in field vole numbers following rabbit declines led to local increases in weasel numbers (Tapper, 1992). Thus, there is evidence to suggest that prey availability is currently limiting at least some species of predator in Britain. Furthermore, the disproportionate reliance on two species implies a degree of vulnerability to stochastic factors such as the large decline in rabbit numbers following the onset of myxomatosis.

We suggest, therefore, that it is important to understand the community structure of our mammal fauna better so that we can estimate the desirable population size for each species, and the ecological consequences of population changes. Increasing the numbers of field voles, the commonest species of mammal in Britain, may be the most important contribution to increasing overall biodiversity. If so, this should be a conservation priority. Enhancing the abundance of the more common species that form the prey base will enable us to maintain and/or re-establish native carnivores. Once species such as the field vole are more abundant, it will be possible to reintroduce carnivores such as the pine marten to those parts of their former ranges where they are currently absent, and which are unlikely to be recolonised naturally (Bright and Harris, 1994).

One of the traits identified in this analysis is that species thought to be at risk from habitat fragmentation were generally rarer than would be expected from abundance/mass relationships, suggesting that these species are already suffering population declines as a result of habitat fragmentation. Thus, we need to understand further the potential impacts of habitat fragmentation on British mammal populations.

It is also clear that the British mammal fauna is heavily skewed towards large herbivores, and that these are generally overabundant already or increasing and likely to become overabundant. This suggests that, in the absence of any large predator, herbivore numbers should be reduced, and that no more large herbivores should be introduced or reintroduced: lynx or wolf would make a greater contribution to restoring an ecological balance than beaver *Castor fiber* or wild boar *Sus scrofa* (Yalden, 1986). Yet there is a consultation document asking for comments on proposals to reintroduce beavers to Scotland, and wild boar have become established in southern England (Anon., 1998a).

Popular species are often used as flagships for conservation, both internationally and nationally. In Britain, many of the species selected for Species Action Plans are popular, and the public is willing to pay for their conservation (White *et al.*, 1997). The value of flagship species has been discussed elsewhere (Leader-Williams and Dublin, chapter 4, this volume). Whilst this approach has had conservation benefits, it is unclear whether the benefits have exceeded the costs. We believe that an objective assessment of the faunal composition of an area, and the stability of the faunal structure, should also play a role in establishing conservation priorities. The preliminary analyses presented here suggest one potential means of achieving that goal.

SUMMARY

The British mammal fauna is heavily skewed towards introduced species, especially larger herbivores. In Britain as a whole, and in each of England, Scotland and Wales, carnivores are less abundant, and small rodents and large herbivores more abundant, than predicted from abundance/bio-mass relationships. Using these analyses to highlight species of particular conservation concern showed that of the four native species/long standing introductions that pose the greatest cause for concern, only two have a Species Action Plan to aid their recovery. One of the other species for which there is no Action Plan is introduced and more common than abundance/ biomass relationships predict it should be. A simple food web suggests that there are too few small mammals (both species and abundance), and it would appear that the comparative rarity of a number of our carnivores is a direct consequence.

We suggest that analyses such as abundance/mass relationships provide a valuable additional means of helping to decide conservation priorities for our mammal fauna. We also argue that conservation priorities must be based on an effective consideration of species interactions.

7

Small mammals and the conservation agenda

ABIGAIL C. ENTWISTLE AND PETER J. STEPHENSON

INTRODUCTION

In recent years the apparent dominance of mammals and birds in the conservation arena has been noted (Wilson, 1992). Whilst focusing on these species may be entirely understandable and defensible given the needs of funding and promoting conservation, such restrictions in conservation focus may not integrate well within a 'biodiversity-led' approach to conservation, and may be more difficult to justify in this context. It has been argued that conservation of species for their intrinsic appeal acts to protect other species within the same habitat (Johnsingh and Joshua, 1994; Leader-Williams and Dublin, chapter 4, this volume). However, under-representation of other species on the conservation agenda may lead to a lack of effective conservation, despite threats equivalent to, or greater than, the more high profile, popular or charismatic species (Ceballos and Brown, 1995). Thus while conservation is succeeding for a limited number of high profile endangered species, lack of similar action may result in a relative increase in the risk of extinction for less popular or charismatic species, which may slide off the conservation agenda. Although large, charismatic species will inevitably remain key flagships for the conservation movement, and the focus for a great deal of emotion from the general public and conservationists alike, the conservation implications for less charismatic species needs to be considered.

Although mammals, in general, appear very well represented on the conservation agenda, attention in fact appears to be directed to a limited number of species. The highest profile mammals are generally large and charismatic, including carnivores, large primates, elephants and ungulates. Some of this bias undoubtedly reflects historical associations, and the evolution of the conservation movement in response to declines in large

African mammals (Fitter and Scott, 1978). Furthermore, these large mammals have intrinsic appeal for both conservationists and the general public (e.g., elephants; Poole and Thomson, 1989). It has also been claimed that the very size of these animals puts them at greater risk of extinction (Coe, 1982; Lawton, 1995), and such threats, coupled with their clear impact on habitats and ecosystems, justifies the conservation attention they receive.

In contrast, smaller mammal species (mass < 1 kg) appear less well represented on the conservation agenda. The small mammal fauna is often seen as a broad assemblage, with the assumption that 'a rat is a rat' (Ceballos and Brown, 1995), and that co-occurrence of species indicates redundancy and ecologically similar roles. This does not account for the unique taxonomic and ecological forms within this large group, and the complimentarity in ecological roles therein. Although there has been increasing recognition of the important role of small mammal species in ecological processes and ecosystem function (including pollination, seed dispersal, predation and prey base; Fujita and Tuttle, 1991; Ceballos and Brown, 1995), this does not appear to have been reflected in how such species are incorporated into conservation programmes. In this context, there is a clear justification to examine the conservation status and particular management needs of small mammals, and to explore means by which conservation programmes could incorporate the conservation requirements of this group.

In this chapter we attempt to explore the conservation status of small mammals relative to the level of conservation attention or direct protection they receive, and to examine whether a focus on large, charismatic species is justifiable from a biological stance, as opposed to a pragmatic one. In doing this we are in no way questioning the obvious threats to large mammals, or challenging the need to focus on their conservation. Rather we want to demonstrate that many of the same arguments can be applied to small mammals. In doing this we hope to raise awareness of the threats facing small mammals, and encourage both researchers and conservationists to take a more active interest in the conservation needs of these species. In addition, we hope that some of the rather more pragmatic reasons why large mammals remain the focus for conservation attention will be clarified.

DISTRIBUTION OF BODY SIZE WITHIN THE MAMMALIA

In general, there is an inverse relationship between body size and species richness (Hutchison and MacArthur, 1959), and in consequence it is ex-

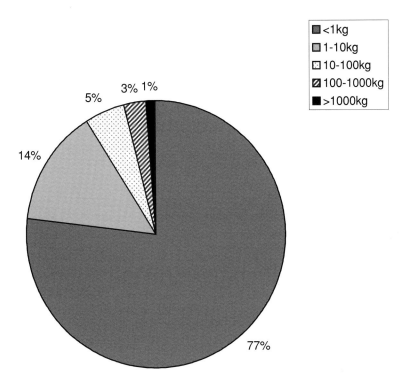

Figure 7.1 The percentage of mammals of different categories of mass, as determined from the literature (Nowak and Paradiso, 1983; Wilson and Reeder, 1993).

pected that smaller organisms will be most common in any community. Analysis of mammal species richness relative to body mass (as an indication of 'size') using data from the mammalian literature (Nowak and Paradiso, 1983; Wilson and Reeder, 1993) demonstrates that most mammals are small, with over 75 % of mammal species having a body mass of less than 1 kg (Figure 7.1). For the purposes of this chapter, species of 1 kg or less will be considered as 'small mammals'. This is a somewhat arbitrary cut-off, but is supported by the number of species in this category, and has been used elsewhere (Barnett, 1992).

Body size, of course, is generally not independent from phylogeny. Thus we tend to find some orders dominated by large species, and others by small ones. Examination of all mammalian orders (classification following Wilson and Reeder, 1993) revealed that nine orders were dominated by species under 1 kg (Table 7.1). These included tree shrews, insectivores, elephants shrews, bats and some smaller marsupial orders. All the 3530 species in these orders will be used as the data set for the rest of the analysis

Table 7.1
Proportion of species in different orders of a mass less than 1 kg

Order	English name	% of species of mass < 1 kg
Monotremata	Monotremes	0
Didelphimorphia	Marsupials	91
Paucituberculata	” ”	100
Microbioteria	” ”	100
Dasyuromorphia	” ”	85
Peramelemorphia	” ”	35
Notoryctemorphia	” ”	100
Diprotodontia	” ”	15
Xenartha	Edentates	14
Insectivora	Insectivores	98
Scandentia	Tree shrews	100
Dermoptera	Flying lemurs	0
Chiroptera	Bats	98
Primates	Primates	23
Carnivora	Carnivores	18
Cetacea	Whales, dolphins	0
Sirenia	Sea cows	0
Proboscidea	Elephants	0
Perissodactyla	Odd-toed ungulates	0
Hyracoidea	Hyraxes	0
Tubulidentata	Aardvark	0
Artiodactyla	Even-toed ungulates	1
Pholidota	Pangolins, scaly anteaters	0
Rodentia	Rodents	94
Lagomorpha	Lagomorphs	41
Macroscelidea	Elephant-shrews	100

in this chapter. This group represents an important component of mammalian taxonomic diversity, and includes a range of monotypic groups – one order, nine families and 279 genera.

THREATS TO SMALL MAMMALS

Small mammals face many of the same threats which affect other groups of fauna and flora, such as habitat loss, pollution, effects of introduced species, hunting and persecution (Lidicker, 1989; Nicoll and Rathbun, 1990; Mickleburgh et al., 1992; Stone, 1995). Small mammals may be particularly prone to habitat loss at a finer level, and the effects of pollution may be greater in this group than among larger species. Furthermore, hunting of small mammals is generally overlooked as an issue.

Habitat loss

The use of habitats by small mammals is dramatically affected by the scale at which these species operate. Within a given habitat, ecological studies have demonstrated that the distribution of many small mammals is strongly associated with the availability of suitable microhabitats, including roosting and foraging sites (Stephenson, 1995; Entwistle et al., 1997). Such microhabitat associations indicate very precise habitat requirements, leading to patchy distributions in response to microhabitat dispersion, and many small mammal species, especially those in rain forest habitats, may have more restricted distributions than previously thought (Nicoll et al., 1988; Stephenson, 1994). Furthermore, specificity may occur for more than one resource (e.g., for foraging areas and roosting sites) and the spatial relationship in the distribution of these different resources may affect distribution of small mammals (Entwistle et al., 1997). Specific microhabitat needs can mean that subtle changes in the habitat structure can lead to drastic effects for small mammal species, and disruption of habitat assemblages (Stephenson, 1993, 1995).

Microhabitat associations also affect the scale at which habitats are effectively fragmented. Following fragmentation, small and subdivided populations are at risk from demographic or genetic effects (Mace and Lande, 1991), which may be higher in small mammals given greater natural fluctuations in their populations (Price and Endo, 1989; Young, 1994). Survival of fragmented populations may be negatively affected by limited dispersal abilities and inability to survive outside habitat patches (Laurance, 1994; Mills, 1995). Habitat specialists, such as small mammals, may be more likely to become isolated, even at small spatial scales of fragmentation (Laurance, 1994).

Microhabitat associations, coupled with limited dispersal abilities, also result in a high number of endemic and restricted range species, with isolated populations associated with specific habitat areas. For example, remnant mountain forests have recently yielded many newly described and highly endemic species (Hutterer et al., 1991) which are likely to be lost if these remnant forest patches are disturbed or destroyed.

Habitat loss and degradation appear to be the greatest threats to small mammal populations, based on recent evaluations (Lidicker, 1989; Nicoll and Rathbun, 1990; Mickleburgh et al., 1992; Stone, 1995; IUCN, 1996). Large-scale degradation of habitats will affect small mammals. For example, many small mammals are dependent on forest habitats, which have undergone severe declines in recent decades (WWF, 1996a). Furthermore, habitat change may also act on small mammals in more insidious

ways, through loss of specific microhabitats, and their increased fragmentation, resulting in isolation of small populations (Fitzgibbon, 1994).

Direct hunting and persecution

Although hunting is traditionally associated with larger mammals, small
mammals have been both hunted and persecuted as pests and carriers of
disease (e.g., declines in the black rat *Rattus rattus* have led to its inclusion
among the ten most threatened rodent species in Europe; Lidicker, 1989).
Small mammals, including the chinchilla *Chinchilla lanigera* (Lidicker,
1989) and the steppe marmot *Marmota bobak* (Bibikov, 1991), have been
hunted for their fur. A number of small mammal species are considered at
risk from commercial trade and are listed under CITES (Wijnstekers,
1995). Small mammals are also targeted as bushmeat – including rodents,
elephant shrews and fruit bats (Fitzgibbon *et al.*, 1995; Suárez *et al.*, 1995;
Entwistle and Corp, 1997), and on occasion may be targeted in preference
to larger species (Njiforti, 1996). Small mammal trapping appears to be
traditional in many areas rather than being solely a response to extirpation
of larger species (Suárez *et al.*, 1995). Although the higher annual productivity of small mammals, particularly rodents, indicates that sustainable
hunting may be possible (Arita *et al.*, 1990; Fa *et al.*, 1995), studies have
indicated measurable impacts of hunting on the populations and distributions of small mammal species (Fitzgibbon *et al.*, 1995; Njiforti, 1996), and
concerns over risks of overhunting have been expressed (Suárez *et al.*,
1995).

Introduced species

Introduced, non-native species of plants and animals (including other
mammals) can severely impact small mammal populations (Dutton and
Haft, 1996; Smith and Quin, 1996) through predation, competition and
direct effects on habitat structure. Such interactions are clear on oceanic
islands, and in Australia and New Zealand, where native small mammal
species have been decimated by the introduction of European carnivores
and rodents (Smith and Quin, 1996). It has also been suggested that non-
native species may pose risks inside isolated habitat islands such as reserves (Goodman, 1995), although evidence for this is conflicting (Stephenson, 1995).

Pollution and pesticide use

The impacts of pesticides and pollution may cause particular threats to
small mammals for two reasons – small body size leading to rapid mobil-

isation of fat resources and the incidence of insectivory in this group. Insectivores are affected by pesticide use through both direct impacts on prey
availability and sublethal build up of residues in the tissues (Clark *et al.*,
1988). Pollution is a particular risk for a number of aquatic small mammals, and may have contributed to population decreases in species such as
the Pyrenean desman *Galemys pyrenaicus* (Poduschka and Richard, 1986;
Stone, 1995). Direct application of insecticides has affected a number of
groups, notably bats (Jefferies, 1972; Racey, chapter 9, this volume).

THREATS ASSOCIATED WITH SIZE?

It is clear that with regard to direct hunting and utilisation of mammals,
large animals are typically at greater risk due to their visibility, and higher
returns from hunting effort. Patterns of loss, based on pre-historical and
historical data, indicate greater impacts on large mammals (Coe, 1982;
Owen-Smith, 1989) and it has been argued that 'Being big is dangerous in
a world dominated by *Homo sapiens*' (Lawton, 1995). Similarly, it has been
inferred across a range of taxa that large species are generally more prone to
extinction (Willis, 1974; Terborgh and Winter, 1980).

In general, life history characteristics and ecological factors relate to
body size (Western, 1979). Certain ecological characteristics of large mammals are intrinsically associated with higher risks of extinction. In general
large mammals are expected to have smaller population sizes (Robinson
and Redford, 1988) thus increasing impacts of stochastic processes (Terborgh, 1974; Terborgh and Winter, 1980), larger area requirements and
lower reproductive rates, restricting the recovery of populations after
crashes (Coe, 1982). In contrast, the life history characteristics of small
mammals may be expected to buffer them from extinction, through higher
population densities, smaller range requirements and high productivity,
and associated intrinsic rates of population growth.

However, such assumptions do not account for differences between orders of mammals in respect to general body size predictions. Taxa such as
bats and insectivores show much lower reproductive rates than expected
from this relationship (Stephenson and Racey, 1995; Racey and Entwistle,
in press) and small mammals occur at a wide range of densities and display
very different range sizes (Gaston and Blackburn, 1995b). In these cases
the broad generalisations based on body size and life history relationships
may not be helpful. Furthermore, when a 'typical' small mammal
life history pattern is considered, the 'live fast–die young' strategy is not
without its associated risks for extinction. Small mammals display greater

natural fluctuations in their populations (Price and Endo, 1989; Young, 1994), leading to risks associated with increased demographic stochasticity. The short generation times typical of many small mammals may reduce persistence time (Pimm *et al.*, 1988) and increase risks of local extinction in response to short-term environmental perturbations. For example, in an animal with a longevity of 12 months, missing one season's breeding through adverse conditions results in local extinction, whereas the lifespan of larger species would buffer them from such effects.

Rather than being based solely on size or population size, it has been suggested that conservation assessments should take into account both density and distribution. In such analyses species displaying both restricted distribution (typical of smaller-bodied species) and low density (typical of larger-bodied species) would be most at risk of extinction (Arita *et al.*, 1990).

Direct evidence from field studies indicates no association between body size and extinction risk (Gaston and Blackburn, 1995b). For example, studies of mammalian extinctions within isolated reserves have demonstrated that body size is not a key factor in predicting extinction risk (Laurance, 1991; Newmark, 1995). In these cases, although initial population size did affect the persistence of species, microhabitat specificity and the tolerance of habitats outside the reserve also affected species survival (Laurance, 1991, 1994). Thus, while some correlates of size (such as population size) do affect likelihood of persistence, it appears that it is ecological factors, rather than size per se that determine the extinction risk of mammals.

CONSERVATION STATUS OF SMALL MAMMALS

General patterns of threat to small mammals were established through review of data in the *IUCN Red List of Threatened Animals* (IUCN, 1986, 1990a, 1993a, 1996). Initial analyses indicated significant increases in the listing of small mammals as threatened, relative to orders dominated by large mammals (Perissodactyla, Proboscidea, Primates, Carnivora, Cetacea, Artiodactyla) over the period 1986–1996 (Figure 7.2). In particular, the number of small mammals listed increased dramatically in 1996, perhaps reflecting a change in the criteria used and the attempt to assess all mammal species (Mace and Lande, 1991; IUCN, 1996).

Analysis of the 1996 List allows some quantification of the extinction threat faced by small mammals. Approximately 70 % of threatened and 78 % of Critically Endangered mammals are small, reflecting the size distribution of species. Overall, a lower proportion of small mammals is con-

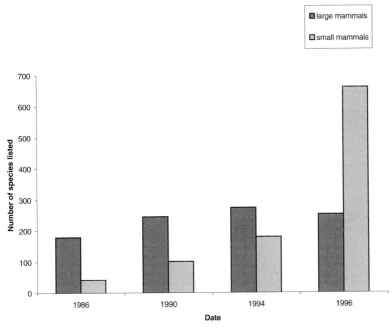

Figure 7.2 Number of species of small and large mammals listed as threatened in the *IUCN Red List of Threatened Animals* (includes all categories of threat except Insufficiently Known, Data Deficient, and Lower Risk) in the years between 1986 and 1996.

sidered threatened (Vulnerable, Endangered or Critically Endangered) compared to other mammals (small mammals 22% threatened [760/3530], other mammals 30% [336/1127]; χ^2 =32.6, $P < 0.01$). However, small mammals are as likely to be Critically Endangered as other mammals, including large mammals (small mammals 4% threatened [132/3530], other mammals 3% [37/1,127]; χ^2 = 0.6, N.S.; large mammals 4% threatened [32/831]; χ^2 = 0.02, N.S.). When the proportions of species threatened in individual orders of small mammals are considered (Table 7.2), they are shown to be as threatened as any group of large mammals. It appears than when all mammals are considered together, the low level of threat among the rodents masks the relatively higher level of threat within other groups such as insectivores (Table 7.2). Similar results have been shown by using a different analytical approach to the data (Mace and Balmford, chapter 3, this volume).

Similar patterns are clear in extinctions recorded in the last 400 years, with data on small mammal extinctions improving over the last decade (Figure 7.3, source IUCN, 1986, 1990a, 1996). A total of 66 small

Table 7.2
Orders of small and large mammals with the highest proportions of
threatened species

Small mammals	Percentage of species listed as threatened	Large mammals	Percentage of species listed as threatened
Microbiotheria	100	Proboscidea	100
Macroscelidea	47	Perissodactyla	58
Insectivora	41	Primates	41
Chiroptera	25	Carnivora	24
Rodentia	16	Cetacea	17

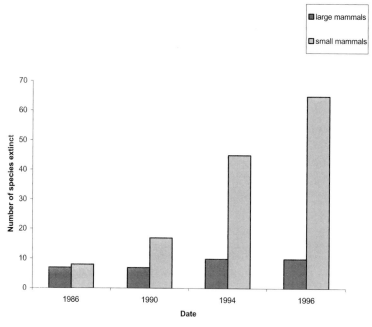

Figure 7.3 Number of species of small and large mammals listed as Extinct in the
IUCN Red List of Threatened Animals in the years between 1986 and 1996.

mammal species are thought have become extinct over the last 400 years –
representing nearly three-quarters of all recorded mammalian extinctions.
Small mammals are just as likely to have gone extinct as other mammals,
including large mammals (small mammal extinctions 2 % [66/3530], other
mammals 2 % [23/1127]; χ^2 = 0.1, N.S.; large mammal extinctions 1 % [12/
831]; χ^2 = 0.7, N.S.).

The evidence above suggests that although small mammals are not as well represented in lower categories of threat (Vulnerable and Endangered), compared to large mammals they are equally likely to be considered Critically Endangered, and have suffered similar levels of extinction. Indeed, once the size of the group is taken into account, it is evident that the majority of mammal species recently lost, and those likely to go extinct during the next 30 years, are small.

CONSERVATION ATTENTION DIRECTED TO SMALL MAMMALS

It is very difficult to assess what constitutes conservation attention. In general, we are defining this as specific action or programmes focused on the group in question. Although wide-ranging habitat-based programmes may address the needs of many species, we wanted to examine the information available on attention directed specifically to small mammals in relation to large mammals. For example, it was noted that while management plans for reserves often highlighted actions for large species, there was rarely a mention of specific management techniques aimed at small mammals. The conservation attention received by small mammals was assessed indirectly from three sources – from publications in four major conservation journals over the last 10 years, from membership of IUCN/Species Survival Commission Specialist Groups and from conservation projects run by major international NGOs.

Publications in conservation journals

Published research in conservation journals reflects attention given to different groups within both a conservation biology and a management context. Representation in journals geared directly to conservation efforts is likely to reflect the interests of conservationists regarding different mammals. Four major conservation journals (*Biodiversity and Conservation, Biological Conservation, Conservation Biology* and *Oryx*) were included in the analysis. All mammal-oriented papers listed in the journals from 1982 (or the first issue, where journals were established after this date) until the end of 1996 were examined, and attributed to mammalian order on the basis of the focus species or assemblage (Figure 7.4). This demonstrated that while the number of papers published on small mammals is increasing, such publications are still under-represented compared to those on large species or assemblages. In this analysis the greatest number of papers (29 %) were focused on carnivores.

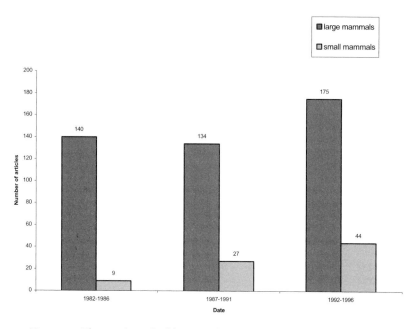

Figure 7.4 The number of publications focusing on large and small mammals respectively which appeared in four conservation journals between the years 1982 and 1996.

It is possible that the analysis may be affected by taxonomic biases of these particular journals. Other specialist mammalian journals (such as *Journal of Mammalogy, Mammalia, Mammal Review* and *Acta Theriologica*) may include more ecological studies on small mammals. However, although many of these papers do provide significant information essential to conservation, few studies in these journals appear to have been designed with conservation as the primary objective. Therefore, it was decided that restricting the analysis to conservation journals limited the consideration to the attention given to small mammals directly in respect to conservation and conservation biology, rather than in a more general ecological context.

Membership of SSC Specialist Groups

IUCN/Species Survival Commission Specialist Groups were set up to identify the conservation priorities within taxonomic groups, using information from a network of international experts. Generally these thematic groups focus on whole orders, but may also review conservation needs of individual species, or on more general themes such as sustainable use. Although the requirements for membership, and level of activity, may vary

Table 7.3
Membership of IUCN/Species Survival Commission Specialist Groups for different orders

Order	Number of Specialist Groups	Total membership	Members per Species
Proboscidea	2	116	58.00
Perissodactyla	4	117	6.10
Carnivora	9	510	1.90
Artiodactyla	8	351	1.90
Primates	1	211	0.90
Cetacea	1	66	0.80
Chiroptera	1	80	0.09
Insectivora[a]	1	31	0.08
Rodentia	1	121	0.06

[a] Includes Macroscelidea and Scandentia.

from group to group, and some groups may be restricted by region, in general it is likely that the size of Specialist Groups will reflect the number of experts active in working on particular orders, and to some extent the likely conservation attention directed to different taxa.

Data were collated from a directory of Specialist Group members produced in 1993 (IUCN, 1993b). These data were used to calculate the number of separate Specialist Groups, number of individual members (accounting for multiple membership), and proportionate membership relative to the number of species in different orders of mammals (Table 7.3). In contrast to the larger-bodied taxa, small mammal orders were only represented by single groups, and generally appeared proportionately less well represented once the number of species in these orders was considered. In particular this contrasts strongly with the attention given to carnivores, which appear to be over represented in terms of both individual groups, and membership.

Projects run by International NGOs

Data were collected from two international conservation NGOs regarding current projects with a mammalian focus. Of these, only one of the in-house projects had a focus on small mammals (action planning for bats; Table 7.4). Of 435 projects listed in WWF's 1996–7 global programme, 29 specifically targeted a particular mammalian species or assemblage – all of which were large mammals (WWF, 1996b). Even within a funding mechanism designed to support work on less charismatic species (The 100% Fund run by Fauna & Flora International) only 17% of mammalian

Table 7.4
The number of species-specific mammal projects run by two international
NGOs (FFI and WWF)

Order	Species	Number of projects
Proboscidea	elephants	11
Perissodactyla	rhinos	8
Carnivora	tigers, other cats, bears, seals	8
Primates	gorilla, drill, tamarin	4
Artiodactyla	ungulates	1
Chiroptera	bats	1
Cetacea	whales	1

projects supported since 1971 have focused on small mammals (Mickleburgh, 1997).

All these sources of evidence indicate that small mammals receive relatively little direct conservation attention – in terms of activity and research, particularly in relation to the size of this group. Or expressed another way '... justifiably or not, large mammals receive a disproportionate share of attention in conservation activity and research' (Young, 1994). The reasons for such a disparity are explored below.

ISSUES AFFECTING CONSERVATION ATTENTION DIRECTED TO SMALL MAMMALS

Lack of knowledge

Despite claims that large mammals are neglected with regard to ecological research (Terborgh, 1988) the evidence to the contrary is clear to anyone who has investigated the literature on most small mammals. Although large scale research programmes have used a limited number of small mammal species as models for examining ecological processes, in general even basic life history and habitat requirements are unknown for most small mammals, particularly tropical species (Nicoll and Rathbun, 1990). In addition, new small mammal species are still being described at a greater rate than large mammals, suggesting that further hidden biodiversity is likely to exist among this group.

A number of factors make research on small mammals more difficult – particularly as many are inconspicuous (due to small size, colouration and difficulties of identification) and show cryptic behaviour, particularly nocturnality. Thorough investigative research beyond simple trapping studies has only recently become possible through the development of new technologies and the continued miniaturisation of transmitting devices.

Common recommendations from IUCN small mammal Action Plans include the need for more surveys to define distributions and populations (Lidicker, 1989; Nicoll and Rathbun, 1990; Mickleburgh *et al.*, 1992). Data on the basic biology, ecology and taxonomy of many small mammals is lacking or inadequate, whereas in larger terrestrial taxa such basic research needs are not usually a prerequisite for conservation (Cumming *et al.*, 1990; East, 1990; Ginsberg and Macdonald, 1990). Lack of research may be one factor contributing to the delay in recognising the degree of threat faced by small mammals over the last decade.

The lack of directly conservation-oriented research for small mammals means that appropriate conservation strategies are often underdeveloped. Research on particular small mammal species has shown how a good understanding of the animal and its requirements can contribute to the development of effective, but not intuitively obvious, management programmes for such species (Holler *et al.*, 1989; Price and Endo, 1989). However we have few generalised guidelines for small mammal conservation, or any understanding to what extent approaches can be generalised for such a diverse group. Research into the means by which assemblages of small mammals can best be maintained is urgently required.

Lack of economic value

One of the main factors underlying the lack of resources and interest directed towards small mammal conservation, is the perceived lack of value of these animals. Small mammals rarely contribute to the economy of a country, and often will have a perceived negative value, when pest species are considered (Ceballos and Brown, 1995). Indeed, the indirect economic importance of many species may not be recognised. For example, bats have been shown to act as key pollinators and seed dispersers for a range of plants which together produce an estimated 448 products of economic importance, with a total value estimated as many millions of dollars (Fujita and Tuttle, 1991). However, governments, institutions and the public rarely see a direct value of conserving such species. Furthermore, although conservation organisations have a broad biological agenda, where biodiversity generally outweighs economic value of species, the range of species requiring attention is not reflected in species-oriented conservation approaches. Most species-focused conservation programmes appear to deal with larger, charismatic 'flagship species', for which the public is willing to provide donations (see Table 7.4). Such species appear to be selected on the basis of their popularity and potential to generate income for conservation, as well as the extent of threat and their value in protecting ecosystems. Indeed, the

Thin-spined porcupine, *Chaetomys subspinosus*, Brazil.
Photograph: Umar O. Santos.

earning power of large mammals should not be underestimated. Surveys by WWF demonstrated that these were just the species that their members preferred to support (D. Warren, personal communication). However, in such circumstances smaller species facing similar threats will not receive the same level of conservation attention.

Public perceptions of small mammals and lack of 'cultural value'

The ability of conservation organisations to promote smaller species may be hampered by their poor public profile. There is little positive publicity of the diversity of small mammal species, and the risks within this group. Instead, there is a tendency for small mammals to be represented by species with more negative associations (rats, mice and bats), and the impression may be that 'a rat is a rat' (Ceballos and Brown, 1995), in contrast to the unique forms among larger mammals such as rhinos and elephants. A study conducted among primary school children in the UK demonstrated that small mammals were among the most disliked species, being considered as 'smelly', 'dirty', 'creepy' and carriers of disease (Stephenson and Entwistle, in preparation). However, those children who owned small pets, such as hamsters and gerbils, displayed much more positive images of small mammals. In contrast, a clear preference was displayed for large, charismatic species, such as tigers, lions, giant pandas and other carnivores, and primates, based on their appearance, and characteristics such as speed, agility, fierceness and, counter-intuitively, 'cuteness'. Large carnivores obviously do have strong cultural associations in Western society, which is also reflected in the conservation programmes supported by the public.

A parallel study in schools in a rural area of Tanzania, close to a park boundary found markedly different perceptions of these species (Stephenson and Entwistle, in preparation). Children liked species that were both aesthetically pleasing and harmless (giraffes and zebras) or economically valued for meat or potential tourist revenue (rabbits, buffalo and rhinos). They disliked larger mammals such as elephants and carnivores (including lions and leopards) as a result of direct dangers posed to life, livestock and agriculture. Nearly all wild animals perceived to come out at night, whether or not they actually did, were disliked and feared. Views towards small mammals were more equivocal: rodents and fruit bats were seen as pests, whereas insectivorous bats were liked because they were thought to eat mosquitoes. Such attitudes were further supported by a study on an island off the coast of Tanzania, where the use of bats for food was reflected in positive perceptions of these species (Entwistle et al., in preparation).

A comparison of the studies from the UK and Tanzania reflects a clear dichotomy between the preferences and priorities of local people, and the preferences of animals in a Western culture, which tend to be reflected in the species-orientated programmes of international conservation organisations. It is not therefore surprising for the need for conflict resolution with local people within a large number of such programmes, and may indicate that their priorities are not always addressed in such programmes based on Western perceptions of value.

ARE CONSERVATION NEEDS OF SMALL MAMMALS MET BY PROTECTED AREAS?

Given the major threats to small mammals include habitat loss, it would seem that protected areas might be an important means to ensure the conservation of a wider range of small mammal species. Most protected areas are developed to conserve biodiversity and natural resources in general. However, where they are formed to conserve species, it is often to save large mammals. Obvious examples include the Selous Game Reserve, Tanzania (African elephant *Loxodonta africana* and black rhino *Diceros bicornis*), Virunga and Garamba National Parks, Democratic Republic of Congo (mountain gorilla *Gorilla gorilla beringei* and white rhino *Ceratotherium simum* respectively), Vu Quang Nature Reserve, Vietnam (soala *Pseudoryx nghetinhensis*), Ujung Kulon National Park, Java, Indonesia (Javan rhino *Rhinoceros sondaicus*), and the series of reserves in northern China (giant panda *Ailuropoda melanoleuca*, see Lu *et al.*, chapter 18, this volume). Protected areas are often set up to protect larger species due to their extensive range requirements, and the assumption that these large areas will also protect other threatened species.

It is not clear how far parks selected on the basis of large mammals act to protect the most threatened small mammals (see Williams *et al.*, chapter 5, this volume). The rarest small mammal species tend to occur in small, isolated areas of habitat – unsuitable for traditional protected areas. In addition, the habitats favoured by those large mammals targeted by such parks may be very different from those showing the highest small mammal diversity. We suggest that in such cases large mammals, such as savannah ungulates and rhinos in Africa, may not be good 'umbrella species' for overall mammalian diversity. Rather, primary forest species, such as primates, may be better umbrellas for small mammals.

The existing management regimes for protected areas rarely take into account the specific needs of small mammals, and may in fact negatively affect these species in some cases, particularly where large mammals are the focus of the park. Overstocking of large mammals may have direct impacts on smaller species. For example, high densities of elephants are known to strongly affect habitats (Cumming *et al.*, 1997), usually resulting in reduced tree cover, and have been shown to reduce bat activity (Fenton and Rautenbach, 1998), presumably through loss of foraging sites in woodland and of potential roost sites. Furthermore, overgrazing by ungulates has been shown to directly affect small mammal diversity and populations (Bibikov, 1991). Specific management requirements of small mammals are rarely written into management plans. Management plans sensitive to small mammals would be likely to consider: fragmentation and connectivity of habitats within parks; promotion of microhabitats as important to specific small mammals or small mammal diversity; limiting impacts of overstocking of large mammals; monitoring and control of effects of invasive species and of pollutant drift from external sources; and protection of potential roost or nesting sites for smaller species. However, further research on the impacts of management techniques is important both for conservation of specific species, and for the development of generalised guidelines.

At present, although protected areas are selected on the basis of overall species richness, time and resources may not be available to assess needs for small mammals. Assessments using 'indicator species' may offer a means to make broad assessments of relative habitat quality and likely species richness in the development of appropriate management strategies within protected areas. In addition, small mammals may benefit from notification and protection of smaller areas of habitat to provide a network of patches for conservation. Among the few protected areas that have been established specifically to conserve small mammals were the series of reserves developed in Russia in the 1920s and 1930s to save the Russian desman (*Desmana moschata*), which was threatened at the time by fur trapping (Stone, 1995). Other examples of potential refugia for small mammals in today's landscapes include graveyards and other traditional sites (Decher, 1997; Entwistle and Corp, 1997), and remnants of natural vegetation on farms (Happold and Happold, 1997). Indeed, networks of interconnected micro-reserves in otherwise affected areas might offer a real hope for protecting a wide range of small mammal species, within an integrated land-use system.

CONCLUSIONS

The evidence indicates that threats to small mammals are as extensive as those faced by large mammals, and that size does not appear to be an important factor directly affecting threat status at a broader scale. However, the lack of conservation attention received by small mammals does not reflect the degree of threat to this group. It appears that the needs of small mammals, in relation to the degree of threat, are not being met by the current conservation agenda.

Large, charismatic species will always have an important role to play as flagships in conservation, especially for fund-raising purposes in developed countries. However, increased attention directed towards smaller, less conspicuous species would serve to achieve balance and broader representation within the mammalian conservation agenda. The apparent priorities promoted by conservation organisations appear to reflect what the public already wants to conserve. There is a danger that it becomes difficult to break out of a circle where conservation organisations are driven by public preferences for species that the organisations themselves have previously promoted as a priority. Pragmatic values, linked to emotional appeal and funding potential, clearly have a role in determining the conservation agenda, and which species are the focus for conservation. We must be aware that decision making within conservation is not just based on objective, scientific assessments of status, but also on the charisma and popularity of the species concerned. However, when the conservation agenda is driven by the general public in Western countries, the values held by local stakeholders about different focal species may not be fully represented.

RECOMMENDATIONS

In addition to an improved profile within conservation, specific recommendations are suggested for means by which small mammal conservation can be promoted within existing conservation programmes, in order to develop a more holistic management approach to mammalian diversity.

- Conservation organisations have an important role in increasing the public awareness of risks to less charismatic species – the power of education with this regard should not be underestimated. Education and awareness campaigns should be aimed at both communities which give funds for conservation projects, and which often have negative attitudes to small mammals, and communities that are recipients of aid for conservation projects, where attitudes may be more equivocal.
- The popularity of certain small mammals, such as gerbils, hamsters and rabbits, could be exploited. In countries where larger native mammal species are few or have been extirpated (e.g., in the UK) small mammals such as hedgehogs, dormice and water voles appear to have popular appeal and effective marketing campaigns for small mammals can be very successful in making these species attractive to the general public (e.g., through the work of The Mammal Society). The potential of smaller species as flagships has also been demonstrated in other countries (including the use of fruit bats on small islands (Action Comores, 1997; Entwistle and Corp, 1997), and conservation agencies might be lobbied to consider supporting model projects that demonstrate the role of smaller, non-traditional, flagship species.
- Captive breeding programmes focusing on small mammals could be promoted, given the apparent greater efficiency and likely success of this technique for small rather than larger species (see Balmford, chapter 16, this volume). Studies of zoo attendance indicate that the small mammal houses may be more popular than otherwise considered (see Balmford, chapter 16, this volume), although further studies may be needed (Ward et al., 1998).
- Protected area managers have opportunities to promote small mammal conservation, within a management approach sensitive to the habitat requirements and threats to small mammals within their protected

areas. Small mammal surveys could be incorporated into protected area management planning, and specific management recommendations for small mammals should be identified such as keeping matrix diversity high, maintaining grazing regimes but avoiding overstocking, maintaining herb and shrub layer, avoiding loss of potential roost sites such as moribund trees, and ensuring connectivity at a microhabitat level.

- Basic research and monitoring on small mammal species is necessary to guide further management activities. Many IUCN/SSC Action Plans indicate priorities for survey and research which would provide information of use to conservation planners and managers on distribution, population densities and microhabitat requirements of small mammals. There are many opportunities to expand surveys and inventories to begin to assess habitat associations, and build up a wider picture of microhabitat requirements of different species. Monitoring of small mammals, particularly identified indicator species, may provide important information that can be interpolated for patterns in wider mammalian diversity with fewer associated costs.
- Future plans and proposed projects for small mammals (including IUCN/SSC Action Plans) might be targeted at a broader level, beyond research and protected areas management, and should ensure regular evaluation to assess success and failure of different strategies for small mammal conservation.

ACKNOWLEDGEMENTS

We would like to thank all those who helped in the schools survey in Tanzania and the UK, especially teachers and pupils, and staff from the WWF Tanzania Programme Office and Tanzania National Parks. We would also like to thank a range of people who have offered constructive advice and discussed many ideas during the development of this chapter, among them Edward O'Keefe, Evan Bowen-Jones, Jessica Worthington-Wilmer, Simon Mickleburgh, Debbie Warren and Mary Shuma. Valuable comments on the text were provided by Simon Mickleburgh and Clare Fitzgibbon.

8

Rare mammals, research and realpolitik: priorities for biodiversity and ecology?

PAUL W. BRIGHT AND PATRICK A. MORRIS

INTRODUCTION

It is sometimes suggested that conservation focusing on rare, charismatic mammals is unsuccessful and unscientific. Although untrue, this is a reminder that a vertebrate-biased, species-centred approach to biodiversity conservation is considered inadequate and obsolete: conservation of landscapes and diversity within and between species is needed to enable sustainable management of ecosystems. The latter strategy should not mean abandonment of high profile (mammal) species, indeed it would be folly to do so. The wider public, who ultimately pay for conservation, find it easier to focus on identifiable species than on more nebulous ecological concepts. There is clear evidence that mammals form valuable conservation flagships. Moreover, research on such species, extending beyond autecology, may greatly benefit biodiversity conservation generally. Nevertheless, conservation should eschew multiple, non-integrated approaches based on the ecology of single species, which may not be of general applicability.

This chapter attempts to integrate three seemingly disparate topics: ecological science, indicators of biodiversity and public support for conservation. We aim to demonstrate that rare mammals lie in a crucial area of overlap between these, so that appropriate policies directed towards rare mammals will have disproportionate benefits for both ecology and the conservation of biodiversity. Our case is based largely on British examples, but the principles arising are probably general.

RARE SPECIES AND ECOLOGICAL SCIENCE

Rare species, as considered here, include those which occur naturally at low population densities, not necessarily as a result of recent population declines.

Model species

Most ecological understanding derives from multiple observations and experiments on a relatively small number of species. Many were selected through convenience or practicality of study (e.g., common small rodents), or because of funding from vested interests (e.g., deer research supported by hunters). Convenience does not necessarily make a species a good model, having traits allowing clear resolution of ecological processes. Probably only a minority of species have been studied because they were, at first sight, good models.

It is not easy to define what constitutes a good ecological model species, compared for example to identifying a useful model for studies of developmental genetics, where few, large chromosomes are a big help. This is because ecology deals with many processes and spatial scales. However, we suggest that species which are either naturally scarce, rare because of human effects on ecosystems, or both, will disproportionately often be good ecological models. This is because rare species frequently exhibit a number of distinctive traits. These are reviewed below, with a brief rationale for their value for research.

- *Distribution confined to specific habitats.* Rare species are frequently intolerant, selecting only the highest quality habitat to which their distribution is restricted (Rosenwig and Lomolino, 1997). Suitable habitat for such species is readily defined. This makes them especially useful for research on metapopulations and large scale processes, where simple but unequivocal identification of suitable and unsuitable habitat patches over large areas is essential. This is a reason for focusing much metapopulation research on rare butterflies with narrow habitat tolerances (Thomas and Harrison, 1992) and why the dormouse *Muscardinus avellanarius* (a threatened, protected habitat specialist) has proved an excellent model for identifying the effects of large scale landscape structure on distribution (Bright et al., 1994; Bright and Halliwell, in preparation).
- *Restricted geographical range and species on the edge of their range.* In the tropics, where the most species occur, geographical range sizes are usually small, and restricted range may be the most widespread trait among rarities. Restricted range species provided an important foundation for current research on biodiversity distribution (Williams and Humphries, 1994). Species at the edge of their range are likely to offer early warning of global climate change, because they will usually be at lower density (Hanski, 1982) and thus highly susceptible to any

environmental perturbation (Elmes and Free, 1994). Restricted geographical ranges and habitat specificity may also both be related to poor dispersal abilities.

- *Low reproductive investment.* Many studies of rare species have reported low levels of investment in reproduction (Gaston and Kunin, 1997). This might result in lower lifetime reproductive success (LRS), or reflect a 'wait and see' strategy; rare species postponing reproduction while conditions are suboptimal, as the edible dormouse *Glis glis* seems to do (Bieber, 1998 and personal observation). Rare species exhibiting such strategies should be excellent models for the increasing number of studies that examine trade-offs between survival and LRS. This is because reproductive output in such species should be very finely tuned to the environment.

- *Populations limited by one or a few factors.* Because of strict habitat requirements, rare species often appear to be limited by only a few factors, notably resources they use consumptively: rare species frequently rely on rare resources. This may be because they are at the apex of food webs (e.g., large carnivores), or because the resources themselves are scarce (e.g. the dormouse; see below). Such single proximate limiting factors mean that rare species should often be sensitive models for studies of population-resource dynamics. Otherwise, such studies yield clearest results when based on very simple systems, like herbivores in deserts (Caughley and Gunn, 1993).

- *High susceptibility to eco-pollutants.* Some rare species form the apex of food webs and therefore accumulate mega-doses of persistent pollutants acquired through the web. The sparrowhawk *Accipiter nisus* and otter *Lutra lutra,* both protected and now recovering well following pesticide-induced declines, are excellent examples (Newton and Wyllie, 1992; Strachan and Jefferies, 1996). Aquatic invertebrates, whose response to pollutants can be easily assayed, are often used as indicators of pollution in aquatic ecosystems. However, there remains considerable controversy over whether species or assemblages are reliable ecotoxicological indicators (Whitehouse et al., 1996), a major limitation being their uncertainty in predicting the effects of new pollutants (e.g., organochlorines in the 1950s and 1960s which wiped out sparrowhawks and otters in many regions). Thus the indicators of pollutants that slip through the invertebrate assay net remain rare species at the apex of food webs. Water supply companies in Britain are recognising this, by using the otter as a bioindicator (Scholey, 1993). More research on rare species as early warning indicators of ecotoxicity is both timely and necessary.

- *Dependency on multi-trophic interactions or coevolved food webs.* A major factor causing loss of biodiversity is chains of extinction in which species are critically, perhaps precariously, dependent on several others (Diamond, 1984b). Many rare species, especially in the tropics, probably fall into this category, and have already demonstrated how dependent complex communities are on 'keystone species' (Gilbert, 1980). They are likely to be increasingly widely researched with the advent of new molecular genetic techniques.

The foregoing list could easily have been structured in other ways and certainly could be longer. It is not our intention to promote rare mammals alone as useful tools in ecology, nor do we suggest that rare species are always and exclusively good model species. Rather, we wish to emphasise that the tractability of *rare species in general* is under-recognised and underused by ecologists. There is considerable scope for increasing use of rare species in ecological research, with concomitant benefits for biodiversity conservation.

THE UNREALISED POTENTIAL OF REINTRODUCTIONS AS EXPERIMENTS

Experiments normally yield greater and more certain insights than observations alone. However, the types of ecological studies that are often important to biodiversity conservation, such as population monitoring and research on large scale distribution, are not readily subjected to experiment. By contrast, reintroductions (including translocations of wild species) represent one of the few fields of conservation biology that can be treated experimentally. Although the value of reintroductions as experiments has been repeatedly extolled in the literature, few reintroductions are truly experimental in featuring different treatments of released animals, incorporating controls and sampling statistically adequate numbers of individuals. This is partly because many reintroductions and translocations of rare species have involved small samples of large mammals which are not readily manipulated. There is perhaps also a reluctance on the part of conservationists to 'experiment' with scarce species, possibly risking mortality. This may be a false economy, since many reintroductions have failed after high mortality amongst released animals (Griffith *et al.*, 1989), for reasons that then remain speculative. They might have succeeded if optimal reintroduction strategies, determined after experimental releases, had been known. Additional costs of treating reintroductions as experiments (Bullock and

Hodder, 1997) should not be a deterrent, as higher rates of successful rein-troduction should result. There is also much to be gained by first studying translocation of closely related surrogate species, but this is rarely done.

Reintroductions as experiments can also yield valuable general ecologi-cal insights, as well as inform reintroduction strategies. This is exemplified by reintroductions and allied research on the dormouse. Many animals are assumed to be strongly food limited at particular seasons, but switching of food preferences as food availability changes seasonally (type III functional responses) may obscure this. The timing of births suggested the dormouse was food limited in early and (especially) mid-summer, following the com-pletion of tree flowering, but prior to the maturation of tree fruits (its main foods; Bright and Morris, 1993). Experiments preceding dormouse rein-troductions involved translocating free-living animals to a site with which they were unfamiliar, to determine the optimum time of year to release this highly seasonal hibernator. The results were unequivocal: dormice released in early to mid-summer failed to feed adequately, rapidly lost body mass and risked high potential rates of mortality (Bright and Morris 1994). Provi-sion of supplementary food reversed declines in body mass. By contrast, dormice released in late summer, who invariably displayed exploratory be-haviour and located food sources, gained body mass and had a high survival rate. The implication is that dormice are strongly food limited in early and especially mid-summer (Bright and Morris 1994). Such unequivocal evi-dence for food limitation would not have been achieved without an experi-mental approach.

A subsequent reintroduction incorporated an experimental comparison of the performance and survival of wild-caught versus first generation cap-tive-bred dormice. Both groups of dormice were from the same genetic source. All were held in cages at the experimental site for eight days before release ('soft release'). We hypothesised that captive-bred animals would perform and survive less well than wild-caught ones (Bright and Morris, 1994). We found that captive-bred dormice initially showed a lower fre-quency of exploratory and restricted-place foraging behaviour. Six weeks after release there were no differences in these behaviours between the two groups of dormice, engendering false optimism as to the fitness of captive-bred animals for reintroduction. However, after four months, survival of captive-bred dormice was half that of wild-caught animals (P. W. Bright and P. A. Morris, unpublished data).

Although the mechanism causing this difference in survival remains uncertain, it has grave implications for the usefulness of captive-bred ani-mals: captives may generally be poorly suited to reintroduction. Without a simultaneous experimentally-based comparison of the two groups of dormice, such findings would probably have been less clear cut. This preliminary research implies that greater investment in appropriate rearing and behavioural training of captive-born mammals might well be cost effective, but this seems to be infrequently attempted. Our work suggests that such efforts will not only be worthwhile with primates (Kleiman, 1989), but also rodents and other less behaviourally complex taxa.

MAMMALS AS INDICATORS OF BIODIVERSITY

It is commonly accepted that groups of 'indicator species' can be used to predict species richness. This is illustrated by the distribution of endemic mammals, birds, reptiles and amphibians in the tropics, which show considerable overlap (Bibby et al., 1992). An analysis using complementary sets, designed to select maximal species diversity within a minimal area, shows that mammals are powerful indicators of bird diversity in sub-Saharan Africa (Williams et al., chapter 5, this volume). The assumption is that such areas represent concentrations of genetic and taxonomic diversity as a whole and so are pre-eminently important for biodiversity conservation. This is probably impossible to test adequately with existing inventories of species occurrence.

Levels of endemism rapidly decline towards the poles and, with some exceptions (e.g., seed plants; Williams et al., 1994), there are few areas of high endemism in temperate latitudes. Other indicators of biodiversity are thus needed (for a review, see Gaston, 1996b). Keystone species should be powerful indicators, since they have disproportionately great impacts, relative to their biomass, on communities and ecosystems (Power and Mills, 1995). The loss of keystone species, by definition, has a cascading effect on the persistence of other members of a community. Extermination of fruit bat pollinators, for example, might lead to the loss of forest trees whose fruits were an essential resource for many frugivores. Here, however, lies a problem with using keystone species as biodiversity indicators: once keystones are gone – indicating a threat to biodiversity – it may be too late to prevent cascading loss of species. This is compounded by keystone species being most often identified after they are lost, as a result of changes to communities (Mooney et al., 1995). Indicator species that forewarn of trouble are thus needed.

We suggest that a more practical, and perhaps frequent, indicator group may be *sequential specialists*, a term first coined in relation to megachiropteran bats by Marshall (1983). Here we use it to signify animals whose fitness wholly depends on a chain of highly specific (not merely different) and mostly ephemeral resources. Sequential specialists may use suboptimal, more generally available, resources (specifically foods) to permit survival during periods of scarcity of optimal resources, but these will not enhance fitness. Fitness will follow the temporal productivity and abundance of serial food types, which may often themselves be scarce. Sequential specialists thus survive tenuously on ephemeral – mostly specialist – resources, a chain which may be rather easily broken.

Although sequential specialists are probably distributed widely among different animal groups (we can find no data on this), there appear to be many mammal instances among frugivorous primates, tropical forest rodents and bats. Two British examples of rare, sequential specialists are given below.

The greater horseshoe bat *Rhinolophus ferrumequinum* forages in ancient woodland in early summer and along the edges of old pastures later in the year, both being habitats of high conservation importance. It appears to track the abundance of a succession of large-bodied insects, its specialised prey, that are rather scare in Britain (Jones *et al.*, 1995). Furthermore, since the greater horseshoe bat has low wing loading, and thus relatively inefficient flight (Norberg and Rayner, 1987), food resources must be available close to roosts, particularly for young bats which have short flight endurance. Thus the species is critically dependent on a seasonal series of insects available in different places, all of which must be close to roosts. This is a demanding requirement in Britain's deforested, intensively farmed landscape, so that the greater horseshoe bat is now restricted to the southwest of England (Corbet and Harris, 1991). Presence of greater horseshoes is therefore probably indicative of the abundance of many scarce larger bodied insects in two key habitat types. Moreover, in winter this species needs another key environmental component, namely caves and similar underground sites in which to hibernate. Its continued presence therefore also underpins the survival of specialised troglobionts.

The dormouse occurs mostly in ancient woodlands, feeding on tree flowers and fruits supplemented with insects, a dietary restriction at least partly imposed by lack of a caecum to digest cellulose-dominated plant tissues (Bright and Morris, 1993; Bright *et al.*, 1994; Bright and Morris, 1996). It is a strictly arboreal forager and, unlike squirrels, not able to forage on the many flowers and fruits that fall to the woodland floor. Most food sources are available for only short periods, such as hawthorn *Crataegus monogyna* flowers which last for around ten days. The dormouse is thus dependent on a series of specialised foods, which only woodlands with a high diversity of tree species provide in continuous succession (Bright and Morris, 1993). In turn we strongly suspect that dormouse abundance correlates with the diversity of woodland phytophagous insects, angiosperms and insect parasitoids, many of which are scarce and poorly mobile. By contrast, the diversity of birds (more mobile), is probably not correlated with dormouse abundance (P.W. Bright, unpublished information). Thus dormouse density is likely to be a good indicator of species richness within woodlands. It is also an excellent indicator of the integrity of ancient landscapes (Bright et al., 1994; Bright and Halliwell, in preparation).

There is a further persuasive reason to use mammals to help monitor biodiversity: the limited mobility of most species, coupled with the great range of body sizes, and thus spatial scales, that they utilise. The former means that mammals are useful indicators of purely local conditions (unlike mobile species), the latter that mammals can be used to assess biodiversity across a range of spatial scales without the confounding effect of using different indicator taxa for different scales. Furthermore the persistence of many mammal (meta)populations is probably contingent upon large scale landscape structure (Bright et al., 1994; Bright and Halliwell, in preparation), a scale at which most of the pivotally important decisions affecting biodiversity are taken (May, 1994).

Thus, we are reminded that some mammals, specifically sequential specialists, can be highly sensitive indicators of biodiversity per se, and that mammals as a group offer important benefits to landscape ecologists and decision makers. We do not suggest that mammals get first prize as biodiversity indicators, but that there is much to be gained from using them as such.

REALPOLITIK: MAMMALS, PUBLIC SUPPORT AND PARTICIPATION

Raising support

Mammals exceed most other taxa in popular appeal. This results largely from their sharing many of our own morphological and behavioural characteristics and through featuring in such classic literature as *Wind in the Willows*, *The Jungle Book* and *Alice in Wonderland*. A poll conducted by the widely read magazine *BBC Wildlife* in 1996 (circulation over 100 000 per month) revealed that a mammal, the otter, was the readers' most popular animal. A bird, the robin *Erithacus rubecula,* came a poor second, despite being a species readers would have frequently observed themselves, whereas the otter would have been seen in the wild by very few. There is obviously

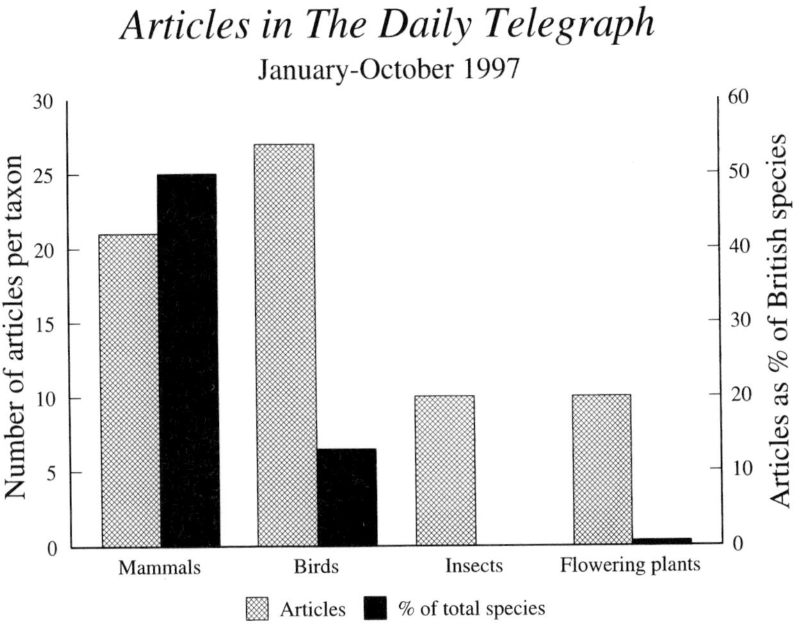

Articles in The Daily Telegraph
January-October 1997

Figure 8.1 Articles featuring different taxa published in the *Daily Telegraph* newspaper. The left *y*-axis (grey shading) shows the total number of articles during January to October 1997 inclusive, the right *y*-axis (black) shows the number of articles as a percentage of the number of species in each taxon found in Britain. Data from the *Daily Telegraph* web site (http://www.telegraph.co.uk), excluding domesticated species and including only one data point for a particular topic per edition.

also great public interest in mammals, even in Britain where species are few and inconspicuous. For instance, in *The Daily Telegraph* newspaper in the year to October 1997 inclusive, more articles were published on mammals, relative to the number of mammal species in Britain, than on birds, insects or flowering plants (Figure 8.1).

Such interest is even reflected in the frequency of spoken and written questions asked by members of the Houses of Parliament. During the year to October 1997 inclusive there were 291 questions featuring wild species of birds, mammals, insects and flowering plants (Figure 8.2). A large majority of these related to birds (81 %), reflecting, we suspect, highly effective lobbying by the Royal Society for the Protection of Birds. There were 29 questions (10 %) featuring mammals; as with birds a disproportionately high frequency of questions compared to the number of species in Britain (Figure 8.2). Few questions featured insects or flowering plants, despite

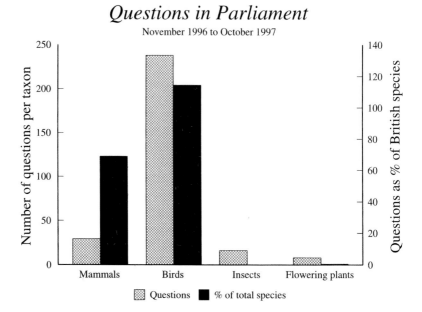

Questions in Parliament
November 1996 to October 1997

Figure 8.2 Spoken and written questions in the Houses of Parliament featuring different taxa. The left *y*-axis (grey shading) shows the total number of questions between November 1996 and October 1997 inclusive, the right *y*-axis (black) shows the number of questions as a percentage of the number of species in each taxon found in Britain. Data from the Parliamentary web site (http://parliament.uk), based on searches of the Common's and Lord's *Hansard* and the Common's and Lord's written questions. Domesticated species are excluded, as are multiple references to a particular taxon in the same debate or written question.

their much larger number of species and larger number that have legal protection.

Although the power of large mammals to command widespread appeal and their value as 'flagship species' has long been recognised, the usefulness of smaller species as flagships has only quite recently become evident. The dormouse provides a clear example of this. A decade ago this species was not featured by the media. Yet as a result of English Nature's National Dormouse Week in 1993 (part of the Species Recovery Programme) 250 articles on dormice were published in newspapers and magazines within a year, and more than three hours of dormouse features were broadcast on television and radio. The coverage was not restricted to Britain, but extended to at least five other countries. A similar species *Glirulus japonicus* in Japan has spawned a cottage industry making dormouse memorabilia and focusing attention on environmental issues and forest loss.

Mammals, large and small, are thus excellent flagship species through which to promote conservation programmes. However, the ability of mammals to garner support for conservation remains underestimated. Research on the relative economic values of threatened mammals in Britain supports this. White *et al.* (1997) investigated people's willingness to pay for conservation using contingent valuation. This method involves setting up a hypothetical market for 'goods' (in this case threatened mammals) that normally have no direct economic value. People are asked to bid for these 'goods' based on information supplied about them. Hence people's bids (willingness to pay) are contingent on the latter. Although the valuation of non-market benefits using such methods remains controversial, the results of White *et al.* are striking. In a telephone questionnaire, people were provided with brief information about the decline and threats to otters and water voles *Arvicola terrestris*. The aims of biodiversity action plans for these species were then stated and people were asked whether they would be prepared to pay a particular amount of money (in the form of a single national addition to taxes) to enable implementation of the plans. From 315 people questioned, the mean willingness to pay was £11.91 for the otter and £7.44 for the water vole. If these values are aggregated across the entire survey population (people in North Yorkshire), £6.4 million and £4.0 million respectively would be available for the action plans. These sums vastly exceed the costs of the action plans suggested in the UK Government's Biodiversity Steering Group report (Anon., 1994a) of £0.8 million for the otter and £1.0 million for the water vole.

White *et al.* (1997) emphasise that such results are prone to many potential sampling biases. Nevertheless, their findings unequivocally demonstrate the power of mammals to attract cash for conservation and the great public support there is for flagship mammal species. We believe that this support should be built on and harnessed for the benefit of biodiversity conservation as a whole, not simply dismissed as obsolete sentimentality.

Involving people

It is easily forgotten that biodiversity conservation is as much about people as wildlife. Because of the flagship status of many mammals (realised and potential), projects involving them can readily engage public participation. There are at least four compelling reasons to promote active participation in conservation programmes by the public. First and most obviously, land owners or managers and local people may hold the key to maintaining the habitat of threatened species or to prevent direct persecution. The roles of the Community Baboon Project in Belize (Horwich and Lyon, 1990) in conserving the black howler monkey *Alouatta pigra* and of British badger groups in combating badger *Meles meles* persecution (Wilson *et al.*, 1997) are excellent examples. Secondly, voluntary participation may provide manpower essential to the completion of conservation projects, and make the most efficient use of available financial resources. We return to this below. Thirdly, engaging public participation, not just armchair sympathy, sends a strong signal to politicians that there is serious, mass commitment among their constituents for conservation programmes. Public participation is thus a sturdy lever for influencing government policies, that should not lightly be ignored by those in power. Finally, the foregoing all feed back positively on one another, so that the effects of promoting each are multiplicative, not additive.

The invaluable benefits of public participation in conservation programmes are evident from the history of recent national surveys and monitoring of mammals in Britain. In the last seven years over 13 000 sites have been surveyed by several thousand volunteers for mammal species of conservation concern (Table 8.1). The Great Nut Hunt of 1993 alone involved over 6000 people, who provided the equivalent of a full-time employee for three years, free of charge (Bright *et al.*, 1996). The National Dormouse Monitoring Programme entails over 100 man-weeks of effort by volunteers each year. These surveys have often entailed quite complex protocols in the field, such as the National Bats and Habitats Survey, yet yielded high quality results as evidenced by subsequent publication in international science journals (Walsh and Harris, 1996a, b). Such work has helped Government agencies in Britain to meet their statutory requirements towards protected mammals (Greenwood 1994), while making highly cost-effective use of relatively meagre financial resources. Indeed calculations by the British Trust for Ornithology suggest that for every £1 spent on organising their public participation surveys, about £20 of fieldwork is completed by volunteers (J. Greenwood, personal communication). There are thus outstanding benefits from seeking active public participation in conservation programmes.

CONCLUSIONS: SYNERGY OF MAMMAL CONSERVATION WITH BIODIVERSITY, SCIENCE AND SUPPORT

We have argued that there are multiple synergistic benefits of using mammals as one focus for biodiversity conservation. These include benefits to ecology and those accruing from public support and involvement in conservation. Our case is based on experience of both applied ecological research

Table 8.1
Surveys and monitoring of mammals in Britain that have involved mass public participation during the last 10 years. Reference to each survey is given, plus the number of sites (e.g., individual woodlands, or 1 km grid squares) surveyed in each case and the approximate number of volunteers involved

Survey and source	No. of sites surveyed	No. of volunteers involved
National badger survey I (Cresswell *et al.*, 1990)	2455	800
National badger survey II (Wilson *et al.*, 1997)	2578	800
The Great Nut Hunt (dormouse survey) (Bright *et al.*, 1996)	1878	6500
National Dormouse Monitoring Programme (P. W. Bright and P. A. Morris, 1992–present)	260[a]	220
National hare survey I (Hutchins and Harris, 1996)	751	550
National hare survey II (R.Temple and S. Harris, unpublished data)	700–800	600
National Bats and Habitats Survey (Walsh and Harris, 1996a, b)	910	*ca* 300
National Bat Monitoring Programme (A. Walsh, personal communication)	934	487
Breeding Bird Survey 1998 (Gregory *et al.*, 1998)	2000	2000
Harvest mouse follow up survey (The Mammal Society, 1996–present, in prep.)	640	170

[a] This is the current total number of site visits per year.

and implementation of conservation programmes that have relied heavily on the voluntary sector and often generated great interest from the media. We argue the case for mammals in the hope of maximising conservation benefits for biodiversity as a whole. This should not detract from the principle of sustainable, integrated management of biodiversity (McNeely, chapter 20, this volume), but rather catalyse increased conservation action.

English Nature's Species Recovery Programme (SRP) provides compelling support in favour of mammals being one important focus for biodiversity conservation (Figure 8.3). The SRP was designed by the Government conservation agency to reverse declines of threatened species. It has been a highly successful programme whose spending has been heavily directed towards mammals, with a high yield of favourable publicity (e.g., the Great Nut Hunt gained more publicity for English Nature than any other of its

English Nature's
Species Recovery Programme

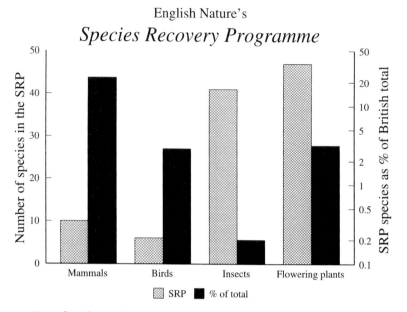

Figure 8.3 The number of species included in English Nature's Species Recovery Programme (SRP). The left y-axis (grey shading) shows the total number of species of different taxa in the SRP up to October 1997 inclusive. The right y-axis (black, note the log scale) shows the number of species as a percentage of species in each taxon found in Britain.

activities to date; Bright et al., 1996). However, there are many other threatened taxa in Britain which a purist might assess as having greater need. There are also far more species among the invertebrates and flowering plants, whose conservation in the name of 'biodiversity' is thus more justified. Yet as Figures 8.1 and 8.2 show, there is little public interest in plants and invertebrates. The fact that the SRP has nevertheless managed to afford to allocate significant resources to these under-appreciated groups owes much to the high profile success of the mammal-led projects which resulted in the SRP attracting annually increased funds during a period of extreme financial stringency on the part of Government. The realpolitik here is clear: saving British 'pandas' may represent a small compromise on scientific principles, but has probably achieved enhanced conservation outcome as well as many other benefits besides.

ACKNOWLEDGEMENTS

Much of the research on dormice described here was supported by English Nature and the People's Trust for Endangered Species, whose support is very gratefully acknowledged. Dr Roger Mitchell (English Nature) kindly supplied information about the Species Recovery Programme, as did Professor Stephen Harris (Bristol University) about surveys. Dr Tony Mitchell-Jones (English Nature) and Professor Paul Racey (Aberdeen University) provided most helpful comments on the manuscript. Finally, we are hugely grateful to the many people who have so effectively participated in national mammal surveys and monitoring, especially of dormice.

PART 3

Conservation approaches for mammalian species and diversity

A range of conservation techniques have been developed and used with the aim of conserving mammals, over the last century. While many early attempts focused on setting up protected areas, from which communities were excluded, the approaches to conservation in general have broadened, building on experience gained. The chapters in this section examine a varied range of approaches to conservation of mammals, including site protection, conservation outside protected areas and *ex situ* techniques.

While protected areas remain high on the conservation agenda in terms of their effectiveness for protection of both species and ecosystems, there is the need to review their impacts, and consider how protected area networks might be improved in future. In addition, other elements of conservation occur at a broader scale – conservation areas can be considered as only one component of a broader landscape used by both wildlife and people. In this respect, approaches such as legislation may be more effective, coupled with sustainable use of wildlife (be it direct or indirect use). Obviously, research has an important place in determining conservation action, and the challenge may be determining how integrated research and conservation policies might evolve. Over recent years, the potential for captive breeding to rescue species threatened with extinction has been explored. The use of *ex situ* techniques may, however, need to be reviewed given its focus on single species, and the need to relate this to broader scale biodiversity targets.

Finally, mammal conservation needs to be considered in the wider global agenda. The final two chapters in this section make the link to socio-economics, political decision making and donor policy. Such approaches highlight the future importance of economics in the conservation of mammals, and the relationships with the larger biodiversity 'market place', particularly given the role of international conventions in guiding the development of conservation policies at the level of national government.

9

Does legislation conserve and does research drive policy? The case of bats in the UK

PAUL A. RACEY

INTRODUCTION

Bats are the most important contributors to mammalian biodiversity in the UK, and are presently afforded a level of legislative protection greater than any other group of mammals. They provide therefore an informative case study on the effectiveness of legislative measures to conserve mammals, and the extent to which such legislation has been led by or has driven research and monitoring.

The aim of this contribution is to assess the extent to which International Conventions, Directives, Regulations and Agreements, as well as domestic legislation, have conserved bats in the UK. It also examines the reverse process – the way in which research on the status, ecophysiology, ecology and conservation biology of bats has resulted in changes in legislation, policy or practice which aims to conserve bats and their habitats.

THE PROTECTION OF WILD CREATURES AND WILD PLANTS ACT 1975

In March 1970, at the Second International Bat Research Conference in Amsterdam, delegates representing 20 countries reported that many bat species in temperate climates appeared to be declining (Punt, 1970) due mainly to loss of habitat, accumulation of pesticides, large scale ringing, and direct killing by man. Insectivorous bats are among the most synanthropic of mammals in that most species establish maternity colonies during summer in buildings, mainly domestic houses, and this may bring them into conflict with the human occupants. They also roost in tree holes, and during winter may hibernate in caves and mines. Since some bats migrate long distances, the conference recommended the adoption of active conservation measures on an international basis. The Fauna Preser-vation Society (now Fauna & Flora International (FFI)) followed this up by asking the Mammal Society to report on the status of bats in Britain. The Mammal Society Bat Group carried out a questionnaire survey of the status of bat roosts which revealed that many were being lost, and that many bats were being killed each year in buildings. The status of two British species, the greater horseshoe bat *Rhinolophus ferrumequinum* and the mouse-eared bat *Myotis myotis* was precarious and they were in danger of becoming ex-tinct in Britain. The report of this survey appeared in *Oryx* (Racey and Stebbings, 1972), and provided the necessary leverage for these two species to be included in The Protection of Wild Creatures and Wild Plants Act 1975, which made it illegal to catch these bats unless licensed to do so by the statutory nature conservation agency (The Nature Conservancy Council – NCC). Although attempts to include the lesser horseshoe bat *Rhinolophus hipposideros* in this Act failed because of inadequate information about its status, only six years elapsed before more effective legislation, involving all British bat species, was enacted. Such legislation was too late however to prevent the extinction of the mouse-eared bat, whose last nursery colony had disappeared by 1980, probably as a result of disturbance, and the last hibernating individual was seen in 1990 (Stebbings and Hutson, 1991; Stebbings, 1992).

THE WILDLIFE AND COUNTRYSIDE ACT 1981

The Wildlife and Countryside Act 1981 (WCA 81) was the UK government's response to The Convention on the Conservation of European Wildlife and Natural Habitats 1979 (The Berne Convention). It protected all 14 bat spe-cies recognised in Britain at the time, and their roosts, from disturbance. In Northern Ireland, the equivalent legislation was the Wildlife (Northern Ire-land) Order 1985. Such protection is more stringent than for any other group of mammals. Not only is it a crime to kill, injure or capture bats, the law on disturbance is stricter for bats than for any other mammals, since it is also a crime to disturb them, unless they are in the living area of a house.

Unlike the 1975 Act, the publicity surrounding WCA 81 was accom-panied by a surge of interest in bats, which was encouraged by conserva-tionists (principally H. R. Arnold, P. W. Richardson and R. E. Stebbings) and resulted in the formation of about 40 local bat groups in the following two years. The activity of these groups was linked by a national coordinating panel whose secretariat was based at the London office of the Fauna and Flora Preservation Society (FFPS, now FFI). The panel was funded jointly for some years by FFPS, The NCC and The Vincent Wildlife Trust. However, when this arrangement proved difficult to sustain, The Bat Conservation Trust (BCT) was founded in 1990 as a fully constituted NGO, whose membership rose steadily to about 3000 in 1998, during which time the number of local bat groups doubled to about 90.

One of the principal requirements of WCA 81 is that householders who are concerned about sharing their dwelling with bats are required to inform the statutory nature conservation agencies (originally The NCC, now English Nature (EN); The Countryside Council for Wales (CCW) and Scottish Natural Heritage (SNH), together with the Environment and Heritage Service in Northern Ireland – referred to collectively as the country agencies). This provides an opportunity for agency staff or bat group volunteers to allay householders' fears, to provide them with factual information about bats and to persuade them to retain bat roosts. In 1982, when WCA 81 was implemented, 30 000 copies of a booklet, *Focus on Bats* (Stebbings and Jefferies, 1982), were distributed in response to enquiries from the public (Mitchell-Jones et al., 1986). Such enquiries also provided a large data set on the distribution of Britain's bats (Mitchell-Jones, 1990; Arnold, 1993) and their roosts, at least 14 000 of which are known in buildings and 1000 underground (Mitchell-Jones et al., 1993). By training and licensing bat workers, the country agencies now exert tight control on activities such as ringing which can only be undertaken for clearly defined research objectives, rather than for general studies of bat movements.

Ten successful prosecutions were brought by The NCC, the police in England and Wales, the procurator fiscal in Scotland, and by the Royal Society for the Prevention of Cruelty to Animals, for infringements of WCA 81 during the period 1985–1998 (Childs, 1998). It is however no longer the policy of the country agencies to take such prosecutions and infringements of the law are now dealt with mainly by police Wildlife Liaison Officers. On a more positive note however, the activities of the country agencies, BCT and Britain's 90 amateur bat groups have brought about a profound change in the public perception of bats. Before WCA 81 the most common telephone request involving bats was for their removal from houses. Since WCA 81 the commonest telephone enquiry takes the form 'I know bats are protected and I don't want to harm them but I am concerned ...'.

WCA 81 also strengthened the protection for Sites of Special Scientific Interest (SSSIs) which were originally among the provisions of the 1949 National Parks and Access to the Countryside Act. Guidelines for the designation of SSSIs for bats were established (Mitchell-Jones et al., 1993) and included all maternity roosts of the greater horseshoe bat and all such roosts of the lesser horseshoe bat containing more than 100 adults, together with all winter roosts of both species containing more than 50 individuals. Any traditional breeding roosts for barbastelles *Barbastella barbastellus*, Bechstein's bats *Myotis bechsteini* and grey long-eared bats *Plecotus austriacus* were also included in the guidelines, together with mixed species hibernacula. In 1993, 72 % of greater horseshoe bats and 53 % of lesser horseshoe bats overwintered in either proposed or designated SSSIs (Mitchell-Jones *et al.*, 1993). Such designation gives the country agencies considerable control over what happens at the site through management agreements with the owner, who receives an appropriate payment for positive management. However, designation of a site cannot prevent it from deteriorating if the owner refuses such an agreement, and as the law stands at present, the country agencies cannot carry out work on the site without the permission of the owner. Nevertheless over 6000 SSSIs had been designated in the UK by 1994, of which 80 in England and 24 in Wales related specifically to bats or included bats among the nature conservation interests of the site (A. M. Mitchell-Jones, personal communication; R. Warren, personal communication respectively).

WCA 81 has been a powerful instrument for bat conservation in the UK and has protected many thousands of bat roosts that would otherwise have been lost as a result of exclusion of bats by householders. It also stimulated the growth of a voluntary conservation movement which has carried out much practical conservation work, and participated in national surveys, results of which have both practical and policy relevance.

Molecular genetics and roost exclusions

If householders are unwilling to share their roof space with bats and cannot be persuaded to keep them, then they have the right to exclude them, provided advice from the country agencies is followed. It has been assumed that bats so excluded will join other colonies. There is little to support this from ringing studies (Neilson and Fenton, 1994; Entwistle *et al.*, in press b) and recent molecular genetic analysis provides strong evidence that it does not happen. Using microsatellite DNA markers, Burland *et al.* (1999) showed that each colony of brown long-eared bats *Plecotus auritus* is a distinct subpopulation. Young remain with their maternity colony which is highly philopatric (i.e. returns to the same roost year after year) and gene flow occurs through extra-colony copulation. Similar results have been obtained from Bechstein's bats (Kerth *et al.*, in press) and mouse-eared bats (Petri *et al.*, 1997).

In some cases, bats have been excluded during pregnancy, after maternity colonies have been established in their historical roosts, and the repro-ductive success of such excluded colonies is likely to be reduced by the disruption of their social organisation and the need to find an alternative refuge. Henceforth, therefore, exclusion should be permitted only after bats have vacated the roost in autumn and after all attempts at persuading the roost owner to retain the bats have failed.

Protection of hibernacula

Bats are particularly vulnerable to disturbance when hibernating. The NCC commissioned research which revealed that bats are not immediately aroused from hibernation by artificial light or noise but will invariably arouse if touched (Speakman et al., 1991b). However, Thomas (1995) re-ported increases in flight activity in hibernacula for up to nine hours follow-ing one- to two-hour surveys. Such arousals are energetically costly, and although bats often arouse naturally from hibernation if the external tem-perature rises above the threshold for insect flight (Avery, 1985; Speakman and Racey, 1989), it is doubtful whether they can replace the energy exp-ended in the arousal process. Installation of grilles at the entrance to caves and mines, which prevent entry by humans, but allow the bats free flight, is a particularly effective means of protecting bats against the disturbance which WCA 81 sought to prevent. Where such disturbance occurs, the numbers of bats using hibernacula increases after grilles have been instal-led (Stebbings, 1969, 1971; Voûte and Lina, 1986). Amateur bat workers have played a major role in the installation of such grilles. In consultation with caving and mine history groups, a Code of Practice has also been produced for those exploring caves or abandoned mines (Hutson et al., 1995).

Many hibernacula have been lost, as a result of their entrances being sealed for safety reasons or by the dumping of domestic refuse. In response to this, several artificial hibernacula have been constructed throughout Brit-ain. These are expensive and although the number of bats using them is low, their success can only be evaluated in the long term. For example the extensive network of underground fortifications constructed at Nietoperek in western Poland prior to and during World War II, is, 60 years later, the largest hibernaculum known in northern Europe, where annual censuses reveal the presence of 30 000 bats of 12 species.

Remedial timber treatments

Another of the tangible successes of WCA 81 is the leverage that it provided in reducing the risk to bats from exposure to remedial timber treatments containing chlorinated hydrocarbons, principally lindane (or gamma-HCH) and pentachlorphenol, applied to roof timbers to kill infestations of wood-boring beetles and wood-rotting fungi respectively (Mitchell-Jones *et al.*, 1989).

When WCA 81 was debated in the House of Commons, the member for Linlithgow, Tam Dalyell, drew attention to this problem and suggested that the companies concerned should adopt a responsible attitude. This intervention led to a great deal of research. Most timber treatment was carried out by a few large national companies, although there were many smaller local operatives, and a thriving DIY market. The mammalian toxicity of chlorinated hydrocarbons was well established by statutory testing on laboratory rodents, but the timber treatment companies concerned refused to extrapolate between mammalian groups and required direct proof of an effect of remedial timber treatments on bats (but declined to work with bat researchers on such an investigation). Working on a small budget provided by The Vincent Wildlife Trust, Racey and Swift (1986) confirmed the very high toxicity of lindane and pentachlorphenol to pipistrelle bats *Pipistrellus pipistrellus* by simulating remedial timber treatments in wooden bat cages. The industry still refused to accept these results on the grounds that the bats had not been allowed free flight to simulate the two hour nightly foraging period (which may have provided an opportunity to metabolise the chlorinated hydrocarbons). In order to resolve the issue, The NCC commissioned The Institute of Terrestrial Ecology to investigate the effect of lindane and pentachlorphenol on pipistrelle bats housed in large free-flight aviaries (Boyd *et al.*, 1988; Shore *et al.*, 1991). The results exactly confirmed (at a cost of two orders of magnitude more) those of Racey and Swift (1986) and the industry agreed to discontinue the use of chlorinated hydrocarbons in bat roosts. In 1988, the government's Advisory Committee on Pesticides also ruled that lindane-based timber-treatment products should be labelled 'dangerous to bats'.

Although a successful result was achieved for bat conservation, it was only after continued exposure of wild bats and a needless series of investigations that resulted in unnecessary deaths of experimental animals. This was particularly unfortunate because alternative insecticides with very low mammalian toxicity and suitable for use in remedial timber treatments were available, in the form of synthetic pyrethroids (Racey and Swift, 1986; Mitchell-Jones *et al.*, 1989). Wider concerns about the safety of lindane and pentachlorphenol also led to their withdrawal from professional and DIY use, assisted by an EC Directive.

A further outcome was that the government established, through its

Health and Safety Executive, an ad hoc Working Group on Bats, Wood Preservatives and Remedial Timber Treatments to oversee the development of protocols for testing remedial timber treatments. A mouse test, the results of which could be extrapolated to bats, was developed and data from such tests have been used to generate models to predict the uptake and likely acute toxic effect of new compounds as they are assessed for registration purposes (Shore et al., 1998). In addition, the sublethal effects of remedial timber treatments was also investigated, and although this is a notoriously difficult experimental area, it was shown that sublethal doses of lindane increased the metabolic rate of pipistrelles (Swanepoel et al., 1999). If this happens when bats are unable to increase their energy intake, energy stores will be depleted and survival imperilled.

THE EUROPEAN BATS AGREEMENT 1991

Part of the function of The Convention on the Conservation of Migratory Species of Wild Animals 1979 (The Bonn Convention) is to develop agreements on the conservation of migratory species that would benefit from international cooperation and management. Migration, in the terms of the Convention, means regular movements across state boundaries. Although bats have not been ringed on the same scale as birds, it is clear that a number of species undertake long-distance migrations on mainland Europe between foraging areas and hibernacula (Strelkov, 1969; 1997 a,b). So far as the UK is concerned, there has been no recovery of a UK-ringed bat from the European mainland or vice-versa, and it has not been easy to distinguish between vagrancy and migration when recording bats on oil platforms and light ships in the North Sea, or in the occurrence of species outside their normal range. The movement of bats between the UK and Europe is of more than academic interest since the discovery of rabies-like viruses in several bat species, principally the serotine *Eptesicus serotinus*, in continental Europe (Amengual et al., 1997). The only such discovery in the UK involved a live Daubenton's bat *Myotis daubentonii* which bit a pregnant bat carer who received post-exposure treatment and suffered no ill effects (Whitby et al., 1996).

The best evidence of migration into the UK is provided by Nathusius's pipistrelle *Pipistrellus nathusii* which moves southwest from the Baltic States to the low countries in autumn. The first breeding colony of Nathusius's pipistrelle was recorded in the Netherlands by Kapteyn and Lina (1994) and since its appearance in Britain in 1969 (Stebbings, 1970), it has been recorded with increasing frequency in summer and autumn on

North Sea oil installations and on the UK mainland (Speakman *et al.*, 1991a, 1993; Rydell and Swift, 1995). Mating calls were recorded in southwest England in 1994 and 1995 (Barlow and Jones, 1996) and in 1997 breeding colonies were discovered in Northern Ireland (Russ *et al.*, 1998) and Lincolnshire. It seems likely therefore that Nathusius's pipistrelle has undergone a range expansion to include the UK in its European distribution.

It is in this context of a changing pattern of migration and the need to protect bats across their European range, that the UK sponsored The European Bats Agreement. Although it is a legal document, the Agreement does not lay down detailed specific actions and targets. Rather it gives broad fundamental objectives which parties to the Agreement are obliged to address and report progress to a meeting convened every three years by its Secretariat.

The fundamental obligations of the Agreement are:

(1) to prohibit the capture, keeping or killing of bats except under permit;
(2) to identify and protect important bat roosts and foraging areas;
(3) to promote public awareness of the importance of bat conservation;
(4) to safeguard threatened bat populations;
(5) to promote research programmes relating to conservation and management, and coordinate these among European countries;
(6) to assess the effect of pesticides on bats, particularly those used in remedial timber treatments;
(7) to adopt and enforce such legislative and administrative measures as may be necessary to give effect to the Agreement.

Although many of these obligations are already being discharged in the UK, as a result of earlier statutes, the protection of foraging areas was an important addition brought about by increasing awareness that such areas are often closer to roosts than may have been previously assumed for such highly mobile animals (Fenton, 1997) and that the foraging habitat of some bat species can be characterised and preferences established (Racey and Swift, 1985). One of the principal benefits of The European Bats Agreement is to provide an intergovernmental forum to address bat conservation issues which may require research to be carried out nationally and internationally. To facilitate this, the Chiroptera Specialist Group of IUCN has established The Coordinating Panel for the Conservation of Bats in Europe. The Agreement is also assisting European countries, particularly those of

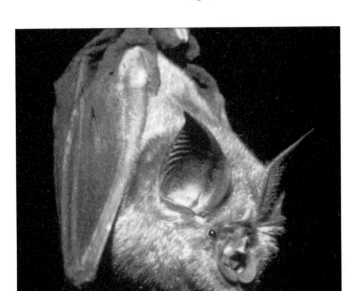

Greater horseshoe bat, *Rhinolophus ferrumequinum*, Great Britain.
Photograph: Paul Racey.

the former Soviet Union, which have not made progress in bat conservation, to do so. At present, there are 14 parties to the Agreement, with a number of others participating fully until the institution of appropriate national legislation allows their full accession.

What has The European Bats Agreement achieved in the first five years of its existence? It provided leverage to obtain EC funding for a LIFE project on bats using the extensive network of underground fortifications around the borders of the Netherlands, Germany, Belgium, Luxembourg and France dating from the Franco–Prussian War (1870–1871) and the two World Wars in this century. The project involves identifying the most important hibernacula of bats and protecting them from disturbance with grilles.

Establishing population trends for bats remains one of the biggest challenges for ecologists and conservationists. Following the establishment of a monitoring programme for lesser horseshoe bats in Wales by CCW, the Department of the Environment contracted the BCT in 1996 to undertake a five year National Bat Monitoring Programme to develop methods for monitoring selected bat species (pipistrelles, Daubenton's bats, Natterer's bats *Myotis nattereri*, noctules *Nyctalus noctula*, serotines, greater and lesser horseshoe bats) and to apply these methods in an attempt to establish population trends. The programme involves harnessing the enthusiasm of the voluntary sector and 900 volunteers have been recruited and, where necessary, trained in the use of bat detectors.

Other initiatives of the European Bats Agreement are a programme for the conservation of underground sites, and attempts to integrate forest management policy and achieve consistency in bat monitoring methodologies. More recently the Council of Europe working in cooperation with the Agreement, as part of its Pan-European Biological and Landscape Diversity Strategy has asked BCT to prepare action plans for the greater horseshoe bat and the pond bat *Myotis dasycneme*.

THE HABITATS DIRECTIVE 1992

The 1992 EC Council Directive on the Conservation of Natural Habitats and of Wild Fauna and Flora is concerned with the maintenance and restoration of favourable conservation status of species listed in its Annexes. For example, Annex II lists animal and plant species whose conservation requires the designation of Special Areas of Conservation (SACs), and includes all the European rhinolophids (Blasius's horseshoe bats *Rhinolophus blasii*, Mediterranean horseshoe bats *R. euryale*, Mehely's horseshoe bats *R. mehelyi*, greater and lesser horseshoe bats) and the following vespertilionids: barbastelles; bent-winged bats *Miniopterus schreibersii*; Bechstein's bats; lesser mouse-eared bats *M. blythii*; long-fingered bats *M. capaccinii*; pond bats; Geoffroy's bats *M. emarginatus*; and mouse-eared bats. All European Microchiroptera are however included in Annex IV of the Directive, which lists animal and plant species of community interest in need of strict protection. The inclusion of bats in these Annexes has resulted in the Habitats Directive becoming one of the principal drivers of research on the conservation biology of bats.

The SACs (together with Special Protection Areas classified under the EC Birds Directive) will constitute a network of so-called Natura 2000 sites. In the UK, proposed SACs must fulfil the criteria for designation as SSSIs. SSSIs currently form an important part of the approach to the conservation of the greater horseshoe bat, 3500 of which occur in southwest England and Wales. Fourteen major maternity colonies are known and the precipitous decline in numbers of horseshoe bats has been halted by the roost protection provided by WCA 81 (Stebbings and Arnold, 1987).

The Habitats Directive is now driving a Species Recovery Programme and associated autecological research. Greater horseshoe bats forage in ancient semi-natural woodland in spring and early summer because it is warmer and insects are more likely to be flying there, but they move to cattle pasture later in summer after the accumulation of dung has resulted in an increase in the number of *Aphodius* dung beetles. Cattle pasture adjacent to a maternity colony is a particularly important foraging habitat for juvenile bats (Duvergé and Jones, 1994; Jones *et al.*, 1995). Ancient semi-natural woodlands within commuting distance of the roost have been designated as SSSIs and management incentives provided by the Countryside Stewardship Scheme for farmers to maintain cattle pasture adjacent to nursery roosts and avoid the use of persistent anthelminthics such as Avermectins, which may reduce the number of dung beetles (Strong, 1992; Mitchell-Jones, 1995; Ransome, 1996). This is an example of the precautionary principle since there is little direct evidence for decreased bat activity over pastures grazed by Avermectin-treated cattle (Chapman *et al.*, 1997). Nevertheless, there is widespread concern in Europe about the use of these treatments (especially when delivered as boluses) and a Berne Convention working group has prepared a Recommendation to control their use.

Article 10 of the Directive obliges member states to improve the ecological coherence of the Natura 2000 network by encouraging the management of features of the landscape which are of major importance for wild fauna and flora. Such features are those which, by virtue of their linear or continuous nature (such as rivers and their banks or traditional field boundaries) or their function as 'stepping stones' (such as ponds or small woods) are essential for the dispersal and migration of wild species and genetic exchange within species. Article 10 in particular has resulted in research in the use bats make of linear landscape features. In the UK national bat habitat survey, Walsh *et al.* (1995) and Walsh and Harris (1996a, b) revealed that bats, predominantly pipistrelles, selected treelines, hedgerows and broad-leaved woodland edge in all landscape types. Verboom and Huitema (1997) and Downs and Racey (1998) showed that pipistrelles made extensive use of treelines during foraging or commuting between roosts and foraging areas and Entwistle *et al.* (1996), Swift (1997) and Schofield (1996, in press) made similar observations for brown long-eared bats, Natterer's bats and lesser horseshoe bats respectively. The study of the use bats make of landscape features and the effect of changes in landscape on their commuting and foraging behaviour is becoming an increasingly important area of research.

There remains, however, widespread concern among bat conservationists that neither the Directive, nor other wildlife legislation, provides adequate protection for bat foraging habitat, despite the stringent protection provided for roosts. A number of studies point to the need to protect such habitat. For example, Entwistle et al. (1997) showed that lactating brown long-eared bats foraged within 0.5 km of their roosts. Such roosts were found in large houses, with complex roof voids, over 100 years old, which often had large gardens with mature deciduous trees, from which the bats gleaned their predominantly lepidopteran prey. Although WCA 81 protects the roosts, no such protection is afforded to adjacent woodland, which may be lost, for example, if the garden is sold off as a building plot.

THE CONVENTION ON BIOLOGICAL DIVERSITY (CBD) 1992

After signing the Convention on Biological Diversity at the United Nations Conference on Environment and Development in Rio in 1992, the UK government launched Biodiversity: The UK Action Plan in 1994 with the aim 'to conserve and enhance biological diversity within the UK and to contribute to the conservation of global biodiversity through all appropriate mechanisms'. However, concerned by the lack of momentum, a group of voluntary conservation organisations prepared a consultative document Biodiversity Challenge which included a list of target species and habitats (Wynne et al., 1993) followed by an action plan (Wynne et al., 1995). Since then the government and the NGOs have worked closely together in advancing the aims of CBD and a list of ca 1500 species of conservation concern has been assembled on the basis of the following criteria:

* threatened endemic or globally threatened species;
* species for which the UK has more than 25 % of the entire population;
* species whose numbers have declined more than 25 % in the last 25 years;
* species that are found in less than 15 1–km squares in the UK;
* species listed in the EC Habitats Directive, the Berne, Bonn and CITES Conventions, WCA 81 or the Wildlife (Northern Ireland) Order 1985.

From this long list, the need to prioritise has led to the production of lists of ca 400 species for which action plans are being prepared and which include pipistrelles, Bechstein's bats, barbastelles, greater and lesser horseshoe bats. The individual species action plans have a steering group of government and non-government specialists to identify priorities and mechanisms for carrying out the obligations of the plans, including the conservation research requirements. These steering groups work in liaison with similar groups established for other species or habitats. The inclusion of bats in the list of priority species will ensure the continuation of research into their ecology, commissioned by the country agencies, or undertaken by universities with research council funding, or by NGOs.

For example the BCT surveyed all available information on the status and distribution of Bechstein's and barbastelle bats which are rare woodland species and drew up recovery plans (Harrington et al., 1995). Schofield et al. (1997) subsequently showed by radiotracking that Bechstein's bats roosted in cavities in mature trees, and foraged entirely in the canopy of broadleaf trees, in both continuous and fragmented woodlands, including treelines and outgrown hedges. Bats commuting between roosts and foraging areas used linear landscape elements but occasionally flew over open pastures.

REFORM OF THE COMMON AGRICULTURAL POLICY (CAP)

The CAP is the basic framework of support for agriculture in the European Union. Introduced in 1957 by the Treaty of Rome, its major aims are to ensure food supplies, to increase the efficiency of production and to provide stability for the agriculture industry. Although the CAP was not originally designed to embrace environmental goals, the Single European Act ratified in 1987 introduced a requirement for environmental protection to be a component of all community policies. Agricultural activity involves over 70 % of the land surface of Great Britain and is a major factor in determining the quality and survival of wildlife habitats in this country. There can be little doubt that agricultural intensification has had an adverse effect on bat populations just as it has on birds (JNCC, 1996). However recent reforms of the CAP have encouraged protection and enhancement of the environment by farmers, particularly through the Environmentally Sensitive Areas (ESA) Scheme, the Farm Woodland Premium Scheme (FWPS), the Set-Aside, Countryside Premium and Countryside Stewardship Schemes. The objective of the ESA programme is to encourage, through financial incentives, agricultural management which is compatible with maintaining wildlife value and landscape. The FWPS encourages farmers to plant new woodlands on land currently in agricultural use to enhance landscape and create new wildlife habitats. Farmers entering the Set-Aside Scheme originally allocated 20 % of their land for five years for rotational or permanent fallow, tree planting or non-agricultural use. However most farmers opted for rotational fallow, which has limited wildlife value and represents a lost opportunity for conservation. The Countryside Premium Scheme makes additional payments to farmers in the Set-Aside Scheme who manage their fallowed land in ways that provide wildlife habitats. All these schemes have potentially beneficial effects on bats, particularly since Walsh and Harris (1996a,b) demonstrated the importance of treelines, hedgerows, woodland edge, scrub and parkland to foraging bats. Currently the BCT is assisting the Central Science Laboratory in an investigation of the use of FWPS plots by bats and how the scheme might be improved to benefit wildlife – an example of policy leading to research.

Annex I of the EC Habitats Directive lists natural habitats whose conservation requires the designation of SACs and includes many of the habitat types listed by Walsh and Harris (1996a,b) such as all types of freshwater and deciduous woodland. The UK Biodiversity Action Plan has also resulted in costed action plans aimed at the conservation of such habitats. These together with the ongoing reforms of the CAP will result in the creation of more habitat suitable for foraging bats.

CONCLUSIONS

There is considerable overlap in the provisions of national and international legislation which benefits bats. Much of this legislation provides effective instruments for the conservation of bats in their roosts and many thousands of roosts have been protected in the UK as a result. The success of such legislation in protecting bats results from the close working relationship between bat biologists and conservationists, legislators and the country agencies responsible for implementing legislation. The voluntary movement has also played a major role in roost protection in the UK and has been strongly supported by the country agencies. However, attention has now turned to foraging habitats and the ways in which agricultural intensification, particularly habitat fragmentation, has adversely affected bat populations and foraging bats. Reform of the CAP provides ways of redressing this and improving the quality of bat foraging habitat. At a practical level, the Joint Nature Conservation Committee has recently commissioned a Bat Habitat Management Handbook for use by land managers (Entwistle et al., in press a).

Research has documented the roosting requirements of some bat species and has shown how bats may be threatened in their roosts by remedial timber treatments, disturbance and exclusions. This has led to changes in policy and practice. Surveys and autecological studies have also revealed that some bat species have habitat preferences or requirements and suggest that their habitats must be protected or enhanced if further declines in bat populations are to be halted. Such protection and enhancement is being carried out only for the foraging habitat of the greater horseshoe bat. Similar initiatives are required for other threatened bat species.

ACKNOWLEDGEMENTS

I am grateful to the following for commenting on earlier versions of this chapter: M. I. Avery, A. C. Entwistle, J. Childs, A. M. Hutson, A. M. Mitchell-Jones, R. Raynor, H. W. Schofield, M. B. Usher, A. L. Walsh, G. Williams and M. R. Young.

10

British mammals: is there a radical future?

DAVID W. MACDONALD, GEORGINA M. MACE
AND STEVE RUSHTON

INTRODUCTION

There are occasions when the comforts of Western Europe tempt the British armchair conservationist to double standards, urging other countries to noble, self-sacrificing conservation efforts on a scale which we would scarcely dream of implementing here. It may be a hackneyed thought, but the ethical certainty that tigers should prowl unfettered in India might be less straightforward if the prowling were in our own backyard! Of course, the UK is an industrialised, over-populated island so perhaps we should not push the argument of practising what we preach to fatuous extremes – but how far should we push it? That is the question we have in mind when asking whether there is a radical future for the conservation of British mammals.

The future of mammals is intimately linked to that of other wildlife, and the landscape in general, and in this chapter we will present some visions for the enhancement of the British environment for mammals, biodiversity and people. We focus on mammals partly because we happen to specialise in them, but largely because their charisma has been important in leading conservation initiatives around the world (see Leader-Williams and Dublin, chapter 4, this volume). In the United States, for example, much spending under the Endangered Species Act has been focused on the protection of charismatic mammals and birds (Brown and Shogren, 1998; Metrick and Weitzman, 1998), whilst the popularity of big game and wilderness for ecotourism in Africa is abundantly clear (see Goodwin and Leader-Williams, chapter 14, this volume). The UK Biodiversity Steering Group has already produced 162 Biodiversity Action Plans for species, with a further 238 proposed. The charisma of mammals should enable them to act as flagships for the conservation of other species highlighted in the *UK Biodiversity Action Plan* (Anon., 1994a) and *Biodiversity Challenge* (Wynne *et al.*,

1995) especially in the most imperilled habitats, such as wetlands and late-successional woodland. Agenda 2000 has the potential to improve the lot of wildlife on farmland. National Parks cover 14 000 km² of England and Wales, and, together with Areas of Outstanding National Beauty (AONBs), encompass 20 % of the UK's land area. The environment, the countryside and wildlife are on the international and national agendas in a big way, so the time is ripe to ensure that mammal conservation has a high priority.

In this chapter we will consider four elements that might contribute to a radical future for British mammals. The first of these is hardly controversial – it concerns the need to foster those mammals we have left. The continuing publication of national Biodiversity Action Plans illustrates this process of fostering, so we will dwell on it no further. The second element, recording and monitoring trends in species' numbers and distributions, is a prerequisite to conserving them; we will cover this topic only in outline as we have recently explored it at length elsewhere (Macdonald *et al.*, 1998a). Next, we consider the importance of scale in conservation, and suggest increasing emphasis on landscape-level processes. We illustrate the potential for predicting the outcome of habitat enhancement by using models of landscapes coupled to models of species' requirements. The changes in the policy and economic environment which might facilitate this vision are outlined, and novel potential sources of public and private funding for the radical future are illustrated. Finally, we consider possibilities for enriching our fauna by reintroduction. The four elements on which this discussion focuses are, thus, the possibilities to foster, record, enhance and enrich Britain's mammalian fauna.

RECORDING SPECIES: THE IMPERATIVE TO MONITOR

Why is it worthwhile to monitor British mammals? We cannot make sensible plans about mammal conservation until we know how many of each species we have, and where they are. Despite heroic efforts for particular species (Strachan and Jeffries, 1993, 1996; Bright *et al.*, 1996; Hutchins and Harris, 1996; Wilson *et al.*, 1997), in the absence of a national monitoring scheme, in general we do not know these basic facts.

Monitoring is the process whereby the distribution and abundance of species is recorded at intervals to reveal changes in their status. Hitherto, the statuses of some terrestrial British mammals have been recorded, and a minority monitored systematically. These surveys, inspired and conducted by a variety of societies, universities and government departments, utilising the enormous energy and skill of both amateurs and professionals, lay a foundation for monitoring mammals. However, there has been no national, coordinated, enduring system for monitoring Britain's terrestrial mammals. Nonetheless, we are blessed with an abundance of robust strands from which such a network might be woven. We have a kaleidoscope of interacting statutory bodies, local authorities, National Parks authorities, national agencies, institutes, and university teams, and there are very important NGOs. Some rest heavily on volunteers or members, and of these The Mammal Society and the Wildlife Trusts must surely be among the guy-ropes of this future net. We have suggested that a national monitoring scheme needs to be innovative, inspirational (to its participants), and integrative – fostering synergy between the diverse players in the mammalogical field (Macdonald *et al.*, 1998a). The task is not only to consider how organisations might best be mustered to count terrestrial mammals, but rather to explore a whole system for gathering, storing, analysing, extrapolating and using these data. These processes are informed by skills ranging from fieldcraft to economics.

The sort of national mammal monitoring network that we envisage has implications beyond the obvious conservation imperative of knowing which species are declining. For example, monitoring will help the UK Government to fulfil its statutory obligations. A variety of international and national conservation laws require monitoring to be effective, or legally commit parties to monitor (Lyster, 1985; Glowka *et al.*, 1994; Macdonald *et al.*, 1998a, b). These include the Convention on Biological Diversity, the EC Habitat and Species Directives, the Berne Convention, the Bonn Convention, CITES, and The Wildlife and Countryside Act 1981. Importantly, under the Convention on Biological Diversity we are committed to maintaining the conservation status of native mammals, and limiting the impact of alien ones, and it is impossible to do either unless we monitor them.

Monitoring will also help to quantify conservation and management problems, providing an interpretative backcloth, fuelling ecological science and preparing for unforeseen problems. Monitoring is part of what we call the Conservation Quartet, the four interdependent ingredients of successful conservation: Research (to crack the problem and identify the solution), Education (to inform society, and influence opinion), Community (to involve the stakeholders) and Implementation (to get the job done). Monitoring, in one guise or another, contributes to each part of the Conservation Quartet. Counting what we have and how it is changing is essential to Research, provides grist for the Educational mill, involves the active participation of Community and will be the yardstick against which the success of Implementation will be judged.

British mammals are exciting, fascinating and important to people in many sections of society. Some are considered assets, others pests, some endangered, others too populous. Yet, the status of the majority of species is insufficiently known to assess trends in their distribution or abundance, or to plan adequately for their management – whether to conserve the imperilled or to control the pestilential. In short, it is necessary to monitor British mammals.

BRITAIN'S MAMMALS IN CONTEXT

Of course, Britain's mammals are a part of a global and regional whole. On a global scale, the diversity that we have within our remit is very small. In our view, this reinforces the responsibility that we have to manage and foster our species in an exemplary manner, and to develop methods and resources to assist managers with greater numbers of species elsewhere in the world. On a regional scale, nearly a third of Europe's 128 species, and six of its seven orders, occur in Britain. Britain has 8.9 % of the palearctic species although it forms far less than 1 % of the land area.

So, we have a need, we have a statutory obligation, and we have the threads with which to weave the mammal monitoring network. Unfortunately, monitoring terrestrial mammals is difficult, because most are shy and nocturnal. However, recent advances in the theory and practice of biology, in computer systems, and in analysis combine to make monitoring British mammals more feasible now than ever before. Certainly, more research is needed to improve methodologies, and particularly to validate indices of abundance, but essentially it is now technically possible to monitor terrestrial mammals. We also believe that the availability of new methods and software tools that readily enable survey and monitoring protocols to be assessed for statistical power and validity, mean that statistical and sampling issues can readily be incorporated into monitoring schemes. Such methods often also prescribe appropriate validation methods, so that the toolbox of sampling techniques can readily be made available for general application. Thus, it appears that a national monitoring scheme is both desirable and feasible. We have developed the details for such a scheme elsewhere (Macdonald *et al.*, 1998a, b), but present here an outline of the proposals. The scheme is called the MaMoNet (Mammal Monitoring Network).

THE MAMONET

The ultimate aim of the MaMoNet is to foster prudent management, and therefore effective custodianship, of Britain's terrestrial mammals, through providing decision makers and practitioners with the information they need to formulate policy and undertake implementation. Obviously any monitoring network must work synergistically with existing schemes, such as The Mammal Society's surveys, and fit within a larger structure, such as the National Biodiversity Network (NBN).

A unifying three-tier grid

The MaMoNet must follow a statistically robust protocol to yield data on national and regional trends in species distribution and abundance. It must make the most of existing historical data, and unite the efforts of government and non-governmental organisations, utilising both amateurs and professionals. It must yield reliable baseline data, be flexible to adjust to areas of rich interest, and foster research into processes underlying mammal populations.

The circumstances of each species differ, and the requirements of a monitoring scheme are varied. To unify this diversity of material and purpose we propose a three-tier system. First, to form a basis for the detection and interpretation of trends in the populations and distribution of each species, the primary requirement is for a Master Sample (gathered from Master Squares, insofar as the fieldwork is likely to be undertaken in map squares of one size or another). Second, because important events might slip through the net if we ignore the interstices of the Master Squares, and also in order to capitalise on sites for which historical data exist, it may be important to monitor some sites outside the Master Squares: we will call these Rich Interest Kilometre Squares (RIKS). Third, because some species are undergoing processes of especial importance in particular places, such as range expansion or interaction with a competing species, it is important to concentrate especially on those places which we term Focus Zones. Examples of Focus Zones might be zones of overlap between red and grey squirrels, *Sciurus vulgaris* and *S. carolinensis* (see Macdonald *et al.*, 1999b), or areas into which muntjac deer *Muntiacus reevesi* are spreading (see Macdonald and Johnson, 1998), or areas into which polecats *Mustela putorius*, or pine marten *Martes martes*, are expanding.

Ideally, the circle will be complete: monitoring will help identify Focus Zones, and will direct the attention of research bodies to the processes responsible for the flux there. In this way, the national monitoring scheme will not only capitalise on detailed research, it will also drive that research. Together, the Master Sample, the RIKS and the Focus Zones comprise the unified three-tier grid of the MaMoNet.

Weaving the MaMoNet

The most difficult issue to resolve in deciding the sampling protocol is how best to deploy the Master Sample. There is no one right answer, so the solution will be a compromise based on evaluating the importance of a variety of pros and cons. Suffice it to say that, in the jargon of statisticians, the protocol could be either random or systematic random (e.g., a randomly positioned regular grid), although the former is statistically simpler to analyse. It should involve a pattern of revisiting at least some sites on successive survey cycles, but should also retain some mobility in sampling sites. Finally, it should accommodate as much historical survey data as possible, especially for species of conservation importance. Other considerations to be weighed in this balance include any biological or logistical advantages either to monitoring all or some species at the same places simultaneously and/or to consolidating several sampling sites in the same locality, and to the survey cycle (which might be seven years). We imagine a burgeoning force of amateur volunteers would be crucial, and that it is equally crucial that their energies are catalysed by a cadre of, say, five full time professional Mammal Monitors.

A system such as the MaMoNet would have many advantages: (1) it could function as a part of, even a framework for, the NBN, or in the worst case it could function autonomously; (2) it could unite professional and volunteer players, facilitating the discharge of government responsibilities and fostering the participation of the voluntary sector; (3) it presents an expandable system, safeguarding the minimum requirements of monitoring, and underpinning the maximum of aspirations for mammal conservation. The MaMoNet would also provide a systematic research tool for investigating processes and could even be expanded throughout Europe as a basis for regional monitoring.

The MaMoNet would enable us to quantify the abundance, distribution and changes in status of British mammals. How could we use these data if we had them? We now turn now to Enhancement and Enrichment of our mammalian fauna.

ENHANCEMENT

If to foster and record the status of British mammals are the first steps to conserving Britain's mammal fauna, then the next is to enhance it. If by fostering we mean to ring-fence the existing populations of threatened mammals so that at worst their status does not deteriorate, by enhancement we mean taking active steps to improve their status. Operationally, planning enhancement requires an understanding of how mammal numbers are likely to change in response to environmental degradation or enhancement. We have developed methods based around Geographical Information Systems (GIS) and Population Viability Analysis (PVA), which we believe may have general applicability for this kind of planning. Having established that it is possible to predict the impact of landscape-scale habitat change, it is then feasible to consider large-scale enhancements for conservation.

Predicting responses to change

Our approach to predicting how a species will respond to a change in its environment has been first to map its current distribution onto detailed habitat maps and then to develop statistical models that allow a robust estimate of its abundance and distribution to be estimated from habitat features alone (Lavers et al., 1996; Rushton et al., 1997). From this model, we can then make predictions about how the size, structure and distribution of the species will alter under certain kinds of habitat change. The species population can then be analysed using PVA techniques (Gilpin and Soulé, 1986; Boyce, 1992). Habitat changes might be a consequence of management imposed to improve the status of the species, in which case we would hope to see an improvement in the PVA forecast after the proposed changes are introduced compared to the PVA outcomes under the status quo. This method thus allows the objective comparison of the relative advantages and disadvantages of alternative habitat management practices, measured in terms of the likely population size or persistence times of resident species.

Case Study 1: the dormouse in the Thames region

Having been the subject of detailed studies (Morris, 1986; Bright and Morris, 1990; Bright et al., 1996), the dormouse, *Muscardinus avellanarius*, provides a good example of how such desktop explorations of ways to examine and enhance the prospects of a species might work. Taking the known distribution of 24 dormouse subpopulations in the Thames catchment, and using data on dispersal (Bright et al., 1996), we compared this version of contemporary reality with a fantasy in which intervention changed management of all woodland to make it desirable for dormice. The subpopulation sizes vary from five or fewer, up to about 120. The web of migration rates between subpopulations was calculated using a migration-distance function parameterised from the literature (Bright and Morris, 1990). This model does not yet take account of the impact of intervening habitats on

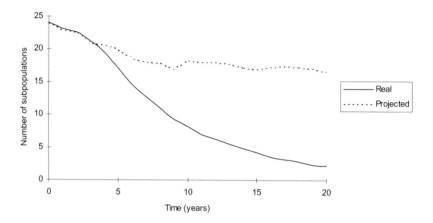

Figure 10.1 Probability curve for population sizes during a 20–year projection of the dormouse population in the Thames area using a metapopulation PVA model (RAMAS Metapop). The curves show the frequency with which each population size was observed during the 20–year period. 'Real' and 'Projected' are alternative habitat management strategies (see text).

migration rates. Nonetheless, it serves to permit us to imagine an ideal world for dormice. The output from such a model is presented in Figure 10.1. The *y*-axis shows the probability that at any time during the next 20 years the population will drop below the critical value shown on the *x*-axis. The critical value that might most interest us is zero – extinction – and here, in the absence of any intervention, the probability of extinction in the next two decades is about 0.28. However, if we imagine these 24 woodlands have been managed to become prime dormouse habitat the extinction risk drops to zero. Our purpose in presenting this example is not to suggest it is realistic (indeed, the instant creation of ancient woodland is clearly fantasy), but rather to illustrate the potency of combined PVA/GIS models for planning conservation enhancement. Nonetheless, in the dormouse case we reveal to policy-makers the likelihood that, if we simply foster and record the current subpopulations of dormice in the Thames catchment, we may preside over their widespread disappearance.

The constraints of small-scale conservation: the possibilities for radical enhancement

In contrast to the vast parks found – and proposed – in some regions, where management can rest on the control of hydrological processes in entire watersheds, conservation in Britain is often confined to small areas requiring intensive management. Conservation of small sites presents general problems, and much of the theory of conservation biology concerns the consequences of small size, fragmentation and isolation of populations (Lawton, 1995). In general, small sites suffer disproportionately from edge-effects (Soulé, 1986; Laurance and Yensen, 1990; Simberloff, 1998a) and for long-term viability it is necessary to manage habitat quality in intervening habitat to maintain stable metapopulation dynamics (Hanski and Gyllenberg, 1993; Harrison, 1994) and to avoid declines due to source–sink dynamics (Pulliam, 1988). Woodroffe and Ginsberg (1998) demonstrate the edge-associated risks for wide-ranging mammals in small sites, while Macdonald et al. (1999a) illustrate the frailty of small, isolated populations likely to be characteristic of small reserves.

Whilst little is known about the effects of fragmentation on British mammals, the processes are likely to be similar to those revealed for vertebrates in America, Asia or Australia (Askins et al., 1987; Diamond et al., 1987; Lawton and May, 1995), and similar principles are illustrated by smaller animals in Britain (Hambler and Speight, 1995a, b). For example, small forest or heathland patches have no core area of typical habitat supporting specialist invertebrates (Webb, 1989), and many woodland species prosper better in big patches, or deeper within woodlands (birds: Bellamy et al., 1996a, b; Hinsley et al., 1996a, b; invertebrates: Ozanne et al., 1997), and the same is probably true of wetlands. As a general rule, forest specialists have dwindled with the loss of native woodland which has occurred since the early Neolithic, 5000 years ago in Britain (Darvill, 1996; Harding and Rose, 1996), and species from successional woodland, woodland edges, and grassland, are also threatened (Shirt, 1987; Thomas and Morris, 1994).

Data for mammals are fewer. There is evidence that the incidence of red squirrels in woodlands is dependent on the size and extent of fragmentation (Verboom and van Apeldoorn, 1990; van Apeldoorn et al., 1994; Celada et al., 1994) and also the separation from other populations of red squirrel (Celada et al., 1994). Similarly, for the ancient woodland specialist the dormouse, fragmentation may play an important role in determining where the species occurs in England (Bright et al., 1996), with woodlands that are widely separated in the landscape having a reduced likelihood of supporting dormice populations (Bright et al., 1996). These principles apply to the fragmentation of riverside water vole Arvicola terrestris habitats (Macdonald and Strachan, 1999). Therefore, while we do not detract for one moment from the crucial efforts to preserve habitat fragments, we also ask what options exist for increasing the expanse of conservation areas in Britain to escape the vortex of small, isolated reserves. Large-scale conservation reduces the conflicts of interest in management characteristic of small reserves (Duffey, 1974), wherein it is generally necessary to manage for just a few successional stages (Duffey and Watt, 1971; Hambler and Speight, 1995a), or a highly intensive rotation (Rushton, 1988; Rushton *et al.*, 1990).

Against this catalogue of obstacles to small-scale conservation, but considering the constraints on a small, over-populated island, is it fruitful to ask what can be done to enhance mammal conservation on a large scale in Britain? The same question has been posed in North America, where massive landscape restoration has been both proposed (Noss and Cooperrider, 1994) and ridiculed. Others have raised this issue in Britain: Whitbread and Jenman (1995) suggest that populations of herbivores might, with minimal intervention, create the mosaic of successional habitats required to support a wide range of currently threatened species in Britain (Thomas and Morris, 1994). Now, and particularly in the context of AONBs, instruments are being conceived for such large-scale conservation (without jeopardising the fine-scale actions required within them) (Brown, 1998). An important example is Agenda 2000.

Agenda 2000, which is an important result of EU enlargement, involves the development of a coherent rural policy, reinforcement of agri-environmental instruments and shifts from price-support to direct payment for environmental benefits provided by farmers. All these are mechanisms to promote sustainable development and involve an increase in the agri-environment, afforestation and early retirement budget from 1.8 billion ECU to 2.8 billion ECU annually. So, at first sight, the paucity of funds available to conservation and the intensity of agriculture throughout the countryside makes the scope for large-scale enhancement of mammalian conservation seem minimal. However, these constraints are the artifices of economic policy and politics. Agenda 2000 illustrates the possibilities. Substantial changes in the farmscape are entirely possible through relatively minor shifts in the Common Agricultural Policy, and mechanisms are conceived of whereby very substantial funds could become available to change radically policy regarding conservation and the wider environment (see below). We conclude, therefore, that consideration of radical and large-scale conservation initiatives is no less sensible in the UK than it is in those parts of the developing world where such proposals are routinely suggested. Ultimately, environmental protection in general, and the enhancement of mammal conservation in particular, are driven by market forces dictated by economic instruments which it is within the power of policy to vary.

Radical, large-scale habitat enhancement for British mammals can, broadly, take two forms. First, there is the possibility of increasing connectivity between isolated populations in a shift towards metapopulation management. The creation of corridors is highly desirable in theory, considering the major importance of dispersal for persistence of small populations by rescue effects and stable metapopulation dynamics (Brown and Kodric-Brown, 1977; Hooper and Harrison, 1998). Empirical evidence of their merit is less abundant, although corridors demonstrably improve the survival of scattered populations of some mammals (Beier, 1993; Henderson, 1985). However, the enthusiasm for corridors is based more on theory than practice, and the extent of their value is debated: for example, in the case of the Florida panther *Puma concolor*, Simberloff and Cox (1987) are sceptical, whereas Noss (1987) is supportive of their cost effectiveness. Where corridors are not effective active translocation is a possibility for the management of some populations.

The second way to escape the penalties of small reserves is to create big ones. In the following section we will explore, using simulations following the logic of the dormouse model presented above, the conservation consequences of virtual environmental policy shifts.

Virtual policy: explorations of possible conservation enhancements

Case Study 2: the water vole

Surveys have revealed a drastic decline in numbers of water voles throughout the UK (Strachan and Jeffries, 1993), and while this is proximately due to predation by American mink *Mustela vison*, the water vole's predicament is exacerbated by loss of riparian habitat (Barreto *et al.*, 1998; Macdonald and Strachan, 1999). This habitat loss is one feature of the general crisis in conservation on farmland that ensued from the post-war miracle of intensified food production (Barreto *et al.*, 1998; Macdonald and Smith, 1991). However, the current policy climate has changed: under the Convention on Biological Diversity, embodied in the Water Vole Species Action Plan (see Strachan, 1999) there is now an imperative to conserve the water vole, and (in addition to reducing the mink factor) to mitigate the impact of agricultural intensification. How might this be achieved?

The Ministry of Agriculture, Fisheries and Food's water fringes scheme seeks to protect water margins from erosion and permit development of tall waterside vegetation, which, as well as stabilising the bank, is also beneficial for wildlife. This policy applies to strips of inbye land bordering still or flowing water, which have a minimum breadth of 12 m if bordering still water, or 6 m, adjoining flowing water. Management requirements include the exclusion of livestock, the control of statutory weeds, prohibition of fertilisers and pesticides for periods of 10 years. How might such schemes, or even more radical ones, benefit water voles and the riparian ecosystem? We have developed a process-based model of water vole populations which illustrates the impact of habitat loss and fragmentation on their population viability (Macdonald and Strachan, 1999; Rushton *et al.*, in press). This revealed, for example, that habitat availability and fragmentation were the most important factors determining water vole presence on the River Windrush. The results suggest that there is an exponential relationship between the likelihood of extinction of the Windrush populations and the extent of habitat fragmentation. This indicates that viability would be increased if we could increase the area of available habitats. The model currently predicts that the Windrush population has a 50 % chance of avoiding extinction over the next 10 years. Doubling the available habitat would decrease this extinction probability to 24 %. The amount of land necessary to bring about this decline in the likelihood of extinction is 118 ha. Along some 20 km of river this is a comparatively small amount relative to the total area of land available in the river corridor. Currently, we are working on the likely economic cost to the farmer of these scenarios.

Case Study 3: restoring the River Cam
Thus far we have focused on water voles, a species-based example, but implicit in our proposals for habitat enhancement is the notion that whole ecological communities should benefit from improvements, albeit perhaps driven by popular enthusiasm for charismatic mammals. Therefore, our next example concerns catchment level management, not individual species. The catchment of the River Cam is dominated (80 %) by intensive arable agriculture. The sort of fringing habitat that is necessary for water voles and other wildlife can also protect in-stream water quality, not only from fertiliser and agrochemical contamination, but also from excess sediment run-off. O'Callaghan (1996) and his team therefore explored the consequences of putting 15 % of the arable land into an hypothetical river corridor scheme.

Within a 25 km × 25 km square of land south of Cambridge a three-stage GIS procedure involved: (1) identifying all blocks of land within 2 km of the river; (2) selecting all land within 100 m of the river, in order to define the 'inner core' of the river corridor to ensure continuity of vegetation; (3) deleting the remaining areas in the 2 km zone if they fell outside the 100 m zone. This 'virtual reality' involved modifying the habitats in the selected corridors such that any already under deciduous woodland remained so, while areas of arable land, pasture and amenity grass (within 100 m of the bank) were transformed to low input grazing pastures, with restrictions on stocking rates and inorganic fertiliser applications, producing either hay-meadow communities (*Festuca ovina–Avenula pratensis*) or grassland (*Agrostis stolonifera–Alopecurus geniculatus*).

The net effects of these simulations on the wildlife value of the Cam were evaluated for riparian bird species. The change in the suitability of the habitat for yellow wagtail *Motacilla flava* was variable; there was little effect along the main channel but predicted increases in suitability along the minor channels following the imposed land use change. The biggest predicted changes were along river corridors previously dominated by intensive arable agriculture wherein the creation of low intensity management grasslands provided additional nesting and feeding sites for the simulated wagtails. In contrast, the habitat suitability for the grasshopper warbler *Locustella naevia* was predicted to increase along the whole of the river network following the introduction of the scheme.

Analyses of this type should not be considered in isolation because they may have considerable implications for agro-economics. For example, the increase in low-intensity grassland created an excess of grazing pasture above the allowable EU limit on the number of livestock. Furthermore, within the river corridor area, the deintensification reduced the simulated profit by £42/ha. Furthermore, even this interdisciplinary model did not take into account all the more subtle consequences of agricultural deintensification. For example, if enhancing water vole habitat involved the creation of more wetland habitat this could have benefits in climate change: wetland in Europe sequesters carbon at some 0.25 tC /ha/yr, but if drained releases it at some 1–10 tC/ha/yr (Adger *et al.*, 1994).

Case Study 4: Red squirrels and woodland habitat creation
In general, East Anglia is a tree-less landscape. This area is interesting in that it also contains a remnant population of the red squirrel. The red squirrel has suffered a serious decline in the UK, at least partly attributable to the introduced grey squirrel, but exacerbated by habitat loss (Reynolds, 1985; Okubo *et al.*, 1989; Rushton *et al.*, 1997). Cambridgeshire has both a low woodland cover and a widespread population of grey squirrels. O'Callaghan's (1996) team considered a virtual policy under which it was decided to take the poorest 10 % of farmland out of conventional agriculture, and to reforest it with a mix of 80 % natural deciduous woodland (for general conservation benefit) and 20 % Corsican pine *Pinus nigra* var. *maritima* (to enhance the prospects for red squirrel conservation).

Figure 10.2 Predicted distribution of grey and red squirrel populations in the River Cam catchment before and after an imposed change in forest cover. Top left – grey squirrels before change; top right – after change in forest cover. Bottom left – red squirrel distribution before change; bottom right following change in cover.

Figure 10.2 shows the predicted current distribution of grey and red squirrels (the latter confined to Thetford) and the distribution of potential new (fantasy) Cambridgeshire forests. It predicts what might happen to the red squirrels if they were provided with the new forests. The simulation suggested that four seemingly viable red squirrel populations would populate this new East Anglian landscape (and of course, the new forests would bring a host of other botanical, entomological and ornithological values). Incidentally, the model of current circumstances also predicts that the Thetford population itself is too isolated to be viable without continual supplementation.

As with the previous river corridor habitat modification example, there are economic ramifications of altering land use for conservation in this way. The models showed that the loss of income throughout the area from converting arable land to forest would amount to £427 000 per annum. This is equivalent to £56/ha. Under the Farm Woodland Scheme, the grant that would be available for planting of this type of forest is estimated at £39/ha, when annualised at a rate of 6% over a 50 year period. Thus the grants presently available for planting broadleaves and conifers are not nearly sufficient to compensate for the costs involved in this change of land use.

Case Study 5: the dormouse in the north of England

As mentioned above, habitat loss, and especially the demise of traditionally coppiced woodland, has contributed to the perilous decline of dormice in Britain. In the north of England dormice remain in an enclave in Allendale within the Tynedale catchment. Combining a GIS map of all suitable dormouse habitat with a model of their population dynamics suggests that the Allendale enclave is unlikely to be viable unassisted. What can be done? We explored a policy which involved enhancing the quality of all the woodland in the locality to improve its suitability for dormice (remembering that coppice is disadvantageous for a lot of invertebrates, lichens and fungi). The result (Figure 10.3) was that the simulated dormice prospered locally, but they still failed to break free from their enclave in the southeast corner. Our suspicion that this is because there are inadequate dispersal corridors to enable the dormice unaided to reach the improved habitat is supported by the impressions of the biologist studying the Allendale population (P. Bright, personal communication). In this case, enhancement of the existing woodland blocks is not enough, and it appears that a network of dispersal corridors is also required.

This example points to the next step in our proposed sequence. Where fostering, recording and enhancing are insufficient, enrichment by intervention may be necessary. In the case of the dormouse, this might involve translocation. For now, however, the point is obvious: namely, it is possible to explore the conservation benefits of radical changes in policy and to calculate the likely costs. The challenge is then to find a metric for converting the pros and cons of a given policy into a common currency. Crucial to this will be an assessment of the existence value of the species to the public, alongside the values of all the other wildlife (wide swathes are likely to benefit species from otters to dragonflies) and aesthetic benefits that would be associated with habitat change.

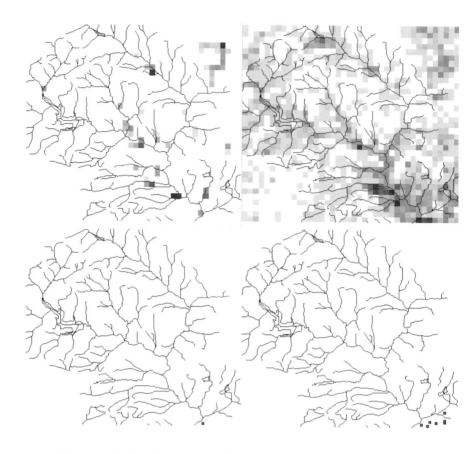

Figure 10.3 Predicted distribution of dormouse in Tyne catchment before and after a change in forest suitability for the species. Top left represents available ancient woodland, top right all available woodland changed to ancient woodland. Colour scale from dark (high) to light (low) area of woodland in each 1 km square of the National Grid. Bottom left – predicted distribution of dormouse under current conditions; bottom right – predicted distribution following increase in area of ancient woodland.

ENRICHMENT

There are instances where conservation is best achieved by leaving wilderness alone. Generally, however, it is already too late for such *laissez faire* conservation, and intervention is required. While intervention may tarnish the notion of pristine wildness, it may be inevitable. An evocative case is the African wild dog *Lycaon pictus* in South Africa. This species is endangered (Woodroffe *et al.*, 1997) and outside the Kruger National Park there are few reserves sufficiently large to support it in South Africa. However, by creating coalitions of game farms, removing the fences between them, but erecting new fences around their shared perimeter (to prevent depredations on neighbouring stock-rearing areas), a series of subpopulations could be created. Fencing these is essential, and so the spectres of overpopulation and inbreeding will ensue. The solution is metapopulation management, whereby wild dogs will intermittently be captured and artificially dispersed between these subpopulations (Mills *et al.*, 1998). This example offers striking insight into the issues associated with enrichment: a superficial look at South Africa might indicate no possibility of creating new enclaves for this imperilled species. However, a series of radical ideas – joining game farms, fencing their borders, and translocating wild dogs – may facilitate substantial enrichment of the fauna, and perhaps even an added source of revenue through phototourism. What then, are the opportunities for enrichment of the mammal fauna in Britain?

The reintroduction of species extirpated from Great Britain during historical times is generally attractive in principle (Morris, 1986), and encouraged by European Union Legislation (Article 22, EC Habitat and Species Directive, EC 92/43). In Britain, high impact 'charismatic' species have been introduced, including the red kite *Milvus milvus* and white-tailed sea eagle *Haliaeetus albicilla*, and culminating in an attempt to introduce the osprey *Pandion heliaetus* to lowland England with seven young adults taken from Scotland (Tomlinson, 1996). In terms of best practice, the practicalities of translocations and reintroductions are dictated by IUCN (1998). The problems of reintroduction are formidable (Yalden, 1993). The most important criteria are that the factors causing the original extinction have been reversed; that a taxonomically, genetically and demographically 'suitable' stock of animals is available; and that sufficient human and financial resources exist to persevere with the reintroduction programme until it has had a reasonable chance of success. There are also veterinary considerations (Woodford and Rossiter, 1993). In the case of British mammals, several species are on the candidate list (Yalden, 1986) including European beaver *Castor fiber*, wild boar *Sus scrofa*, wolf *Canis lupus*, and European lynx *Lynx lynx*, and each illustrates different problems.

On the face of it, reintroducing these large mammals to Britain is not a sensible option in conventional terms (i.e., if the primary aim of reintroduction is to establish a viable, free-ranging population in the wild, of a species, subspecies or race, which has become globally or locally extinct, or extirpated, in the wild). However, our remit is to consider whether there is a radical agenda for the enrichment of Britain's mammalian fauna, and we are mindful that these large mammals have an aesthetic appeal to a wide public that is potentially enormous (and potentially highly profitable in terms of ecotourism and sport hunting). We are also mindful of the conservation potential unleashed by the example (see above) of the metapopulation management of the African wild dogs in South Africa. Let us, then, consider briefly lessons learnt from the reintroduction of large mammals elsewhere in Europe.

The European beaver

The European beaver was eradicated in Britain by the sixteenth century, and being easily susceptible to hunting was similarly lost from much of western Europe (Macdonald *et al.*, 1995). Macdonald and Tattersall (1999) have reviewed arguments for and against the reintroduction of this species to the UK. As a tool for predicting the likely viability and spread of introduced beavers, we have again used both PVA and GIS-based models (Macdonald *et al.*, in press; South *et al.*, in press), and, in collaboration with Scottish Natural Heritage, we have used these models to explore the feasibility of reintroducing beavers to Scotland.

A simulation of the viability of reintroduced beaver populations at selected sites was performed using a process-based population dynamics model integrated into a GIS. The GIS system revealed locations in the Highlands with suitable deciduous forest associated with fresh water, and dispersal corridors, and then iterated through the population dynamics model to simulate how introduced beavers might spread through that landscape. Each block of suitable habitat within the landscape was modelled as having separate subpopulations of families of beaver. Four simulation scenarios illustrate variations on the theme of carrying capacity and dispersal distance, demonstrating that even in the very best location, only 40–60 animals were present after 50 years (Figure 10.4). The number of subpopulations that established was never more than a handful and only three sites in the Highlands supported more than 10 individuals.

We conclude that to secure the long-term viability of reintroduced beavers in Scotland is likely to require habitat enhancement. In the meantime, it is likely that reintroduced beavers would have to be the subject of population management, in the form of regular supplementary releases. That, however, is scarcely an unusual situation in the UK: most nature reserves are heavily managed, and some successful instances of bird conservation rely on indefinite management. This level of intervention might strike the purist as somehow unnatural, but seems to us no worse than presiding over an ever-dwindling countryside with an impoverished mammal fauna.

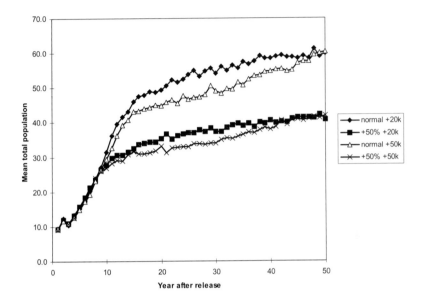

Figure 10.4 Predicted population size of beaver following release at one site in Scotland under two carrying capacity (normal and +50%) and two dispersal (20 km and 50 km) scenarios.

In our judgement, the reintroduction of the beaver to the UK is not seriously controversial. Of course, there are pros and cons (and we judge that on balance they favour reintroduction, see Macdonald and Tattersall, 1999). Of course, also, attention given to the glamour of a new reintroduction should not steal resources from the conservation of our existing fauna. Equally, it would be foolish to suppose that reintroduced beavers would not bring some irritations and require interventionist management which will raise questions regarding welfare. Nonetheless, the level of nuisance they might cause is unlikely to be great, and all the evidence is that, where necessary, they can easily be removed (*vide* the ease with which they have been widely extirpated). The situation is very different regarding some other candidates for reintroduction, where the drawbacks are potentially much more dramatic and less manageable.

Wild boar

While the reintroduction of free-ranging lynx and wolves on mainland Britain remains a fantasy, approximately 120 wild boar are already living around the Kent–Sussex border (MAFF, 1998). These animals are likely to have escaped from exotic meat farms during the major storm in 1987, and are thought to be breeding successfully. Their presence forces an urgent re-examination of the desirability of large, potentially dangerous animals in the English countryside. Wild boar were once native in the UK and were a prestigious quarry species. However, they became extinct in Britain by the end of the seventeenth century, probably due to the actions of pig farmers, and the loss of habitat (Rackham, 1986). The establishment of new wild boar populations has predictably met with mixed reactions from the local communities. These range from fear for human safety; to allegations of livestock predation; to amusement when a wild boar was caught mating with domestic free-range sows; to considerable enthusiasm for the arrival of a once-native species.

In attempting to evaluate the potential consequences of wild boar rein-troduction, it is sensible to consider the experiences of continental Europe. Wild boar have continued to thrive in many countries, and have also been reintroduced to several areas for hunting (e.g., Boitani *et al.*, 1994). Al-though Germany, Poland, Russia, France and Spain all suffer agricultural damage from wild boar, the animals are considered to be an economic asset (Tisdell, 1982). In many countries, farmers are compensated for crop losses caused by the rooting of boar. It is notable that there are no documented cases of wild boar predating lambs, nor of disease being transmitted be-tween wild boar and domestic pigs. Wild boar can conflict with the conser-vation of certain rare flora (particularly woodland bulbs), but it remains to be seen whether, on balance, they are considered environmentally benefi-cial. Even in the UK, there are recent reports of captive wild boar being used in a Scottish country park to control long grass, remove unwanted weeds, and break up the soil, thus allowing natural regeneration of pine (Anon., 1997).

In contrast, most of the concerns about the environmental and econ-omic threats posed by wild boar to farming and native wildlife are based on experiences with feral pigs. These animals were introduced as exotic spe-cies to many parts of the world, including Australia, New Zealand and Hawaii, and now are serious pests. In Australia, the economic cost to agri-culture is estimated at over $100 million per annum (Choquentot *et al.*, 1996). Although wild boar and feral pigs are both subspecies of *Sus scrofa*, feral pigs are larger, have greater litter sizes and can breed throughout the year. They are known regularly to prey on lambs (O'Brien, 1985; Choquen-tot *et al.*, 1997), and can damage native flora (Brown, 1985). However, whether these experiences can be extrapolated to wild boar in Britain is questionable. Perhaps a more important issue is whether sufficient areas of suitable habitat are available in Britain to support viable, self-sustaining wild boar populations (Leaper *et al.*, 1999).

Wolves

There is a full literature on wolf reintroductions in North America (Fuller, 1989) and the increasing rarity of wolves in Europe makes them a strong candidate for reintroduction. The 100 km² Isle of Rum, 19 km from the mainland, is often mooted as a site for wolf reintroduction to Britain. When acquired by the Nature Conservancy Council, Rhum had a population of 1500 deer of which 16 % starved each winter, but an annual cull of about 250 deer has since reduced winter mortality to about 4 %. The culled deer on Rum (25 500 kg) might therefore sustain a population of 19 wolves eating 3.6 kg/day. Such a population might (Mech, 1966) or might not be viable. Estimates of the area needed to sustain a viable wolf population range from 10 000 to 13 000 km² (Soulé, 1986). However, most relevant to our discussion are the wolves of the 544 km² Isle Royale in Lake Superior, which immigrated from Ontario across the ice in the winter of 1947–48. Between 1959 and 1974 the population numbered 17–31 wolves and contained one or two reproducing packs. The population increased steadily in the 1970s, peaking in 1980 at 92 wolves/1000 km². Numbers dropped to 14 wolves in 1980–1982, then stabilised at 20–24 (Peterson and Page, 1988). Estimates of deer consumption range between 15, 16.6 and 36.7 deer/wolf/year (Mech, 1970; Pimlott, 1967). There has been some debate regarding the population density that wolves introduced to Rum might reach (e.g., maximum 92/1000 km² in the 1980s on Isle Royale; Peterson and Page, 1988), but doubtless such a closed population would undergo violent predator–prey cycles that would probably be unacceptable to the wider public. It would therefore be necessary to calculate, and manage for, a desired balance of wolves and deer. Keith (1983) provided a model to predict the number of ungulates required per wolf to maintain a stable ungulate population, given a certain harvest by hunters. To judge by other studies, the answer might be a ratio of about 100 deer/wolf (Pimlott, 1967)

Zimen and Boitani (1979) point out that human population is not necessarily incompatible with the survival of wolves (in the Abruzzi region of Italy, wolves survive alongside 29 people/km², whereas they have been exterminated amongst 1.33 people/km² in Sweden).

The European lynx

The European lynx was exterminated from western Europe, surviving only in Scandinavia, Slovakia and the Pyrenees. However, they have been reintroduced with varying success to Slovenia, Austria (Styria), Germany (Bavarian Forest), Slovakia (Moravian Forest), Italy (Gran Paradiso), Switzerland (Alps, Jura) and France (Vosges) (Cop, 1992; Breitenmoser and Breitenmoser-Wursten, 1993). The German project failed, and those in Switzerland, Austria, Slovenia and France are supported by compensation schemes which reimburse farmers for stock losses. The best documented reintroductions are those in Switzerland (Breitenmoser *et al.*, 1993; Breitenmoser and Haller, 1993). Officially, nine male and seven female lynx were released at four sites between 1971–1976, but at least nine others were released clandestinely at five other sites. There are now two populations: one in the Jura mountains to the north, covering 5000 km², which has spread also into the French Jura, and one in the Alps in central/western Switzerland, occupying about 10 000 km², which has spread into both France and Italy. In all, there are believed to be 50–100 adult lynx in Switzerland, and a further 60 dead animals have been reported over the 20 years. From 1973 to 1988, compensation has been paid on 4442 sheep, 16 goats and 15 other livestock, but studies of the diet show that roe deer *Capreolus capreolus* and chamois *Rupicapra rupicapra* are the principal prey; of 88 prey items, discovered by following radio-collared lynx, 48 were roe deer, 30 chamois, five hares *Lepus europaeus*, two sheep, two marmots *Marmota marmota*, and one red squirrel. While the reintroduction of lynx is thus feasible, and may offer general lessons, it seems totally impractical in the UK in unfenced areas.

Eco-parks

Enrichment of British mammal faunas has occurred *de facto* and perhaps haphazardly, for otters *Lutra lutra*. Carefully planned translocation is feasible, and already underway for dormice, and planned for water voles. More controversially, it is on the agenda for pine marten. Clearly, in historical times, it was commonplace to translocate mammals, especially quarry species, to bolster their numbers. For example roe deer and hares have been much shuffled around the UK. Some such translocations were highly ill-conceived, such as the hedgehogs *Erinaceus europaeus*, introduced to North Uist (D. Jackson, personal communication). Indeed, it is not long ago that the introduction of aliens, such as grey squirrels, muntjac deer, or even edible dormice *Glis glis*, rabbits *Oryctolagus cuniculus*, and fallow deer *Dama dama*, was thought of as desirable. The proposal to reintroduce the European beaver is different from these now seemingly cavalier escapades: it rests on a meticulously scrutinised evaluation following detailed guidelines within international legislation (Macdonald and Tattersall, 1999). But what of the larger, charismatic mammals we have mentioned?

Clearly, experiences elsewhere reveal that it is feasible to reintroduce species such as wolf, lynx, boar (and even bear *Ursus arctos*) that were recently members of the British fauna. To enrich our fauna with these species strikes us as a thrilling prospect, and one likely to generate ecotourism revenue. It also strikes us as plainly out of the question in the context of the intensive agriculture that typifies the vast majority of Britain. Do these species then drop from the radical agenda for conservation in Britain, or indeed, western Europe? We suggest there is no reason in principle why they should.

Conservation, like the rest of environmental management, is often the result of market forces: if the public attaches sufficiently high existence value to wolves in Britain, or if they are believed to have sufficient revenue-generating capacity, then there are clearly ways ahead. If, as we suggest, these large mammals would be unacceptable free-ranging, then the answer is simply to create fenced parks, following the inspiration of the example of wild dogs in South Africa, and indeed expansive game reserves elsewhere (where, incidentally, the cost of predator-proof fencing was approximately £2000/km). How large would such a reserve have to be? The experience of Isle Royale tells us that for several decades wolves have thrived on an island of 500 km². In an era of new community forests in Britain, large-scale restoration of that order of magnitude is demonstrably not out of the question. Of course, to keep predators in balance with their prey (and genetically viable) would require management, but neither this nor the capital costs of fencing are beyond the realms of possibility – indeed, as a form of land management, the costs are small in terms of farm subsidies within the Common Agricultural Policy as we discuss below.

Note, we are not saying that fenced wilderness parks are a priority for British conservation. We merely point out that on this small and industrialised island there is a tendency to think small about conservation, while advising big to those in developing countries. If the notion of taking a cluster of marginal farms out of production, and creating there a park where tourists can hear wolves howling or, going back even further in history, watch forest bison *Bison bonasus*, is what the consumer wants from our environment, then it is not impossible to create it.

'FREE' British Wildlife

In raising this last, and most extreme step in our radical agenda, our purpose is largely to be provocative. The sequence, Foster, Record, Enhance and Enrich includes many unprovocative, and indeed essential, steps, within the acronym FREE. To Foster our mammalian fauna is an obligation under the Convention on Biological Diversity, and few could surely dissent from the view that without Recording what we have we can neither monitor its status nor plan its preservation. Furthermore, in a countryside embattled and impoverished by agricultural intensification, and the fall-out from industrialisation, the notion that we should enhance the well-being of our mammals is scarcely controversial, and indeed is embodied in the UK government's Species Action Plans. However, it is under the topic of Enhancement, which in practice generally means habitat restoration, that there is a real opportunity to be both radical and realistic. If we wish a new arterial system of river corridor habitat swathing our waterways, we can have it. If we want to convert entire farms into a linked network of wildlife havens we can do it, and perhaps even more profitably than they are currently used for agriculture. The use of the countryside in Britain is the result of an economic structure driven by policy and the smallest tweak of that policy can revolutionise the prospects for conservation. All this is possible. The fact that it is also possible in principle to enrich our fauna with wolves or lynx in large fenced eco-parks may be true, and may be headlineworthy, but is less important than the general point that there is no need to think small when it comes to managing the environment.

STATUTORY MECHANISMS

Of course, several of the ideas we present here are part of a convergent evolution with thinking in the broader conservation community as the focus shifts from sites to landscapes. There is therefore an emerging legislative framework within which ideas for large-scale mammal conservation can sit. We will summarise these briefly.

First, the 1992 EC *Habitats and Species Directive*, transposed into UK law in 1994/5, introduced the designation of Special Areas of Conservation (SACs) as a requirement of member states. Together with Special Protection Areas (SPAs) designated as a requirement of the 1979 Birds Directive, these sites will form the Natura 2000 network throughout Europe. The goal is to maintain or restore natural habitats and wild species at a favourable conservation status. While there is no doubt that some SACs/SPAs are large and made up of several Sites of Special Scientific Interest, many are small or are mosaics of spatially separated sites; these latter are a step towards, but do not culminate at, landscape conservation.

The second major British commitment stems from the 1992 United Nations Conference on Environment and Development, producing the

Convention on Biological Diversity, which, in 1994 led to the publication of *Biodiversity: the UK Action Plan* (Anon., 1994a). The commitment to conserve and 'where practicable' enhance wild species and wildlife habitats, includes such relevant elements as the 'greening' of the Common Agricultural Policy, financial incentives to encourage environmentally sensitive forms of agriculture and encouragement of the adoption of environmentally beneficial management practices. The whole countryside philosophy, and the concept of zonation, stems from this plan, and has spawned English Nature's *Natural Areas Programme*. Natural Areas share common features of landscape and biodiversity, and the programme complements the Countryside Commission's *Countryside Character Programme* based on areas with a common landscape character. The two maps are combined into a single map for England, which divides the country into (40–50) units representing natural and cultural dimensions of the landscape, and complements the 20 *Natural Heritage Zones* in Scotland and *Landmap* in Wales.

Clearly, then, the current intellectual framework for thinking about conservation is compatible with the sort of widescale enhancement plans we suggest should be on the radical agenda for mammal and other conservation in Britain. But within this framework, do mechanisms exist to pay for such initiatives? Within the UK there are two broad policy instruments to promote the deintensification of agricultural production. First, the designation of *Environmentally Sensitive Areas* (ESAs) within which farmers are compensated for returning to traditional, less-intensive methods of production. Second, those associated with the CAP reforms, in particular the set-aside provisions of the *Arable Area Payments* scheme. For example, there are 22 ESAs, in parallel with which the *Countryside Stewardship Scheme* provides farmers with payments to sustain the beauty and diversity of the landscape, improve and extend wildlife habitats, restore neglected land or features, and create new habitats and features. Despite reform of the CAP allowing Arable Area Payments to be made for set-aside land, the potential for conservation was low until *MAFF's Habitat Scheme* for former five-year set-aside provided an annual subsidy to maintain and enhance land of wildlife value (including six water fringe areas). In Scotland the equivalent is the *Countryside Premium Scheme*. In Wales the *Tir Gofal* all-farm scheme will combine ESAs and *Tir Cymen* into an all-Wales scheme (Tir Cymen attracted 2800 farms in limited pilot areas, so the potential of Tir Gofal is tremendous).

Considering the existing options, the MAFF Habitat Payment in 1998 ranges from a basic payment of £275/ha for former set-aside land, through £405/ha for water fringe-withdrawal of arable land from production and

£435/ha for extensive grassland management on current arable, to up to £525/ha for saltmarsh. However, although all these schemes represent a level of support for the wider countryside that would have been unimaginable 20 years ago (Macdonald and Johnson, in press), the sums are not large in the context of large environmental projects. Where might we find innovative sources of finance to support a radical agenda for conservation?

FROM VISION TO REALITY: FINDING FUNDS

Large scale projects, especially the sort of habitat enhancements we propose, will be expensive. Is it conceivable that they can be paid for? Despite the past being far from promising, and conservation typically being blighted by trifling budgets, we see grounds for optimism. European and nationally funded large area schemes, such as support of the North York Moors National Park, have already revolutionised protection of AONBs. For example, European Objective 5b designation brought £9.6 million to England's five northern National Parks (and thereby levered a total investment of £25.7 million). For the future, and most obviously, reform of the CAP offers huge opportunity. Agenda 2000 may see the end of set-aside and bring instead further agri-environmental benefits. The 1996/7 basic area payment was £338.03/ha for set-aside (there are, for example, 11 000 ha of set-aside in Sussex, costing about £3 million per annum). While set-aside does have some value to wildlife (Best *et al.*, 1997; Baines *et al.*, 1998; Sotherton, 1998; Tattersall *et al.*, 1999), we suspect that such large sums might be better spent on more useful habitat enhancements than the growing of rank grassland.

In fact, for agricultural and political reasons, quite apart from environmental ones, the time is ripe for the whole basis of payments to change. The options for such change raise huge questions in economics, so our point is merely to highlight the enormous implications for conservation, and the opportunity for innovation. To take just one example, there might be virtue in a generous 'out-goers' scheme for those wishing to leave farming in marginal areas: paying them to return their land to a self-sustaining near-natural system might be cheaper for the Treasury than paying continual high subsidies; it might also offer revenue generating ecotouristic opportunities and, if planned on a landscape scale, it might even create opportunities for metapopulation management, along with corridor creation, for some species. In fact, EC Regulation 20/79 already allows for early retirement of farmers and might facilitate this idea (as might Articles 10–12 of the Rural Development Regulation).

In addition to reform of the CAP, other novel funds are emerging for mammal conservation in Britain. The Heritage Lottery Fund (HLF) and the Landfill Tax (both of which could provide 75 % of costs of habitat enhancement) are significant potential sources. Restoration clearly preserves aspects of the National Heritage. Since 1995, only 7 % of the HLF's budget has gone to countryside and nature conservation. This is likely to change. For example, the Tomorrow's Heathland Heritage project, managed on behalf of HLF by English Nature, will allocate £14 million over three years. The Government now has budgeted £750 000 for English Nature's Species Recovery Programme, and Scottish Natural Heritage has equivalent support. We see huge potential for conservation through both the EU and HLF; large sums of money are already on stream. Admittedly much of this is directed at farmland, but the potential for conservation on farmland is immense (Macdonald and Smith, 1991; Macdonald and Johnson, in press). However, woodland restoration, creation and management is being fostered through the Woodlands Grant Scheme and the EU Life Fund, amongst others. This can be targeted at priority species and habitats (e.g., new native woodland) through the various Woodland Improvement Grants (e.g., Project III for woodland management), and through Supplements and Challenge Funds. The question arises as to whether a sufficient proportion of this funding is directed to mammal conservation. We think it is not.

In addition to the HLF and the EU, there is another source of big money in society: industry. Increasingly, business is involved in the environment and environmental politics, and this involvement includes biodiversity (UK Round Table on Sustainable Development, 1998). It seems likely that whether voluntarily, or through the instruments of regulation or taxation, industry will increasingly be required not merely to limit, but also to repair its impact on the environment. Therefore, it strikes us as sensible to ask whether mechanisms exist whereby industry might become more involved in environmental enhancement.

Linking restoration and pollution offset

Climate change is a threat to wildlife internationally, and Britain, with 1 % of the world's population, produces some 2 % of the CO_2 emissions. Under the agreements reached at Rio (1992), Kyoto (1997) and Buenos Aires (1998), Britain must reduce its net emissions, and plans to do this partly by enhancement of natural sinks for CO_2 (Anon., 1994b). Some believe this might provide spin-off benefits for wildlife, but others are sceptical (Adger et al., 1997b). Nonetheless, to the extent that afforestation might be a beneficial form of habitat enhancement for some British mammals, the topic of carbon sequestration is relevant. The cost of planting forestry to sequester carbon in Britain has been estimated at *very* roughly £10/t C (£3/t CO_2) (Adger and Brown, 1994; Adger *et al.*, 1997a, b). If a small fraction of the 150 million tonnes of carbon Britain releases each year were disposed of in forestry at this price, millions of pounds might be available for afforestation. This possibility raises two linked questions: would this forest creation significantly (1) enhance conservation and (2) diminish carbon levels? If so, diminishing climate change and enhancing habitat creation might share a common mechanism.

Britain is currently expanding its forests at 20 000–30 000 ha per annum (Anon., 1994b). These trees will be a sink for carbon only so long as they keep growing; thereafter, they will become, instead, a carbon store. Furthermore, the ideal forest for carbon sequestration is far from that which is ideal for wildlife: the best sequestration rates are achieved by fast-growing, generally exotic species, with low parasite / herbivore burdens, growing on good, fertile, well-watered land (see Brown *et al.*, 1996). For example, poplar, grown on an industrial scale in short-rotation coppice on good agricultural land in Britain, would sequester at 5 tC/ha/year. One million hectares of such 'woodland' could sequester only 3 % of Britain's annual emissions (Adger and Brown, 1994; Cannell and Dewar, 1995) – yet this is over 4 % of the land surface. The biophysics of the carbon cycle are very complicated with the result that despite afforestation, between 1947–1980 UK forestry was not a net CO_2 sink because soil carbon was released as land was prepared for planting (Adger *et al.*, 1994; Adger and Brown, 1994). Overall, the benefits to the global carbon dioxide budget from even massive forestry activity within Britain seem likely to be trivial (Brown *et al.*, 1996; Adger *et al.*, 1997b).

Therefore, while it would be foolish to dismiss the potential, and not least the public appeal, of the idea of carbon offset afforestation, we suspect that this mechanism is unlikely to contribute significantly to carbon offset in the UK, and is therefore unlikely to fund on a large scale tree planting suitable for conservation. Furthermore, woodland creation is only one type, albeit an important type, of habitat enhancement required by the radical agenda for mammal conservation.

Mitigation banking

While it seems to us the carbon offset does not offer significant hope as a means of paying for radical enhancement of British mammal habitats, the concept behind such swaps may be crucially relevant. Related concepts already operate. For example, in North America the process called mitigation banking allows the development of land if an even greater area of similar or better land is purchased by the developer and protected in perpetuity. This thinking need not be restricted to swapping land, but could embrace the trading in permits between environmental 'goods' and 'bads' of any type, including pollutants, habitats and species, with relative values set by scientists and society. Obviously, such a scheme would require strict regulation, and should under no circumstances provide a soft option for developers and polluters. Furthermore, the financial value of conservation is very hard to measure (Brown and Shogren, 1998), and calculations of environmental damage and opportunity costs will also be difficult (Brown *et al.*, 1996). However, since it is inescapable that trade will create environmental costs, there will always be opportunity for society to require these to be compensated if a suitable metric can be found for doing so. Indeed, the Clean Development Mechanism for tradable carbon credits agreed at Buenos Aires in 1998 illustrates the topicality of such mechanisms. These swaps might be direct (one piece of land for another), but more likely the trade will not be like for like (carbon emissions might be swapped for habitat restored). Industry causing an environmental 'bad' might pay for a corresponding environmental 'good' through an 'Environment Fund', operating not dissimilarly to the HLF. The costs of environmental damage, or its mitigation would be swapped for conservation cost and action. In the case of carbon, conversion could involve payment to the Environment Fund in direct relation to tonnes of carbon emitted. This might involve agreement on the value of the economic damage done per unit of CO_2 (estimated at $50–100/t C; Houghton, 1997); or the market value of carbon offsets per unit CO_2 (e.g., $20–£20/t C); or the cost of the cheapest method to offset CO_2: tropical forest protection (estimated at $0.4–15/t C) (Brown *et al.*, 1996). If approximately 154 million tonnes of carbon per year from Britain were linked to payment at $0.4–15/t, somewhere between $62 million and $2.3 billion would be available for the Environmental Fund each year!

In this context it is interesting to ask how much conservation projects might cost. Multi-million pound projects have been supported by the EU, especially in the Northern Parks, and the HLF has donated more than £500 000 to the Gower's AONB. The UK government's plans to create between 1994–97 an additional 60 000 ha of woodland were costed after grant subsidy at £90 million (this is an area equivalent to a forest of 20 × 30 km, and thus bigger than Isle Royale – see above – or 6000 km, of woodland corridor 100 m wide). Allowing natural regeneration along a 100 m wide corridor through Grade 2 arable land might cost £40 000/km for land purchase. Currently, a 12 000 ha estate in the Cairngorms is on sale for £7 million. Taking some southern examples, albeit at a smaller scale, there are guidelines for likely transaction and management costs. At Pinkhill Meadow in Oxfordshire a plan to create a mosaic of wetland habitats including permanent and temporary water, gravel islands, mudflats, reedbeds, wet grassland and scrub cost £112 000 for only 2 ha. The cost to restore an ancient water meadow system, Sherbourne Water Meadows, and thus improve the ecological value of the floodplain, was £120 000 for 57 ha. To restore 2.5 km of the River Cole channel from a straightened and deepened profile into a meandering, shallow profile and to re-establish natural integration of the river with its floodplain cost £140 000 for 25 ha (Driver, 1997). The Royal Society for the Protection of Birds (RSPB) has recently raised £600 000 towards restoration of 103 ha of Otmoor, Oxfordshire, with £500 000 from the HLF.

The costs of all these projects are high in the context of current conservation spending, but they are trifling in the context of the costs of carbon emissions alone, not to mention the wide array of other sources of environmental damage for which society might decide the polluter should pay.

CONCLUSIONS

Britain is a small island on which a great deal has been achieved for mammal conservation, much of it by working at a local scale. Often, this involves effort at a particular site, with a focus on one species. The achievements of this concentrated focus on a small scale are legion: our purpose has not been to diminish this approach, but rather to raise the question of whether these vital building blocks can be assembled into a fortress for the nation's conservation estate. The shortage of funding that characterises much of conservation work, and acceptance of the fact that conservation can only be squeezed into small corners of the countryside, may unnecessarily limit the canvas on which conservation plans are drawn. Too small a focus risks, on the one hand, missing opportunities for radical change and, on the other, a preoccupation with minutiae akin to treating the external symptoms of a systemic disease. In this case, the underlying cause of the 'disease' is often insufficient and overly fragmented wild habitat, and the cure may require action at the scale of landscapes. We have sought to draw attention to the exciting prospect that fundamental changes could be achieved by tackling conservation at the scale of landscapes or catchments. This is in accord with modern thinking, embodied in the concepts of Natural Areas, on behalf of the statutory agencies for conservation. The public, business and government all now have options for environmental damage mitigation and conservation enhancement which could make a real difference to the systemic problems that could be cured by habitat enhancement.

A radical agenda for landscape level conservation of mammals, and other wildlife too, is by definition a big job. Furthermore, it is a long-term operation. However, it is not unrealistic. We sense a growing realisation, clearly embodied by the Climate Change and Biological Diversity Conventions, that the environment is everybody's problem, and that its protection must be paid for. Society has the power to require the adjustment of economic instruments better to foster environmental goals; the reform of the Common Agriculture Policy is an obvious starting point. The 'greening' of such regulatory instruments could cost society rather little while revolutionising the budgets available to conservation. In short, we think it may be timely to stand back from the local focus of some conservation thinking, lest we be found to have fiddled while Rome burned, and to explore the mind-game of a more radical future for British mammal conservation. That exploration might usefully progress through the steps of fostering, recording, enhancing and enriching the fauna: a succession which we hope is memorably captured in the acronym FREE British Mammals. With the help of charismatic mammals, the possibility is there to win a radical future for British wildlife generally.

ACKNOWLEDGEMENTS

Part of the inspiration for this chapter came from discussions on mammal monitoring with Steve Gibson and Tom Tew of the JNCC, and from the team that worked with us on the MaMoNet project funded by DETR and JNCC, all of whom we thank. The other part came from conversations with those concerned with economic instruments to promote environmental policy, notably Dieter Helm and David Slater of OXERA Environmental Ltd. The chapter benefited hugely from the tireless energies of Clive Hambler and Sophie Stafford, and also from comments on earlier drafts by Ian Brown, Alastair Driver, Steve Gibson, Fiona Mathews, Gus Mills, Mike Packer and Francoise Tattersall.

11

Conservation of large mammals in Africa. What lessons and challenges for the future?

PHILIP MURUTHI, MARK STANLEY PRICE, PRITPAL
SOORAE, CYNTHIA MOSS AND ANNETTE LANJOUW

INTRODUCTION

How can single species conservation efforts in Africa be given greater effectiveness? In this chapter, we ask what lessons might be learnt from past efforts spent on conserving specific populations of large mammals and suggest future conservation action. Our case studies are the elephant *Loxodonta africana* of Amboseli in southern Kenya; the mountain gorilla *Gorilla gorilla berengei* in the Democratic Republic of Congo (DRC), Rwanda and Uganda; black rhinoceros *Diceros bicornis* in Kenya; and the hirola antelope *Damaliscus hunteri* in Kenya. We have selected these particular case studies because they are familiar to us. Our organisation, the African Wildlife Foundation (AWF), has had a long-term commitment to the conservation of these species and their habitats. The four case studies illustrate successes and problems in African species and ecosystem conservation. With the exception of the hirola, all the study species have either stable or increasing populations after experiencing alarming declines in the recent past.

CASE STUDY 1. ELEPHANTS AT AMBOSELI IN KENYA

The Amboseli elephant population has been monitored continuously since 1972. The population declined in the 1970s due to poaching and drought (Moss, 1988, 1994; unpublished data). A reversal in the downward population trend has occurred since the beginning of 1979 with the population now growing dramatically (Figure 11.1). The Amboseli elephant population is growing at an annual rate of 3.9 % through breeding alone (C. Moss, unpublished data)

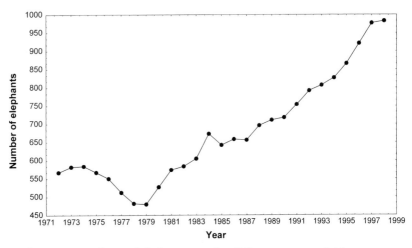

Figure 11.1 Population of elephants at Amboseli from 1972 to 1998. The population declined in the 1970s due to poaching and drought. A reversal in the downward population trend has occurred since the beginning of 1979 with the population now growing dramatically.

Until the mid- to late-1970s, the Amboseli elephant population was little disturbed by human activity. Their movements were natural, seasonal events resulting in relatively minor effects on the habitat (Western and Lindsay, 1984). Poaching in the 1970s led to the confinement of elephants inside the park (Laws *et al.*, 1975). However, with increased security and tolerance by local Maasai people, Amboseli elephants are now spending much more time outside the park, ranging on Maasai Group Ranches and across the border into Tanzania.

In 1973, after many negotiations with central government, the Maasai vacated 390 km² of land which then became Amboseli National Park. Because most of the swamps are located inside the park, this move denied the Maasai their dry season grazing. The Maasai were promised adequate water supplies outside the park. They would also be compensated for the cost of tolerating wildlife grazing on their group ranch lands, and obtain direct economic benefits through development of wildlife viewing and tourist campsites and through services provided by the government. According to Lindsay (1987), between 1983 and 1985 three rhino and over 20 elephants were speared by Maasai in protest against the park and inadequate water supplies. The conflict situation has not abated and between January and November 1997, at least 15 elephants, representing over 75 % of the population's mortality for the period, had been killed in conflict situations with local people (C. Moss, unpublished data).

Lessons learnt

As elephants continue to utilise communal lands, long-term means must be sought to alleviate antagonism between nature preservation and the needs of Maasai people for land and adequate livelihoods. The Amboseli area urgently requires a land use policy, developed with full participation of the Maasai, to cater for an expanding range of interests and for the benefit of local people and wildlife conservation. Through such a policy, and efforts to encourage coexistence outside the park, pressure on habitat inside the park will be reduced to allow regeneration of vegetation. After all, the park was not designed to be a self-sufficient unit but as part of a multiple land-use system (Western, 1973).

At Amboseli, conflicts occur over shared resources such as space, water and forage or over crop damage in cultivated fields east of the park. Wildlife managers should understand the nature of conflicts between humans and wildlife and seek innovative ways to mitigate them. One successful approach being applied by AWF in the Amboseli area is a 'consolation scheme' under which a landowner whose livestock is killed by an elephant is paid for the loss in order to prevent retaliatory spearing of elephants. We should also build upon the positive attitude that Maasai have towards wildlife with which they have coexisted for centuries (Kangwana, 1993). The increase in the elephant population since 1979 runs against the continuing collapse of elephant populations elsewhere, a measure of the protection given by the Kenya government and the Maasai around Amboseli. The task now is to maintain such a positive attitude given the transition in lifestyles that the Maasai are undergoing (Kituyi, 1990; Western, 1994).

At the country level, Kenya and Tanzania should develop common transboundary initiatives aimed at conserving wildlife, and to foster cooperation and security. The population of elephants and the Maasai community straddle their common border. International forces and a strong expatriate lobby within Kenya have influenced conservation at Amboseli (Western, 1994). International funding has enabled Cynthia Moss to conduct 25 years of research on Amboseli elephants. Through her work supported by AWF, the elephants are well-known all over the world with a positive benefit in increased numbers of tourists visiting Amboseli. Tourism has made a significant contribution to the conservation of Amboseli elephants. Through it Amboseli National Park and its wildlife earn both the local and national governments significant revenue. When tourism grew at 22 % per annum between 1965 and 1969, it contributed more than 70 % of the local Kajiado County Council's income (Western, 1969). The Maasai leadership and national government see the park and its wildlife as valuable resources which they strive to protect.

CASE STUDY 2. MOUNTAIN GORILLAS

The mountain gorilla population is divided into two subpopulations separated by less than 25 km. One is found in the Bwindi Impenetrable National Park (BINP), covering about 330 km² in Uganda. The other, in the Virunga Volcano Region (VVR), straddles three national parks in three countries: Mgahinga Gorilla National Park in Uganda (27 km²); Volcano National Park in Rwanda (125 km²); and Virunga National Park in DRC (approximately 250 km²). There are about 600 mountain gorillas, about 300 of which are in the BINP (Butynski and Kalina, 1993; IGCP, unpublished data).

Threats to the mountain gorillas include poaching, forest encroachment, disease, inbreeding, refugee crises, civil unrest and institutional instability (Kalpers, 1991). Gorilla habitat is under pressure from humans seeking land and forest products. VVR and BINP are located in a region that has over 300 people/km² with a high rate of population increase, and this is putting pressure on the natural resources (Werikhe *et al.*, 1997). Threats to mountain gorillas increased during the crisis in Rwanda from 1994 to 1996, and the subsequent mass exodus of over one million refugees into DRC. Thousands of people were entering the park each day on the DRC side, harvesting wood for fuel, construction and furniture, hunting for food and in at least one case, killing a gorilla to obtain an infant for subsequent sale. This serious threat decreased when the refugees left the camps in 1996. However, the institutions responsible for protected area management are only just starting to regain their momentum and funding, training and institutional capacity and are still relatively weak.

The mountain gorilla is especially susceptible to human diseases, as its genetic makeup is close to that of humans. Paradoxically, groups regularly visited by tourists have the highest rates of reproduction (Barnes, 1994) and this may be because these groups are better protected from poachers than those not regularly visited. Additionally, because they occur in small populations, mountain gorillas face the risk of inbreeding.

In 1990, the consortium members of the Mountain Gorilla Project (MGP) (AWF, Fauna & Flora International and World Wide Fund for Nature–International), which since 1979 had operated only on the Rwanda side of the VVR, established the International Gorilla Conservation Programme (IGCP) to cover all three countries where mountain gorillas occurred. The IGCP is not solely a 'single-species rescue mission', but a mechanism for increasing cooperation between protected area authorities and their partners in the region, and developing a regional approach to conservation of a shared habitat. The IGCP promotes the conservation of the mountain gorilla as a 'flagship species' of the afro-montane forest and as a source of tourism-based revenue for the region. The programme operates through protected area authorities in each country.

Activities of the IGCP include park management (gorilla and habitat protection at field level), institutional capacity building, developing integrated regional processes and tools, promoting local community participation in conservation, and improving policy context for environmental management. Wherever possible, activities are coordinated within the three countries, and approaches and methods are harmonised. The IGCP has supported regular meetings between field-based park staff of the three countries and worked with the protected area authorities to develop a framework for regional collaboration in the transfrontier areas of the VVR. This Integrated Regional Conservation Framework is a primary objective of the IGCP.

Lessons learnt

The approach of forming a coalition of conservation organisations to work towards the protection of a threatened habitat and flagship species throughout its entire range, has proved effective and necessary in this volatile and difficult region. By pooling the different approaches, strengths and expertise of each IGCP coalition member into one programme, the knowledge, experience and resources available are increased. Although the different management styles and approaches of each of the organisations can have costs on the coalition, they enable the programme to benefit from flexibility which would not be obvious were only one organisation involved. Sharing the responsibility for funding of the IGCP enhances the ability of each organisation to raise funds, thus adding to sustainability and ability to make long-term commitment to conservation of the species and its habitat.

Financial flexibility and diversity must be built into long-term conservation programmes. Each IGCP coalition member contributes equally to the 'core budget' but the programme also raises funds from outside sources for specific activities. Increasing the number of sources of funding increases financial security for the IGCP, and ensures that its activities do not become 'donor driven'. This is critical because politics can influence the willingness of donors to fund conservation activities. The IGCP concentrates on developing a regional framework for conservation within the three countries, which lack a common conservation strategy for mountain gorillas and their habitat. The area is small enough to be managed cooperatively, and the ecological, socio-economic, cultural and ethnic set-up in the area is more or less uniform across the borders. Finally, gorilla tourism is an important source of revenue in each of the three countries, thus providing an opportunity for collaboration. The benefits of regional cooperation, be it as a 'Peace Park' or a transfrontier protected area, are numerous (Kalpers and Lanjouw, 1997). The IGCP has supported regional and bilateral meetings, unofficial encounters and attendance at conferences/meetings to ensure that the protected area authorities are communicating at all levels.

The weak national economies of the three countries reduce the ability of the protected area authorities to be effective. The IGCP has provided equipment for both the field staff and offices, as in the case of Rwanda in August 1994 after the genocide and civil war. The IGCP provides technical assistance to develop policies for nature-based and gorilla tourism programmes and works towards increasing the involvement of local communities in conservation activities. In Rwanda, the IGCP has brought other partners (CARE–International) into the arena with the protected area authorities and ministries responsible for the environment, to link conservation activities with development for local communities. These activities aim at sustainable parks through bringing benefits of conservation to those upon whom it is ultimately dependent.

The IGCP has found that when providing technical advice and focusing on the development of institutional capacity, the long-term relationship of trust that it builds with protected area authorities is fundamental. After they lost most of their equipment and facilities during the genocide, Rwanda's Organisation de Tourisme et des Parcs Nationaux (ORTPN) contacted the IGCP for help in developing short- and medium-term plans for the authority. The IGCP facilitated a planning meeting, followed up by a 'partner meeting' involving other potential donors to OPTPN leading to the development of emergency programmes to protect parks and mountain gorillas. In DRC, after the change in government in early 1997, the IGCP performed the same role again for the Institut Congolais pour la Conservation de la Nature (ICCN).

CASE STUDY 3. THE BLACK RHINO IN KENYA

The world population of black rhinos declined from around 65 000 in 1970 to 2400 in 1995, a fall of 96 % (Emslie, 1996). This decline was primarily due to poaching. The current world population of black rhino is about 2500 individuals in four strongholds – Kenya, Namibia, South Africa and Zimbabwe. Of the estimated 1500 rhino in Kenya in 1980, only 381 remained by 1987. As populations of black rhinos in Kenya continued to decline in spite

of extensive conservation measures, it became clear that only effective security of each population would provide long-term hope.

Subsequently, due to the intensified anti-poaching efforts and transfer
of animals into secured sanctuaries begun in 1985 (Western, 1987), the
population has risen to the present estimated 430 rhinos. Populations inside sanctuaries have increased, through breeding at about 4 % per annum
since 1991, while those outside sanctuaries have decreased during the same
period (Brett, 1991).

An overall objective of the Kenya rhino programme is to manage the
country's rhinos as a metapopulation thus maintaining long-term genetic
diversity and demographic stability. A more immediate objective is to attain
a population of 600 black rhino by the year 2000 (Emslie, 1996). Activities
towards these goals are undertaken through cooperation between the
Kenya Wildlife Service (KWS), non-governmental organisations (NGOs),
and private landowners. Representatives of these organisations sit with
many KWS staff on the National Rhino Management Committee. This de-
liberates on all rhino conservation matters and agrees on subsequent conservation action to be undertaken by KWS as the implementing
government agency. NGOs also provide assistance to the rhino programme
through direct funding and supplying equipment for monitoring rhinos
and maintenance of sanctuaries.

Monitoring is important in order to keep track of changes in the population and to act promptly if individual rhino are known to face a particular
risk of being poached. It is also important that Kenya's rhinos are to be
managed as a metapopulation. At present however, monitoring is far from
perfect as the Kenya rhino programme suffers staff and vehicle shortages.
Large areas may not be covered and individual rhinos not protected.
Monitoring in the field is complicated because some rhinos are not marked
and thus cannot be individually identified. Additionally, the difficult terrain
and thick vegetation make it impossible to locate individuals at frequent
intervals and make a quick and accurate assessment of the total number of
rhino in an area.

There are 17 locations in Kenya with rhino, seven of which are unfenced. Of the country's 430 rhinos, 314 are found in fenced areas at an
overall density of about 0.24 rhino/km². The rest are found in unfenced
areas at an overall density of 0.06 rhino/km². With adequate security in
place, the ultimate aim would be to move rhinos bred within sanctuaries to
help repopulate areas where populations have been wiped out by poachers.
After rhino numbers exceeded their carrying capacities in a few sanctuaries, Kenya undertook the first rhino 'free release' at Tsavo East National

Park in 1993 and 1994. This 'free release' has been successful and this population is increasing through breeding. Kenya's sanctuary approach to rhino conservation has reversed population declines and contributed to returning rhinos to areas where they can roam without the confines of fences. Rhino populations that have shown no growth need special attention. Very small or fragmented populations show little prospect for growth. Isolated individuals should be captured and moved to other areas to augment the viability of existing populations. In other Kenyan rhino sanctuaries, numbers have not increased in spite of the absence of poaching. Rhino populations in some newly established sanctuaries have shown slow growth or no breeding at all. Finally, some populations such as those of the Maasai Mara cross the international border into adjacent Tanzania. Their protection depends on collaboration between the two countries.

Lessons learnt

Security and monitoring remain by far the most important considerations for rhino conservation in Kenya. Security must always be high especially in fenced areas where many rhino are concentrated within relatively small areas making them vulnerable to poaching. Continuous monitoring and frequent censuses are necessary for effective rhino management. Monitoring must be made more effective, for example, by combining foot patrols with vehicle and aircraft patrols. Furthermore, there is need to research the use of modern technologies for tracking rhinos (du Toit, 1996). Towards this end, AWF has supported the design and field testing of a suitable radio collar for rhinos at Madikwe Game Reserve in South Africa and the use of Global Positioning Systems (GPS) for accurate patrol work in Natal. At the Waterberg Plateau Park in Namibia, AWF is supporting a creative scheme in which rhino monitors are paid incentive money commensurate with their productivity in rhino monitoring and surveillance.

Overall, Kenya's rhino programme should instigate priority activities that achieve the goal of attaining a population of 600 animals by the year 2000, before any genetic management of populations. The present population falls short of the 7.5 % net annual growth rate necessary for the metapopulation to achieve the target for the year 2000. The programme should be managed flexibly, thereby assessing conservation actions and if necessary modifying approaches. Inadequate monitoring will result in an inability to manage rhinos as a metapopulation. Managing as a metapopulation will require good knowledge of sex-ratios, age structure and individuals. Managing rhinos to maintain genetic diversity will involve moving individuals between sites and might jeopardise their demographic performance because of the potential negative effects of handling. Furthermore, experience shows that moving animals between established populations is a very high risk activity. With adequate monitoring in the field, a Population Habitat Viability Analysis (PHVA) will help formulate a metapopulation strategy through which all rhinos would be managed interactively to maintain genetic diversity and demographic stability. Individuals from isolated and small populations should be moved to sanctuaries for their safety and contribution to breeding.

We need to understand other factors limiting rhino population growth. It is suspected that declines in carrying capacity, especially in a few fenced areas, have led to a drop in reproductive rates (Brett, 1991). The assessment of carrying capacity for rhinos needs updating. This is also necessary if surplus rhinos are to be removed from areas where the population is approaching carrying capacity. To accomplish this, it is necessary to improve ecological monitoring. Rhino sanctuaries should be managed even if it means removing other species, such as elephants, which from the rhino's perspective cause habitat deterioration.

Success in rhino conservation shows that pooling expertise, experiences and funds from many stakeholders is necessary to counteract threats to conservation. At the regional level, there is a need to facilitate the exchange of expertise and information between countries. Kenya's success with the sanctuary model shows that in-country breeding in almost natural conditions is possible and makes it easy to return rhinos to the wild when security permits.

CASE STUDY 4. THE HIROLA ANTELOPE IN KENYA

The hirola, a critically endangered antelope species, is confined to a small area of the plains in the Garissa district of southeastern Kenya (IUCN, 1994; East et al., 1996). The status of the population in Somalia is not known (Magin, 1996). During the 1980s, conservationists noticed an impending crisis due to a marked decline in estimates of the hirola population (Hillman et al., 1988: figure 2). However it was not until 1995 that the Kenya Wildlife Service conducted an aerial census specifically for the species. The Hirola Task Force (HTF) was formed in late 1995 as a response to the crisis. The HTF hired a consultant to the Species Survival Commission of IUCN who developed a recovery plan for the hirola (Magin, 1996). The recovery plan summarised available information on the ecology and status of hirola, and presented a strategy for its in situ and ex situ conservation.

Hirola are threatened by poaching, competition with livestock, range

Mountain gorilla, *Gorilla gorilla beringei*, Democratic Republic of Congo.
Photograph: Ian Redmond.

deterioration, disease and lack of information on population status (Magin,
1996). Faced with difficulties in conserving the hirola in its original range
due to prevailing insecurity, the HTF resolved to translocate about 100
hirola to safer grounds and bolster the survival chances of the estimated 50
to 80 individuals in Tsavo East National Park.

The first translocation was completed successfully in August 1996
when 35 hirola were captured north of the Tana and 30 released in Tsavo

East National Park. Subsequent translocation of hirola to Tsavo East National Park was stopped through a court injunction filed in the Kenya High Court by the local residents within the hirola's natural range who objected to the transfer of the species (*Daily Nation* newspaper, Nairobi, 30 August 1996). The survival of the population at Tsavo East is of interest. For reasons yet to be understood, the translocated hirola population experienced losses approaching 50 % and had no surviving young (Soorae, 1997).

Lessons learnt

The hirola is facing the risk of extinction and more concerted national and international efforts are needed to avert this crisis. Implementation of the Hirola Recovery Plan (Magin, 1996) is a very high priority in international antelope conservation. Meanwhile, frequent censuses and monitoring are necessary in order to understand the current population status. Security must be effective before threats to hirola conservation can be addressed in their original range.

With the prevailing bad security situation in the hirola's original range, the translocation to Tsavo East National Park may be critical to saving the hirola from extinction. Further translocations should be considered if and when finances, legal decisions and local community support allow. The support of local communities and politicians must be won before any future translocation is undertaken. Monitoring and research is needed to understand factors limiting hirola population growth in Tsavo East National Park and appropriate measures taken to remedy the situation.

An evaluation of past conservation efforts and the translocation of 1996 being prepared by the HTF will be very informative for future conservation action. There is a need to evaluate the success of the various methods used in capturing, moving and releasing the animals and documentation of the causes of mortality. Population and habitat viability modelling is necessary to allow an evaluation of the probability of extinction of the hirola populations and the likely impacts of management interventions.

GENERAL LESSONS FOR CONSERVATION OF LARGE MAMMALS IN AFRICA

Lessons learnt through the four case studies show that the conservation of a large mammal species should be considered within an overall focus on conservation of habitats and the overall threats facing the species in the area. The approach must be multidisciplinary. To de-emphasise the boundaries between protected areas and surrounding pastoral lands with the aim of ensuring that wildlife continues to have access to areas outside parks and reserves, landowners must be given incentives to tolerate or welcome the situation. For the elephant, the two fundamental conservation concerns are how habitat can be effectively secured for elephants and how to mitigate human–elephant conflicts. An effective conservation approach has to integrate ecological knowledge, working with traditional Maasai institutions (starting at the neighbourhood level), training of individuals at all levels, and capacity building of local Maasai communities to improve their ability to manage and benefit from wildlife/elephant conservation. This approach is working for the outreach project in support of elephant conservation in the Amboseli area being undertaken by AWF.

All these case studies show that political support is key to the success of large mammal conservation in Africa. All stakeholders should participate fully. The success of the 'consolation scheme' at Amboseli can be attributed to the participation of the local Maasai at all stages of its planning and implementation. On the other hand, the case of the hirola illustrates that poor security, and political pressures from local communities can hinder conservation efforts. The Hirola Task Force had garnered enough national and international resources to carry out the translocation in 1996, but it was impossible to complete the transfer without the approval of the local population.

Where the habitat spans international borders (e.g., with the mountain gorilla, black rhino and elephant), the approach should be regional. A common vision is needed between countries that share wildlife populations if conservation is to be effective. This vision should also be shared and encouraged by other partners in conservation as illustrated by the successful work of the IGCP.

Conservation of large mammals in Africa will benefit from innovative approaches such as those in monitoring and surveillance (black rhino), funding (mountain gorilla) and partnerships (all case studies). Where monitoring and surveillance are key to the survival of the species, there will be need to incorporate modern technology in conservation efforts to make them cost-effective and accurate. Working in a politically volatile region, the IGCP has found that it needs to have flexible funding in order to respond to crises. Financial diversity and flexibility reduce the vulnerability of the conservation programme and decrease its tendency of being 'donor-driven'. The conservation programme needs to have a diversity of activities, so that it can concentrate on different approaches, objectives and needs at different times, responding to the situation and circumstances. Strategic partnerships formed in response to specific conservation needs are useful for large mammal conservation in Africa as illustrated by the IGCP, the Hirola Task Force and the Kenya Rhino Management Committee. Such partnerships need not be formed in response to crises, as they would also be very useful in undertaking preventative conservation.

Programmes for the conservation of African large mammals develop long-term relationships with the different partners and stakeholders to ensure their sustainability. For the IGCP, finding appropriate staff who know the region and can tolerate upsets is the key to success. Finally, a conservation programme should establish a permanent presence in its region of operation, and keep information flow open and multidirectional. The conservation of large mammals in Africa stands to benefit enormously from the exchange of experiences and lessons learnt from the various projects such as those in conflict mitigation, and application of research findings to management.

12

Which mammals benefit from protection in East Africa?

TIM M. CARO, MARCEL REJMÁNEK AND NEIL PELKEY

INTRODUCTION

East Africa has one of the most developed networks of protected areas in the world, including well-known national parks such as Tsavo, Queen Elizabeth and Serengeti and famous game reserves such as the Selous (Siegfried et al., 1998). Many of these areas were originally set up for sport hunting in the early part of the twentieth century because professional hunters were attracted to places of high mammal abundance where it was easy to shoot trophy species (Selous, 1908; Roosevelt and Heller, 1922). Subsequently they became national parks or game reserves in the 1950s, 1960s and 1970s. These hunting grounds were often dry season refuges for mammals, attracted to a swamp (e.g.. Amboseli and Katavi) or river (e.g., the Nile and Great Ruaha Rivers) that held water year-round. Exceptionally, some hunting areas encompassed entire migratory routes such as the Serengeti Plains. When these areas came under formal protection, governments effectively inherited the legacy of sportsmen's choices of where best to hunt mammals. In this chapter, we investigate how effective these protected areas are in conserving mammals by asking three interrelated questions: (1) how well do these areas protect mammal diversity?; (2) which mammal species currently benefit most from protection?; and (3) which aspects of protection are the most important in conserving mammals in contemporary protected areas?

In recent years, there has been an increasing number of studies attempting to identify sites of high conservation value (Vane-Wright et al., 1991). These centre on locating places of maximal overlap in the distribution of species as an index of species richness (Williams and Gaston, 1994; Williams et al., 1996a), as well as locating areas of endemism (Thomas and Mallorie, 1985; Balmford and Long, 1994; see also Prendergast et al., 1993).

Obviously, the practical success of these research efforts ultimately depends on the political will to set these areas aside from future development. In light of this, it is extremely important to determine the extent to which existing protected areas coincide with areas of special conservation interest. Here we ask whether choice of protected areas based on mammal abundance in times past matches contemporary concern about protecting biodiversity in East Africa (Bibby *et al.*, 1992). We focus on mammals because they are a well documented taxonomic group in the region. If large mammal abundance is a poor predictor of larger mammal diversity (i.e., species richness), the network of protected areas in East Africa will need to be expanded to protect additional diversity before it disappears.

The purview of a fully protected area includes protecting features of topographical interest from destruction, wilderness habitat from agricultural and urban development, and animal and plant populations from hunting, collecting and other forms of exploitation. The effectiveness of protected areas in fulfilling these objectives depends, in part, on preventing encroachment and, in part, on the pressures outside area boundaries since an absence of external threat lessens the importance of protection, at least for the time being. In the second part of this chapter, we investigate the effectiveness of protection at two spatial scales: in a remote national park in western Tanzania; and across ten different census zones covering the whole country.

Even in fully protected areas that legally prohibit exploitation of resources, enforcement occurs at different levels both between and within them, ranging from parks and reserves with a well equipped ranger force, backed up by working vehicles and rifles; to those of benign neglect where patrols are rare or absent; to those in which the guardians illegally hunt and cut timber. Using variation in anti-poaching effort, researchers have recently begun to explore the most important aspects of anti-poaching in conserving large mammals in Africa. In the final part of the chapter, we collate these studies in order to identify common elements of anti-poaching that are most effective in conserving mammals in East Africa.

METHODS

Conservation areas in Tanzania

Much of the data presented in this chapter come from Tanzania. In that country, there are five main types of conservation area. National Parks (NPs) allow no settlements or human activities and these laws are enforced by Tanzania National Park rangers. Game Reserves (GRs), under the Department of Wildlife, are subject to the same legal restrictions except that they allow for limited hunting under licence, usually by tourist visitors, for approximately six months of the year (PAWM, 1995). Game Reserve laws are enforced year round by game scouts stationed at a headquarters and sometimes at outlying posts. Game Controlled Areas (GCAs) allow for settlement, cattle grazing and some timber extraction, as well as regulated hunting by tourists and residents. Regional and District Game Officers are normally responsible for issuing hunting permits to residents. Open Areas (OAs) are similar to GCAs except that some contain permanent settlements; as a result, firewood collection is more extensive. Forest Reserves (FRs) allow for hardwood extraction under licence and resident hunting. In general, laws pertaining to GCAs, OAs and FRs are rarely enforced owing to shortage of funds from central government.

Mammal abundance and diversity

To explore the association between large mammal abundance and diversity, we used both a small and detailed data set restricted to Tanzania, and an expanded data set covering Kenya, Rwanda, Tanzania and Uganda. The first consisted of population sizes of mammal species, mostly ungulates, in nine protected areas: Burigi–Biharamulo GRs, Katavi NP, Mikumi NP, Mkomazi GR, Ngorongoro Conservation Area, Ruaha NP, Selous GR, Serengeti NP and Tarangire NP (Figure 12.1). Data were collected using standardised aerial surveys conducted between October 1987 and 1994 by the Frankfurt Zoological Society, Serengeti Ecological Monitoring Programme and Tanzania Wildlife Conservation Monitoring (see Norton-Griffiths, 1978; SEMP, 1988a, b; Campbell and Borner, 1995 for details). Date of surveys and sources of information are listed in Caro *et al.* (1998a) but for one exception: we used an average of three counts to calculate ungulate population sizes in Ngorongoro Conservation Area (April 1987, October 1987 and March 1988; SEMP, 1988a, b). Elephant numbers across Tanzania were taken from counts made in 1987 (SEMP, 1989). We felt comfortable in using both NPs and GRs in this analysis as densities of large mammals differ little between the two sorts of area (Caro *et al.*, 1998a).

Many of the mammal populations migrate outside of the protected areas during periods of the year, thus the season in which an aerial survey is carried out can affect the population count within an area. For most protected areas, more than one survey had been conducted, so we took a mean for wet season counts and a mean for dry season counts, and then averaged these means.

Our expanded data set consisted of these nine areas in Tanzania in

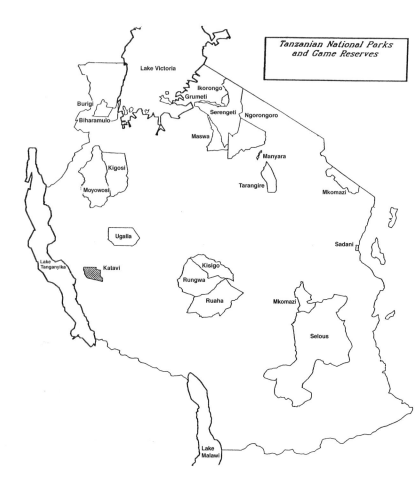

Figure 12.1 Location of national parks and game reserves in Tanzania used in this study.

addition to three from Uganda, three from Kenya, one from Rwanda and an additional one from Tanzania. Data were obtained from the literature as follows: Queen Elizabeth NP (Field and Laws, 1970; Eltringham and Wood-ford, 1973; Eltringham, 1977; Eltringham and Din, 1977); Kidepo NP (Ross *et al.*, 1976); Toro GR (Verner *et al.*, 1984); Tsavo NP (Leuthold and Leut-hold, 1976); Nairobi NP (Foster and Kearney, 1967); Lake Nakuru NP (Kutilek, 1974); Akagera NP (Spinage *et al.*, 1972); Manyara NP (Prins, 1996). In parks where more than one census was reported, we took an average. Despite these data coming from many sources and thus differing in quality, and being collected over a 26-year period and therefore being subject to environmental variation, they were the only data on mammal densities in the region that were available.

Biomass data were obtained from female bodyweights in Estes (1991). Following general procedure, female weights were multiplied by 0.75 to represent the weight of an average individual of that species (Schaller, 1972). For each species, average individual weight was multiplied by total estimated population size for an area to give an estimate of each species' biomass in that area. These figures for each species were subsequently added together and divided by the area of the NP or GR to yield a total biomass expressed in kg/km². Information on size of protected areas were collected from Serengeti Ecological Monitoring Program (SEMP) and Tanzania Wildlife Conservation Monitoring (TWCM) reports, from East (1988) or from sources listed above.

Data on the presence or absence of large and medium-sized mammal species (see Table 12.1) were obtained from many published and unpublished sources (M. Rejmánek, unpublished) and extended using detailed distribution maps in Kingdon (1977) and East (1988). Where possible, distribution data were cross-checked with researchers who were or had recently worked in these areas (Serengeti, Ngorongoro, Katavi: T. Caro, F. Selous and S. Creel; Mikumi: G. Norton; Tanzania protected areas: A. Rodgers; Uganda protected areas: M. Rejmánek and J. Baranga). Mammals were classified into definitely present, probably present, or absent. We combined the first two categories as this gave the same result as restricting ourselves to the first measure only.

Species benefiting from protection: ground surveys

A detailed study was conducted in and immediately adjacent to Katavi National Park in Mpanda District of Rukwa Region, western Tanzania between September 1995 and December 1996 (Caro, 1999a). The area consists largely of miombo, dry forest habitat (Rodgers, 1996) with a single distinct wet season. The study area consisted of four conservation areas: a NP, a GCA, a FR and an OA. To determine densities of mammals in these four conservation areas, a total of 2953 km of transects were driven in a Land Rover at < 10 km/hour along the same established but minor tracks once during every month of the study except April and July 1996; transects ranged in length from 0.7–31.1 km (X= 11.5 km, N= 20 transects) (Caro, 1999a, b).

During each transect a note was made of all species of mammal seen that were larger than a rat (Table 12.2). As soon as a mammal was sighted,

Table 12.1

Mammal species examined in this chapter

Common name	Latin name	Difficult to census? air	Difficult to census? ground	B	G	A
Small antelope*						
duiker	*Cephalophus and Sylvicapra* species	Yes	Yes	+	+	+
oribi	*Ourebia ourebi*	Yes	Yes	+	+	+
steenbok	*Raphicerus campestris*	Yes	Yes	+		+
klipspringer	*Oreotragus oreotragus*	Yes	Yes		+	
Baboon*						
olive	*Papio anubis*	No	No	+		+
yellow	*Papio cyanocephalus*	No	No	+	+	+
Buffalo	*Syncerus caffer*	No	No	+	+	+
Bushbuck	*Tragelaphus scriptus*	Yes	Yes	+	+	+
Bushpig	*Potamochoerus porcus*	Yes	Yes	+	+	+
Small carnivore[a]		NA	Yes	+		
Eland	*Taurotragus oryx*	No	No	+	+	+
Elephant	*Loxondota africana*	No	No	+	+	+
Gazelle*						
Grant's	*Gazella granti*	No	No	+		+
Thomson's	*Gazella thomsoni*	No	No	+		+
Gerenuk	*Litocranius walleri*	No	No	+		
Giraffe	*Giraffa camelopardalis*	No	No	+	+	+
Hartebeest*						
Coke's	*Alcelaphus buselaphus*	No	No	+	+	+
Red	*Alcelaphus caama*	No	No	+		+
Hippopotamus	*Hippopotamus amphibius*	Yes	Yes	+	+	+
Impala	*Aepyceros melampus*	No	No	+	+	+
Kudu*						
Greater	*Tragelaphus strepsiceros*	Yes	No	+	+	+
Lesser	*Tragelaphus imberbis*	Yes	No	+		+
Lion	*Panthera leo*	Yes	Yes	+		
Small mammal[b]		NA	Yes	+		
Mongoose[c]		NA	Yes	+		
Oryx	*Oryx gazella*	Yes	Yes	+		

Table 12.1
(cont.)

Common name	Latin name	Difficult to census? air	ground	B	G	A
Kob	*Kobus kob*	No	Yes	+		
Reedbuck*						
Bohor	*Redunca redunca*	Yes	Yes	+	+	+
Southern	*Redunca arundinum*	Yes	Yes	+		+
Rhinoceros	*Diceros bicornis*	No	Yes	+		
Roan antelope	*Hippotragus equinus*	No	No	+	+	+
Sable antelope	*Hippotragus niger*	No	No	+	+	+
Sitatunga	*Tragelaphus spekii*	Yes	Yes	+		
Spotted hyaena	*Crocuta crocuta*	Yes	Yes		+	
Topi	*Damaliscus lunatus*	No	No	+	+	+
Vervet monkey	*Cercopithecus aethiops*	NA	No	+		
Warthog	*Phacochoerus aethiopicus*	Yes	No	+	+	+
Waterbuck	*Kobus ellipsiprymnus*	No	No	+	+	+
Wildebeest	*Connochaetes taurinus*	No	No	+		+
Zebra	*Equus burchellii*	No	No	+	+	+

B: biomass study; G: ground censuses; A: aerial censuses; + denotes used in this chapter. NA denotes not counted from the air. * species were combined in the national survey comparisons; species groupings are referred to as species in the text.
[a] Leopard (*Panthera pardus*), wild dog (*Lycaon pictus*), serval (*Leptailurus serval*), ratel (*Mellivora capensis*) and side-striped jackal (*Canis adustus*) combined; [b] Hare (*Lepus capensis*) and squirrel combined; [c] Banded (*Mungos mungo*), dwarf (*Helogale parvula*), black-tipped (*Galerella sanguinea*) and marsh mongoose (*Atilax paludinosus*) combined.

the vehicle was stopped and a record was made of the number of individuals within the group. To calculate the area of each transect, a nearly continuous record was made of the distance at which mammals could be seen on each side of it. Thus, at the start of the transect, the observer estimated the distance at which an adult warthog, *Phacochoerus aethiopicus*, would still be visible and wrote this down for right and left hand sides of the track; estimated distances were checked repeatedly against markers at base camp. Five hundred metres was set as the maximum distance visible on each side. Subsequently, area was calculated by multiplying transect widths by lengths for each side of the transect and summing them. For each species

Table 12.2

Mean densities of mammals per km^2 inside and outside Katavi National Park (KNP); N refers to number of transects. Also shown are z values and P values on Mann–Whitney U tests

Species	Inside KNP (N=7)	Outside KNP (N=13)	z value	P value
Antelope (small)	0.06	0.38	−1.646	N.S.
Baboon	0.01	0.07	−0.191	N.S.
Buffalo	21.15	3.81	2.874	0.004
Bushbuck	0.04	0.03	2.589	0.010
Bushpig	0.07	0	2.947	0.003
Carnivore (small)	0.04	0	2.947	0.003
Eland	1.45	0.01	3.580	< 0.001
Elephant	1.96	0.03	3.399	0.001
Giraffe	2.17	0.68	2.906	0.004
Hartebeest	0.35	0.90	−0.683	N.S.
Hippopotamus	5.15	0	3.385	0.001
Impala	0.72	1.18	2.559	0.011
Kudu (Greater)	0.01	0.02	−0.380	N.S.
Lion	0.07	0	2.947	0.003
Mammal (small)	0.01	0	1.977	0.048
Mongoose	0.21	0.13	1.524	N.S.
Reedbuck	0.39	0.08	1.757	N.S.
Roan antelope	0.19	0.08	2.185	0.029
Sable antelope	0	0	0	N.S.
Spotted hyaena	0.19	0	4.231	< 0.001
Topi	2.13	0.09	3.166	0.002
Vervet	0.47	0.10	1.348	N.S.
Warthog	1.34	0.56	2.582	0.010
Waterbuck	4.28	0.18	3.394	0.001
Zebra	5.64	0.81	2.794	0.005

or constellation of species, density was calculated by adding the total number of individuals seen on a given transect and dividing by the area visible. For each transect and for each species, average densities were calculated across all 14 months over which data were collected. These mean densities for the seven transects in Katavi NP were then compared to 13 transects driven in the other three conservation areas outside the Park.

Species benefiting from protection: aerial surveys

We also examined densities of mammal species (see Table 12.1) in NPs and GRs across the whole of Tanzania and compared them with those in GCAs and OAs using the same aerial censuses as those in the biomass calculations (see above). These four types of conservation area were found in ten census zones: Burigi–Biharmalo; Katavi; Mkomazi; Moyowosi–Kigosi; Ruaha–Rungwa–Kisigo; Sadani; Selous–Mikumi; Serengeti–Maswa–Ikorongo–Grumeti; Tarangire; and Ugalla (Figure 12.1) (see Caro *et al.*, 1998a, b for details). Rainfall, vegetation type and human population pressure vary geographically across Tanzania but are fairly similar within each census zone. To take account of this variation, we used each census zone as its own control. Thus for each individual aerial census within a census zone, we calculated each species' density over the total area irrespective of conservation area within that zone. We then calculated densities in each type of conservation area within that census zone, and subtracted each from the census zone overall density to yield a standardised density for that species in each conservation area. If more than one survey of a census zone had been conducted, we calculated the average of standardised scores for each conservation area for wet and dry season counts separately, and then took an average of these seasonal averages. Statistical tests were conducted on these average standardised scores (see Caro *et al.*, 1998a).

Aspects of protection

To determine the way in which protection affects mammal populations, data on anti-poaching efforts were collected by visiting several NP and GR local headquarters and head offices in Tanzania. Records included the annual budget allocated and number of patrols conducted per month between 1981 and 1992, and the number of rangers or game scouts, officers and wardens present, and the number of working vehicles and working rifles in 1992. These figures were subsequently divided by the area of each NP or GR to yield densities of people or items per km^2. These densities were then matched to mammal densities as determined by the mean of mean wet and mean dry season densities across seven areas for which both types of data were available: Mikumi NP; Ruaha NP; Tarangire NP; Mkomazi GR; Moyowosi–Kigosi GR; Rungwa GR; and Selous GR. These represented a wide geographic spread of protected areas across the country. Data from other areas in Tanzania, and from other countries, were gleaned from the literature.

RESULTS AND DISCUSSION

Does mammal abundance predict mammal diversity?

We first plotted number of large and middle-sized mammal species against size of protected area since it is known that species number increases with area (MacArthur and Wilson, 1967). As expected, mammal species number

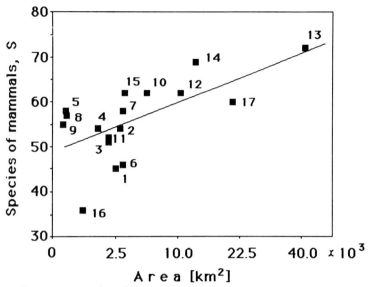

Figure 12.2 Number of mammal species in 17 protected areas in east Africa plotted against size of protected area. $S = 49.07 + 0.109 \, (\sqrt{\text{Area}})$. 1. Akagera NP; 2. Burigi-Biharmalo GRs; 3. Katavi NP; 4. Kidepo NP; 5. Manyara NP; 6. Mikumi NP; 7. Mkomazi GR; 8. Nairobi NP; 9. Nakuru NP; 10. Ngorongoro Conservation Area; 11. Queen Elizabeth NP; 12. Ruaha NP; 13. Selous GR; 14. Serengeti NP; 15. Tarangire NP; 16. Toro GR; 17. Tsavo NP.

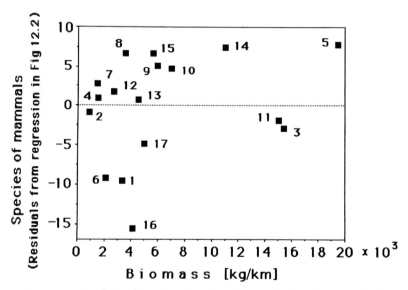

Figure 12.3 Residuals of number of species of mammals from the regression in Figure 12.2 plotted against large and middle-sized mammal biomass. Protected areas as in Figure 12.2.

was significantly related to area ($N=$ 17 protected areas, r^2 = 0.412, $P < 0.001$; Figure 12.2). We then plotted the residuals of species number from this regression against biomass/km² (Figure 12.3). There was no significant association between mammal biomass and the number of mammal species once area had been controlled for ($N=17$, r^2 = 0.071, N.S.). Admittedly, our samples were restricted to areas with medium to high densities of mammals (in parks and reserves), and there may be a positive association between abundance and diversity at low densities. Nevertheless, within this network of protected areas, and controlling for area, there were similar numbers of mammal species in analysed areas irrespective of mammal biomass.

In East Africa, biomass increases with productivity as determined by rainfall (Coe *et al.*, 1976; East, 1984). In contrast, the number of species increases and then declines with increasing rainfall (Western, 1991), although the reasons for this are poorly understood (see Rosenzweig, 1995). Plotting diversity against abundance, one might therefore expect a positive association at low abundance and a negative one at high abundance but we found no indication of this in our data set.

From a conservation perspective, lack of association between mammal abundance (principally large ungulate abundance) and larger mammal diversity suggests that the current network of protected areas in East Africa, initially established for reasons of high mammal biomass, may not be particularly effective at conserving larger mammal diversity. To protect biodiversity better in East Africa, we need to know where sites of species richness, sites of high endemism and areas of biological uniqueness lie and specifically target them for protection (Pomeroy, 1993; Turpie and Crowe, 1994). For example, the Eastern arc of mountains in Tanzania contains many endemic species in a number of taxonomic groups (Lovett, 1993; Stuart *et al.*, 1993) and is now being given conservation priority. Fortunately, NPs and GRs in East Africa are still being gazetted in the 1990s. In Tanzania, for instance, the Udzungwa NP in Tanzania was established in 1990, and several new national parks have been recently gazetted in Uganda. Thus there are still opportunities for setting up protected areas in locations of high biodiversity in the region.

Which mammal species benefit from protection?

Table 12.2 shows the densities of mammals inside Katavi National Park and densities immediately outside. Out of a total of 25 species or species groupings, 17 occurred at significantly higher densities inside the Park including two large carnivore species. Prior analyses showed that this was not the result of differential sampling in different months when mammals might have moved into the Park; nor could differences in vegetation account for these results (Caro, 1999a).

Elsewhere in Tanzania, illegal hunters prefer to kill ungulates that are large and numerous (Arcese *et al.*, 1995). When the 18 ungulate species in the Katavi ecosystem were ranked according to body weight, species living at significantly higher densities inside Katavi NP than outside appeared to be large, but not significantly so (Median test using Fisher's procedure, $P =$ 0.132; Table 12.3a). Across the whole of Tanzania, areas that both prohibited settlement and were protected by guards (i.e., NPs and GRs combined) contained significantly higher densities of nine out of the 20 ungulate species than did GCAs and OAs combined. These species were buffalo ($Ns =$ 17,40 conservation areas respectively, $Xs =$ 2.93, 1.39/km^2, Mann–Whitney U test, $z =$ 3.524 on standardised scores, $P <$ 0.001), bushbuck ($Ns =$ 11,25, $Xs =$ 0.01, 0.02/km^2, $z =$ 2.617, $P =$ 0.009), eland ($Ns =$ 15,37, $Xs =$ 0.19, 0.09/km^2, $z =$ 2.718, $P =$ 0.007), giraffe ($Ns =$ 17,40, $Xs =$ 0.20, 0.22/km^2, $z =$ 2.059, $P =$ 0.04), hartebeest ($Ns =$ 17, 40, $Xs =$ 0.51, 0.15/km^2, $z =$ 3.506, $P <$ 0.001), hippopotamus ($Ns =$ 10,18, $Xs =$ 0.31, 0.12/km^2, $z =$ 2.639, $P =$ 0.008), roan antelope ($Ns =$ 11, 18, $Xs =$ 0.07, 0.02/km^2, $z =$ 2.880, $P =$ 0.004), waterbuck ($Ns =$ 16,37, $Xs =$ 0.11, 0.16/km^2, $z =$ 3.701, $P <$ 0.001) and zebra ($Ns =$ 17, 40, $Xs =$ 1.40, 0.93/km^2, $z =$ 3.445, $P <$ 0.001). Taken together, these species were heavier and therefore carried greater quantities of edible flesh than species whose densities were not significantly affected by protection (Median test using Fisher's procedure, $P =$ 0.032; Table 12.3b). In short, nationwide, almost half of the ungulate species counted showed higher population densities in areas that contained a guard force and prohibited settlement but this effect was more marked for species of larger body weight.

Tables 12.3a and 12.3b show a strong congruence in which particular species benefit from protection in the Katavi ecosystem and across the ten census zones in Tanzania. Hippopotamus, buffalo, giraffe, eland, roan antelope, waterbuck, zebra and bushbuck were found at significantly higher densities in areas under protection at both the local and national scale. Studies at both spatial scales suggest that absence of active protection results in the differential loss of large meat species from wilderness areas in Tanzania. An alternative explanation, that NPs and GRs were specifically set up to protect concentrations of large mammal species and might therefore be expected to hold higher densities of these species, can only partially explain these results. This is because protected areas were never precisely situated on areas of high mammal abundance; their exact boundaries were

Table 12.3a
Ungulates separated by whether their densities were higher in Katavi National Park, and by body weight

	Compared to median ungulate body weight	
	Higher	Lower
Species for which densities were significantly higher in Katavi National Park	Elephant Hippopotamus Giraffe Buffalo Eland Roan antelope Zebra Waterbuck	Topi Bushpig Warthog Impala Bushbuck
Species for which densities were not significantly higher in Katavi National Park	Sable antelope	Greater kudu Coke's hartebeest Bohor reedbuck Duiker

Table 12.3b
Ungulates separated by whether their densities were higher in areas under protection across the whole of Tanzania, and by body weight

	Compared to median species body weight	
	Higher	Lower
Species for which densities were significantly higher in areas under protection	Hippopotamus Giraffe Buffalo Eland Roan antelope Zebra Waterbuck	Hartebeest Bushbuck
Species for which densities were not significantly higher in areas under protection	Elephant Sable antelope Wildebeest	Kudu Topi Bushpig Warthog Reedbuck Impala Gazelle Small antelope

determined more by socio-political considerations than by relative densities. Thus we might expect mammal densities in adjacent unprotected areas to be high in many cases as well. A second alternative, that large species are attracted to protected areas for environmental reasons, water or

Table 12.4
Spearman rank order correlation coefficients between densities of various aspects of anti-poaching effort and mammal densities across seven protected areas in Tanzania

Species	Budget	Rifles	Officers and rangers	Working vehicles	Patrols
Buffalo	—	0.600	0.600	0.829**	0.700
Elephant	—	0.257	0.029	0.200	—
Giraffe	−0.029	0.143	0.179	0.107	0.086
Hartebeest	−0.486	−0.107	−0.321	−0.429	0.086
Impala	—	−0.257	−0.257	−0.029	—
Kudu	—	−0.143	−0.200	−0.371	—
Reedbuck	−0.580	−0.396	−0.523	−0.523	−0.116
Warthog	−0.486	−0.143	−0.286	−0.393	0.086
Waterbuck	—	−0.143	−0.286	−0.286	—
Zebra	0.714	0.714*	0.679*	0.821**	0.829**

$N = 6$ or 7 areas; — sample size too small to test. $* P < 0.1$, $** P < 0.05$.

forage for instance, seems untenable given that densities of many middle-sized mammal species do not follow this pattern. Moreover, animals are free to move between protected and unprotected adjacent areas as none of the areas were fenced.

Other evidence supports the working hypothesis that poachers preferentially target large meat species. Examining poached animals discovered by rangers in the Serengeti NP, Arcese *et al.* (1995) showed that illegal hunters preferred larger species to smaller ones. Similarly, Dublin *et al.* (1990) showed that poachers removed approximately 85% of buffalo from the northern Serengeti. Caro (1999a) found that densities of larger species increased with distance from a centre of poaching activity. These studies and results presented here suggest that illegal hunters are responsible for differences in large mammal densities inside and outside protected areas. Apparently, then, the presence of guards in an area, be it a NP or GR, does deter meat poachers and selectively benefits large meat species.

Which aspects of protection are most important?

To determine which aspects of protection were primarily responsible for the higher densities of meat species in protected areas, we examined the relationship between anti-poaching effort/km^2 and species' densities across a subsample of protected areas. There were no significant associations between protected area budget/km^2 and mammal densities (Table 12.4), nor between the number of rifles or rangers/km^2 and mammal densities except in the case of zebra. Densities of buffalo and zebra were signifi-

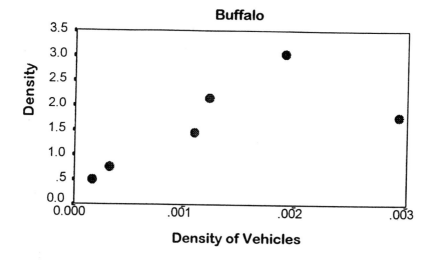

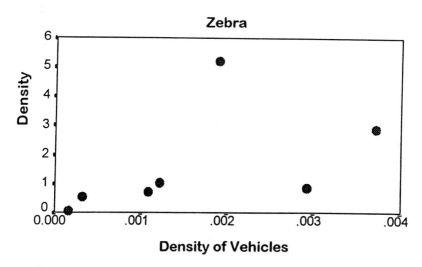

Figure 12.4 Densities (numbers/km²) of buffalo and zebra plotted against density of working vehicles in areas of Tanzania protected by rangers or game scouts.

cantly positively correlated with density of working vehicles however ($N = 6$ legally protected areas, $r_s = 0.829$, $P = 0.042$; $N = 7$, $r_s = 0.821$, $P = 0.023$ respectively; Figure 12.4). Zebra densities were also significantly associated with the number of patrols/month ($N = 6$, $r_s = 0.829$, $P = 0.042$). These results are interesting because buffalo are one of the most important meat species in Tanzania.

Table 12.5

Summary of the effects of different aspects of anti-poaching effort on the success of detecting and arresting illegal hunters. Katavi: this study; Serengeti: Arcese *et al.* (1995); Luangwa: Leader-Williams *et al.* (1990a) and Jachmann and Billiouw (1997) respectively

Area:	Katavi	Serengeti	Luangwa	Luangwa
Species hunted:	Meat spp.	Meat spp.	Elephant and rhino	Elephant
Budget				X
Scout number		X		X
Scout pay				X
Patrol effort	X	X	X	
Vehicles	X	X	X	
Investigation				X
Departure time		X		
Season		X		

Although it is possible that central authorities provide more equipment and encourage greater effort in areas with higher mammal densities, other studies of anti-poaching in east Africa suggest that it is anti-poaching effort that has a positive effect on wildlife. In Serengeti NP, Arcese *et al.* (1995) found that more arrests were made when patrols contained intermediate numbers of rangers (9–15); that frequency of patrols, mixed vehicle and foot patrols, and early departing patrols were most successful at apprehending meat poachers; and that success was highest during the dry season when mobility of rangers was greatest (Table 12.5). In the Luangwa Valley, Zambia, Leader-Williams *et al.* (1990a) found that more days spent on patrol per unit area reduced elephant and rhinoceros (*Diceros bicornis*) poaching, and that vehicle patrols had greater success at making arrests than foot patrols (Table 12.5). More recently, Jachmann and Billiouw (1997) working in the same area found that the total law enforcement budget, scout density, cash rewards given to scouts on arresting poachers, and personal emoluments all reduced illegal killing of elephants. Days spent following up leads also had the same effect (Table 12.5).

These studies were carried out in different areas, investigated different types of poaching and used different methods, however two common themes emerge (Table 12.5). Success at detecting and arresting poachers is clearly enhanced by patrol effort, however measured, and by numbers of working vehicles.

African buffalo, *Syncerus caffer*, Uganda. Photograph: Sybil Sassoon.

CONCLUSIONS

Protected areas perform differing conservation services with the passing of time. Originally, the older NPs and GRs in east Africa were set up to prevent overexploitation of large ungulates and carnivores by expatriate hunters. Nowadays, in more populated areas, they protect habitat from many human activities such as tree felling, agricultural encroachment and expanding settlement (Brotein and Said, 1995). In less populated areas, they prevent activities such as overhunting and hardwood exploitation. Mammalian biomass in these older protected areas is not correlated with biodiversity, as measured by species richness of large and medium-sized mammals, suggesting the famous reserves and parks are not exceptional reservoirs of mammalian diversity. Nonetheless, we did not measure diversity of other taxonomic groups. Newer protected areas, on the other hand, such as Kakamega, Sokoke and the Usambara forests are sites of high endemism. They have been identified specifically for their biological uniqueness and have few large mammals in abundance.

East African NPs and GRs have been unsuccessful in protecting black rhinoceros (Western and Vigne, 1985; Leader-Williams, 1988; Western, 1992) and have been only partially successful in preventing exploitation of elephants (Douglas-Hamilton, 1987; Barnes and Kapela, 1991; Prins *et al.*, 1994). Our analyses show, both at the local and national scale, that they are currently very successful in protecting large meat species from the exploitation that occurs outside their borders. Data from the Katavi ecosystem indicates that carnivores also benefit from this protection (Table 12.2) probably as a result of the larger prey base there. Currently, protected areas have far less of a conservation impact on middle-sized ungulates, both at the small and large scales, because these species are not yet heavily impacted by illegal hunters. In future, however, we speculate that NPs and GRs will be important repositories for these species too, if local hunters turn their attention to smaller game in unprotected areas.

Studies that have examined the effectiveness of anti-poaching efforts in east Africa suggest that the frequency of patrols is important in apprehending poachers. Among mammals, large meat and trophy species therefore stand to gain the most from such patrols. In addition, the density of working vehicles is critical to the success of patrols. Although the number of anti-poaching studies are few, and more research is needed, it is clear that providing and maintaining anti-poaching vehicles and encouraging frequent patrols are key to effective protection of mammals in protected areas of east Africa.

ACKNOWLEDGEMENTS

We thank the Government of Tanzania, the Department of Wildlife, Serengeti Wildlife Research Institute, Tanzania National Parks, and Ngorongoro Conservation Area Authority for permissions. We thank Peter Arcese, Monique Borgerhoff Mulder, Ken Campbell, Pete Coppolillo, Scott Creel, Brian Farm, Paule Gros, Craig Packer, Herbert Prins, Bethany Woodworth and Truman Young for commenting on various parts of the manuscript.

13

The role of Transfrontier Conservation Areas in southern Africa in the conservation of mammalian biodiversity

JOHN HANKS

INTRODUCTION

It is now widely accepted that the mammals of Africa face a bleak future, a consequence of a combination of factors directly and indirectly influenced by the activities of man (Balmford *et al.*, 1995; Happold, 1995). These factors can be grouped under six main headings.

Habitat loss associated with agricultural development and human settlement

Africa has the highest population growth rate of any major region in the world and the lowest prevalence of contraceptive use. This high rate of growth has resulted in unprecedented human demands for food, fuel, shelter and water, and a level of land transformation by pastoral, agricultural and urban development and by alien plant encroachment that has destroyed or fragmented natural habitats throughout the continent (WRI, 1994). For example, in the lowlands of the Western Cape in South Africa, only 6 % of renoster shrubland and 14 % of fynbos are currently untransformed (Rebelo, 1992).

Civil unrest

Protected areas have all too often been severely disrupted by military actions, with a concomitant loss of biological diversity (Westing, 1992). Some of the civil wars have been exacerbated by external interventions, and have left many people dead, in exile or exposed to famine (Williams, 1997). In southern Africa, Angola, Mozambique, and to a lesser extent Zimbabwe and Namibia all experienced several years of savage conflict, a guerilla war which had, and still has, a profound effect on economic relations with bordering countries, and on internal post-independent economies.

Poor management of designated protected areas

The majority of Africa's protected areas are inadequately funded and are unable to maintain basic infrastructure and facilities at an acceptable standard for international tourism. Furthermore, a combination of a chronic shortage of funds coupled with poorly motivated and inadequately trained staff has made it increasingly difficult, if not impossible, for protected area managers to safeguard valuable endangered species, or even in some cases to prevent human encroachment.

Vulnerability of fragmented small habitat islands

There is a growing body of literature on the vulnerability of fragmented small habitat islands designated as protected areas. Even if all the other factors which could impact on mammal populations are brought under control, a combination of genetic and environmental factors, coupled with the vulnerability of isolated populations to various wildlife diseases, may undermine the long-term viability of the isolated populations (Soulé, 1987; Khan et al., 1997).

Lack of a national commitment to the conservation of mammalian biodiversity

Of the world's 35 poorest countries, 29 of them are in Africa south of the Sahara. Some face a situation of absolute poverty. For example, Mozambique's economy since its independence from Portugal in June 1975, has suffered not only from the damaging effects of nearly 17 years of war, but also from drought, floods, famine, the displacement of millions of people and a severe scarcity of foreign exchange and of skilled workers. As a consequence, Mozambique became one of the poorest countries in the world, heavily reliant on foreign credits. The vast majority of Mozambicans live below the poverty line, and social indicators are among the lowest in Africa. In 1995, according to estimates from the World Bank, the country's gross national product (GNP) was US$1513 million, equivalent to only $88 per head (Cravinho, 1997). Conservation budgets are low or non-existent under such circumstances.

Overhunting

Populations of mammals have been eliminated from vast areas of Africa as a result of overhunting. For example, in 1650, elephants *Loxodonta africana* were widespread in South Africa in all suitable habitats, with the exception of the more arid central regions and the grasslands of the Free State. The growth of the ivory trade and the emergence of professional ivory hunters reduced or eliminated elephant populations from most of South Africa by 1920 (Robinson, 1992).

This chapter will outline the development of Transfrontier Conservation Areas in southern Africa in relation to the recent establishment of the Peace Parks Foundation, and will describe how the threats to mammalian biodiversity outlined above can be addressed through this initiative.

THE ORIGIN OF THE PEACE PARKS FOUNDATION AND THE DEVELOPMENT OF TRANSFRONTIER CONSERVATION AREAS IN SOUTHERN AFRICA

The concept of transborder protected area cooperation through the establishment of 'peace parks' is not a new one. IUCN – The World Conservation Union had long been promoting their establishment because of the many potential benefits associated with them (Westing, 1993; Hamilton *et al.*, 1996). In 1988, IUCN's Commission on National Parks and Protected Areas had identified at least 70 protected areas in 65 countries which straddled national frontiers (Thorsell, 1990). In June 1990, WWF South Africa was requested by the Government of Mozambique to carry out a feasibility study of the possibility of a permanent link being established between some of the protected areas in southern Mozambique and their adjacent counterparts in Swaziland, South Africa and Zimbabwe. It was completed and submitted to the Government of Mozambique in September 1991 (Tinley and van Riet, 1991). The report was discussed by the Mozambique Council of Ministers, who recommended that further studies were required to assess fully the political, socio-economic and ecological aspects of the feasibility study. The Government of Mozambique then requested the Global Environment Facility (GEF) of the World Bank to provide assistance for the project, which was granted. The first mission was fielded in 1991, and in June 1996 the Bank released its recommendations in a report entitled *Mozambique: Transfrontier Conservation Areas Pilot and Institutional Strengthening Project* (World Bank, 1996a).

The report suggested an important conceptual shift away from the idea of strictly protected national parks towards greater emphasis on multiple resource use by local communities by introducing the Transfrontier Conservation Area (TFCA) concept. In short, TFCAs were defined as relatively large areas, which straddled frontiers between two or more countries and covered large-scale natural systems encompassing one or more protected areas. Very often both human and mammal populations traditionally migrated across or straddled the political boundaries concerned. In essence,

242 | J. Hanks

TFCAs extended far beyond designated protected areas, and could incorporate such innovative approaches as biosphere reserves and a wide range of community based natural resource management programmes (World Bank, 1996a). The Peace Parks Foundation subsequently adopted this new paradigm.

As a result of the political constraints prevalent in southern Africa at the time of the initiation of the GEF funded programme in Mozambique, only limited attention could be given to the development of formal links between the three main participating countries, and unfortunately this persisted throughout the duration of the study. Two years after the election of Nelson Mandela, South Africa was experiencing a rapid and significant growth in its nature-based tourism industry, but very few of the benefits associated with this growth were being made available to Mozambique. These concerns prompted Anton Rupert, the President of WWF South Africa, to request a meeting with President Chissano, and this was held on 27 May 1996. Rupert emphasised the significant economic benefits that could accrue to Mozambique if the proposed TFCAs were implemented. The Maputo discussions were followed by a Transfrontier Park Initiative meeting in the Kruger National Park on 8 August 1996 under the joint Chairmanship of Mozambique's Minister of Transport and Communications, Paulo Muxanga, and South Africa's Minister of Transport, Mac Maharaj, where it was agreed that the two countries, together with Zimbabwe and Swaziland, should cooperate to realise the economic benefits of the proposed TFCAs.

Towards the end of 1996, it became clear to WWF South Africa that interest in the peace park concept was not only growing within the country, but also in the neighbouring states. For the first time, *southern* Africa was being seen as a tourist destination, not just South Africa or other countries on their own, and an integral part of this vision was the development of TFCAs or peace parks involving all of South Africa's neighbouring countries (de Villiers, 1994; Pinnock, 1996). The Executive Committee of WWF South Africa came to the conclusion that unless a separate body was set up to coordinate and drive the process of TFCA establishment and funding, these areas would not receive the attention that was required to make them a reality on the ground. Accordingly, the Peace Parks Foundation was established on 1 February 1997 with an initial grant of Rand 1.2 million (US$260 000) from Anton Rupert to facilitate the establishment of TFCAs in southern Africa.

OBJECTIVES OF THE PEACE PARKS FOUNDATION

The Peace Parks Foundation has been constituted and established in South Africa as an Association incorporated under Section 21 i.e., a company 'not for gain'. It has virtually all the powers of a normal company, but cannot have shareholders, and no profits can be paid to supporting members. The Foundation is managed by a Board of Directors under the Chairmanship of Anton Rupert, and has eight Honorary Patrons, namely President Mogae (Botswana), His Majesty King Letsie lll (Lesotho), President Muluzi (Malawi), President Chissano (Mozambique), President Nujoma (Namibia), President Mandela (South Africa), His Majesty King Mswati lll (Swaziland), and President Mugabe (Zimbabwe). The overall objective of the Foundation is to fund and facilitate the development of Transfrontier Conservation Areas, placing particular emphasis on the promotion of regional peace and stability, the creation of new jobs associated with the anticipated growth of tourism in southern Africa, and the conservation of biological diversity. The countries involved in the initial phase of the Foundation's programme are Botswana, Lesotho, Malawi, Mozambique, Namibia, South Africa, Swaziland, Tanzania, Zambia and Zimbabwe.

LEVELS OF SUPPORT REQUIRED FOR THE ESTABLISHMENT OF TFCAs

For TFCAs to become a reality, support is required at five levels.

Political

TFCAs involve a unique level of international cooperation between the participating countries, particularly on sensitive issues related to the opening of international boundaries. An open commitment by each Head of State is an essential prerequisite for the TFCA to succeed. To avoid the danger of the perception of 'top-down planning', an active advocacy programme is also required to obtain political support at the local or community level.

Regional

Within each region, the relevant international bodies have a key role to play in facilitating the process. Within southern Africa, the Southern African Development Community's support for the TFCA process is of paramount importance.

Technical

Within each TFCA all the relevant 'technical' responsible agencies must be consulted and involved, including the conservation departments and government departments responsible for immigration, police, home affairs, customs, health, etc.

Local communities
All local communities in and adjacent to the TFCAs must be consulted at the start of the development process and at all subsequent stages of development. Every effort should be made to ensure that significant economic benefits of TFCAs are made available to neighbouring communities, with particular attention being given to making them partners in the business opportunities that will open up.

Financial
TFCAs are expensive to establish and run successfully. Financial support must be forthcoming from the State, with perhaps the bulk of the funding coming from private sector investments and bilateral and multilateral aid agencies.

Following discussions in South Africa with the Boards of the KwaZulu Natal Nature Conservation Service (Natal Parks Board) and South African National Parks (National Parks Board), and with conservation agencies in neighbouring countries, seven potential TFCAs were identified for initial support by the Foundation (Figure 13.1). Each of these has the potential to make a contribution to the improvement of the conservation status of mammals in southern Africa, particularly in terms of all the advantages associated with a significant increase in the size of the designated protected areas, and a joining together of fragmented habitats. In the text that follows, the first six are listed from the west to the east of the region, ending with the Drakensberg/Maloti TFCA to the south. Further information on community involvement and the existence of land resource claims in each of these areas is given in Greeff (1998).

TRANSFRONTIER CONSERVATION AREAS SUPPORTED BY THE PEACE PARKS FOUNDATION IN 1997 AND 1998 AND THEIR RELEVANCE TO THE CONSERVATION OF AFRICA'S BIODIVERSITY, PARTICULARLY MAMMALIAN BIODIVERSITY

Richtersveld / Ai-Ais TFCA
This proposed TFCA spans some of the most spectacular scenery of the arid and desert environments of southern Africa, incorporating the Fish River Canyon (often equated to the Grand Canyon in the USA) and the

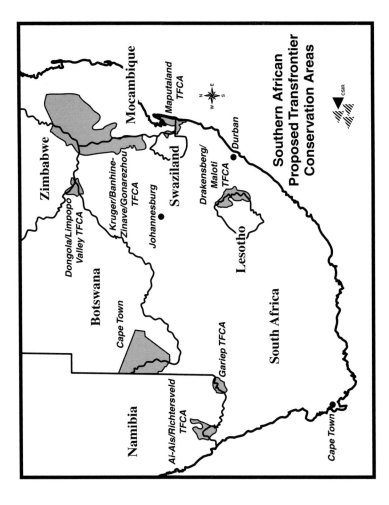

Figure 13.1 Map showing location of proposed Transfrontier Conservation Areas in southern Africa.

Ai-Ais hot springs. It is 6222 km² in extent of which about 1902 km² (31 %) are in South Africa, and the remainder (69 %) in Namibia. It comprises the Richtersveld National Park in South Africa, which was proclaimed in 1991 as South Africa's only fully contractual national park, and the Ai-Ais Nature Reserve in Namibia, which was proclaimed in 1986. The Namibian conservation authorities have been approached informally by the South African National Parks Board on the subject of the formal establishment of the proposed TFCA, but no agreement or joint management plan exists.

Many of the species of fauna found in the area are adapted to withstand the harsh, arid climate (between 15 and 300 mm of rain each year, and summer temperatures well over 40 °C). Fifty-six species of mammals have been recorded, of which eight are listed in the South Africa Red Data Book (Smithers, 1986), including the aardwolf *Proteles cristatus,* the brown hyaena *Parahyaena brunnea* and Hartmann's mountain zebra *Equus zebra hartmannae.* Six species are endemic to the southern Africa subregion, a particularly common example being the dassie rat *Petromus typicus* which is confined to the South West Arid Zone where there is suitable rocky terrain habitat. The mountain ground squirrel *Xerus princeps* has a similar range to the dassie rat, excepting that the only place in which it has been recorded in South Africa is in the Richtersveld National Park. Along the Orange River predators such as leopard *Panthera pardus,* caracal *Caracal caracal* and black-backed jackal *Canis mesomelas* still occur in reasonable numbers. However, with the exception of klipspringer *Oreotragus oreotragus,* ungulates are uncommon (van Jaarsveld, 1991; Acocks, 1988; Skinner and Smithers, 1990; Powrie, 1992; NPB, 1996; Gelderblom *et al.,* 1997).

The two designated conservation areas involved are relatively recent acquisitions to southern Africa's network of protected areas, and their combination in the TFCA will make a significant contribution to the consolidation of protected land in the Namib Desert biotic zone (Meester, 1965) and the mammals associated with it.

Gariep TFCA

This is the least developed of all the seven proposed TFCAs, and is still at the concept stage. The Namibian and South African conservation authorities have accepted the concept of the TFCA, but no formal discussions have taken place. As with the Richtersveld/ Ai-Ais, the area is also centred along a stretch of the Orange River which forms the international boundary between South Africa and Namibia. The proposed TFCA is 2774 km² in extent, of which 2007 km² (72 %) are in South Africa, and a further 767 km² (28 %) in Namibia. It comprises an arid area characterised by broken terrain with deep sandy dry river gorges flowing down to the Orange River from both sides. Inland on the South African side are relatively untransformed areas of typical Namaqualand Broken Veld, with a unique 'forest' of *Aloe dichotoma* (Acocks, 1988; Bezuidenhout, 1997; Gelderblom *et al.*, 1997).

Of particular significance to conservation of mammalian biodiversity is the potential of this TFCA as a major new sanctuary for the black rhinoceros *Diceros bicornis* and possibly for Hartmann's mountain zebra. Black rhino have declined from an estimated 100 000 in 1960 to approximately 2400 in 1995 (AfRSG, 1996). The Gariep TFCA contains extensive areas of ideal black rhino habitat, and introduced animals would be relatively easy to protect (by virtue of being surrounded by commercial farms and the TFCA's remoteness from areas of significant human population). The Peace Parks Foundation funded a feasibility study of the proposed TFCA, which was completed in June 1998 (Jardine and Owen, 1998). The study examined current patterns of land-use, the conservation importance of the area, and potential threats to biodiversity. The Foundation is waiting for advice on this matter from the Board of South African National Parks before any further action is taken.

Kgalagadi Transfrontier Park

In contrast to Gariep, this TFCA was formally established by the governments of South Africa and Botswana in April 1999. This TFCA has been *de facto* in existence since 1948 through a verbal agreement between South Africa and Botswana, and is comprised of the Kalahari Gemsbok National Park in South Africa (proclaimed in 1931), and the Gemsbok National Park in Botswana (proclaimed in 1971), and subsequently extended to incorporate the Mabuasehube Game Reserve. The Kgalagadi Transfrontier Park Management Plan was reviewed and approved by the two conservation agencies early in 1997. The Plan provides a basis for cooperative tourism ventures, and proposes the sharing of entrance fees equally by both countries. An integral feature of the new agreement is that each country will provide and maintain its own tourism facilities and infrastructure, giving particular attention to developing and involving neighbouring communities (NPB (South Africa) and DWNP (Botswana), 1997). The park is 37 991 km² in extent, of which 9591 km² (27 %) are in South Africa with the remainder (73 %) in Botswana. The Transfrontier Management Committee is in the process of establishing a Section 21 company 'The Kgaladai Transfrontier Park Company' to manage and control the financial aspects of the programme.

The area represents a large ecosystem relatively free of human influence, an increasingly rare phenomenon in Africa. The 60 mammalian species recorded include large herds of ungulates, mainly gemsbok *Oryx gazella* after which the national park gets its name, springbok *Antidorcas marsupialis*, and blue wildebeest *Connochaetes taurinus*, and to a lesser extent red hartebeest *Alcelaphus buselaphus* and eland *Taurotragus oryx*. These ungulates and an abundance of rodents support many carnivores and the TFCA has built up a deserved reputation as one of the few ecosystems in southern Africa where a variety of large predators can be maintained. Leopard, brown hyaena, and spotted hyaena *Crocuta crocuta*, lion *Panthera leo*, cheetah *Acinonyx jubatus*, bat-eared fox *Otocyon megalotis* and the highly endangered wild dog *Lycaon pictus* are all well represented (Eloff, 1984; Main, 1987; Acocks, 1988; Mills and Haagner, 1989; Mills, 1991; Gelderblom *et al.*, 1997; NPB (South Africa) and DWNP (Botswana), 1997).

The absence of man-made barriers between the two components of the TFCA has provided a conservation area large enough to maintain significant nomadic and migratory movements of wild ungulates, and predation by large mammalian carnivores, two biological features that were once widespread in the savannahs and grasslands of southern Africa.

Dongola / Limpopo Valley TFCA

This proposed TFCA is 4872 km² in extent, of which 2561 km² (53 %) is in South Africa, 1350 km² (28 %) is in Botswana, and 960 km² (19 %) is in Zimbabwe. The TFCA is centred at the confluence of the Limpopo and Shashe Rivers, and is made up of a complex mosaic of land ownership. It incorporates land owned by the state, National Parks Board and private landowners in South Africa, including the Venetia Limpopo Nature Reserve owned by De Beers Consolidated Mines Ltd (Carruthers, 1992). Most of the private landowners on the Botswana side have indicated their willingness to participate in the TFCA, and they have the support of Botswana's Department of Wildlife and National Parks. Prospects appear equally as encouraging in Zimbabwe. The South African authorities have had preliminary discussions on the implementation of the TFCA with their counterparts from the two neighbouring countries, but no formal agreements have been concluded, and no joint development plan exists.

The TFCA has excellent potential as a 'big five' conservation area. Viable populations of lion, leopard and cheetah still occur, and the population of nearly 1000 elephants in Botswana is the largest population on private land in Africa. Ungulates already present include eland, impala *Aepyceros melampus*, blue wildebeest, Burchell's zebra *Equus burchellii*, Sharpe's grysbok *Raphicerus sharpei*, and steenbok *Raphicerus campestris*, and there is suitable habitat for both black and white rhino *Ceratotherium simum*. The area has 19 Red Data Book mammals (Robinson, 1995; Gelderblom *et al.*, 1997). Introductions of mammals into the Venetia Limpopo Nature Reserve include 44 elephants from 1991–1994, 10 roan *Hippotragus equinus*, 10 sable *Hippotragus niger* and 20 tsessebe *Damaliscus lunatus* in 1994, and 15 wild dog in 1992. All the introductions have been successful except the wild dog, which increased to 27 in 1992 before disappearing completely the following year (M. Berry, personal communication). A major constraint to the movement of animals in the area is the presence of the veterinary cordon fence and an electrified military barrier on the South African side of the Limpopo River, and this needs to be addressed urgently. Once established, this TFCA has the potential to be a significant sanctuary for wild dog, black rhino and elephant and for the 16 other Red Data Book species. Wild dog and elephants in particular would benefit from the larger area of the TFCA.

In December 1998, the Peace Parks Foundation purchased an 865–hectare farm in the Limpopo River in South Africa for incorporation into the new Vhembe/Dongola National Park, and will continue to do all it can to assist the South Africa National Parks Board with purchase of land to establish this essential core area.

Kruger / Banhine – Zinave / Gonarezhou TFCA

This is the largest of the seven proposed TFCAs. It is 95 712 km² in extent, of which 69 208 km² (72 %) is in Mozambique, 19 458 km² (21 %) in South Africa, and 7019 km² (7 %) in Zimbabwe, and it will create one of the most substantial and impressive conservation areas in the world. As described at the start of this chapter, discussions between South Africa and Mozambique at a variety of levels have been taking place since 1990. A Transfrontier Committee was established in 1997 involving representatives from the conservation agencies from the two countries, but no formal agreement is in place. The Global Environment Facility (GEF) Trust Fund has granted US$5 million to Mozambique for the Transfrontier Conservation Areas Pilot and Institutional Strengthening Project. There is a total commitment to this TFCA from all the relevant South African and Mozambican authorities, and considerable progress should be made with the initial phases of the project in 2000.

With more species of big game than any other tract of land of equivalent size, the TFCA has the potential to become one of Africa's premier ecotourism destinations. The South African side will incorporate Africa's first national park, the Kruger National Park, which was proclaimed on 31 May 1926, and a number of privately owned areas on the western boundary of the park. Zimbabwe's portion of the TFCA will include a small area of communal land and the Gonarezhou National Park, which was proclaimed as a reserve in 1968 and obtained national parks status in 1972. In Mozambique the TFCA will incorporate the Coutada 16 Wildlife Utilisation Area immediately adjacent to the Kruger National Park (shortly to be gazetted and put out to public tender for its development and management), the Zinave National Park, which was originally proclaimed as a safari hunting area in 1962 and as a national park in 1972, and Banhine National Park which was established in 1972. It will also include a large area of state owned communal land with a relatively low population density. Kruger National Park alone is one of the major areas of vertebrate diversity in southern Africa, with 147 species of mammals, 505 species of birds, 51 fish species, 35 amphibian species and 119 reptile species. It is one of the few protected areas in southern Africa capable of maintaining a natural large carnivore/prey system, which will be enhanced considerably once the whole TFCA is in place. Significant populations of mammals in the Kruger National Park include 1500 lion, 2000 spotted hyaena, 8320 elephants, 2200 white rhinos, 250 black rhinos, 32 000 Burchell's zebra, 2200 hippos *Hippopotamus amphibius*, 5000 giraffe *Giraffa camelopardalis*, 1500 warthog *Phacochoerus aethiopicus*, 16 640 buffalo *Syncerus caffer*, 3500 kudu *Tragelaphus strepsiceros*, 1500 waterbuck *Kobus ellipsiprymnus*, 14 000 blue wildebeest and over 100 000 impala. Other ungulates include eland, nyala *Tragelaphus angasii*, bushbuck *Tragelaphus scriptus*, roan, sable, tsessebe, steenbok, mountain reedbuck *Redunca fulvorufula*, Sharpe's grysbok, klipspringer, suni *Neotragus moschatus*, oribi *Ourebia ourebi*, red duiker *Cephalophus natalensis* and common duiker *Sylvicapra grimmia*. Within the park alone are 18 Red Data Book mammal species. Unfortunately, there has been a recent increase in tuberculosis due to *Mycrobacterium bovis* in several of the mammal species in the Kruger National Park in addition to buffalo, and this could delay the implementation of the proposed TFCA. The Gonarezhou National Park has a similarly diverse vertebrate fauna, although the total number of species and of individuals is lower. The many years of civil war in Mozambique coupled with recurrent droughts and a serious lack of management capacity has resulted in the reduction or even complete elimination of most of the large and medium-sized mammals from Zinave and Banhine National Parks and from the intermediate areas. The extent of the decline is difficult to determine because no systematic surveys have been carried out in this part of Mozambique for over 20 years.

Blue wildebeest, *Connochaetes taurinus*, South Africa.
Photograph: Sybil Sassoon.

Elephants and several species of ungulates used to move freely between South Africa, Mozambique and Zimbabwe. At one stage it was estimated that 10–15 % of the Kruger National Park's elephant population moved into Mozambique during the wet summer months, returning as the waterholes dried up. These movements came to a stop when the fencing of the entire eastern boundary of the Kruger National Park was completed in 1976 (Pienaar *et al.*, 1966; Greyling and Huntley, 1984; Branch, 1988; Sinclair and Whyte, 1991; Carruthers, 1995; Jacana Education and the National

Parks Board, 1996; Nel, 1996; Gelderblom *et al.*, 1997; I. J. Whyte, unpublished data).

On the Mozambique side of the border priority activities must address the problems of increasing human encroachment into the area, ongoing poaching, a lack of staff, funds and capacity to rehabilitate and restock the existing designated protected areas, and deforestation for fuelwood and charcoal production. Existing settlements will be incorporated into the TFCA, and no attempt will be made to force people to relocate to other areas. Rather, every effort will be made to develop outreach programmes to offer people opportunities to work with conservation and/or tourism development activities. The Peace Parks Foundation has provided the Mozambique government with two fully equipped mobile homes for use by staff in the Zinave National Park, and has allocated approximately US$100 000 for a community-based conservation and ecotourism project adjacent to Zinave. With 72 % of the proposed TFCA in Mozambique, considerable investment will be required in infrastructure development and capacity building before the area can realise its enormous potential as one of the world's greatest sanctuaries for mammalian biodiversity conservation and for nature-based tourism. With the removal of fences from the eastern boundary of the Kruger National Park, there will be a gradual and natural restocking of mammals in the areas immediately adjacent to the Park, but both the Banhine and Zinave National Parks in Mozambique will require substantial mammal restocking programmes.

Maputaland TFCA

This proposed TFCA straddles the border between South Africa, Mozambique and Swaziland. It is situated on a low-lying coastal plain between the Lebombo Hills in the west and the Indian Ocean in the east, and offers a unique combination of big game, extensive wetlands and coastal areas. The TFCA is 4195 km^2 in extent, of which 317 km^2 (8 %) is in Swaziland, 2783 km^2 (66 %) is in Mozambique, and 1095 km^2 (26 %) is in South Africa. As with the Kruger TFCA, discussions at a variety of levels on the Maputaland TFCA involving South Africa, Mozambique and Swaziland have been taking place since 1990. The GEF allocation of US$5 million will also cover developments in Mozambique for this TFCA as well. The proposed TFCA will eventually incorporate Hlane National Park, and the Mlawula, Simunye and Mbuluzi Nature Reserves, a small section of Sisa Ranch and Malahleni dispersal area, all of which have been incorporated into a new conservancy. The Maputo Elephant Reserve in Mozambique was established in 1932, and was subsequently increased in size in 1969. All the remainder of the land in the country is state-owned communal land, with a relatively low population density. In South Africa, the Ndumu Game Reserve was established in 1924, and the Tembe Elephant Reserve in 1983.

The consolidated area will be particularly important for elephant conservation. Tembe (160 elephants) and Maputo Elephant Reserve (approximately 270 elephants) are the only indigenous populations remaining on the coastal plains of southern Mozambique and KwaZuluNatal (South Africa), and the two would be linked together, re-establishing traditional seasonal migrations between the fertile Maputo River floodplain and the two protected areas. The 102 species of mammals include both black and white rhino, and other Red Data Book mammals include samango monkey *Cercopithecus mitis*, suni and red duiker. Unfortunately, severe poaching has reduced or even eliminated several species of large mammals from the Mozambican side, presenting an important opportunity for mammal restocking programmes, particularly of buffalo, hippo, tsessebe, Burchell's zebra, blue wildebeest, roan, sable, oribi, waterbuck, eland, kudu, impala, bushbuck, steenbok, suni and nyala. When ungulates are established, cheetah and wild dog can follow (Bruton and Cooper, 1980; Acocks, 1988; Mountain, 1990; World Bank, 1996a; van Wyk, 1996; Gelderblom *et al.*, 1997).

The Peace Parks Foundation has already committed approximately US$30 000 for the funding of salaries for a senior ranger and eight game scouts for two years in the Maputo Elephant Reserve (a project it is carrying out with the assistance of the Endangered Wildlife Trust's Mozambique office) and will give priority to other requests from the Mozambique Government for this area. On 9 July 1997, the Peace Parks Foundation convened a meeting in Swaziland to introduce the concept of TFCAs in general, and to discuss Swaziland's involvement in the Maputo TFCA in particular. The meeting was unanimous in its support for the TFCA, and set up a committee to further the establishment of the proposed conservancy in the area. The Foundation had subsequently allocated approximately US$9000 for a detailed investigation into the establishment of the conservancy.

Drakensberg / Maloti TFCA

The Drakensberg is the highest region in South Africa. The proposed TFCA is 8113 km^2 in extent, of which 5170 km^2 (64 %) is in Lesotho and 2943 km^2 (36 %) is in South Africa. The establishment of the TFCA has been under negotiation since 1982, and the negotiations are ongoing. It will contain the largest and most important high altitude protected area in

254 | J. Hanks

the subcontinent, supporting unique montane and subalpine ecosystems. On the South African side of the border, a number of provincial nature reserves have been combined together with state forests, wilderness areas and nature reserves proclaimed in terms of the Forest Act to form the Natal Drakensberg Park. This is now being managed by the KwaZulu Natal Conservation Service as a statutory protected area. On the Lesotho side, the Sehlabathebe National Park ranks as a schedule IV protected area in terms of IUCN protected area categories. Portions of the alpine belt of Lesotho have been earmarked as a Managed Resource Area in terms of the Managed Resource Order No.18 of 1993.

The proposed TFCA is home to a variety of ungulates, including bushbuck, eland, reedbuck *Redunca arundinum*, mountain reedbuck, grey rhebok *Pelea capreolus*, klipspringer, black wildebeest *Connochaetes gnou* and oribi, although numbers are generally low. The entire Natal Drakensberg Park has already been accepted for listing under the Ramsar Convention as a wetland of international importance. The harsh climatic conditions have deterred permanent settlement within the TFCA with the exception of a few recent isolated exceptions, although the Lesotho side is used in the summer months for grazing (Hilland and Burtt, 1987; Acocks, 1988; IUCN, 1990b; Bainbridge and Motsami, 1995; Gelderblom *et al.*, 1997; Smith, 1997).

DISCUSSION

All of the seven proposed TFCAs can make a major and lasting contribution towards the conservation of southern Africa's mammalian biodiversity. They address the six main threats to Africa's mammals outlined in the introduction as follows.

Habitat loss

There should be a significant reduction in habitat loss associated with agricultural transformations and human settlement when the communities living within and/or adjacent to the TFCAs embrace the management objectives of these areas and become partners in their development. The promotion of the alleviation of poverty through the creation of jobs in and around the TFCAs can slow or even halt habitat loss. Very poor people, struggling at the edge of subsistence levels of consumption and preoccupied with day-to-day survival, have limited scope to plan ahead, and often have little choice but to degrade or overexploit any available natural resources (Mink, 1993).

Civil unrest

Civil unrest, which has characterised the life of millions of people in southern Africa over the last two decades, has a better chance of being reduced when the 'peace parks' are fully operational. The unprecedented level of political support from eight Heads of State in the region should greatly facilitate the process. The surrounding communities from a diverse range of nations and cultures will be given a new opportunity to cooperate regularly to promote a wide range of economic benefits associated with the daily operations of the TFCAs.

Poor management

The poor management of protected areas in much of Africa has come about because of a drastic reduction in budgets and a lack of suitably qualified and motivated staff. Without adequate financial resources, a national protected area network is little more than a list on a piece of paper. Each TFCA has the potential to earn considerably greater revenue from increased tourism than if each of the protected areas continued to operate in isolation. If this increased revenue is ploughed back into the areas concerned, and the TFCAs take full advantage of cost savings associated with sharing capital equipment and skilled manpower, inadequate budgets should no longer be an excuse for poor management. An essential prerequisite to TFCA establishment is the provision of adequately trained staff. The recently opened Southern African Wildlife College[1] is uniquely positioned to address the urgent need for capacity building in this field throughout southern Africa.

Fragmentation

The vulnerability of fragmented and isolated habitat islands is directly addressed by the establishment of most of the proposed TFCAs, particularly when they bring together protected areas that are separated by communal

---

[1] The mission of the Southern African Wildlife College is to provide protected area managers from southern Africa with the motivation and relevant skills to manage their areas and associated wildlife populations sustainably and in cooperation with local communities. The two-year training programme covers a broad range of management skills, including law enforcement, infrastructural management, people management (including tourism), neighbour relations and community development, administration (including financial and personnel management), anti-poaching operations and a wide range of wildlife management skills.

lands or commercial farmland, as is the case with the Kruger/Banhine–Zinave/Gonarezhou TFCA, the Maputaland TFCA and the Dongola/Limpopo TFCA.

Lack of national commitment

The lack of a national commitment to the conservation of mammalian biodiversity has been largely brought about by the seeming irrelevance of all biodiversity conservation to the leaders of African states. TFCAs present an exciting new opening to show that these enlarged areas set aside for the conservation of biodiversity represent not only the optimum form of land-use, but the only option for the marginal drier areas that is economically viable and ecologically sustainable. In most of the TFCAs, mammals are an integral part of development plans. In the larger TFCAs, such as in the 95 712 km^2 of the Kruger/Banhine–Zinave/Gonarezhou TFCA, the introduction of biosphere reserves, developed in cooperation with local communities, is an additional powerful incentive to promote biodiversity conservation (Batisse, 1997). In January 1999, the Peace Parks Foundation established a specialist micro-development facility, wholly dedicated to identifying, developing and arranging finance for community based ventures in and around the TFCAs. This has the potential to build up equity partners in local communities, introducing a sense of ownership, which is long overdue.

Overhunting

Overhunting of selected valuable species should be reduced with an improvement of the management of protected areas, the introduction of a national commitment to mammalian biodiversity conservation and a reduction of civil unrest.

The development of TFCAs elsewhere in Africa deserves full support from the international conservation community. It is encouraging to see the recent enthusiastic response to the study initiated by the United States Agency for International Development to assess transboundary conservation in southern Africa, coupled with moves by Malawi, Tanzania and Zambia to participate in TFCA development.[2]

---

[2] Further information on the USAID study and other TFCA developments in Africa can be obtained from Werner Myburgh at the Peace Parks Foundation (wernerm@ppt.org.za).

14

Tourism and protected areas – distorting conservation priorities towards charismatic megafauna?

HAROLD J. GOODWIN AND NIGEL LEADER-WILLIAMS

INTRODUCTION

Protected area (PA) managers can face a dilemma between promoting tourism to earn revenue and promoting effective measures to conserve species, habitats and biodiversity. Indeed, many PA managers have a dual mandate to balance out these two sometimes conflicting demands. The root cause of this problem lies with the underlying aesthetic or socio-economic reasons why many PAs were originally established, often as a focus for nature- or wildlife-based tourism, rather than as a focus for biodiversity conservation (Leader-Williams et al., 1990b). Many PA managers already devote much energy to reconciling the management of tourism with the management of habitat and species (Zebu and Bush, 1990). In future, this task is likely to become more difficult as increasing volumes of tourists venture into ever more remote places, including PAs that are attracting an increasing market share of the tourist industry.

The terms 'nature tourism', 'wildlife tourism' and 'ecotourism' are often used interchangeably, and incorrectly. Nature and wildlife tourism (hereafter 'wildlife tourism') is often just assumed to comprise tourism that involves international travel by people from rich developed countries to wildlife areas in poorer developing countries, as a means of providing much needed foreign exchange for hard pressed national economies, and earnings for poor rural people, as well as a reason for justifying the upkeep of wildlife in PAs (Giongo et al., 1993). However, a wider view of wildlife tourism encompasses all forms and scales of tourism that involve the enjoyment of natural areas and wildlife. Wildlife tourism includes, as a principle aim, the consumptive or non-consumptive use of wild animals in natural areas, whether these are protected or unprotected. It may be high volume mass tourism or low volume/low impact tourism, it may generate high economic returns or low economic returns, be sustainable or unsustainable, domestic or international, and based on day visits or longer stays (see Roe *et al.*, 1997).

Ecotourism has emerged in recent years as a widely used buzz-word, but much confusion has surrounded its precise meaning (see Roe *et al.*, 1997). Many users have adopted ecotourism as a generic term to describe tourism that has, as its primary purpose, experience of an unspoilt natural environment (Jenner and Smith, 1992). Some users also incorporate a desire within use of the term ecotourism to minimise negative environmental impacts (Orams, 1995). However, more correctly ecotourism can be defined as low impact nature tourism that contributes to the maintenance of species and habitats either directly, through a contribution to conservation, and/or indirectly, by providing revenue to the local community sufficient for local people to value and therefore protect their wildlife heritage area as a source of income (Goodwin, 1996).

In this chapter, we first outline the general development of the tourist industry, of the different forms of wildlife tourism in particular, and of the dilemmas that this poses for PA managers. Next we examine the extent to which the expectations of visitors, the approach adopted by the tourism industry in marketing wildlife tourism, and the desires of the visitor in their destinations may cause a distortion of priorities towards charismatic mammals. We then review whether visitor expectations cause undue impacts upon mammals. Finally, we conclude with some suggestions as to how these distortions may be minimised. The chapter concentrates upon non-consumptive tourism in developing countries in the tropics and, given the nature of this volume, distortions that are evident towards mammals in terrestrial PAs throughout the whole wildlife tourism industry. The chapter devotes little space on the more general topic of how wildlife tourism may be turned into ecotourism, aspects of which have been well covered recently elsewhere (Ashley and Roe, 1998; Goodwin *et al.*, 1998).

TOURISM, WILDLIFE TOURISM AND PROTECTED AREAS

The development of tourism

The Oxford Dictionary defines a 'tourist' as 'one who makes a tour..., especially for recreation; one who travels for pleasure or culture, visiting a number of places for their objects of interest, scenery or the like'. Tourists have travelled throughout history. However, large scale tourism did not occur until the Industrial Revolution, when affordable rail travel and the offer by employers of paid holidays for their staff, stimulated the development of seaside resorts in Europe and the United States that catered for a new class of domestic tourists (Pearce, 1981). Larger scale international tourism began to develop in the early 1900s. Aeroplane technology developed during the two World Wars led to more affordable and long distance air travel. Tourism has now grown into a mass industry, because of affluence among the industrialised nations of the West and the Asia Pacific region, and the associated increase in disposable income and leisure time. Besides advances in transport technology (Pearce, 1981), the development of tourism has been further associated with cheap oil and the entry of multinational companies to the industry (Hunter and Green, 1995).

Tourism now generates over 10% of the world's gross domestic product, and employs one in nine workers worldwide (WTTC, 1994). The exponential growth in the global tourist industry can be gauged by the numbers of international tourist arrivals. These have risen from 25 million in 1950, to 183 million in 1970, to 450 million in 1991 and to 594 million in 1996, and to a predicted 650 million by the year 2000 (Murphy, 1985; Lindberg and Hawkins, 1993; WTO, 1998). However, these figures comprise all international arrivals, including business travellers who may not be touring in the spirit of the Oxford Dictionary definition. Largely as a result of business travel, almost 70% of international arrivals are to developed countries. Nevertheless, international arrivals to developing countries now account for an increasing share of the global figure, some 24% in 1980 and 30% in 1995 (WTO, 1996). The scale of domestic tourism, including day trips, is less well documented in readily available statistics. However, estimates from the late 1980s suggest that expenditure on domestic tourism accounts for approximately 90% of total tourism expenditure (Hunter and Green, 1995), and this sector is also predicted to rise dramatically (Ceballos-Lascurain, 1996).

Despite its huge growth, the tourist industry has proved no panacea for development, and incurs costs as well as benefits. A vital concern for developing countries is the high 'leakage' of tourism-generated foreign exchange, some 55 to 90% of which benefits foreign-owned tour operators, hotels and airlines in developed countries (Koch, 1994). Furthermore, public concern has focused on the impacts of mass tourism, both on the natural environment and on the culture of local people. These concerns led to the emergence of alternative forms of tourism, which tended to be small-scale and 'low key', with an emphasis on locally owned, traditional accommodation (Pearce, 1994), intended to cater for the 'alternative travel-ler seeking intimate but non-destructive contact with foreign cultures and environments' (Pleumarom, 1994).

The development of wildlife tourism

Wildlife tourism can encompass a range of activities, including bird watch-ing, wildlife viewing, photographic and walking safaris, reef diving, whale watching, trophy hunting and sport fishing. Wildlife tourism may be achieved through many different forms of transport, including on foot, by vehicle, boat or balloon. Wildlife tourism may be purposeful or may also include tourists who visit wildlife areas as an incidental part of a broader trip. For example, many tourists book a combination beach and safari holi-day in Kenya. Business trips may also involve visits to wildlife areas that are casual diversions rather than the prime motivation for visiting a country.

Overall, wildlife tourism is an important component of the interna-tional and domestic tourism industry. Wildlife tourism accounts for 20–40 % of international tourist arrivals, depending on the region (reviewed in Roe et al., 1997). Wildlife tourism is also very important for many domestic tourists, including those on day trips. However, as with tourism more gen-erally, statistics are often not available to determine what proportion of wildlife tourism is of domestic origin. However, it is likely to be very high in some countries, with nationals making up around 15–25 % of wildlife tour-ists in Canada, and some 90 % of visitors to the NPs in Thailand, India and South Africa (Ceballos-Lascurain, 1996).

As with tourism generally, wildlife tourism is likely to increase in im-portance and scale (Giongo et al., 1993). Furthermore, recent surveys sug-gest that wildlife tourism may also attract an increasing share of the market. Favoured destinations have shifted in the last 20 years towards developing countries, especially those rich in biodiversity. Central America, the Amazon, southern and eastern Africa, south and southeast Asia are notable growth areas for wildlife tourism. Key habitats and species are thought to have an undeniable influence on the popularity of wildlife tourism destinations (Risk and Policy Analysts Ltd., 1996). However, wild-life tourists focus on African savannahs as their major destination, as these provide the highest concentrations of easily accessible, readily visible large mammals. In contrast, wildlife tourism has been slower to develop in rain-forests. In Latin America, for example, rainforests provide difficult access to wilderness areas and have been weakly marketed. Furthermore, the species of interest to most tourists are secretive in their habits and less well known than their African counterparts. Equally, a number of more unusual tourist destinations with good visibility, such as the Antarctic, are becoming increasingly popular (Marsh, 1991).

Wildlife tourism in protected areas

Conservation biologists define protected areas (PAs) as predominantly natural areas established and managed in perpetuity through legal or customary regimes primarily for the conservation of biological diversity and natural resources. However, many PAs were originally established for a variety of aesthetic and socio-economic reasons, often as a focus for tourism (Myers, 1972). In other words, the siting of individual PAs or of whole PA networks in both developed and developing countries has seldom been determined by nature or biodiversity conservation priorities alone. In turn, this has led to many ad hoc reservations and an unsystematic coverage of biodiversity within national PA networks (Leader-Williams et al., 1990b; Pressey, 1994).

The world's first National Park (NP) was established at Yellowstone in the USA in 1872, as a 'public park or pleasuring ground for the benefit and enjoyment of the people'. Soon afterwards four Canadian NPs were established in scenic mountainous areas on the initiative of railroad companies wishing to increase their tourist traffic. These and several other Canadian NPs established subsequently have been the focus of, rather than removed from, economic development (Bella, 1987). Besides tourism, other pragmatic and socio-economic considerations, such as agricultural suitability, have also been important motives in establishing and siting PAs (Usher, 1986; Leader-Williams et al., 1990b; Hunter and Yonazon, 1993). Thus, PAs and networks established by default rarely afford comprehensive coverage of a nation's biological diversity (Pressey, 1994). Moreover, PAs with a socio-economic basis to their establishment are inherently weak in their provision for nature conservation, and conflicts can result between the need to preserve and the need to make a profit.

Nevertheless, tourism has long been advocated as a sustainable use for PAs, on the basis of a symbiotic relationship that can be created between conservation and tourism (Budowski, 1976). PAs are perhaps the prime sites for wildlife tourism as the legislative regimes under which they were established offer investors a longer-term guarantee of maintaining their attractions. In turn, international wildlife tourism can contribute enormously to the management of PAs, particularly in developing countries. Benefits can include foreign exchange revenue, employment opportunities and stimulation of economic activity. The trend of developing tourism in more natural settings continues, and PAs are obviously among the prime attractions for tourists, in both developing and developed countries (Giongo *et al.*, 1993). For example, the United States National Parks System is the world's largest tourist attraction (WTO and UNEP, 1992), while Australia's Great Barrier Reef NP attracts around 500 000 visitors a year (Jenner and Smith, 1992).

The goals of wildlife conservation may, however, at times be diametrically opposed to those of social sustainability. Hence, wildlife conservation objectives, even when stated in utilitarian terms of promoting tourism, may also have social implications. The designation of PAs in developing countries may contribute greatly to conserving wildlife and attracting tourists, but at the cost of excluding local communities from traditional practices such as nomadic pastoralism, cultivation and gathering wood, grass, medicinal plants and minor forest products, and so on (Leader-Williams *et al.*, 1990b). For example, pastoralists have been displaced from traditional grazing lands in Kenya and Tanzania through the creation of PAs. Indeed, Nairobi and Amboseli NPs in Kenya were excised from land that had provided dry season grazing and permanent water sources for the Maasai (Berger, 1996). In protesting their dissatisfaction, the Maasai have even killed important components of the wildlife resource upon which the tourism industry depends (Cater, 1993).

Patterns of wildlife tourism may also have negative impacts upon particular areas. For example, Kenya's reputation as a wildlife tourism destination is heavily dependent on just a few PAs, which then produce revenue for the wildlife authority upon which the less visited PAs in a more extensive system depend. Such unevenly distributed patterns of visitation can have serious implications for carrying capacities in heavily visited sites. The potential problems caused by tourism are increasingly recognised in PA management plans for key destinations such as the Galapagos Islands and Mount Kilimanjaro (Roe *et al.*, 1997), as well as by national wildlife and tourism policies (Ceballos-Lascurain, 1996).

Hence, one of the major challenges for wildlife tourism is how to ensure that PAs are financially self-sufficient without detracting from their primary function of preserving biodiversity and natural values (Goodwin *et al.*, 1998). To achieve this, it is usually necessary to encourage private sector investment and provide local communities with a vested interest in wildlife tourism. The labelling of land as a national park or some other category of PA may well serve to increase visitation to a wildlife area. However, if wildlife authorities are constituted as departments of central government, this may not necessarily produce any direct connection between revenues generated by visitors and operating budgets available for wildlife conservation by PA managers. In such situations, revenues earned from PAs accrue directly to the central treasury, and PAs are managed with budgets that are allocated centrally, and that take account of other national priorities such as health, education and communication. Equally, wildlife authorities in countries such as Kenya and South Africa have been created as parastatals and executive agencies, in which pricing and revenue are becoming more important to PA managers. In such situations, tourist viewing preferences and the demand that they represent will become increasingly significant as PA managers place greater reliance on the revenue earned from visitors.

WHAT DO TOURISTS WANT TO SEE?

Tourists book for, and depart on, their journeys with a set of expectations that is partially shaped by the travel industry, which in turn responds to tourist expectations. Hence, tour operators have a major role in presenting destinations to tourists, and can have a major influence on the volume of traffic to a particular site (Goodwin et al., 1998). The marketing of destinations is largely carried out by international tour operators overseas and by local tour operators in the metropolitan centres of the host country, by people and institutions remote from the destinations. Once the tourist is in the destination, they also develop further expectations, which in turn may cause the managers of those destinations to vary their management policies. It has been suggested previously that the successful marketing of wildlife tourism appears to be related to the predictable occurrence of certain target species within a relatively restricted area. Wildlife tourists expect a reasonable guarantee of seeing a particular key species or species group before they visit a location in any substantial numbers (WTO and UNEP, 1992). The following is believed to summarise the attitude of many wildlife tourists:

> The vital word in wildlife tourism is 'big'. People who travel the world to see animals want them to be large, and preferably deadly, or they want to see huge numbers. There is another vital ingredient. You must be able to get close up. Distant wildlife does not sell, the experts agree (Newlands, 1997).

Nine students studying for the MSc in Conservation Biology at the Durrell Institute of Conservation and Ecology (DICE) in the UK have examined such assumptions. Their studies have been undertaken at various points along a chain, from perceived expectations of visitors, to marketing by tour operators, to tourist expectations during the actual visit to a PA. They have focused on various destinations in Asia and in Africa, but used largely similar methodologies,

Table 14.1

Data available from DICE surveys of tour operators, and tourists *in situ* on expectations, marketing and visitor preferences with regard to wildlife tourism in different protected areas

Country of destination	International tour operators	Local tour operators	Tourists *in situ*	Author
India	Based in UK			Filgueiras, 1997
			Keoladeo	Goodwin *et al.*, 1998
Indonesia		Padang	Siberut	Liman, 1996
			Komodo	Goodwin *et al.*, 1998
Madagascar			Kirindy Forest	Teelen, 1996
Tanzania	Based in UK			Mafuru, 1997
Zambia	Based in UK			Clarke, 1997
			Luangwa Valley	Butler, 1996
		Lusaka	Kafue	Mwenya, 1996
Zimbabwe	Based in UK			Pirie, 1996
			Hwange	Andersen, 1995
			Gone-re-zhou	Goodwin *et al.*, 1998

enabling comparison across destinations. These students collected data from surveys of UK-based and local tour operators, from content analysis of the brochures of these operators, and from tourist surveys conducted in PAs (Table 14.1). We predicted that there would be considerable variation between countries and continents in what was marketed and attractive to tourists, because of the different visibilities, habitats and landscapes, cultures and peoples, and abundances of wildlife in the different situations. However, when tourists wished to see wildlife, there would be considerable interest in viewing large charismatic mammals. In this section we summarise some of these data, to expand upon an already published study of expectations during actual visits to a more limited range of sites in Asia and Africa (Goodwin *et al.*, 1998).

Tour operators views of clients' expectations

Postal surveys of UK-based tour operators showed that those marketing India believed their clients were attracted primarily by culture and history. They placed much less emphasis on encountering wildlife and adventure, and made no mention of wildlife abundance. In contrast, those marketing Zimbabwe believed three key elements were of primary importance in making southern African countries attractive for their clients, namely encounters with wildlife, abundance of wildlife and an element of adventure. Tour operators believed that encountering authentic India or Africa, and the exotic or unusual were similarly important to both destinations, although not of primary importance. Being able to undertake a range of activities and meeting local people were felt to be of more importance to those visiting southern Africa than India, but again these elements were not of primary importance. Very little emphasis was placed by tour operators on their clients' wish for luxury, good food or home comforts in either destination (Figure 14.1).

In terms of perceived preferences for seeing different species of wildlife, tour operators featuring India believed their clients would most wish to see a tiger and Indian avifauna, followed by elephants and leopards. Tour operators featuring southern Africa believed their clients would most wish to see the 'Big Five' of elephant, rhino, lion, leopard and buffalo, the concept generated by big game hunters at the turn of the century (Mellon, 1975), whether they mentioned these species collectively or singly. There was felt to be little interest among those visiting southern Africa in seeing birds or other smaller mammals. Thus, apart from the wish to see birds in India, most tour operators believed their clients would wish to see the respective charismatic and dangerous large mammal species on each continent (Figure 14.1). We will now move to examine the visual topics that tour operators most use in their brochures, in response to perceived expectations of their clients.

Marketing through brochures

The brochures of UK-based tour operators selling tours to India portrayed very different visual topics to those selling tours to Tanzania, Zambia and Zimbabwe (Figure 14.2). Equally, even among the three African countries, there are finer grain differences in visual presentation of topics, although a relative consistency emerges when compared with India. The visual topics in brochures advertising India are more heavily dominated by aspects of the country's culture and history, and by its people, than by brochures advertising the three African countries, which place the most emphasis on African fauna. However, brochures for both India and the three African countries place similar emphasis on both landscapes, and on facilities and services in support of tourism. There is little emphasis in visual displays of flora or of sport (Figure 14.2).

Among the fauna portrayed in UK-based tour operators' brochures advertising India, pictures of the tiger, elephant and camel predominate. Similarly, within brochures advertising the three African countries, visuals of large mammals almost completely predominate, although there are variations between the three countries in terms of the proportions of elephants, large cats and rhinos portrayed. There are very few portrayals of birds

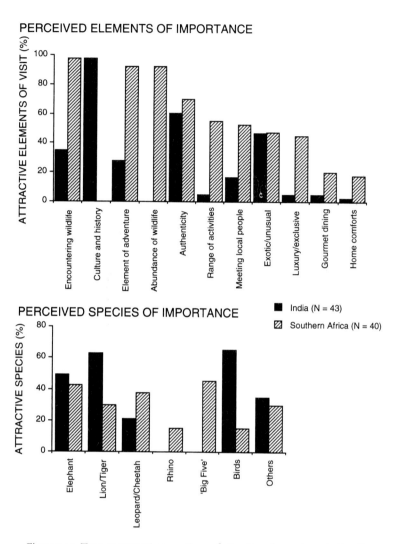

Figure 14.1 Tour operators' perceptions of attractive elements and attractive species for wildlife tourists, based on questionnaires administered to UK-based tour operators sending tourists to India and southern Africa/Zimbabwe (data from Pirie, 1996; Filgueiras, 1997). Tour operators were asked, in their own view, what elements make a tourist's visit to that region or country attractive, and what species (or species groups in the case of southern Africa only) of wildlife tourists to India and Zimbabwe most wish to see. The differences for both elements and species between India and southern Africa/Zimbabwe were highly significant ($\chi^2 = 99.69$ and 22.63, df = 9 and 5, both $P < 0.001$; the analysis for species omitted the Big Five for Zimbabwe).

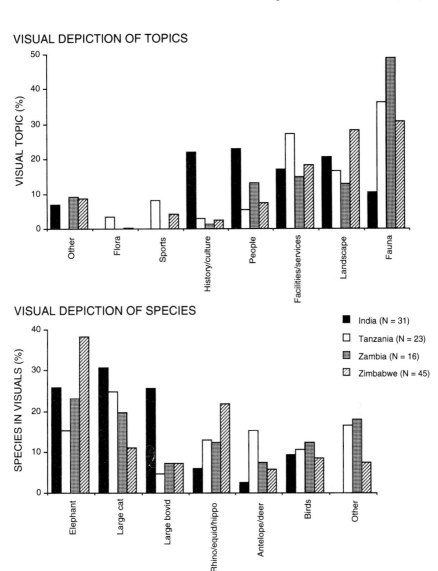

Figure 14.2 The visual depiction of destinations in India and Africa, including Tanzania, Zambia and Zimbabwe, in the brochures of UK-based tour operators (data from Pirie, 1996; Clarke, 1997; Filgueiras, 1997; Mafuru, 1997). Brochures were examined both for the range of topics covered in pictures of the destination and, within the fauna category, for the species of animals depicted. The difference in the topics depicted between India and Africa was significant (χ^2=20.46, df=6, $P < 0.001$).

or other mammals for India or for any of the African countries (Figure 14.2).

This marked difference between marketing continents was maintained in the two more limited studies that have been undertaken among local tour operators. Indonesian tour operators in Padang marketing trips to Siberut believed their clients were most interested in local culture (71 %) and trekking (57 %), while wildlife was of little interest (14 %). However, all local tour operators sought improvements in opportunities for wildlife viewing, in order to promote more tourism to Siberut (Liman 1996). Zambian tour operators in Lusaka marketing trips to Kafue considered that wild animals (100 %), birdlife (58 %) and river scenery (50 %) were the most important features (Mwenya 1996). We will now move to examine what tourists in PAs most wish to see.

Preferences of tourists in protected areas

Surveys of international tourists about their motivations for visiting three NPs were expected to reflect more strongly the features that attracted them to the NP, than would a survey conducted among the general population of international tourists in the respective countries (Goodwin et al., 1998). At Keoladeo in India, most (45 %) visitors were interested in culture, while wildlife interested fewer (30 %) visitors. Similarly in Komodo in Indonesia, most (57 %) visitors were interested in culture, fewer (19 %) were interested in landscape, while very few (7 %) were interested in wildlife. Wildlife is most significant in Zimbabwe where 66 % of tourists in Gona-re-zhou rated wildlife as the most important motivation for travel, this was followed by landscape (20 %) and culture (9 %).

This broad difference between the two continents of Asia and Africa is further amplified when published data are shown with additional data from MSc theses (Figure 14.3). Cultural and people-related aspects are of most interest to visitors in three Asian PAs. Wildlife is of secondary, and habitat and landscape of tertiary, interest in the Indian PA of Keoladeo, while habitat and landscape is of secondary, and wildlife of tertiary, interest in the two Indonesian PAs of Komodo and Siberut. The interests of visitors change markedly in the five African PAs. Cultural and people aspects are of tertiary importance, or are not even mentioned as being of importance, by visitors to African PAs. In the rainforest habitats of Madagascar, habitat and landscape considerations are of primary, and wildlife of secondary, interest in Kirindy Forest. However, in the woodland savannah habitats of Zambia and Zimbabwe, wildlife is of primary interest in the four NPs of Kafue, South Luangwa, Gona-re-zhou and Hwange (Figure 14.3).

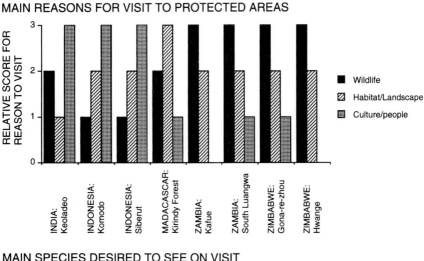

Figure 14.3 The expressed elements and species of interest for visitors to protected areas in India, Indonesia, Madagascar, Zambia and Zimbabwe (data from Andersen, 1995; Butler, 1996; Liman, 1996; Mwenya, 1996; Teelen, 1996; Goodwin *et al.*, 1998). The different studies of the main reasons why people visit different areas were carried out by a mixture of methods that involved both mean scores and percentages that were not directly comparable. Hence, the interest of visitors in wildlife, habitat and landscape, and culture and people for the eight sites are given relative scores by order of importance, irrespective of method, with 3 = most important, 2 = second important, and 1 = least important (where culture and people were not mentioned, no score is given). Visitors to Kirindy Forest and South Luangwa ranked the importance of particular species or species group on a scale of 1–5 in their decision to visit, and results are shown where mean scores exceed 3.80.

Even though visitors to Madagascar and mainland Africa sites have different wishes with regard to experiencing habitats and landscape, and wildlife, tourists to Kirindy Forest most wish to see the endemic large mammals, namely the lemurs, while putting lesser emphasis on vegetation and birdlife. As expected, visitors to the savannah woodland area of South Luangwa most wish to see the large mammals, and place most emphasis on the large cats, elephants and giraffe, followed by hippos, spotted hyaenas and buffaloes (Figure 14.3). Of the traditional 'Big Five', the black rhino did not feature among the most desired mammals because it is almost certainly locally extinct in South Luangwa, while buffaloes appear lower down the list of non-consumptive tourists than on the list of hunters.

Tourists in South Luangwa also noted that seeing few animals close up from vehicles, seeing rare species, followed by being in a wild landscape and night game drives were the factors most important in their stay (Butler, 1996). Given the expectations directed towards mammals on the part of the tourist industry and of the visitors themselves, we now move to consider whether this has consequences for the management of tourist impact in PAs.

DO TOURISTS CAUSE IMPACTS ON WILDLIFE?

The types of disturbance to wildlife caused by tourists depend upon a range of factors including its predictability; its frequency and magnitude; when it occurs within the daily activity cycle or life cycle of a particular species; the type of tourist activity, for example, foot safaris, boating, hot air ballooning; and upon the type of tourist (see Roe et al., 1997). Wildlife tourists may intentionally seek out the species they wish to see, and when tourist activities occur during sensitive times in the life cycle, for example, nesting, or when they involve close approaches to wildlife for the purposes of identification or photography, the potential for disturbing individuals is high. Equally, some impacts may be very difficult to identify, due to lack of baseline data and the inherent complexities of ecological systems, or the long term and cumulative effects of those impacts. Furthermore, animal responses to human disturbance differ between individuals, and even between situations for a single species. Even when an impact from tourism is quantified successfully, a further difficulty may arise in determining if that impact is biologically important in the long term. Thus, a disturbed animal may feed or nest elsewhere, or a road graded through woodland may quickly revert to woodland when that road is no longer used. Nevertheless, a few studies have quantified some form of environmental impact arising from wildlife tourism. Here we examine if the expectations of visitors (see preceding section) and deliberate actions on the part of tour guides skew the direct impacts of tourists towards the mammals most tourists wish to see. We do not consider unwitting impacts, such as the transmission of diseases between tourists and animals, or the indirect impacts of wildlife tourism, for example localised changes in habitats as a result of off-road driving, trampling or littering, or the impacts from associated infrastructure, such as development of lodges and roads, all of which have been reviewed elsewhere (Roe *et al.*, 1997).

Most available studies of direct impacts of tourism upon wildlife do indeed focus upon mammals, with a smaller number focusing on birds (Table 14.2). Elephants, hippos and giant otters are locally disturbed by boat trips offered around lodges. Hippos are particularly sensitive to disturbance since they rest during the day, while giant otters appear similarly prone to disturbance since they feed during the day. Buffalo and lion are caused considerable distress by balloon safaris in East Africa. Primates, such as Sulawesi black macaques and spectral tarsiers, are significantly affected by tourists on foot. The feeding of Indian rhinos may be disturbed by tourists on elephants' backs.

For many wildlife tourists, observing a top predator stalking and securing a kill may be the highlight of their trip, but the desire to view such activities affects certain predators (Table 14.2). For some species, data on disturbance is largely inferred and anecdotal, for example studies of leopards. In the case of the cryptic and generally nocturnal leopard, such disturbances are likely to be insignificant in terms of their overall range and abundance. However, the diurnal cheetah is less common and widespread, and more prone to disturbance in the smaller and more open PAs (Table 14.2). Equally, in larger and more wooded areas, tourists appear to cause the cheetah less disturbance (Caro, 1994).

CONCLUSIONS

The growth in international and domestic tourism will result in increasing visitor pressure on PAs, and management priorities are likely to shift accordingly. Published work and student theses have shown that the tourist industry and wildlife tourists themselves have a set of expectations on desirable elements in their visits to PAs. While no research has yet been done by our group on destinations in Latin America, and considerable gaps remain in what has so far been achieved elsewhere (Table 14.1), the contrasts between the existing data for Asia and Africa are instructive. Tourists who

Table 14.2
Some species upon which direct disturbance in their feeding, breeding and resting patterns has been described (reviewed in Roe et al., 1997)

Species	Disturbance	Area	Country	Reference
Cheetah	Vehicle-viewing	Amboseli	Kenya	Henry, 1980
Cape buffalo Lion	Balloon trip		Kenya	Sindiyo and Pertet, 1984
Masked booby Red-footed booby Blue-footed booby	Walkers	Galapagos	Ecuador	Burger and Gochfeld, 1983
Galapagos albatross	Walkers	Galapagos	Ecuador	de Groot, 1983
Leopard	Game-viewing	Ruhuna	Sri Lanka	Santiapillai et al. 1982
Ruddy shelduck	Canoe trip	Chitwan	Nepal	Hulbert, 1990
Hippopotamus	Boat trip	Selous	Tanzania	Rohs, 1991
Cheetah	Game-viewing	Masai Mara	Kenya	Muthee, 1992
Giant otter Jaguar Lowland tapir	Boat trip	Manu	Peru	Dunstone and O'Sullivan, 1996
Elephant Black rhino	Boat traffic	Matusadona	Zimbabwe	McIvor, 1994
Indian rhino	Elephant rides	Chitwan	Nepal	Lott and McCoy, 1995
Sulawesi black macaques Spectral tarsiers	Walkers	Tangokoko	Indonesia	Kinnaird and O'Brien, 1996

Leopard, *Panthera pardus*, Kenya. Photograph: Sybil Sassoon.

visit forested natural environments in Asia experience more limited visibility than those who visit savannah Africa. Tour operators expect their clients interested in India to find culture and history more attractive (Figure 14.1), and market these aspects more heavily in their brochures (Figure 14.2), than for clients interested in Africa. Even in PAs, tourists in Asia wish to concentrate more on cultural and people aspects than on landscape and wildlife, while tourists in savannah Africa are primarily interested in wildlife (Figure 14.3). This is despite the fact that the African countries so far included in our studies do not lack in very important cultural or historical attractions (e.g., Kilwa in Tanzania, Livingstone's memorial in Zambia, or Great Zimbabwe).

Despite these broad differences between forested Asia and savannah Africa, the expectations of clients, the marketing strategy of tour operators and the wishes of tourists in PAs are mainly directed towards wishing to see the native large mammal faunas of each area, whether in Asia or Africa (Figures 14.1, 14.2 and 14.3). The wish to see birds and vegetation may also be assumed, marketed or expressed in forested situations in Asia or in Madagascar, but the underlying basis of tourist expectations nevertheless lies with large mammals. These desires would also appear to have important consequences for the impacts caused by, or on behalf of tourists wishing to see the charismatic mammals (Table 14.2). Hence, there is evidence here that charismatic megafauna may distort the management priorities of those PAs that are present or future foci of wildlife tourism. A comprehensive future study that investigated management practices and priorities among PA managers with high and low levels of wildlife tourism would be instructive.

The question remains for conservationists and PA managers whether they wish to attempt to re-focus this interest on the part of tourists from individual, charismatic species to wider habitat, landscape and biodiversity concerns. Such an enterprise would require considerable effort all the way along the tourist chain from expectation, to marketing to actual visit. For example, UK tour operators thought it important to show their clients a range of different habitats during their visit to Zimbabwe, perhaps in recognition of the linkage between habitats and species (Pirie, 1996). However, this would also require considerable changes in the material included in brochures. Tourists inside PAs also believe that additional facilities would enhance their visit, for example the labelling of trees and provision of interpretative centres (Butler, 1996; Liman, 1996; Mwenya, 1996; Teelen, 1996), all of which could help to focus on wider biodiversity issues than the present desire to concentrate on viewing large mammals.

Conservationists and PA managers recognise that tourism is a major management issue and they will deploy increasing amounts of time and resources to its management. An additional concern, and one not discussed fully in this chapter, is to turn wide-scale nature tourism into ecotourism, if PAs managers are to be enabled to harness this major industry to help meet conservation objectives and to restrain it from damaging the 'attraction'. Local communities bear the opportunity costs of living adjacent to PAs and the direct costs associated with living with large mammals, which damage crops and which endanger human lives. Tourism is one means by which local communities can diversify their economies and gain from the protected species. We hope that we have shown how the tourism industry and visitors to PAs can be used to develop awareness of the importance of habitat and more general biodiversity issues.

ACKNOWLEDGEMENTS

We thank Ina Andersen, Cheryl Butler, Marcus Clarke, Raquel Filigueiras, Puspa Liman, Nyamakumbati Mafuru, Lackson Mwyena, Frances Pirie and Simone Teelen for their dedicated work while they were Master's students at the Durrell Institute of Conservation and Ecology. Cheryl Butler and Matthew Walpole prepared figures used in the conference presentation.

15

Integrating hunting and protected areas in the Amazon

RICHARD E. BODMER

INTRODUCTION

This chapter looks at the conservation of Amazonian wildlife and considers how local communities and wildlife hunting can be consistent with protected areas. The rationale is that: (1) local people need to be involved in wildlife conservation, because they are the ones who hunt animals for subsistence food and monetary income (Western and Wright, 1994; Child, 1995; Bodmer *et al.*, 1997b); (2) hunting will be compatible with conservation only if animal populations are not overhunted (Bodmer, 1994; Robinson and Redford, 1994a); and (3) to ensure that animals are not overhunted, communities must themselves set aside non-hunted areas to act as sources for heavily hunted areas (Bodmer and Ayres, 1991; Hill and Padwe, in press). These non-hunted areas are in fact community-based protected areas that are in accord with the needs of local people and of wildlife conservation.

Protected areas are important for the conservation of tropical forests (McNeely *et al.*, 1994a; Amend and Amend, 1995). Unfortunately, many governments are often unable to manage existing protected areas, because of lack of money and political pressure by local communities and business interests who use natural resources and oppose protected areas (Barzetti, 1993; Mansour *et al.*, 1995). Management of many protected areas is shifting from policies that exclude local communities to those that involve them (Wells and Brandon, 1992; Barzetti, 1993; Redford and Mansour, 1996).

A novel paradigm is needed to set aside new protected areas of tropical forest. This new system of protected areas would likely involve local communities and their use of natural resources. However, before promoting community-based protected areas it is necessary to show how resource use by local communities can lead to protected areas that conform with the conservation of animals and plants, and the subsistence and monetary needs of the people. Indeed, community-based efforts should not be promoted if attempts at community-based conservation lead to overexploitation, habitat destruction, and the degradation of protected areas, because of uncertainties with sustainable use and/or difficulties of accommodating social and economic realities.

This chapter looks at ways to incorporate wildlife hunting with community-based protected areas in the Amazon forests. Local people throughout the Amazon use wildlife as an important source of subsistence meat and as a way to earn income by selling meat in local markets. Hunters get the greatest amounts of wild meat from five ungulate species: the red brocket deer *Mazama americana*; grey brocket deer *Mazama gouazoupira*; collared peccary *Pecari tajacu*; white-lipped peccary *Tayassu pecari*; and lowland tapir *Tapirus terrestris* (Bodmer et al., 1994). These ungulates are also important components of the Amazonian ecosystem and help maintain forest structure through seed dispersal (Fragoso, 1994).

Data from a long-term field project in the Peruvian Amazon were used to look at the relationships between local people, hunting and protected areas. The first question that needs to be asked is: are ungulates being overhunted? This was examined using an analysis, known as the harvest model, that compares harvests to estimates of animal production. The hunting was then evaluated further by looking at the riskiness of the harvest levels. This was done using a stock-recruitment analysis.

Information on overhunting was then used to look at management techniques that could remedy overuse. One promising solution for overhunting combines non-hunted and hunted areas. Animals from non-hunted areas could replenish hunted areas if animals are overhunted. Thus, if local people desire long-term use of wildlife for their subsistence and monetary needs they should set up and maintain these non-hunted areas.

STUDY DESIGN

Two representative areas of northeastern Peru were used as in-depth study sites. These sites include the major landscape characteristics (flooded forest and upland forest) and human features (ribereño culture) of the region (Padoch, 1988; Chibnik, 1994). One area was in and around the upland forests of the Tamshiyacu–Tahuayo Community Reserve (RCTT) and the other in the flooded forests of the Pacaya–Samiria National Reserve (RNPS)

(Figure 15.1). The two areas had rural people who used natural resources and showed an interest in participating in the projects.

The Pacaya–Samiria National Reserve is a 2 000 000 ha flooded forest. In the Reserve, a site with persistent hunting was studied near the villages of Maipuco, Nueva Esperansa and San Antonio along the Marañon River (Maipuco site) and a site with slight/no hunting near the village of Dos de Mayo along the Samiria River (Samiria site). Studies were carried out between 1993–1996. All of the ungulate species except the grey brocket deer occurred in the Reserve.

The Tamshiyacu–Tahuayo Community Reserve is mainly in upland non-flooded habitats. In the forests in and around the Reserve, a site with persistent hunting was studied near the villages of Chino and San Pedro along the Qb. Blanco and upper Tahuayo Rivers (Tahuayo/Blanco site) and a site with slight/no hunting near the villages of Carolina, Esperanza and San Philipe along the lower reaches of the Yavari Miri River (Yavari–Miri site). Studies were carried out in this area between 1989–1997. All five ungulate species occurred in the Reserve.

The study design used both descriptions and experiments. The experimental design compared persistently hunted sites with slightly hunted/non-hunted sites (Bodmer et al., 1997a). The treatment in this design was hunting pressure, since habitat was kept as constant as possible within the upland sites and within the flooded forest sites.

Overhunting of ungulates was examined in the study areas using the following approaches:

(1) A harvest model compared production with a known harvest in a specified catchment area, which provided a direct measure of overhunting.

(2) A stock-recruitment model evaluated the riskiness of the ungulate harvests by examining harvest levels in relation to maximum sustained yield (MSY) estimates.

(3) A source-sink model evaluated the need for non-hunted areas as a way to remedy overhunting.

METHODS

Hunting pressure

Information on hunting pressure was obtained by involving hunters with data collection. Hunters participated by collecting skulls of animals they

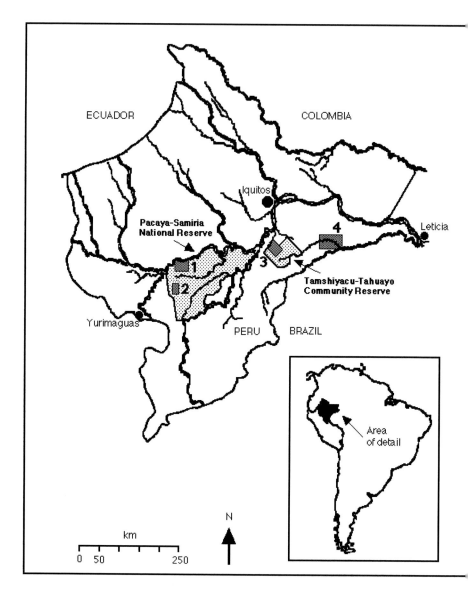

Figure 15.1 Map of northeastern Peru showing the flooded forest sites with (1) persistent hunting (Maipuco), (2) slight hunting (Samiria), and the upland sites with (3) persistent hunting (Tahuayo/Blanco) and (4) slight hunting(Yavari–Miri).

hunted. Hunters labelled the skulls by the sex of the individual, the date hunted, and the location of the kill. This method provided information on the number of individuals hunted (harvest) and the area used by hunters (the catchment area). An error margin was added to the hunting pressure to account for animals hunted, but not recorded either by skulls or interviews. Skulls from hunted animals were placed in the Zoology Museum at the Universidad Nacional de la Amazonia Peruana.

Densities and abundances

Transects were used to calculate abundances of ungulates and estimate their densities. Trails were cut in the forest and censused. Hunting trails were avoided during censuses. Transects were censused in the morning and evening, and records were taken of the number of animal groups sighted, the number of individuals in each group, and the perpendicular distance of the first sighting to the trail.

Abundance was measured as the number of groups sighted per km of line transect censused. Densities were estimated using the DISTANCE method, which is the most widely used method to evaluate tropical wildlife populations (Buckland et al., 1993; Wilson et al., 1996).

The Samiria site had 756 km of census, the Maipuco site 1031 km, the Yavari Miri site 482 km, and the Tahuayo/Blanco site 626 km, altogether a total of 2895 km.

Reproductive parameters

Reproductive productivity (average number of young /female/year) was calculated from data on reproductive activity of females and used information on: (1) number of gestations per year; and (2) gross productivity (number of foetuses/number of adult females examined) (Gottdenker and Bodmer, 1998).

HARVEST MODEL

A harvest model compared the harvest and production of ungulates in the persistently hunted sites and helped to predict overhunting. The model used production estimates from reproductive productivity and population density. Harvest data and catchment areas gave an estimate of hunting pressure (individuals harvested/km^2). We assumed that a maximum of 60 % of production could be harvested without overhunting for very short-lived species, 40 % for short-lived species and 20 % for long-lived species (Robinson and Redford, 1991). Peccaries and deer were considered short-

Table 15.1
An example of the harvest model used for peccaries in the Tahuayo/Blanco
and Maipuco study sites

	Collared peccary *Tayassu tajacu*	White-lipped peccary *Tayassu pecari*
Tahuayo/Blanco		
Gross productivity	0.76	0.57
Number of gestations/year	2.00	1.65
1/2 density (ind/km²)	0.70 ± 0.15	3.3 ± 1.45
Annual production (ind/km²)	1.06 ± 0.23	3.10 ± 1.36
Hunting pressure (ind/km²)	0.33	0.33
% of production harvested	31 ± 10	11 ± 8
Maipuco		
Gross productivity	1.02	0.51
Number of gestations/year	1.88	1.69
1/2 density (ind/km²)	0.33 ± 0.19	0.95 ± 0.47
Annual production (ind/km²)	0.63 ± 0.36	0.82 ± 0.40
Hunting pressure (ind/km²)	0.03	0.10
% of production harvested	5 ± 2	12 ± 4

lived, and we assumed that a maximum of 40 % of production could be
harvested without overhunting. In contrast, lowland tapir were considered
long-lived animals and we assumed that a maximum of 20 % of their production could be harvested without overhunting.

An example will illustrate the harvest model (Table 15.1). Female collared peccaries shot by hunters had a gross productivity in the Tahuayo/
Blanco study site of 0.76 foetuses/animal and in these forests they had an
average of 2.00 gestations/year (Gottdenker and Bodmer, 1998). This resulted in an annual reproductive productivity of 1.52 young/female/year.
The reproductive productivity was then multiplied by half of the density of
collared peccaries, since we assumed that half of the population in the
Tahuayo/Blanco site were females. The product, annual production, was
then divided into the annual hunting pressure of 0.33 collared peccary
hunted/km². This yielded the percentage of production taken by hunters,
which in this case was 31 % of the collared peccary production. This was
below the 40 % maximum for a short-lived species, which suggested that
hunters were not currently overharvesting collared peccaries in the
Tahuayo/Blanco site.

The harvest model showed that white-lipped and collared peccaries
were not overhunted in both the persistently hunted areas of upland and
flooded forests (Table 15.2). The percent of production harvested from red

Table 15.2
Percent of production taken by hunters in the flooded forest site
of Maipuco and the upland site of Tahuayo/Blanco. The
proportion of production that can be harvested sustainably is
assumed to be 40 % for deer and peccaries and 20 % for
lowland tapir

	% of production taken by hunters	
Species (common names)	Maipuco	Tahuayo/Blanco
White-lipped peccary	12 ± 4	11 ± 8
Collared peccary	5 ± 2	31 ± 10
Red Brocket deer	37 ± 10	38 ± 6
Grey Brocket deer	—	38 ± 9
Lowland tapir	400 ± 200	140 ± 53

and grey brocket deer were both close to the 40 % limit in the persistently hunted upland forest, and for red brocket deer in the persistently hunted flooded forest. Harvests of red and grey brocket deer were just outside the limits of overhunting. In contrast, lowland tapir were overhunted in both the persistently hunted areas of upland and flooded forests, with well over 100 % of production being harvested. This meant that the base population of lowland tapir was being depleted in these sites, which was obviously unsustainable.

The harvest model is a useful way to evaluate overhunting in an area, because it uses information on production and harvests from field sites. However, the model does not consider density-dependent effects of production (Robinson and Redford, 1994b). Density-dependent relationships help determine levels of production that can be harvested at different population sizes. A stock-recruitment model was used to evaluate the population size of ungulates and examine whether harvesting at that population size was a risky or safe hunting strategy.

STOCK-RECRUITMENT MODEL

The stock recruitment model assumes that production varies predictably with population size. If recruitment is density-dependent then production is maximised at some population density below K, the carrying capacity (Caughley, 1977). This density, termed the density of maximum sustainable yield (MSY), is determined by the shape of the curve of recruitment against population density (McCullough, 1987). Managing populations to achieve MSY is risky. Any overharvesting would result in a deceased base population the following year, and if continued, quickly lead to extirpation of the population (McCullough, 1987). For the same reason, harvesting species at population levels lower than the MSY point is risky. However, harvesting species with large base populations (to the right of MSY) is a safe strategy that should be used (Caughley and Sinclair, 1994).

Amazonian ungulates are K-selected species and they should have density-dependent recruitment that responds to the relationships between rate of increase and population size (Caughley, 1977). An adaptation of the stock-recruitment model was therefore used to examine the riskiness of hunting. The shape of the recruitment curve has not been defined for Amazonian ungulates. Nevertheless, the approach can be used to provide an estimate of the state of a hunted population (N/K). Densities (N) of a hunted population can be compared to the carrying capacity (K) of a population and to an estimated MSY. In turn, this can help determine whether hunting is on the safe or risky side of the MSY.

Carrying capacities (K) of Amazonian ungulates were assumed to be similar to densities at the slightly/non-hunted sites of Yavari Miri and Samiria. The MSY for Amazonian artiodactyls was assumed to be at 60% of K, because empirical studies on artiodactyls usually have MSY at this level of K (McCullough, 1987; Robinson and Redford, 1991). The MSY for lowland tapir was assumed to be at 80% of K, because tapir have little variation in their reproductive productivity which would result in an MSY closer to K. Densities of Amazonian ungulates in the persistently hunted sites were then compared to the estimated K and MSY.

In the upland forests of Tahuayo/Blanco densities of collared peccary, red brocket deer and grey brocket deer were above the predicted MSY and on the safe side of the stock-recruitment model (Table 15.3). Therefore, both the harvest and stock-recruitment model suggested that current harvests of collared peccary, and red and grey brocket deer in the upland forests of Tahuayo/Blanco were not resulting in overhunting.

In contrast, densities of white-lipped peccary in the upland forests of Tahuayo/Blanco and densities of white-lipped and collared peccary and red brocket deer in the flooded forests of Maipuco were below the predicted MSY and on the risky side of the stock-recruitment model (Tables 15.3 and 15.4). While the harvest model predicted that with the current offtake these species were not being overhunted, the stock-recruitment model predicted that current harvests should be lowered so populations could increase to levels above the predicted MSY.

The densities of lowland tapir in both the upland forests of Tahuayo/Blanco and the flooded forest of Maipuco were below the predicted MSY

Table 15.3
The stock-recruitment analysis for ungulates in the Tamshiyacu–Tahuayo
Community Reserve.
K was estimated from densities at the Yavari Miri site. N is the density in the
persistently hunted site of Tahuayo/Blanco. Maximum sustained yield (MSY) is given
as the percent of K. Strategies were either risky or safe

Species	K	MSY (%)	N/K (%)	Strategy
White-lipped peccary	13.1 ± 5.8	60	50	risky
Collared peccary	1.6 ± 0.5	60	87	safe
Red brocket deer	0.94 ± 0.3	60	75	safe
Grey brocket deer	0.24 ± 0.1	60	87	safe
Lowland tapir	0.91 ± 0.3	80	45	risky

Table 15.4
The stock-recruitment analysis for ungulates in the Pacaya–Samiria National
Reserve.
K was estimated from densities at the Samiria site. N is the density in the persistently
hunted site of Maipuco. Maximum sustained yield (MSY) is given as the per cent of K.
Strategies were either risky or safe

Species	K	MSY (%)	N/K (%)	Strategy
White-lipped peccary	8.1 ± 2.7	60	18	risky
Collared peccary	1.8 ± 0.4	60	22	risky
Red brocket deer	0.5 ± 0.03	60	19	risky
Lowland tapir	0.06 ± 0.02	80	50	risky

and on the risky side of the stock-recruitment model (Tables 15.3 and 15.4). In the case of the lowland tapir, both the harvest and stock-recruitment models indicated that current harvests were overhunting tapir and should be lowered. The harvest model clearly showed that hunting should be lowered to attain a sustained offtake, while the stock-recruitment model suggested that hunting should be lowered so tapir populations could increase to levels above the predicted MSY.

The harvest and stock-recruitment models should be viewed as indicators and their numeric results should not represent precise values, but general trends. Indeed, our understanding of tropical ecosystems is still very incomplete and analyses of hunting must incorporate uncertainties, especially with species-specific models that assume closed populations. At the same time, local people want to know how many animals they can hunt so they can feed their families. Used with caution these models can help local people determine levels of hunting.

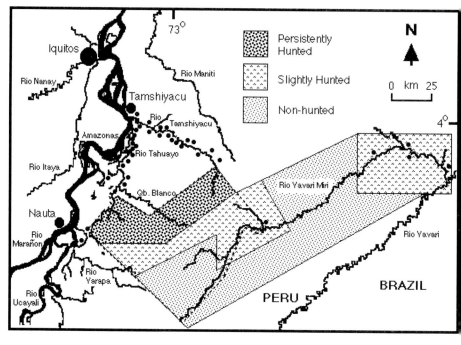

Figure 15.2 Map of the Tamshiyacu–Tahuayo Community Reserve and its surroundings, which was used to estimate the size of the source and sink areas. The dots represent villages and the dashed lines show the official boundaries of the reserve.

SOURCE–SINK STRATEGY

The harvest and stock-recruitment models showed that hunting should be lowered on Amazonian ungulates to attain a sustained offtake and increase populations to levels above the predicted MSY. Setting non-hunted areas adjacent to hunted areas can help remedy this overhunting and is known as the source–sink strategy, with unhunted source populations being able to replenish hunted (or sink) areas (McCullough, 1996).

The effectiveness of the source-sink strategy was evaluated using examples from the Tamshiyacu–Tahuayo Community Reserve and the Pacaya–Samiria National Reserve. Both reserves have non-hunted areas adjacent to hunted areas. Non-hunted areas may produce a surplus of Amazonian ungulates that can move into areas of persistent hunting.

For example, the Tamshiyacu–Tahuayo Community Reserve and its surroundings can be divided into three types of hunting zones: (1) a persist-

Table 15.5
Results of the harvest model for lowland tapir in source and sink areas in and around the Tamshiyacu–Tahuayo Community Reserve

Category	Persistently hunted sink	Slightly hunted source	Non-hunted source	Slightly hunted plus non-hunted source	All areas source–sink
Approximate area (km²)	1700	4000	5300	9300	11 000
Density (ind/km²)	0.21	0.91	0.91	0.91	0.80*
Hunting pressure (ind/km²)	0.07	0.02	0.0	0.01*	0.02*
% of production harvested	140	16	0	8	18

* indicates that densities and hunting pressures are weighted averages between sites.

ently hunted area of 1700 km²; (2) slightly hunted areas totalling 4000 km²; and (3) non-hunted areas totalling 5300 km² (Figure 15.2). The non-hunted and slightly hunted areas are potential source populations for the persistently hunted area. The size of hunting zones were estimated from data on harvests and catchment area collected from hunters over the past eight years.

The effectiveness of the source-sink strategy was examined for lowland tapir populations in the reserve, because tapir were the most overhunted of the Amazonian ungulates. The harvest model showed that in the persistently hunted site of Tahuayo/Blanco 140 % of lowland tapir production was hunted. This was clearly a sink area. In the slightly hunted sites an estimated 16 % of lowland tapir production was hunted, which was below the 20 % limit (Table 15.5). The slightly hunted sites could therefore be considered as part of the source area. Thus, the non-hunted sites where 0 % of production was hunted, and the slightly hunted sites together made up the aggregate source area. Hunters were taking an estimated 8 % of the lowland tapir production from this aggregate source area, which was well within sustainable levels. Within the entire source-sink area including the persistently hunted, slightly hunted and non-hunted sites hunters were taking an estimated 18 % of lowland tapir production. This suggested that overhunting in the persistently hunted area could be remedied by source areas, and hunting of lowland tapir in the entire source–sink area appeared to be sustainable.

Currently, there is no information on whether lowland tapir are actually moving between the hunting zones. However, continued persistence of tapir in the Tahuayo/Blanco site suggests that recruitment by immigration from the source area is important for the persistently hunted site. In addition, the tapir population in the persistently hunted area is considerably younger than that in the slightly hunted area (Bodmer, 1995), which suggests that younger animals might be moving from the source to the sink. The way local people hunt tapir concurs nicely with the source–sink model. Tapirs are the largest terrestrial wildlife species in the Peruvian Amazon and are important sources of subsistence and commercial meat for local people. This makes it difficult for local hunters to curtail current tapir harvests. Indeed, it would be unlikely that a hunter would not shoot a tapir if he encountered one in the forest. Thus, a source–sink strategy is a management alternative that agrees with the reality of local hunters.

The effectiveness of the source-sink strategy was also examined with peccary and deer populations. The risky hunting levels of peccary and deer in the persistently hunted areas suggested that these animals were at risk of overhunting. However, if a management strategy includes the slightly hunted and non-hunted source areas this risky strategy is acceptable, because the source areas could replenish overhunting of the persistently hunted populations if necessary.

In these examples, the source–sink strategy is used in conjunction with harvest and stock-recruitment models to manage Amazonian ungulate populations. The harvest and stock-recruitment models are used in persistently hunted areas to obtain an idea about the sustainability of the harvests. In contrast, the source–sink strategy is used to set aside non-hunted and slightly hunted areas to safeguard against overhunting.

COMMUNITY-BASED CONSERVATION

Community-based conservation must acknowledge the use of natural resources by local people and include their subsistence and monetary needs. However, community-based initiatives will only lead to conservation if natural resources are not overharvested. Recently, much attention has been given to the subsistence and monetary requirements of local people and their need to attain an improved life as part of sustainable development (Robinson, 1993). There is no doubt that this is of utmost importance, especially in light of community-based conservation. Of equal importance, is recognising that better information is needed on the biology of ecosystems and species (FitzGibbon, 1998). Community-based conservation will undoubtedly fail if the biology of natural resources is not adequately taken into account.

If communities rely on wildlife for their well-being, future conservation will require that it is not overhunted. Biological studies, such as the one described in this chapter are needed to help communities determine levels of hunting that allow them to use wildlife populations. Indeed, communities often ask biologists how many animals they can hunt to maintain wildlife resources for the long-term (personal observations). In addition, it is unrealistic to assume that hunters can manage wildlife by themselves in the complex natural systems of tropical forests. Thus, community-based management is likely to function best if it is co-managed with researchers assisting local people with technical aspects of wildlife management (Bodmer and Puertas, in press). Unfortunately, many local people become discouraged with managing wildlife when it becomes clear that there is not enough information available to determine hunting levels. One of the greatest challenges of conservation today is to give local people adequate information that they can use to better manage their use of natural resources.

COMBINING HUNTING WITH PROTECTED AREAS

In this chapter the harvest and stock-recruitment models and the source-sink strategy were used to help resolve overhunting by local people. Non-hunted areas are an important component to curb the effects of overhunting. Local communities who live in the vast expanses of western Amazonia naturally recognise the value of setting aside non-hunted areas as source populations, especially when they realise how these areas will help guarantee the long-term use of their resources. Communities who set aside non-hunted areas do so because it fits with their ambitions to use resources and their subsistence and monetary needs. These non-hunted areas are a type of community-based protected area.

In contrast, most of the currently existing protected areas have had little or no involvement of local people (Dixon and Sherman, 1990; Redford and Mansour, 1996). The current protected area strategies usually set goals to protect 10 % of natural areas (McNeely et al., 1994b). Governments are finding it difficult to reach this level of protection, because of economic and social constraints (Barzetti, 1993). The non-hunted areas set aside by communities could easily exceed this 10 % level and protect much larger areas, especially in western Amazonia. The persistently and slightly hunted areas could act as corridors between non-hunted areas, thus creating a landscape matrix that allows for movement of wildlife.

Funds for wildlife management and protected areas are often limited in tropical countries. Non-hunted areas set aside by local communities use economic incentives and are much less expensive than state run, top-down programs (Bromley, 1994). However, these community-based protected areas must include studies on the biology of animal populations, because it is essential that animals are not overhunted (Bodmer, 1994; Robinson and Redford, 1994b; FitzGibbon, 1998).

The current system of protected areas should be maintained to help conserve biodiversity (McNeely et al., 1994a). However, in addition to this current strategy, a new community-based strategy of protected areas should be set up that is based on the non-hunted areas that communities set aside to remedy overhunting. This would greatly enhance current conservation efforts.

ACKNOWLEDGEMENTS

I am indebted to the tremendous support provided by the communities of the Reserva Comunal Tamshiyacu–Tahuayo and the Reserva Nacional Pacaya–Samiria, who participated with this project; and to Rolando Aquino, Pablo Puertas, César Reyes, Alfredo Begazo, Tula Fang, Nicole Gottdenker, Jessica Coltrane and Etersit Pezo who helped with the field-work; and to Julio Curinuqui and Gilberto Asipali for their dedicated field assistance. The following organisations provided logistical and financial support for the projects: University of Florida's Programs in Tropical Conservation, the Department of Wildlife Ecology and Conservation and the Center for Latin American Studies; Instituto Nacional de Recursos Naturales – Peru; the Universidad Nacional de la Amazonía Peruana; the Asociación para la Conservación de la Amazonía; the National Geographic Society; The Nature Conservancy; the Wildlife Conservation Society; the Chicago Zoological Society; AIF-WWF/DK, Programa Integral de Desarrollo y Conservación Pacaya Samiria; the Fundación Peruana para la Conservación de la Naturaleza; and the Rainforest Conservation Fund.

16

Priorities for captive breeding – which mammals should board the ark?

ANDREW BALMFORD

INTRODUCTION

Zoo-based captive breeding can help conserve only a small minority of threatened mammals. Although the world's zoos have considerable resources at their disposal (with a combined operating budget estimated at four to six times that of all protected areas in the tropics; CBSG, 1992), there are many other demands on zoo space and money. Beside captive breeding, responsible zoos strive to educate the general public about animals and their conservation. They are often centres of scientific research, and they are increasingly involved in raising funds for *in situ* conservation programmes (Hutchins *et al.*, 1995). Most fundamentally, zoos must continue to attract large numbers of visitors simply in order to remain open. These and other considerations mean that only around 15% of mammal spaces in zoos are currently devoted to threatened species (Magin *et al.*, 1994). Even under the most optimistic scenarios about how much this proportion will increase, and how large captive populations must be to retain their long-term viability, it is unlikely that the world's zoos will be able to establish and maintain long-term breeding programmes for more than around 200 mammal species out of a total of 500 species of tetrapods (Conway, 1986, 1995; Sheppard, 1995). Yet 1096 mammal species (and over 2500 tetrapod species) are already known to be threatened with extinction (IUCN, 1996); the true total is likely to be far higher (Mace and Balmford, chapter 3, this volume).

Thus if zoos are to maximise their contribution to conservation through captive breeding, they must develop rational priorities for *ex situ* conservation. In practice, even existing selection criteria, which stress the need to focus on threatened and flagship species and on groups with which zoos already have husbandry experience (IUDZG/CBSG, 1993;

Seal *et al.*, 1994), may not be adopted. For instance, there is little evidence that zoos have so far devoted disproportionate space to threatened species (Magin *et al.*, 1994). Moreover, critics argue that current guidelines fail to address many of the main challenges facing captive breeding (Rahbek, 1993; Snyder *et al.*, 1996). The aim of the present chapter is to summarise recent collaborative work I have been involved with, in an attempt to stimulate a wider debate on priorities for captive breeding (for further details, see Balmford *et al.*, 1995, 1996, in press). In particular, here I try to identify additional criteria for species-selection which explicitly tackle the biological and economic realities of captive breeding, and consider how far meeting these goals is likely to conflict with other constraints on zoo activities. Most of the results are discussed largely in the context of mammal conservation, although each of the main points is of wider taxonomic relevance.

The first part of the chapter examines three very basic concerns which should be addressed when selecting species for *ex situ* conservation. Only quite rarely do mammal populations build up more quickly in captive-breeding programmes than under effective conservation in the wild; some *ex situ* programmes are still net consumers of the species they are trying to breed (Balmford *et al.*, 1995). Thus a first criterion is the need to pick threatened species which are likely to breed reasonably rapidly and reliably in zoos. A second consideration is cost-effectiveness. We know that conserving threatened mammals through captive breeding costs around an order of magnitude more than effective *in situ* conservation (Balmford *et al.*, 1995); economic considerations are also one of the main constraints limiting the overall capacity of zoos for captive breeding. I therefore look in detail at what sorts of mammal species are relatively cheap to keep in captivity, both in terms of short-term maintenance requirements, and long-term costs of entire breeding programmes. Last, the successful re-establishment of wild populations is seen by many as the most important end-product of captive breeding (Tudge, 1992; IUDZG/CBSG, 1993; Ebenhard, 1995). However, a recent analysis revealed that only five mammal reintroductions (representing around 11 % of all attempts) have so far been successful (when success is defined as achieving a self-sustaining population of 500 individuals; Beck *et al.*, 1994). In order to improve this situation, the third criterion proposed is that captive breeding should explicitly target those species with realistic prospects of successful reintroduction over the short to medium term.

The second section of the chapter moves on to consider whether zoos already meet these criteria for species-selection, and asks how far any necessary shift in the composition of zoo collections is likely to have an adverse impact on zoo attendance. I consider what sorts of species are needed in order to attract visitors into zoos, and then present data from surveys at three zoos looking at what interests people once they are inside zoos. The results are mixed. The bad news is that the existing composition of zoo collections appears to be biased towards species which breed rather poorly and at high cost, and that little consideration is paid to the likelihood of eventual reintroduction. The good news is that the data on zoo visitors indicate that reversing this situation need not necessarily conflict with the need for zoos to operate profitably.

THREE NEW CRITERIA FOR SPECIES SELECTION

Criterion 1: Species which breed

One self-evident requirement of a successful captive-breeding programme is that the target species breeds reasonably quickly and reliably in captivity. Captive populations are typically founded by relatively few individuals, but rapid population growth thereafter reduces both the genetic and demographic risks associated with such a bottleneck (Ballou and Foose, 1996). Because of this we examined whether we might be able to predict a species' likely reproductive performance in captivity from a readily-measured attribute such as body size. We pooled data extracted from studbook analyses (using SPARKS software – ISIS, 1993) and zoo census reports, and then compared mean intrinsic rates of population growth (r) with the body mass of a range of threatened species. We looked only at threatened species already held in coordinated breeding programmes, we considered only one species per genus, and we took care to exclude data from periods in which zoos were seeking in any way to limit population growth (Balmford et al., 1997; for more detailed methodology, see Balmford et al., 1996).

The results were unsurprising: as has long been established for free-ranging populations (e.g., Fenchel, 1974), we found a clear negative relationship between rates of population increase and body mass (Figure 16.1). For mammals, over 30 % of the variance in population growth can be predicted from body size alone ($r^2 = 0.36$, $N = 32$ species, $P < 0.001$; note that this result is not artificially inflated by the inclusion of four genera of rhinos, as excluding all but one still consistently yields $r^2 > 0.30$, $P < 0.001$). If all non-mammalian species for which data are available are also included, the result becomes even stronger ($r^2 = 0.44$, $N = 50$ species, $P < 0.001$; for details of the species, see Balmford et al., 1996). The message is simple: to achieve consistently high rates of population growth, *ex*

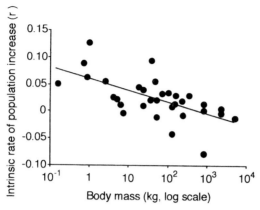

Figure 16.1 Intrinsic rates of population growth of threatened mammals in captivity, as a function of body mass. All points are for species held in coordinated breeding programmes and exclude data from periods when zoos were actively seeking to limit population growth.

situ programmes should concentrate where possible on smaller-bodied taxa.

Criterion 2: Species which are cheap

There are several different components to the overall costs of long-term captive-breeding programmes, but the most straightforward is simply the annual *per capita* cost of keeping an animal alive and healthy in captivity. We collated all available published estimates of *per capita* maintenance requirements (Conway, 1986; Harcourt, 1986; Kleiman *et al.*, 1991), and supplemented these with additional data from London Zoo (P. Pearce-Kelly, personal communication). When we compared these with body mass, the results were again unsurprising: the annual cost of keeping individual mammals alive in captivity shows a clear increase with body size (Figure 16.2; $r^2 = 0.55$, $N = 11$ species, $P < 0.01$). Once more, the pattern is even more striking when data on birds, reptiles, amphibians and invertebrates are included as well ($r^2 = 0.82$, $N = 26$ species, $P < 0.001$). Thus smaller-bodied species are not only better breeders, but they also cost less to keep than their bigger counterparts.

However, against these two benefits of targeting smaller animals must be weighed the fact that on average, larger-bodied species have longer generation lengths. This is important, because the rate at which populations lose genetic variability is directly correlated with their generation length (Soulé *et al.*, 1986). This in turn means bigger-bodied species can in principle be kept in lower numbers (and hence conceivably at lower overall cost)

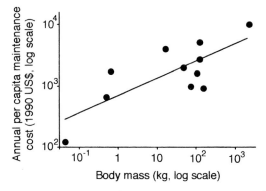

Figure 16.2 Annual *per capita* maintenance costs of mammals in captivity, as a function of body mass. Costs are adjusted to a 1990 dateline using the standard technique of applying the US GDP deflator index.

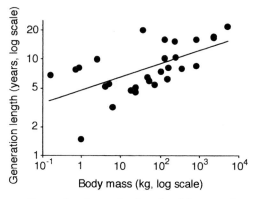

Figure 16.3 Generation lengths of threatened mammals in captivity as a function of body mass.

than smaller-sized species, yet still retain long-term genetic viability (Soulé *et al.*, 1986; Tudge, 1992). We used our studbook analyses to check that in our sample, generation length was indeed greater for the bigger species. As predicted, we found that among our threatened mammals, generation length increased with increasing body mass (Figure 16.3; $r^2 = 0.34$, $N = 28$ species, $P < 0.001$; for all species combined: $r^2 = 0.35$, $N = 46$ species, $P < 0.001$). Is this effect strong enough to offset the disadvantages of concentrating on bigger animals?

In order to examine the overall impact of body mass on total conservation cost, taking into account its effects on breeding rate, on *per capita* cost and on generation length, we next constructed an integrated genetic and economic model which costed entire, idealised breeding programmes for

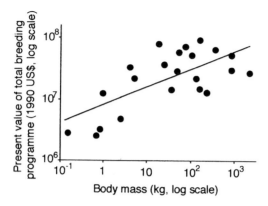

Figure 16.4 Present values (again in 1990 US$) of entire, idealised breeding programmes for threatened mammals, as a function of body mass.

each of our threatened species. Full details of the model are published elsewhere (Balmford et al., 1996), but in essence it involved asking what size initial captive populations of 25 genetically effective founders of each of our species would have to grow to and then remain at in order to retain 90 % of their initial heterozygosity over a period of 100 years. We assumed that the proportion of heterozygosity lost per generation approximated to $1 / 2N_e$ (where N_e is the genetically effective population size; Wright, 1931). The output of this stage of the model was a series of population profiles which varied between species, depending on their observed generation length and rate of population growth. We then costed these idealised programmes, using estimates of the likely ratio of effective to census population size (N_e/N), and information on annual *per capita* costs from the literature and from adoption fees requested by zoos; future expenditure was discounted at 4 % per annum. The final product was a set of figures for the present value of the whole of each programme, which represented the total amount of money which would have to be invested now, in order to meet all anticipated programme costs over the next 100 years (see Balmford et al., 1996 for details).

The results were again clear cut. The overall, long-term costs of idealised breeding programmes increased substantially with increasing body mass (Figure 16.4; for mammals: $r^2 = 0.44$, $N = 22$ species, $P < 0.001$; for all species combined: $r^2 = 0.60$, $N = 37$ species, $P < 0.001$). Thus the benefits of keeping large-bodied species with long generation lengths are in practice entirely swamped by their high *per capita* maintenance requirements and poor breeding performance. As a consequence, the present value of an entire *ex situ* programme for golden lion tamarins *Leonto-*

pithecus rosalia, for instance, is estimated to be only one-fifth that of a pro-gramme for gorillas *Gorilla gorilla*. When all the effects of body size are taken into account, it is clear that zoos should be able to target more species per conservation dollar by focusing their attention on relatively small-bodied species. Other factors will undoubtedly be important in explaining inter-specific differences in programme costs, but the high proportion of variance accounted for just by body mass argues that it should be a key concern in selecting species for cost-effective captive breeding.

Criterion 3: Species which can be reintroduced

If successfully re-establishing wild populations is the eventual goal of cap-tive breeding, can we identify what sorts of species are more amenable to reintroduction? Many assessments of what makes reintroductions, intro-ductions and translocations successful have been published over the past decade (Griffith *et al.*, 1989; Short *et al.*, 1992; Beck *et al.*, 1994; Kleiman *et al.*, 1994; Wilson and Stanley Price, 1994; Veltman *et al.*, 1996; Wolf *et al.*, 1996; Green, 1997; Primack and Drayton, 1997). Some biological at-tributes of the species concerned, including aspects of their ecology and life history, do appear to be important, but only in certain analyses. More con-sistently, reintroduction success increases with several management-related factors, including the number of individuals released, the total number and timespan of the releases, and the level of investment in subse-quent monitoring. Reintroductions are also more likely to succeed where the time spent in captivity is minimal, further underlining the importance of selecting species capable of rapid *ex situ* population growth.

But by far the strongest single determinant of the fate of reintroductions is the availability of high quality habitat in which the threats to the species have been eliminated (Short *et al.*, 1992; Kleiman *et al.*, 1994; Wilson and Stanley Price, 1994; Primack and Drayton, 1997). We therefore make a distinction between more readily reversed threats (such as overexploitation, the impact of introduced species, or small-scale habitat degradation – which experience shows can sometimes be halted, leaving behind intact but vacant habitat for reintroductions), and less reversible threats (such as large-scale habitat clearance). Even if the latter are stopped, the subsequent recovery of unoccupied habitat for reintroductions will take a great deal of time. We suggest that wherever possible, captive breeding should focus on species challenged primarily by more rather than less reversible threats (see also Wilson and Stanley Price, 1994; Mace and Balmford, chapter 3, this volume).

298 | A. Balmford

MEETING THESE CRITERIA

So how far does the existing portfolio of *ex situ* programmes already address the concerns that have just been raised, and to what extent might any recommended shift in zoo collections conflict with the need for zoos to continue to attract large numbers of visitors? The criteria we have looked at reduce to two simple recommendations: that given a choice, zoos should target smaller- rather than larger-bodied threatened species, since these will probably breed better and cost less; and that zoos should select species facing relatively reversible threats, because such species are more likely to be successfully reintroduced.

Species which can be reintroduced

In thinking first about whether zoos target mammal species facing more readily reversed threats, we looked in detail at those primates, carnivores and ungulates covered by IUCN/SSC Action Plans and IUCN/SSC/CBSG Conservation, Assessment and Management Plans (CAMPs). For each threatened species and distinct subspecies, we identified whether the primary threat listed was large-scale habitat loss (which we suggest is very hard to reverse, except over the long term), or some other, more reversible challenge (as outlined above; see also Mace and Balmford, chapter 3, this volume). We then further classified each species or subspecies according to whether it was the subject of a coordinated breeding programme (using data from de Boer *et al.*, 1993; Wiese *et al.*, 1993).

If captive breeding focuses on mammals with greater potential for reintroduction, then the proportion of threatened species and subspecies already in *ex situ* programmes should be greater among those facing more reversible threats than among those threatened by large-scale habitat loss. In practice, this is not the case (Figure 16.5). In each of the three groups we looked at, species and subspecies threatened primarily by habitat clearance were just as likely as other taxa to be targeted by captive-breeding programmes (for primates: Fisher's exact $P = 0.11$; carnivores: $\chi_1^2 = 0.03$, N.S.; ungulates: $\chi_1^2 = 0.95$, N.S.). Thus established *ex situ* efforts do not appear to be directed towards species that are more likely to be successfully reintroduced; nevertheless, we suggest that gradually reversing this pattern should in principle be quite possible.

Species which breed reliably and at low overall cost

The issue of actively targeting smaller-bodied species is more complex. To date, it appears that zoos have done quite the reverse. At a coarse taxonomic

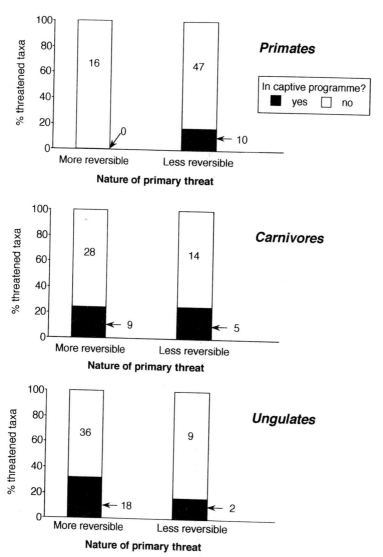

Figure 16.5 The representation of threatened species and subspecies of primates, carnivores and ungulates in established captive-breeding programmes, depending on whether the primary threat they face in the wild is more or less reversible (see text for details).

scale, threatened mammals are far more likely to be selected for captive breeding than are threatened species from other groups (number of established programmes for threatened mammals and non-mammals, compared with the distribution of threatened species as whole: $\chi_1^2 = 247.3$,

$P < 0.001$; Balmford *et al.*, 1996). Moreover, within the mammals, the percentage of an order's threatened species and subspecies that are already the subject of an *ex situ* programme is positively correlated with the order's average body size ($r_s = 0.75$, $N = 9$ orders, $P < 0.05$; Balmford *et al.*, 1996). Thus captive initiatives are far more likely for large-bodied threatened species (such as ungulates or primates) than for smaller-bodied ones. Importantly, these results are not simply a reflection of more attention being paid to larger-bodied threatened species because these are more severely threatened: both patterns are equally strong when re-examined just for endangered species (Balmford *et al.*, 1996); and anyway, there is little clear evidence so far that the level of threat is any higher for mammals in general (or large-bodied mammals in particular) than for smaller-bodied species (Entwistle and Stephenson, chapter 7, this volume; Mace and Balmford, chapter 3, this volume).

One potentially very good reason why zoos apparently pick bigger animals for captive breeding could be that they are responding to the perceived preferences of their visitors. The public may be more likely to go to zoos displaying large-bodied species, and second, once there, may be more interested in those exhibits containing large and charismatic birds and mammals. Although these propositions are entirely reasonable, there is a surprising shortage of objective data with which we can begin to test them.

Preferences of the zoo-going public

There is a particular lack of data on the first issue here – the question of what sorts of species are best able to attract visitors into zoos in the first place. Although large charismatic taxa such as primates, cats and ungulates probably are important, unambiguous information is generally unavailable. For example, interpreting general analyses of animal popularity (such as Morris, 1960) is hampered because these do not examine preferences in the context of a zoo visit, and because animals that are generally disliked (such as snakes and spiders) can be as effective at drawing the public into zoos as animals that are generally liked. More recent interview-based surveys of the popularity of animals with visitors to Zürich and Chester zoos in part get around these problems, and report a generally positive relationship between a species' size and its popularity (Ward *et al.*, 1998; Balmford, in press). Nevertheless, even these results cannot be used directly to identify the most profitable species for zoos to use in attracting the public, because as well as generally being more popular, larger-bodied animals will cost more to keep (see above).

The most direct and appropriate way of exploring the cost-effectiveness of different animals in attracting visitors would be to compare zoo attendance before and after the opening of one or more major new exhibits (taking into account any differences in exhibit cost). Intriguingly, one of the very few studies to begin taking this approach found that imaginative displays of small-bodied species can substantially increase zoo attendance (Yajima, 1991). More work along these lines is clearly needed.

The second issue – what interests visitors once inside zoos – is more straightforward to assess. Looking first at London Zoo, we arranged for teams of undergraduate students to conduct repeated, systematic censuses (35 in December 1993, 30 in July 1994) of the distribution of visitors across each of the main groups of exhibits. The mean percentage of visitors at each exhibit is, of course, a direct reflection of how the average visitor distributes their time within the zoo, and was surprisingly consistent between winter and summer (correlation between winter and summer scores for % visitors at each exhibit: $r_s = 0.87$, $N = 10$ exhibits, $P < 0.01$). Importantly, the exhibits were grouped so that each cost the zoo very roughly the same amount to maintain: thus our results provide a measure of the benefit to the zoo, in terms of visitor interest, per unit investment in an exhibit.

When we looked at how interest in the different exhibits varied with the size of the species on display, we failed to uncover any evidence that exhibits of bigger-bodied animals were more popular. The mean percentage of visitors per exhibit (averaged across winter and summer) was unrelated to body size ($r_s = -0.01$, $N = 10$ exhibits, N.S.); indeed the aquarium and the reptile house, which display precisely those sorts of smaller-bodied species which our analyses suggest deserve wider representation in *ex situ* initiatives, were both among the three most popular exhibits in the zoo. Likewise, small mammals were more popular than ungulates, elephants or rhinos. In practice, the only good predictor of visitor numbers that we could identify at London was exhibit location: visitor numbers decreased as distance from the gate increased ($r^2 = 0.69$, $N = 10$ exhibits, $P < 0.01$). Importantly, after controlling for this position effect statistically, the residual percentage of visitors per exhibit remained independent of the body size of the species they contained (Figure 16.6a; $r_s = -0.19$, $N = 10$ exhibits, N.S.).

The London data thus call into question the widely-held notion that displays of large-bodied species are necessarily more interesting to the general public, but come from a single zoo studied over a relatively short interval. In order to examine the generality of this result, we have run similar assessments at other UK zoos. At Whipsnade, a large, open zoo which concentrates on big mammals, 30 censuses in July 1994 again failed to uncover any obvious relationship between visitor numbers at different

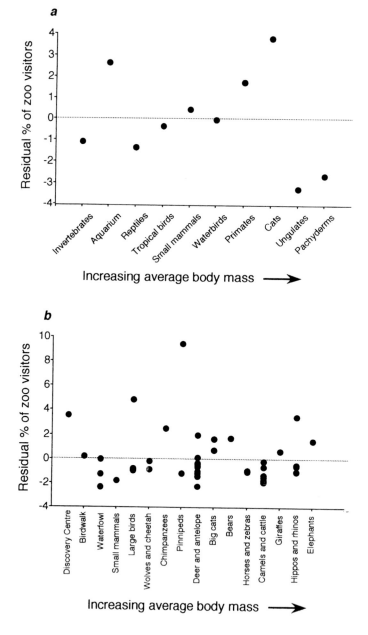

Figure 16.6 The mean percentage of zoo visitors at different exhibits, as a function of the average body mass of the animals on display. Data are for (a) London; and (b) Whipsnade. In both cases, plots show residual visitor numbers, after controlling for statistically significant effects of exhibit location.

exhibits and the body size of the species they contain (correlation between the mean % of visitors at exhibits and the ranked body mass of their inhabitants: $r_s = 0.00$, $N = 45$ exhibits, N.S.). There is a similar, albeit weaker relationship with exhibit location to that seen at London (% visitors at each exhibit versus mean distance from gate and playground: $r^2 = 0.10$, $N = 45$ exhibits, $P < 0.05$), but after controlling for this, once again there is no evidence that residual visit numbers are in any way correlated with species' body mass (Figure 16.6b; residual % of visitors versus ranked body mass: $r_s = 0.04$, $N = 45$ exhibits, N.S.).

More detailed analyses are possible using data from Dudley Zoo, a relatively small, urban collection. Here, data from 25 censuses conducted in March and April 1997 revealed a weak positive correlation between mean visitor numbers per exhibit and ranked body mass (for all exhibits: $r_s = 0.25$, $N = 47$ exhibits, $P < 0.10$; but for those containing mammals only: $r_s = 0.26$, $N = 33$ exhibits, N.S.). However, as was also the case at Whipsnade (but not London), we were unable to lump up the Dudley exhibits into similarly expensive groups, and so this initial result (like the results of simple questionnaire-based surveys discussed above) is confounded by differences in the costs of exhibit maintenance. Data on actual costs at Dudley were unavailable, so instead we estimated the relative cost of each exhibit from the number of animals they contained, and the average adoption fees which three different zoos (London, Chester and Edinburgh) requested from the public for maintaining the species on display. We have shown elsewhere that, though imperfect, this method is a statistically reliable procedure for estimating true maintenance requirements (Balmford et al., 1996). It revealed that total maintenance costs of the Dudley exhibits showed a clear increase with the body mass of the species they contained (for all exhibits: $r_s = 0.57$, $N = 47$ exhibits, $P < 0.001$; for those containing mammals only: $r_s = 0.62$, $N = 33$ exhibits, $P < 0.001$). Before going any further, we therefore controlled for this effect by dividing mean visitor numbers at each exhibit by our estimate of its maintenance costs, to derive an index (in visitor numbers / £) which like the figures from London, reflected each exhibit's relative benefit to the zoo in terms of visitor interest per unit investment.

This ratio covaried with several, potentially non-independent attributes of the exhibits, and so to explore these relationships more thoroughly we constructed a multiple regression model (after log-transforming the index to achieve normality). Overall, this accounted for half or more of the variance in our cost-adjusted index of visitor interest (for all exhibits: $r^2 = 0.48$, $F_{4,40} = 11.13$, $P < 0.001$; for mammal exhibits only: $r^2 = 0.64$, $F_{4,26} = 14.09$,

$P < 0.001$). Whether we looked at all exhibits or just those housing mammals, the model revealed that four variables were all independently related to variation in visitor numbers controlled for cost (see Figure 16.7 for the three most interesting relationships). As at London and Whipsnade, our index varied with exhibit location (for all exhibits: $t = 3.26$, $P < 0.01$; for mammal exhibits: $t = 3.44$, $P < 0.01$). Visitor numbers per unit investment also increased with the activity and visibility of the animals in the exhibit (when this was scored from 1 for consistently invisible animals through to 5 for consistently visible and active ones – for full scheme see legend to Figure 17.7a; for all exhibits: $t = 3.97$, $P < 0.001$; for mammals: $t = 4.81$, $P < 0.001$). Cost-adjusted visitor numbers increased with the extent of labelling at an exhibit (when measured as the number of words – Figure 17.7b; for all exhibits: $t = 2.75$, $P < 0.01$; for mammals: $t = 2.96$, $P < 0.01$). Finally, and most interesting, controlling for cost, we found that visitor numbers per exhibit actually decreased with the body size of the animals on display (Figure 17.7c; for all exhibits: $t = 4.43$, $P < 0.001$; for mammals: $t = 5.82$, $P < 0.001$). Thus at Dudley, after taking the costs of maintaining different-sized animals into account, it appeared that larger-bodied species made for less profitable exhibits than did smaller-bodied species.

DISCUSSION

I believe that the results summarised here carry three important messages. First, looking at the current composition of zoo collections, our work and that of others (e.g., Magin *et al.*, 1994) show that the largely ad hoc preferences followed to date lead to the concentration of scarce zoo resources on species that are often not threatened, that commonly breed relatively slowly in captivity, that will cost a great deal to maintain over the long term, and that will often be extremely difficult to return to the wild. Second, our results indicate that reversing this situation and trying to focus *ex situ* efforts more efficiently will require the identification and adoption of new and robust selection criteria. In my view these must reflect, among other concerns, the likely reproductive performance and maintenance requirements of different species in captivity, as well as the threats which the species face in the wild.

Third, although the data on zoo visitor behaviour are still limited, they indicate that addressing the sorts of issues raised here need not necessarily conflict with other financial considerations. We evidently need more direct work on what sorts of exhibits are most cost-effective at attracting visitors (as opposed to interesting them once they are in a zoo). But even if these

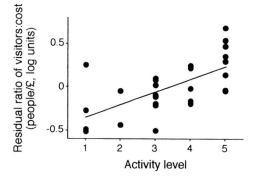

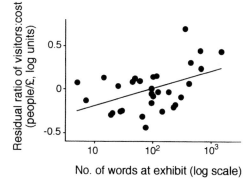

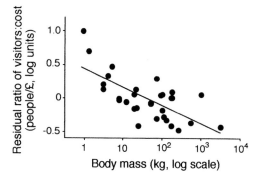

Figure 16.7 The mean number of visitors (controlling for exhibit cost) at different mammal exhibits at Dudley Zoo, as a function of the activity level of the animals (where 1 = invisible, 2 = visible but motionless, 3 = occasionally active, 4 = generally active, 5 = always active), the number of words used in labelling the exhibit, and the body mass of the species on display. In all three cases, plots show residual visitor numbers, after controlling for the statistically significant effects of exhibit location and the other two variables in the model.

studies indicate that zoos must maintain some large-bodied species in order to draw in the public, this requirement need only define a minimum set of exhibits. Our data on what interests visitors once inside London, Whipsnade and Dudley suggest that much remaining zoo space could be usefully redirected from larger-bodied species towards smaller animals. This need not compromise zoo profitability because, controlling for cost differences, exhibits of large mammals appear no more popular with the public than displays of smaller-bodied animals. Importantly, it is worth noting that these latter results have recently been replicated in new data from Chester Zoo, as well as in reworked data from Zürich Zoo (Balmford, in press).

Taken together, these findings suggest that captive breeding schemes could usefully place much more emphasis than at present on relatively neglected but rewarding non-mammal groups such as fish, amphibians, reptiles and particularly invertebrates. However, even among the mammals, zoos might increase the impact of their captive-breeding efforts by giving more attention than at present to threatened species in fast-breeding groups such as rodents and insectivores or highly social ones such as the bats.

The criteria outlined here are not intended to be a complete prescription of future priorities for captive breeding. Rather our intention has been to stimulate a rational, data-driven debate within the zoo community about what species it is best placed to help conserve, and how. Many will disagree with particular criteria put forward in this chapter. There are also a whole series of additional considerations that bear on species selection which I have not discussed. In terms of captive breeding, other major concerns include: further determinants of a species' maintenance requirements (such as social organisation and diet); whether or not a species is local to the area where captive breeding is planned (which has implications in terms of the risks of both domestication and disease; Snyder *et al.*, 1996); and whether (particularly in the case of large mammals such as cetaceans) it is considered ethical to keep the species in captivity in the first place. More widely, I agree with other authors (e.g., Hutchins *et al.*, 1995) that captive breeding may well be less important than other key conservation roles of zoos, such as education, and fund-raising for *in situ* conservation (Balmford *et al.*, 1995). A comprehensive set of species-selection criteria for zoos must clearly address these goals as well. The extent to which any of these important objectives are achieved, however, will increasingly depend on replacing existing, largely ad hoc priorities with selection criteria explicitly designed to maximise the overall contribution which zoos can make to the effective conservation of species and their habitats.

ACKNOWLEDGEMENTS

Many of the ideas presented here were developed in close collaboration with Georgina Mace, Sarah Blakeman, Nigel Leader-Williams and Michael Green. I thank Stephen Morris for devising the economic formula, and Paul Pearce-Kelly, Dave Clarke, and very many helpful studbook holders for access to unpublished data. Esther Barrett, Deborah Cox, Jon Hadley, Beatrix von Meier, Shelley Murray, Henry Nicholls, Juliet Owens and Anna Woodd collected the zoo visitor data with the kind permission of the Directors of London Zoo, Whipsnade Wild Animal Park, and Dudley Zoo, and with considerable help from the staff at all three collections. Comments from two anonymous referees and Abigail Entwistle improved the manuscript.

17

A recipe for species conservation: multidisciplinary ingredients

ANNA T. C. FEISTNER AND JEREMY J. C. MALLINSON

INTRODUCTION

It is clear that the burgeoning human population is having an increasingly negative impact on the world's biological diversity. The impact is felt both globally and locally and may result in degradation of entire ecosystems or loss of individual species. Moreover, many threats to biological diversity are synergistic. Independent factors, such as logging and overhunting, combine additively or multiplicatively to make a situation worse (Myers, 1987). When populations are reduced, genetic and demographic effects work together – as a small population becomes inbred, reduced survival and reproduction are likely, and the population declines further, becoming increasingly vulnerable to demographic variation and stochastic events. This negative feedback effect has been termed the 'extinction vortex' (Gilpin and Soulé, 1986), and results in increasing susceptibility to extinction.

Ensuring the continued functioning of ecosystems is the main aim of conserving biodiversity, but in this chapter we are taking a species-oriented approach. However, even ensuring the long-term survival of an endangered species can be extremely complex. Even where species decline can be attributed to a single cause, such as overhunting (e.g., of whales and rhinoceros), experience has shown that stopping hunting can be anything but simple.

Effective conservation requires an exchange of knowledge and technology, a building of consensus, a bringing together of expertise from several professions, disciplines and organisations, and the mobilisation of resources (Westley and Vredenburg, 1997). This clearly implies an approach which combines the resources of several disciplines in a collaborative way.

The potential disciplines involved in a conservation programme can be viewed as the ingredients in a recipe for effective conservation, and the collaborative approach necessary as the ambience and organisation of the kitchen in which several chefs are working simultaneously. In the first part of this chapter we briefly review some important ingredients and then discuss ways of ensuring that the chefs are at least following the same recipe! Later we describe case studies from the work of the Jersey Wildlife Preservation Trust, now known as the Durrell Wildlife Conservation Trust, which illustrate this approach.

CONSERVATION BIOLOGY

The widespread realisation of the threats to global biodiversity has highlighted not only the urgent need for conservation action but also the requirement for information on which to base rational preventative and restorative measures (Ryder and Feistner, 1995). Conservation biology is a multidisciplinary science that has developed to deal with the crisis confronting biological diversity (Primack, 1993). It has two main goals: to investigate human impacts on biological diversity; and to develop practical approaches to reducing the rate of extinction (Soulé, 1985, 1986; Wilson, 1992). It is thus trying to find answers to specific questions occurring in actual field situations, e.g., determining the best strategies for protecting endangered species, for designing nature reserves and for reconciling the needs of local people with conservation aims.

The disciplines of taxonomy, population biology and ecology are central to conservation biology. However, the ubiquity of human impact on the environment has meant that a much broader range of disciplines, more focused on human issues, is now included, for example, environmental law, ethics and economics, social sciences such as anthropology, sociology, socioeconomics and geography, and the management of learning as applied to conservation education and professional training (Primack, 1993). A large number of topics is thus relevant to conservation biology, but in the context of a species-oriented conservation programme, a few key ingredients can be identified.

CONSERVATION PROGRAMME INGREDIENTS

Every conservation programme is likely to need to address both biological and anthropological factors. Ingredients on the biological side will involve *field research* – to find out the distribution, status and behavioural ecology of the species in question, and *habitat management* may also be needed – for example in cases where degradation has occurred, restoration, replanting, removing exotics, providing additional nest/roost sites and food provisioning. *Management of the wild population* may also be a component and includes release programmes such as translocations and reintroductions, and metapopulation management. In crisis situations it may be necessary to establish a *captive breeding* programme as a safety-net and *research in captivity* is usually required to increase knowledge on both the basic biology and the management of the species.

Addressing the anthropological factors may involve components of *in-country education*, particularly in schools and through awareness raising, and *professional training* to build in-country capacity for conservation (research, education, management, etc.). *Community participation* is crucial where protected areas/threatened species are close to human populations and for local people to support conservation efforts. Finally *government agreements* are frequently an important political aspect of a conservation programme. These human-centred components may later build to include environmental legislation and rural development initiatives.

It may not be necessary for all ingredients to be added simultaneously. For example, in a crisis situation, political will and basic field research may be the initial steps. Awareness, education and captive breeding may follow, and as the programme develops, reintroduction, government agreements, legislation and habitat management may follow. However, even adopting such a multidisciplinary approach may not work if the various actions and actors are not coordinated or part of a coherent programme. Therefore, at the outset of any conservation planning process efforts are needed to ensure that a common goal is identified and that roles and communication channels are clear.

COOPERATIVE PARTNERSHIPS

The pervasive nature of human impact means that local people and institutions should be an integral part of any planning process aimed at mitigating effects of environmental degradation (Caldecott, 1996). Collaboration between institutions represents a challenge for organisations which work in traditional, competitive contexts (Rabb and Sullivan, 1995). Academic scientists, non-governmental organisations (NGOs), conservation organisations and government agencies concerned with endangered species are no strangers to competition. Even when the ultimate goal is shared, many attempts to save species become bogged down in ideological and political disputes (Alvarez, 1993), and with increasing numbers of individuals and/or groups involved, the potential for conflict increases, even among conservationists who are supposedly on the 'same side'.

Conservation problems are complex, ownership/jurisdiction is unclear, multiple interested parties (stakeholders) must agree to find a solution, and they need to do so in an open, non-hierarchical forum. In addition, collaborations which bring together stakeholders from different cultures must deal with cross-cultural sensitivities (Brown, 1991; Westley and Vredenburg, 1997). As McDowell (1996) stated 'The most innovative ideas can be grouped under four 'P's: partnerships, people, politics and the private sector'.

HOW TO ACHIEVE CONSENSUS?

Achieving this necessary collaborative coordinated approach is not easy, although a recent paper has demonstrated how partnerships between government and NGOs can successfully promote species and habitat recovery efforts by using integrated task-oriented teams (Kleiman and Mallinson, 1998). Team composition (field biologists, educators, conservationists and administrators) encourages multidisciplinary, flexible, risk-taking, collaborative and 'bottom-up' approaches to problem solving and participatory decision making.

However, there is also a tool which has been specifically designed to help achieve consensus in planning for conservation action: the Population and Habitat Viability Analysis (PHVA), developed by the IUCN/SSC Conservation Breeding Specialist Group (CBSG).

THE PHVA PROCESS

The objectives of the PHVA workshop process are to assist local managers and policy makers by bringing together people from many disciplines – biologists, wildlife managers, scientists, government officials, funding NGOs, socio-economists, captive breeding specialists, and educators – in order to develop a set of conservation objectives and management plans for the species in question (Ellis and Seal, 1995).

PHVA workshops are held in the range country of the species, by invitation from, and in collaboration with, the local wildlife agencies responsible, and are generally attended by 10–40 people. The workshop uses a variety of tools, including a stochastic population simulation computer program called VORTEX (Lacy, 1993), which is used to examine the effect of an array of variables on the genetic structure, demography, and risk of extinction of the population(s) (Ellis and Seal, 1995). Over the last few years, CBSG has conducted or participated in 125 + such workshops in 50 countries, and these have proved successful in building collaboration and consensus among disparate groups. In future, CBSG is planning to increase participation so that social factors, such as demography, land use, culture and economics, are included in the modelling and planning processes (CBSG/SSC/IUCN, 1997). A detailed review of CBSG's role in inter-organisational collaboration and problem solving in the conservation arena is given by Westley and Vredenburg (1997).

Most PHVAs focus on a single species, or small group of taxa. A species-oriented approach can be used to effect biodiversity conservation if by protecting the species a significant number and diversity of additional plants and animals also benefit. The chosen taxon becomes a flagship species (Dietz et al., 1994).

In order to act as a flagship, a species should be native to a region with high species richness and endemism, and preferably with habitat still reasonably intact; it should possess behavioural and physical traits that endear it to the people whose support for conservation action is desired; and have ecological characteristics that link its conservation closely with that of its habitat and additional species (Dietz et al., 1994).

Until relatively recently the term 'flagship species' usually implied a charismatic megavertebrate, often mammals such as pandas, elephants, tigers, rhinos, whales, etc. (Leader-Williams and Dublin, chapter 4, this volume). However, although recognising the considerable appeal of such spectacular animals, through good communication, even 'low visibility' projects, with diminutive endemic species, have the potential to mobilise people and governments to conserve endangered species and threatened habitats (Durrell and Mallinson, 1987; Dietz et al., 1994, Entwistle and Stephenson, chapter 7, this volume). Animals that are 'naturally appealing' (such as koalas and primates, with their round faces and cuddly, furry appearance) or that can be made to seem special through effective public relations exercises (such as black-footed ferrets and Livingstone's fruit bats), can be used to generate support for conservation. People can associate/identify much better with animals that they find appealing, distinctive or special, and it is often more productive to stimulate and foster this interest in a single species (and to undertake habitat protection on the back of it) than to try to garner support for the concept of biodiversity preservation. The flagship species we present as case studies are all of small mammals weighing less than 8 kg.

Table 17.1

Summary of the components of conservation programmes based round small mammals as flagship species

Component	Golden lion tamarin	Pigmy hog	Alaotran gentle lemur	Livingstone's fruit bat
Field research	✓ extensive	✓ distribution range use	✓ extensive	✓ distribution
Wild population management	✓ reintroduction translocation			
Habitat management	✓		✓ small-scale restoration	
Captive breeding	✓ in/ex country	✓ in country	✓ in/ex country	✓ ex country
Research in captivity	✓	✓	✓	✓
In-country education	✓		✓	✓
Professional training	research education	research captive breeding	research education	monitoring education
Community participation	✓		✓	✓
Government agreement	✓	✓	✓	✓

CASE STUDIES

The case studies, from the conservation work in which the Durrell Wildlife Conservation Trust is involved, illustrate the use of various key ingredients in the conservation programmes based on a flagship species (Table 17.1) and emphasise the informal and formal collaborative partnerships necessary for effective conservation.

The golden lion tamarin

Lion tamarins (golden lion tamarin *Leontopithecus rosalia*, golden-headed lion tamarin *L. chrysomela*, black lion tamarin *L. chrysopygus* and black-faced lion tamarin *L. caissara*) are small (< 700 g) primates which inhabit the remaining fragments of the once widespread Atlantic rainforest of Brazil's southeastern coast. A recent study in southern Bahia recorded over 450 species of trees in a 1 ha plot – the highest tree biodiversity in the world (Thomas and de Carvalho, 1993). Of the original continuous forest, once nearly 16 000 km long and occupying an area of more than 1 000 000 km², only 2 % remains (Seal *et al.*, 1990; Rylands, 1993–94).

The golden lion tamarin (GLT) has been used as a flagship species for the conservation of Brazil's Atlantic forest. The Golden Lion Tamarin Conservation Program (GLTCP), is an initiative of the Smithsonian Institution, National Zoological Park, Washington DC. It uses a broad multidisciplinary approach (Table 17.1) which has been coordinated, collaborative and long-term. Much of the planning has used the PHVA process.

The GLTCP has significantly increased the amount of protected Atlantic forest in Rio de Janeiro State by about 38 % (2300 ha) (Ballou *et al.*, 1998). In addition, in 1998 the Golden Lion Tamarin Association (the Brazilian NGO Assoçião Mico Leão Dourado) was instrumental in getting Fazenda União, a ranch of over 2400 ha of forest owned by the Federal Railroad Company, where GLTs from habitat fragments are being translocated, decreed a Biological Reserve, thus increasing by 23 % the protected habitat for the species (Kierulff and de Oliveira, 1996; Ballou *et al.*, 1998).

By the end of 1998, there were 300 GLTs surviving as a result of the reintroduction programme. Ninety-five per cent of the reintroduced population comprised wild-born tamarins and this will increase (Ballou *et al.*, 1998). The total wild population of GLTs including reintroduced animals, has risen from about 200 to over 800. The scientifically managed captive population of 488 individuals in 143 zoos worldwide, provides additional security for the species (Ballou *et al.*, 1998).

However, the future of GLTs will remain precarious unless more forests can be protected and degraded habitat restored. The goal of the GLTCP is to establish some 2000 GLTs in the wild and gain protected areas totalling 23 800 ha. Other objectives include: reducing deforestation; permanently conserving at least part of the privately owned forests in the area; reducing fires in forests and cleared areas in the region; reducing commerce in the species; and reducing illegal hunting within protected areas.

As a result of using the GLT as a flagship species, the spin-offs for biodiversity conservation include studies of the fauna and flora of the Atlantic forest (Kierulff *et al.*, 1991); conservation education programmes for the local communities (Dietz and Nagagata, 1995); professional training of conservation biologists (Kleiman *et al.*, 1990); a forest protection and rehabilitation programme (Rylands, 1993–1994); and a greater understanding of GLT biology.

The success of the GLTCP can be clearly attributed to planning through the PHVA process and to collaboration between individuals and organisations. The Brazilian Federal Environment Agency (IBAMA), works closely with the four lion tamarin International Recovery, Research and Management Committees (IRMCs), and with both local and international NGOs. Several strategies, developed for the first time in the lion tamarin programmes, may serve as models for other conservation programmes (Mallinson, 1997). For example, this is the first time that (1) a government has recognised, by law, IRMCs as technical advisers on both wild and captive populations of endangered species; (2) the title to all individuals which form part of internationally scientifically managed populations, are owned by the people and government of the country where the species are endemic; and (3) an international fund has been established to which all *ex situ* holders of individuals of an endangered genus are annually requested to contribute, to support in-country conservation work. Since the Lion Tamarins of Brazil Fund's inception in 1991 it has raised more than US$160 000.

The GLTCP highlights how bringing several disciplines together in a collaborative situation and using a flagship approach can promote public attention and support, culminating in the preservation and conservation of both animals and habitat (Rylands, 1993–1994).

The pigmy hog

The pigmy hog *Sus salvanius* is an 'indicator species' for the improved management of early successional grasslands of the northern Indian subcontinent (Oliver and Narayan, 1996). It is also one of the subcontinent's most threatened species, and is classified as Endangered (IUCN, 1996). Some considered the pigmy hog extinct, until in April 1971 a dramatic reappearance after a fire represented a reprieve for the world's smallest member of the pig family, weighing approximately 8 kg and standing about 23 cm at the shoulder.

In May 1971, the Trust and the Fauna Preservation Society (now Flora & Fauna International, FFI) combined forces to provide technical advice to the newly formed Assam Valley Wildlife Scheme, which was attempting to establish captive breeding programmes for pigmy hogs on tea estates and at Gauhati Zoo (Mallinson, 1971).

In 1976 a pair of pigmy hogs was taken to Zurich Zoo, on breeding loan from the Government of Assam (Schmidt et al., 1978). Although five young were successfully reared, by 1984 all had died and no viable captive population remained in Assam. In the late 1970s, Oliver (1980) carried out extensive field research on the status and distribution of the pigmy hog, which resulted in conservation recommendations being adopted by Assam's Forestry Department. In 1984 at IUCN's General Assembly, the pigmy hog was chosen as one of the world's 12 most endangered animals.

An Action Plan for the Conservation of the Pigmy Hog was drafted by the IUCN/SSC Pigs and Peccaries Specialist Group (PPSG) in April 1985, at the invitation of the then Joint Secretary for Wildlife at the Union Ministry of Environment and Forests, New Delhi. Nearly 10 years later, during which political, motivational and regional security problems hampered its implementation, the recovery programme was finally formally approved. The Pigmy Hog Conservation Programme (PHCP) is being conducted under a formal International Conservation Management and Research Agreement (ICMRA) between PPSG, the Trust, Assam State Forest Department and the Union Ministry of Environment and Forests. This is the first agreement of its kind in India.

The Action Plan has several objectives: (1) to promote the future protection and management of the species and its habitats; (2) to conduct wide-ranging field status surveys; (3) to establish a captive breeding and research programme; (4) to initiate medium to long-term field studies to investigate the species' behavioural ecology; and (5) to establish parameters for improved habitat management for the pigmy hog, and for maintaining biodiversity.

The PHCP has already made substantial progress since the ICMRA was signed in 1995. Major developments include: the construction of the Pigmy Hog Research and Breeding Centre (PHRBC) at Basistha, Assam; the monitoring of radio-tagged hogs in Manas Sanctuary; the establishment of a successful captive breeding programme at the PHRBC (the population has grown from six to 69 individuals); and the initiation and development of long-term ecological and management studies of tall grasslands, and of connecting them for better protection and management of grasslands and their remnant hog populations (Oliver *et al.*, 1997).

This multi-institutional collaborative programme is also contributing to the conservation of other endangered species which share the hogs' habitat, including the hispid hare *Caprolagus hispidus*, Indian rhinoceros *Rhinoceros unicornis*, chital *Axis porcinus* and Bengal florican *Syphicotides indica*. The future development of research sites for controlled burning of the thatch to discover the best way to manage the grassland habitat has, as its long-term goal, to benefit both local people and the conservation of biological diversity.

The Alaotran gentle lemur

The Alaotran gentle lemur *Hapalemur griseus alaotrensis* is a small (<1300 g) primate restricted to the marsh vegetation around Lac Alaotra, Madagascar's largest lake, and is Critically Endangered (Mittermeier *et al.*, 1994b).

The Trust became involved with this taxon in 1990 when, following the St. Catherine's Workshop recommendations (Wharton *et al.*, 1988), an expedition to capture Alaotran gentle lemurs to found an *ex situ* captive breeding programme (CBP) as a safety net was undertaken (Durrell, 1991). This endeavour was part of a long-term collaboration with the Malagasy Government, which began with the signing of a joint protocol of collaboration in 1983 (Bloxam and Durrell, 1985). Ten animals were imported, and all remained the property of the Malagasy Government.

Very little was known about the lemur in the wild so an early priority was to undertake field research to establish its conservation status. In 1993 and 1994 three studies were carried out with the cooperation of the Ministry of Animal Production and Water and Forests. These established that the total population size was about 7500 individuals, divided into two subpopulations (Mutschler and Feistner, 1995). The main threats were habitat destruction and hunting (Feistner and Rakotoarinosy, 1993; Mutschler *et al.*, 1995) and the lemurs lived in small groups, were folivorous (Mutschler *et al.*, 1998) and territorial (Nievergelt *et al.*, 1998). The development of a multidisciplinary conservation programme, from these early beginnings in field research and captive breeding, is described in detail by Feistner (1999).

Work at Alaotra indicated that heightening awareness about the unique and threatened nature of its fauna would be beneficial to biodiversity conservation in the region. In collaboration with the World Wide Fund for Nature (WWF) and the Malagasy authorities, a poster was produced featuring the lemur, and some 2000 examples were distributed around the lake. Informal follow-up two years later indicated that awareness had increased.

The CBP was successful, and a further import of wild-caught animals was authorised and undertaken in March 1997 to increase the number of founders. Lemurs were also established at two in-country institutions. The CBP is managed cooperatively through a European Endangered Species Programme and international studbook (Feistner and Beattie, 1998). The captive lemurs have also been the focus of a research programme on infant development and nutrition.

Research in the field continued with a long-term study of behavioural ecology (Mutschler, 1998) and the extended field presence provided the opportunity to train local university students. Positive signs of protection of wild lemurs, like reduced hunting pressure, in and around the study sites, are evident. The tendency from substantial animal losses (-20%) in one study population in late 1995, to an increase ($+11\%$) in 1996 and 1997 was probably linked to the permanent presence of researchers and their open communication with the local people (Mutschler, 1997).

Alaotra is not only an area of biological importance, but is also an important economic centre for fishing and rice production, and has a growing human population. However, in areas where state control is weak, conservation action and sustainable resource use can only work if there is consensus about management decisions among the vast majority of resource users. Dialogue and discussions with local people have been a key aspect of developing community activities around Alaotra (Rakotoniaina, 1998; Durbin, in press). More frequent and formal environmental awareness campaigns were started, including a joint project with the Ministry of Education Program Office for Environmental Education, and involved teacher training and exhibitions of traditional art and craft work using natural materials from the marshes. The lemur was given cultural and symbolic importance in many of the products (Durbin, 1999). Community activities have resulted in a traditional law to prevent overfishing and to protect marshes, and village initiatives for habitat restoration. At a regional level, there is now a federation of local NGOs promoting the designation of Lac Alaotra as a Ramsar site.

The degradation in the fauna and flora of Lac Alaotra has been documented in several studies (Young and Smith, 1989; Pidgeon, 1996) and several species are already in severe decline or locally extinct (e.g., birds: *Aythya innotata, Nettapus auritus, Tachybaptus ruficollis, Platalea alba*; fish: *Rheocles alaotrensis, Ratsirakia legendrei*; plants: *Nymphaea stellata*; Pidgeon, 1996). Effective conservation of the Alaotran gentle lemur, now a flagship species representing the whole marsh ecosystem, will thus have major spin-offs for biodiversity conservation in the region. In turn a healthy ecosystem will provide a sustainable living for the thousands of people of Alaotra.

Livingtone's fruit bat

Livingstone's fruit bat *Pteropus livingstonii* is endemic to the Federal Islamic Republic of the Comores (RFIC) and its known distribution is restricted to the upland forests of the islands of Anjouan and Moheli. The species is Critically Endangered (IUCN, 1996) and has been given highest priority rating for its conservation in the IUCN Action Plan for Old World Fruit Bats (Mickleburgh *et al.*, 1992). Survival of Livingstone's fruit bat is dependent on the integrity of the upland forests, which provide feeding and roosting sites, and also support other endemic fauna.

Livingstone's fruit bat is large (weight 600–800 g with a forearm length of 170–183 mm) and black, with orange eyes and round ears (Young *et al.*, 1993). It is an impressive sight soaring on thermals and has been developed as a flagship species for the upland forests.

Surveys carried out in 1988 (Thorpe *et al.*, 1988) confirmed previous reports of the low population levels of the bat. In 1990, the Trust, in collaboration with the Centre Nationale de Documentation et de Recherche Scientifique des Comores (CNDRS) and the Government of the RFIC, began efforts to bring a population into captivity for breeding as a safety net. At that time, it was estimated that only 120 bats remained on Anjouan (Carroll and Thorpe, 1991) and that the Moheli population had probably been wiped out by cyclones in 1983 and 1984 (Carroll, 1992). Between 1990 and 1995 a total of 17 bats was captured to found the captive population at Jersey Zoo. The Government of the RFIC retains official ownership of all animals involved in the CBP.

The CBP has been successful and bats have been distributed to a second collection. Research on the captive bats has also been an important component, and has covered social interactions, infant development and nutrition.

Very little is known about Livingstone's fruit bat, and so during capture and other expeditions, field research was undertaken on bat ecology. Information has been obtained on population estimates, timing of reproduction, feeding ecology and morphometrics (Carroll and Thorpe, 1991; Reason and Trewhella, 1994; Trewhella *et al.*, 1995; Clark *et al.*, 1997).

The upland forests are not only important for their biological diversity but also for the human population, through acting as watersheds. Deforestation has resulted in only 11 of Anjouan's 45 original rivers still flowing year round (IUCN, 1993c). However, due to a rapidly increasing human population and a demand for land for subsistence agriculture, forest destruction continues. Environmental awareness and community education is thus important. A variety of materials has been distributed, including stickers, posters, slide packs, lesson plans, a video and bat identification sheets (Action Comores, 1993, 1994, 1997). Training of Comorien personnel in both research and community education techniques has also been undertaken (Action Comores, 1997).

In order to highlight the conservation problems and to stimulate and guide conservation efforts an IUCN Species Action Plan was produced (Carroll *et al.*, 1995) and distributed in both English and French.

Strategies being developed to expand the conservation programme include: establishment of an in-country field base for further research on the fauna and upland forest habitat and possibly for captive breeding; further development of partnerships with the government and CNDRS; the integration and development of partnerships with other local and national organisations such as the Comorien NGO ULANGA, FFI, IUCN/SSC Chiroptera Specialist Group and with international agencies; the development of informal local protection agreements, hopefully to be followed by legislation; expansion of environmental education; further development of the CBP; and further research in captivity on biology and management of Livingstone's fruit bat.

This programme is in the early stages, but several components are already in place. Unfortunately in-country activities are currently 'on hold' due to the political instability in the region. However once resumed, the effective conservation of Livingstone's fruit bat, a flagship of the upland forests in the RFIC, should result in important benefits for the flora and fauna of the region as well as for the people.

DISCUSSION

The need for conservation action is at an all-time high as we approach a sixth 'extinction spasm' (Myers, 1987). Not only is species loss occurring, but changes in major global support systems (global warming, marine and atmospheric pollution, etc.) are being documented. It is clear that repairing the damage, and/or stemming and preventing further loss is crucial, as was finally recognised in the Rio convention.

In this chapter we have argued that successful conservation undertakings are characterised by shared objectives and open communication and usually require a creative and multidisciplinary approach. The case studies illustrate examples where this approach has been successfully implemented.

With the goal to preserve as much as possible of the biological richness of the Earth within the context of sustainable development, we need to strike a better balance between well-meaning conservation groups and the people interacting with the habitats and species they are trying to protect. This should translate into people who live in the area being fully involved in defining the problems and the feasible solutions, in selecting the chosen remedies, designing the work, allocating responsibilities and sharing in the benefits (Peters, 1996). The in-country PHVA workshops try to bring this about.

With an increasing number of conservation operatives in the global arena, the level of institutional competition, both for funds and credit/publicity, appears to be intensifying. This competition diverts time, energy and financial commitment from what should represent amicable partnership endeavours and can compromise conservation initiatives. The pressure to secure funds and keep a high public profile often results in individual organisations claiming 'success' where results have relied on team effort, and where credit to several major partners, including in-country participants, would be more appropriate.

Imperialistic approaches, arrogance, insensitivity to cultural traits and local requirements, and personal agendas, are all problems facing practitioners of inter-organisational conservation programmes. As Adams and McShane (1992) record: 'More often than not, scientists and conservationists have overtly gone about their business, ignoring each other as well as the people affected by their decisions'.

Partnership links between activities in country and *ex situ* are critically important (Mallinson, 1991). Funding, support, breeding facilities and expertise may be provided externally, whereas local insight, expertise, education, implementation and political will may be provided internally. Where captive breeding is a component, this can take place both in country and *ex situ*. There is a growing need to look at total populations, and to develop metapopulation management programmes.

Cooperative approaches promote and support biodiversity conservation through joint programmes of research, capacity building and conservation activities. Collaboration between institutions represents the optimal employment of their resources and skills (Prance, 1997). Ultimately, the success of our attempts to repair and hold together the world's threatened ecosystems, will depend on strategies achieved through collaboration and consensus.

What has the panda taught us?

LU ZHI, PAN WENSHI, ZHU XIAOJIAN, WANG DAJUN
AND WANG HAO

INTRODUCTION

No other animal has drawn as much attention from the general public, conservation organisations and governments as the giant panda. The panda has become a symbol of conservation. In the past two decades, intensive panda research and conservation projects have been conducted to save the species, and these have demonstrated how scientific information can help with designing a correct conservation strategy. The panda habitat falls into a region that is rich in biodiversity. Conserving the giant panda also benefits thousands of other animals and plants, some of them endemic to the region. In addition, panda habitat protects the watersheds of the upper Yangtze River, and with it the livelihoods for millions of people downstream. The threats to the species are habitat degradation and poaching. Conservation is more of a socio-economic issue than a scientific one. Because of its charisma, the panda is a good vehicle to deliver a conservation message, educate the public and raise funds. Panda conservation demonstrates the process of how a conservation concept can become reality and how a species-focused conservation effort can contribute to biodiversity conservation in a country.

SCIENTIFIC RESEARCH TO IMPROVE CONSERVATION DECISIONS

Giant pandas *Ailuropoda melanoleuca*, once widely distributed in southern and eastern China, northern Vietnam and northern Myanmar, are now only found in six fragmented mountainous areas in Shaanxi, Gansu and Sichuan Provinces of western China. It was estimated in the late 1980s that there were about 1000 animals in the wild within a habitat area of

13 000 km². Habitat loss was 50 % between the early 1970s and late 1980s. (MoF and WWF, 1989).

Most panda fossils, some up to 3 million years old, have been found in warm-temperate and subtropical areas at an elevation of 500–700 m, areas that are now heavily populated by humans. Today, typical panda habitat consists of the mixed coniferous and broad-leaved forests with an under-storey of bamboo, at altitudes from 1500 m to over 3000 m. Distribution at low elevations is limited primarily by human settlements and agriculture, whereas the highest distribution extends to the upper limit of bamboo.

During the 1980s, information on panda life history was collected in the Wolong and Tangjiahe Reserves, Sichuan Province (Schaller *et al.*, 1985, 1989; Schaller 1986, 1993). Since 1985, long-term research has re-vealed panda population dynamics and social behaviour in the Qinling Mountains, Shaanxi Province (Pan *et al.*, 1988; Lu 1991, 1993; Lu *et al.*, 1994; Pan, 1995; Pan *et al.*, in press). Studies were also conducted on the genetic diversity of panda populations (Lu Zhi, Pan Wenshi and S. O'Brien, unpublished data). These studies have provided a basic understanding of panda biology, upon which a conservation strategy must be based. It has also helped to clarify or correct misunderstandings and misconceptions about pandas, and accordingly has influenced conservation measures. The following examples illustrate this.

Bamboo flowering

In the 1980s, bamboo in panda habitat mass-flowered and died, following its natural life span (Johnson *et al.*, 1988). This phenomenon caused much concern. A campaign of 'Rescuing Pandas' began and public donations were received from all over the world. At that time, it was also decided to build over 10 'Rescue Centres' to help look after sick and starving pandas and keep them in captivity until the bamboo recovered. Rewards were pro-vided to villagers who rescued pandas. Was the mass-flowering of bamboo a fatal threat to pandas? As a carnivore, the panda has unusual food prefer-ences, in that it depends almost completely on bamboo. The bamboo diet provides pandas with just enough energy for survival but with little safety margin in terms of energy (Dierenfeld *et al.*, 1982; Lu, 1991). The nutri-tional strategy of pandas is based on obtaining energy from low-quality food: the animal usually spends up to 14 hours per day eating some 12–15 kg of bamboo leaves and stems, or 23 kg of shoots (Schaller *et al.*, 1985; Lu, 1991). Even so, a panda population consumes only about 2–3 % of the bamboo biomass in its habitat.

Flowering is a normal part of the life cycle of bamboo and happens once every 40 to 100 years, depending on the species. There are nearly always at least two species of bamboo available as food in a panda habitat. For example, there are two or three species of bamboo in Qinling, at least five species in Pingwu and the Minshan Mountains, and 13 in the Liangshan region. Bamboo flowering usually occurs in only one species at a time, leaving other species as alternative food. Pandas have, of course, depended on bamboo for several million years. During bamboo flowering and die-off, the panda's reaction has been to switch its diet to another species of bamboo and to expand its home range (Johnson et al., 1988). The 1980s national survey of panda populations and habitats estimated that around 20–30 % of the bamboo in the habitat had flowered. This flowering did not cause shortage of food for pandas, and it is clear that the key for panda conservation remains protection of the habitats (MoF and WWF, 1989).

The 'Rescue Centres' not only cost a significant amount of conservation money, but also removed many pandas from the wild, and this could have reduced the viability of populations and interfered with social structure. Subsequently, the captive population bred relatively poorly and it is still not self-sustaining (see below). Few animals have been returned to the wild, and thus the wild population has not received any benefit from the rescue measures. Records in the panda studbook show that, from 1983 to 1986, 42 pandas were brought into captivity. Most have now died but 17 remain alive. The research results were presented to conservation authorities, and in 1986 the building of rescue centres was stopped. Later, rewards for rescuing pandas also ceased. However, if the habitat were so fragmented that only one species of bamboo remained, the panda would run the risk of starving during bamboo flowering. Habitat protection, therefore, is the key to preventing such a disaster occurring in future.

Abandoned panda infants

Among the 'rescued' pandas, more than 50 % were young, less than 2.5 years old. Often, when a panda infant was seen alone, it was considered to have been abandoned by its mother. Of 69 pandas caught between 1980 and 1989, 35 were less than 2.5 years old and of these 16 subsequently died, while one was released. So far, only five out the 35 females have bred successfully (Xie and Gibbs, 1997).

The research in Qinling, using radio telemetry, documented in detail the interactions between wild panda mothers and their infants. From the observation of four female pandas and their six cubs, it was noted that mothers often left their cubs alone in a den or in a tree while they foraged. Cubs were normally left for four to eight hours, but sometimes for up to 52

Table 18.1
Captive breeding record for giant panda

Date	Total number in captivity	Wild caught	Captive-born /survived more than one year	Breeders (♂:♀)	Captive-born breeders (♂:♀)
1979	215	178	37 / 7	15 (6:9)	0
1989	360	247	113 / 31	45 (18:27)	6 (0:6)
1997	454	269	185 / 75	66 (28:38)	11 (1:10)

Data summarised from Xie and Gipps (1997) *The Giant Panda Studbook.*

hours (Lu *et al.*, 1994). These findings was presented to conservation authorities and a recommendation was made not to 'rescue' infants (Lu *et al.*, 1994). Since 1994, few infants have been taken from the wild.

Reproduction (captive versus wild)

It is a general impression that pandas are doomed because they cannot breed well and because panda mothers are so careless with their babies that they often die accidentally. The idea that 'sex is a problem' makes a good news headline.

The captive breeding record of giant pandas has been poor. Although great progress has been made since 1991, problems continue. Most adults that have grown up in captivity have not been used in breeding, especially in natural mating, as they are either unable to mate or are not interested. Table 18.1 summarises information from *The Giant Panda Studbook* (Xie and Gibbs, 1997). Between 1936 and 1997, 454 pandas have been kept in captivity, 269 of which were wild caught and 185 captive-born. Only 75 have survived more than one year in captivity. So far, only 66 pandas in the captive population have been involved in breeding. Among them, only 11 breeders are captive-born (14.7 % of the total number of captive-born animals surviving for more than one year). In September 1997, there were 117 pandas living in captivity, of which 25 had been involved in breeding (18 wild-caught and seven captive-born). Twenty-one animals were less than four years old, and thus too young to breed. This left 71 animals (74 % of adults) that were of breeding age but who had not been able to breed. Meanwhile, infant mortality in captivity remains high, sometimes reaching 40–45 % (Xie and Gibbs, 1997).

Poor reproduction and high infant mortality are the main reasons why the captive population is not self-sustaining. The question is whether the lack of successful reproduction, as shown in captivity, is the reason the species is endangered in the wild. Does the survival of the species depend on human help with breeding, such as through artificial insemination or even cloning? Research on the life history of the panda in the wild provides a completely different picture (Pan et al., 1988; Lu, 1991, 1993; Lu et al., 1994; Pan, 1995; Zhu, 1996; Pan et al., in press).

Giant pandas are basically solitary animals. Each adult has a well-defined home range, with an average area of 9.8 km² for females and 23.7 km² for males in the Qinling Mountains (Lu, 1991). The home range of one male may cover that of several females. Home ranges of adult females usually overlap, although each female tends to have a core area of its own, while the home ranges of males are more exclusive (Schaller et al., 1985; Lu, 1991; Pan et al., in press).

Pandas are polygamous. The mating season is between March and May and once one female is in oestrus, several males may approach to seek an opportunity to mate. There is an obvious hierarchy among males, but one female still has the chance to mate with several males. It was observed that females sometimes also make their own choices about with whom to mate (Schaller et al., 1985; Lu, 1991; Pan et al., in press). Although pandas are solitary animals, individuals have frequent direct or indirect social interactions with their neighbours. Scent markings and vocalisations are the main modes of communication. Fights between two adult males or females also occur outside of the mating season.

Young are born in August and September. After giving birth, females often do not eat for a number of days, the longest observed period was 25 days. The whole time that a panda mother spends in the den is dedicated to holding, licking and nursing the newborn cub (Lu, 1992). Panda cubs spend 1.5 to 2.5 years with their mothers, a period during which they learn many of their social and environmental skills. The period of such learning extends well after independence, as when, for example, a young male may follow an adult male for weeks or even months (Lu, 1991, 1992).

Using radio telemetry and direct observation, information on population dynamics was collected in Qinling between 1989 and 1997 (Pan et al., in press) (Table 18.2).

Although it is difficult to determine what percentage of adults actually left offspring in the population, all showed reproductive behaviour. A female gives birth every two to three years. Among the nine cubs observed (Table 18.2), only one died before the age of 1.5 years. Infant mortality was much lower than that recorded in captivity. In addition, long-term monitoring showed that the Qinling panda population remained stable or increased

Table 18.2
Parameters of the study population of giant panda in Qinling

Parameters		Cubs	Subadults	Adults (reproductive)	Old (post-reproduction)
Age (years)	Female	0–1.5	1.5–4.5	4.5–19.5	> 19.5
	Male	0–1.5	1.5–4.5	4.5–16.5	> 16.5
No. of months monitored		108	124	680	9
No. of individuals observed		9	7	20	1
No. of deaths observed		1	1	4	1
Average death rate per year		10.6%	9.3%	6.8%	75.7%
Age structure (% in each age group)		24%	19%	54%	3%

over the past 15 years while commercial logging in habitat was severe in some locations (Lu 1991; Pan, in press). This research leads to a conclusion that if the panda can be left alone in its wild habitat which can support a viable population, that population will survive.

With the above information, we may estimate why the success of captive breeding is unsatisfactory:

(1) Over 50% of the wild-caught captive pandas were captured as young. These pandas missed the important learning experience through social behaviour. As captive-born pandas, they are often forcibly weaned and separated from their mothers at six months so that the mothers will come into oestrus again. Again, cubs are deprived of behavioural learning, leading perhaps to poor breeding responses in captivity. Moreover, pandas in captivity are often kept separately in cages without social interaction among individuals. Learning and social stimulation is often considered to be an important component in an animal's behavioural development.

(2) Most zoos have only a few pandas, often only a pair, which makes polygamous mating impossible – both females and males have no choices even if the pair do not match each other.

(3) For many years, pandas have been fed with highly nutritious food such as porridge, which is quite different from their high-fibre natural diet. A rich diet and lack of exercise might also have an impact on reproductive performance.

(4) Many zoos keep pandas in cages or small enclosures, which have caused psychological problems.

Low reproduction in captive populations may be a result of a combination of the above.

Between 1986 and 1995, blood and hair samples were collected from 62 pandas from Qinling, Minshan, Qionglai, Liangshan and Xiangling, as well as from captive-born animals. A molecular genetic study was carried out on these samples in order to assess the genetic diversity of the panda at both a species and a population level. Different methodologies were applied, such as mitochondrial DNA restriction fragments length polymorphism (RFLP), DNA fingerprints, mitochondrial DNA D-Loop sequencing, and microsatellite DNA (short tandem repeats) polymorphism analysis. The preliminary results showed that:

- The species genetic diversity value was comparable to outbred populations but close to the lower level for such populations.
- Among the populations of different mountain regions, the level of genetic diversity followed the order: Qionglai > Minshan > Qinling.
- The differentiation between the populations was not significant, which indicated that the period of isolation between the populations had not been long. However, the Qinling population had a specific mitochondrial DNA RFLP genotype, and each of the three populations (Qinling, Minshan, Qionglai) had 'signature alleles' among the microsatellite loci, which could be useful for identifying an individual's origins.
- The genetic diversity among the captive born pandas (from zoos) was comparable to wild populations.

To sum up, the impression of the panda's low reproduction is from the captive population. Reproduction in wild panda populations remains at a much higher level than in the captive population (Table 18.3).

All the above examples show the importance of accurate scientific information in conservation decision making. False information and misconceptions could lead to the adoption of inappropriate conservation measures. It also needs to be recognised that much information has to be collected over an extended time period. In order to establish a scientific decision making mechanism, the World Wide Fund for Nature (WWF) is now supporting a dynamic database on the giant panda population and its habitat, which includes a national survey in all panda ranges, setting up of a monitoring system for panda populations, habitat and threats, a GIS database and a long-term research project on population dynamics and behaviour.

Table 18.3
Summary of the recorded difference between wild and captive pandas

Items	Wild pandas	Captive pandas
Social interactions	Males and females may be familiar to each other through scent marking, occasional contacts and get-together during mating; males establish hierarchy through fighting in and out of mating season	Isolated
Mating system	Polygamous	Usually pairs, males often incapable of natural mating, artificial insemination applied
Behavioural learning of young	Wean at age 1–1.5; follow mothers for 1.5–2.5 years and observe mating events in the area	> 50 % wild-born caught as cubs; captive-born usually weaned at six months then are isolated from other adults
Diet	Bamboo	High nutrition food
Daily activity	14 hours for feeding	Much less time being active
Infant mortality	Low	High
Living conditions	Free ranging, each with defined home ranges	Cages and enclosure
Adult behavioural expression in reproductive activities	100 % adults	26 % adults
Population status	Stable or slight increase if the habitat protected and poaching reduced	Not self-sustaining

CONSERVATION DEALING WITH ROOT CAUSES

Intensive conservation efforts, along with the involvement of WWF, began in the early 1980s, with scientific research followed by a national survey of populations and habitats, in order to understand the actual threats and the basic needs in panda conservation. It has been revealed that pandas have unique adaptations to their habitats, and that their reproduction is adequate in the wild, with populations remaining stable or increasing slowly when their basic needs for survival are met. As a species, it is not suffering inbreeding depression. The threats to the species are from human activities, principally habitat destruction and poaching (Schaller *et al.*, 1985; Pan *et al.*, 1988; MoF and WWF, 1989).

With limited financial resources, conservation efforts have to focus on the main threats. Therefore, panda conservation must strive to eliminate adverse human impact on the wild populations rather than concentrate on captive breeding which so far has not been able to maintain a self-sustaining population.

With healthy wild populations of over 1000 pandas, 'panda cloning', an issue that has been recently raised as a solution to saving the species, is unnecessary. Even if all the technical obstacles were overcome, adding cloned pandas to viable wild populations would not significantly help the species. The problem that 'panda cloning' intends to solve, reproduction, is not the main threat to the species.

To address the main threats, a national panda conservation plan was jointly developed in 1989 by the Ministry of Forestry of China and WWF. Among other suggestions, it recommended an expansion of protected areas. Since 1993, the Chinese government has established 17 new panda reserves. Together with the existing ones, a total of 33 panda reserves cover nearly 50 % of the panda habitat. However, much habitat is still not protected and here there is intensive commercial logging conducted by both state and local or private companies. For example, in the largest panda county, Pingwu, three reserves only cover about 20 % of the habitat. Logging is conducted by county-owned logging companies, community-owned logging farms and individual contractors. Logging practice has become more and more intensive since the county's revenue has to be generated locally following the economic reform in the late 1980s. Unsustainable logging is the biggest threat to the panda habitat. The conflict between local economic development and conservation is a basic worldwide issue.

During 1997, an integrated conservation and development project (ICDP) was initiated in Pingwu by WWF and its partners. The project involved broad issues, including land and resource tenure, decentralisation of government power, people participation, public awareness, policy change toward sustainable forest resource use, sustainable land use and alternative livelihood development. The recent natural forest logging ban that was issued by China's State Council made it a reality that all logging in the panda habitat had been stopped. This, on the other hand, added pressure to the livelihood development. The ICDP certainly showed the complex nature of conservation.

PANDA CONSERVATION BENEFITS

Protect the panda, protect rich biodiversity and watersheds

The southwest temperate forests where the panda habitat is located contain perhaps the highest level of biodiversity at this latitude in the north hemisphere. It also supports endemic species, such as takin *Budorcas taxicolor*, golden monkey *Pygathrix roxellana*, red panda *Ailurus fulgens* and the Chinese monal *Lophophorus lhuysii*. The habitat also serves as an important watershed, upon which millions of people in the lowlands depend. Therefore, protecting the giant panda will also ensure biodiversity conservation and a secure life support system for many people. WWF has made an evaluation of priority areas, or 'ecoregions', for biodiversity conservation. Over 200 ecoregions were selected as the 'Global 200'. China's southwest temperate forest ecoregion was chosen among the top five in need of support. Panda conservation will be a key component of this ecoregional approach.

Raising awareness

Conservation is more of a socio-economic issue than a scientific one. In a country like China, with a huge population and rapid economic growth, conservation is faced with extreme pressures. In China's conservation history, the panda has played an important role in educating the public and raising awareness. As a 'national treasure', the panda is a good vehicle to deliver conservation messages, not only to the public, but also to decision makers and donors. A 'flagship species' that has drawn so much attention will also be in a better position to ensure improvement of conservation policies and legislation in the country.

Never say die: fighting species extinction

KATHY MACKINNON

INTRODUCTION

Should we ever give up on a species? The simple answer to this question is no. The global community seems to agree. More than 170 countries have now ratified the Convention on Biological Diversity and thus committed to conserve and sustainably use biodiversity which means that individual species within those countries' boundaries should be secure. Some countries have even enshrined this principle in their legislation. The United States, for instance, has an Endangered Species Act under which it is not permissible to decide to allow a species to go extinct. If only it were so simple. In the twentieth century alone 319 animal species, including 20 mammals, have become extinct globally. More worryingly, another 140 species of mammals are endangered and likely to become extinct in the near future, more than twice the number of mammals that have gone extinct over the last 400 years (Groombridge, 1992).

What do we mean by giving up on a species? The staircase to extinction has many steps. At what point is it fair to say that we (or the species) have given up? Steller's sea cow *Hydrodamalis gigas*, the quagga *Equus quagga* and the Caribbean monk seal *Monachus tropicalis* have all reached the bottom of that staircase and become globally extinct, the latter as recently as 1962; they are now known only from museum specimens. Yet other species have been exterminated in the wild but still survive in captivity. At least some of these species have the potential to be reintroduced to their native habitats. Père David's deer *Elaphurus davidianus*, for instance, was eliminated in the wild, discovered in captivity in 1861, bred in zoos worldwide and recently reintroduced to China.

Where on the extinction staircase should we place those rare and threatened species, including many charismatic large mammals, which are no longer found in many parts of their former range or survive only in small isolated populations? Once a population of a species has been so reduced that it is no longer reproductively viable, then in effect that species is doomed to extinction at that site, even though some individuals still survive – the 'living dead' phenomenon described by Janzen (1986). Add together multiple local extinctions and suddenly a species is on the brink of global extinction. Given the numerous local extinctions recorded over the past few decades it seems clear that in reality we are giving up on species all the time – at least at the local level.

Nobody knows exactly how many species there are; estimates range from 5 million to 10 million, 30 million or even 100 million (Heywood, 1995). What is known is that only 1.8 million species have been described so far and of these only 4500 are mammals. Of all known mammals and birds, 1 % have become extinct in the last 100 years, indicating the trend in biodiversity loss the world is facing (Groombridge, 1992). Although new mammals are still being discovered, for example the Vo Quang ox or saola *Pseudoryx nghetinhensis*, and the giant muntjac *Megamuntiacus vuquangensis*, from the forests of Indochina (Timmins *et al.*, 1998), local extinctions of well-known species occur on a daily basis. As more of the world's natural habitats are lost and more mammal species become threatened, the dilemma of which species to save, where, when and how, will become more acute. It is unlikely that the global conservation community will ever give up on charismatic species such as rhinos, pandas and tigers, but we will need to be increasingly innovative and cost-effective to ensure conservation of lower profile species and their habitats. While this chapter focuses primarily on mammals, many of the lessons apply equally well to other animals and plants.

SPECIES LOSS: THE CAUSES OF EXTINCTION

The five principal causes of species extinction at the local or global level are: habitat loss and fragmentation; habitat degradation including pollution (a particular problem in marine and freshwater habitats); overexploitation through harvesting and hunting; secondary extinctions; and the impact of introduced alien species. Often these threats are inter-related and most threatened species face at least two or more (Groombridge, 1992). Climate change may become a sixth force in the twenty-first century, but is not yet recognised as a major' contributing factor, except perhaps in the case of amphibians (Blaustein and Wake, 1990).

Almost all natural habitats throughout the world are being degraded or converted to human-made landscapes. The most species-rich of all terrestrial habitats, lowland rainforests, are under particular pressure. The old growth tropical forests of west Africa, India, the Philippines and Madagascar, and the Atlantic forests of Brazil, all rich in endemics, have already been reduced to less than 10 % of their original areas (J. MacKinnon, 1997; Terborgh and van Schaik, 1997). In spite of the increased worldwide attention to tropical rainforests there is no indication that the rate of loss or degradation is slowing (Whitmore and Sayer, 1992; Aldhous, 1993; J. MacKinnon, 1997). In many countries tropical rainforests are unlikely to endure outside protected areas beyond the next 35–40 years (Terborgh, 1992).

Habitat loss almost invariably leads to habitat fragmentation, restricting plants and animals to 'islands' of habitat, often too small to support viable breeding populations. A 90 % reduction of habitat will result in the almost immediate loss of about half of the species found in that area (Wilson, 1992). Once fragments have become isolated from sources of colonisation, however, species loss continues, often rapidly, through the process of secondary extinctions. Depending on the size of the remaining fragment, 90 % or more of the initial species complement can ultimately disappear (Diamond, 1984b). Larger mammals and predators at the head of the food chain are some of the first to disappear (Lovejoy et al., 1983). The effects of fragmentation on species loss are further exacerbated as new access roads for logging or regional development open up wilderness areas to pioneer farmers, hunters and harvesters and lead to further land clearance and unsustainable harvesting of forest species.

For most of human history, humankind has been impacting on other species. Overhunting was responsible for the demise of the mammoths and mastodons of North America, the giant lemurs of Madagascar, giant kangaroos of Australia, the ground sloths and glyptodonts of North and South America and many of the native birds of Hawaii and other Pacific islands (Olson and James, 1982; Martin and Klein, 1984; Wilson, 1992). More recently, the international trade in furs reduced species such as chinchilla Chinchilla spp., giant otter Pteronura brasiliensis, vicuna Vicugna vicugna, and many cat species to very low levels (Hemley, 1994). Tropical forest species are especially prone to extinction since they often occur at very low densities (Whitmore, 1984). Even traditional hunting by indigenous people can reduce primates and other mammal and bird populations to very low densities or eradicate populations completely, a phenomenon recorded in tropical forests from the Amazon to Borneo (Redford, 1992; Bennett et al., 2000).

The deliberate or accidental introductions of exotic species to new ecosystems have also led to extinctions of native species, especially on oceanic islands and in freshwater systems. Introduced European foxes in Western Australia have almost eradicated local marsupial populations (Burbridge and Mackenzie, 1989). Competition between native red and introduced grey squirrels, *Sciurus vulgaris* and *S. carolinensis*, in England and Wales has led to local extinctions of red squirrel populations (MacKinnon, 1978). The brown tree snake *Boiga irregularis*, a native of Australia, New Guinea and the Solomon Islands, reached Guam about 50 years ago and has since extirpated nine of the island's 13 native forest birds (Anon., 1998b). Eradicating introduced species can be a costly and difficult task, well illustrated by the long-term Australian campaign to control and eradicate introduced European rabbits *Oryctolagus cuniculus*.

SETTING PRIORITIES FOR CONSERVATION

All species are not equal in terms of their distinctiveness, their functional roles within the ecosystem, the degree of threat they face, their conservation needs or importance to humankind (economic or cultural). Certain categories of species are particularly vulnerable to extinction because of characteristics such as large body size (Erdelen, 1988), need for large home ranges (e.g., big cats) and seasonal migration patterns. Also vulnerable are species with: narrow geographic ranges, such as island endemics; only one or a few remaining populations (e.g., gorilla *Gorilla gorilla*); small or declining population size and low population densities (e.g., orangutan *Pongo pygmaeus*); specialised feeding niches (e.g., giant panda *Ailuropoda melanoleuca*); or little genetic variability (e.g., cheetah *Acinonyx jubatus*). Other species may be at risk because they aggregate (e.g., herds of bison *Bison bison*); are commonly hunted or harvested or depend on old growth habitats that are under pressure from logging and agricultural encroachment. A species may exhibit several of these characteristics. Thus the Javan rhino *Rhinoceros sondaicus* has large body size, low population density, a large home range and inhabits tropical rainforests threatened by logging and agricultural expansion. Because of hunting for its valuable horn, this species has been reduced to only two small populations throughout its former range. Like many other extinction-prone species it is a particular focus of conservation efforts.

The loss of a single species may have far-reaching impacts. It is difficult to predict the effects of loss of any single species on other species (animal or plant) and ecosystem functions, whether they occur in species-rich or species-poor ecosystems. We do know, however, that in Mauritius the formerly common tree *Calvaria major* has not produced seedlings naturally since its obligate seed disperser, the dodo *Didus ineptus*, was hunted to extinction 300 years ago (Temple, 1977). A species may have a suite of biological characteristics which allow it to function in multiple roles, shaping ecosystem structure and processes and helping to maintain ecosystem health. The impacts of some key species on their communities and habitats are well-documented: moose *Alces alces* and reindeer *Rangifer tarandus* on boreal and Arctic ecosystems; sea otters *Enhydra lutris* in Californian and Arctic kelp forests; predators in biological control; the role of large carnivores in maintaining densities of herbivores and seed predators at levels below the available food supply and the impacts of major grazers and browsers on grassland ecosystems (Heywood, 1995). Among mammals, bats and several small marsupials are known to be essential pollinators while many are important seed dispersal agents for ecologically and economically important tree species (Fujita, 1991; MacKinnon *et al.*, 1996). Losing such key species will clearly have an impact on the structure and functioning of their ecosystems.

The key question for conservationists, however, should not be which species to save but how to better focus conservation efforts for maximum effectiveness to maintain as much biodiversity as possible. This will involve a realistic assessment of traditional approaches (both *in situ* and *ex situ*) as well as weighing the costs and benefits of new approaches to conservation, sustainable use and more equitable sharing of the benefits. For different species different options, or suites of options, may be more or less appropriate, depending on current threats and national or international willingness to pay, either in cash and compensation (conservation organisations, zoos, international donors) or opportunities forgone (local communities, private landowners and national governments). The feasibility of success for any option should be paramount in deciding how to proceed.

PROTECTED AREAS: CORNERSTONES OF BIODIVERSITY CONSERVATION

For many species protecting adequate and connected habitat will be the single most important way to ensure their long-term survival. Conservationists have long debated where and how much habitat needs to be protected to conserve all species. Biodiversity is not distributed uniformly; centres of biological richness or endemism can be recognised. Numerous texts have been prepared on setting conservation priorities (MacKinnon and MacKinnon, 1986a, b; Dinerstein *et al.*, 1995; Johnson, 1995; J. MacKinnon, 1997). Often sites and habitats that are important for conservation of one taxonomic group may be important for others. Thus there is considerable overlap between areas of endemism of birds, amphibians and mammals in Africa and for birds, amphibians and reptiles in Central America (Bibby *et al.*, 1992). Nevertheless it is not always useful to rely on one indicator group alone. South African reserves established to protect the large mammal fauna, for instance, provide almost no protection for the unique fynbos flora of the Cape Floral Kingdom (Rebelo and Siegfried, 1990). Moreover since we do not know the distribution, or value, of all species, conservation efforts cannot be restricted to biological hotspots alone. It is important to conserve representative samples of habitat throughout all biogeographic regions, to protect both restricted range species and those that are more common and widespread. Reviews of protected areas throughout Africa, Asia and Latin and Central America show that whereas remote mountain regions are often fairly well protected, the more species-rich lowland forests and wetlands, including coastal mangroves, are often poorly represented in protected area networks (MacKinnon and MacKinnon, 1986a, b; Dinerstein *et al.*, 1995; J. MacKinnon, 1997).

The size of individual reserves and the representativeness of any national protected area network will usually be a trade-off between protecting as much remaining natural habitat as possible and minimising conflict with competing land uses – see Box 19.1. The size of reserve needed to protect a viable population of any given species will depend on the species ecology, including habitat and range requirements. While small mammals may be able to maintain viable populations in relatively small areas, large mammals often require very large ranges. Asian elephants *Elephas maximus* and Sumatran rhino *Dicerorhinus sumatrensis* may need an area of 600 000 ha to maintain viable populations in tropical forests (K. MacKinnon, 1997). Even larger areas may be needed for top predators. A viable population of jaguars *Panthera onca*, say 500 individuals, requires somewhere in the order of 1 000 000 ha of suitable habitat (Terborgh and van Schaik, 1997). This is not to say that large mammal populations cannot be maintained in smaller reserves but the smaller the area, the more effort and expense must be given to management. Such management requirements may include habitat manipulation (controlled burning, waterhole construction and maintenance) or translocation and reintroductions of new stock, a strategy that has worked well for white and black rhinos, *Ceratotherium simum* and *Diceros bicornis,* in southern Africa (MacKinnon *et al.*, 1986). Since few protected areas are large enough to protect the full extent and range of habitats that large mammals require, it is important to look at other solutions. Increasingly conservationists are proposing a landscape approach

African elephant, *Loxodonta africana*, Kenya. Photograph: Sybil Sassoon.

to species conservation. Thus for the tiger *Panthera tigris* it has been suggested that conservation strategies should focus on large tiger conservation
units that may include one or more protected areas and adjacent wildlands,
including areas that straddle international boundaries (Dinerstein *et al.*,
1997).

It is often suggested that current protected area systems may be good
for protecting the larger charismatic mammals but not so good for smaller
mammals (Entwistle and Stephenson, chapter 7, this volume). In fact a
truly representative protected area system should provide good protection
for all mammals as well as other animals and native plants. A review of the
distribution of Bornean birds and mammals (other than bats) shows that
almost all are represented in at least one of the island's protected areas
(MacKinnon *et al.*, 1996). Other island, country and regional reviews give a
similar picture (Petocz and de Fretes, 1983; MacKinnon and MacKinnon,
1986a, b; Round, 1988). Even in Indochina, where protected area networks
are among the least adequate in Asia, most large mammals, including endemics and threatened species, are recorded from at least one reserve
(MacKinnon and MacKinnon, 1986b).

Simply designating areas as national park or reserves, however, is not
sufficient to ensure effective protection and long-term conservation of their
habitats and wildlife. Even where forests seem intact and healthy they may

Box 19.1. Nicaragua: Linking development with conservation to protect the path of the Jaguar

The MesoAmerican Biological Corridor, sometimes called Paseo Pantera (Path of the Jaguar), is a corridor of tropical rain forests, pine savannahs, mountain forests and coastal wetlands that extends from Mexico to Colombia. In addition to the jaguar, South America's largest cat, the corridor provides habitat for thousands of other resident animals and plants, rare and threatened species such as tapirs (*Tapirus* species), and harpy eagles *Harpia harpyja*, and wintering habitat for Nearctic breeding birds. It is also home for hundreds of thousands of people, many of them indigenous tribes, who subsist from farming and harvesting forest products and other natural resources.

Within Nicaragua the corridor of natural habitats extends almost unbroken along the Atlantic coast. Soils are fragile with little agricultural potential and human population levels are low. Only 390 000 people, about 10 % of Nicaragua's population, live in the Atlantic region. Until recently there has been only limited exploitation of the Atlantic region's natural resources – small scale forestry, mining, fisheries and limited agriculture. The civil war and the ensuing peace led to resettlement of indigenous and non-indigenous communities, land allocations to retired militia and the advance of the agricultural frontier into Nicaragua's tropical forests. Pressures to open up Nicaragua for more extensive logging, mining, fishing and transport routes are further threatening the rich biological resources of the Atlantic region.

The Nicaragua Atlantic Biological Corridor Project is the first of four Global Environment Facility (GEF) projects in Central America being prepared with the assistance of the World Bank. The $7.1 million grant from the GEF is supplying the incremental costs of protected areas and conservation-based land use in the corridor as part of an integrated development and conservation project that is valued at $30.5 million. The project is also supported by a credit from the International Development Association (IDA) and bilateral funding from the Netherlands, Canada and the Nordic countries. The IDA funding will support improved agriculture in the more densely populated Pacific region of Nicaragua to alleviate rural poverty and improve productivity, thus reducing the need for emigration to the Atlantic corridor and thereby curbing expansion of the agricultural frontier and clearing of Atlantic forests. The agricultural development project helps to address the root causes of biodiversity loss by reducing the need for more agricultural land, thus reducing pressure on the biologically rich Atlantic corridor. This project makes development work for conservation in an exciting initiative that will promote conservation of both biodiversity and ethnic cultures in one of the most intact parts of the MesoAmerican corridor (World Bank, 1997).

be empty of larger mammals and birds as a result of hunting, either for subsistence or commerce (Redford, 1992; Robinson and Bennett, 1999). A 'paper' park is no park at all. Gazetting a park but providing no resources for staff to protect and manage it is often equivalent to giving up on the species and habitats within it, especially when pressures from resource exploitation, agricultural encroachment and hunting are intense. This challenge has now been taken up by the World Bank in partnership with World Wide Fund for Nature (WWF) and other NGOs as part of a new Alliance for Forest Conservation and Sustainable Use. The Alliance goal is to work with client countries to achieve the following targets by the year 2005: establish 50 000 000 ha of new protected areas; strengthen management in 50 000 000 ha of existing 'paper' parks and establish 200 000 000 ha of the world's production forest under independently certified sustainable management.

THE CHALLENGES OF *EX SITU* CONSERVATION: CAPTIVE BREEDING AND REINTRODUCTIONS

The best, easiest and cheapest way of protecting species is usually the protection and management of their natural habitats. Sometimes, however, wild populations have become so small or isolated that they may need active management and/or the introduction of new blood. Under these circumstances *ex situ* conservation efforts can be an important part of an integrated conservation strategy to protect endangered species (Feistner and Mallinson, chapter 17, this volume). In recent years zoos and other conservation organisations have given increasing attention and funding to captive breeding schemes. Indeed the apparent decline in the species extinction rate over the last two decades may be attributable to conservation actions that have involved taking the last wild individuals into captivity (Groombridge, 1992). There have been some noteworthy successes and such programmes have played a vital role in conservation of some endangered species, e.g., Arabian oryx *Oryx leucoryx* (Stanley-Price, 1989). Moreover zoos can and do play an important role in raising awareness and support for conservation for particular species and protected areas. Nevertheless captive breeding schemes should be seen as a supplement rather than an alternative to *in situ* species protection (MacKinnon and MacKinnon, 1991). They should not be allowed to divert attention and funding away from *in situ* conservation efforts nor to become an excuse for giving up on conservation of a species in the wild.

  Ex situ conservation is not cheap and may not be a practical strategy for many species. The cost of maintaining African elephants *Loxodonta africana* and black rhinos in zoos is up to 50 times greater than protecting the same number of individuals in east African national parks (Leader-Williams, 1990). It costs approximately US$2000 a year to keep a rhino in captivity compared to US$200 per animal annually for protection and management in the wild in the Luanda Valley, Zambia (Stanley-Price, 1993). Moreover the costs per wild rhino will decrease as rhino numbers increase, the natural rate of increase is generally higher in well-protected wild populations and there is less risk of disease. Furthermore the protection of a large area of natural habitat brings ecosystem benefits, including protection of other native animal and plant species (MacKinnon and MacKinnon, 1991). Such considerations have led to the decision to return wild-caught Sumatran rhinos from US and UK zoos, where captive breeding programmes have failed, to Way Kambas National Park in Indonesia. The rhinos will be released into a large enclosure within their natural habitat so that they can be well protected and monitored under these semi-captive conditions and eventually released fully into the wild.

As the Sumatran rhino case illustrates, it is not always easy to persuade wild-caught animals to breed in captivity. If captive breeding schemes are successful, however, then wildlife managers are faced with a much greater challenge, returning captive-bred animals to the wild. A detailed study of 198 mammal and bird reintroduction programmes conducted between 1973 and 1986 found that reintroductions were more likely to be successful for game species (86 %) than threatened or endangered species (44 %); for wild-caught animals (75 %) than captive-bred animals (38 %); for herbivores (77 %) than for carnivores (48 %); for releases that occurred in better quality habitat; and for releases in the core of the species historic range rather than in peripheral or other areas (Griffith *et al.*, 1989). A second survey (Beck *et al.*, 1994) which looked only at the reintroduction of captive-born animals within the historical range of the species judged that only 16 out of 145 reintroduction projects (11 %) were successful, i.e., led to a self-maintaining population of 500 individuals. According to this study successful reintroductions require the release of large numbers of animals over many years. It may also be worth noting that it is probably easier to introduce animals into arid and semi-arid savannah habitats, which support high biomass, than into tropical rainforests where species densities are naturally low and carrying capacity may already have been reached.

Reintroductions and translocations are only practicable if the original threats or causes of extinction have been removed and adequate habitat remains and is well protected. Translocation of surplus individuals or family groups from overstocked habitats (e.g., well-protected small reserves) can allow habitat recovery and help to restock other areas, where the species has become locally extinct. Releasing captive-bred animals into the wild is generally more difficult than translocations since in addition to the traumas of capture and release the animals have to contend with learning new skills for which captivity may have ill prepared them (Kleiman *et al.*, 1991). Given the difficulties of reintroduction, relying solely on captive breeding schemes may be equivalent to giving up for some species.

One of the greatest problems facing many species is that most of their natural habitat has been lost or disturbed by human use and settlement so that there are few suitable areas for reintroduction. Tigers breed prolifically in captivity and the current zoo population probably equals or exceeds that in the wild. Nevertheless it would be difficult and even dangerous to release these captive-bred animals because they no longer fear and avoid people. Yet tigers are an extremely resilient and fast breeding species and wild populations can recover quickly if given adequate protection. Populations of Siberian tigers *Panthera tigris altaica*, in the Russian Far East, once considered seriously threatened, recovered within a few years once protection was improved for the tigers and their prey base (Miquelle *et al.*, 1999).

For large carnivores and many rainforest species, focusing on protecting populations in the wild is a far more viable option than reintroduction schemes. Figure 19.1 shows how effective protection of Sumatran rhino reserves will protect some of Sumatra's last remaining blocks of forest. As well as Sumatran rhinos, Gunung Leuser reserve alone protects 382 bird species (80 % of Sumatra's resident birds) and 105 mammals (75 % of the island total). This includes 39 rare, threatened and endemic birds and 19 rare and endemic mammals. Effective protection of all the rhino reserves in Sumatra can be expected to make a major contribution to protecting that island's biodiversity. Similarly Ujung Kulon, home to one of the last populations of Javan rhino, also protects three endemic primates (Javan gibbon *Hylobates moloch*, Javan surili *Presbytis comata* and Javan lutong *Trachypithecus auratus*) as well as half the Javan bird fauna. The peninsular park also protects important populations of endangered mammals such as banteng *Bos javanicus* and wild dog *Cuon alpinus*. Elsewhere 'flagship species' such as elephants and tigers have been used to attract international funding for conservation efforts, including resources from the Global Environment Facility (GEF) – see Table 19.1.

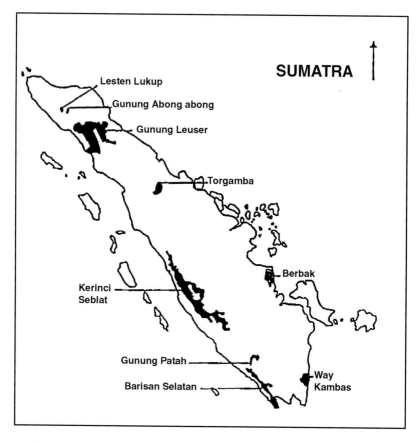

Figure 19.1 Sumatran parks and reserves with populations of Sumatran rhinos.

SUSTAINABLE USE OF SPECIES AND ECOSYSTEMS

Less than 10 % of the world's terrestrial ecosystems lie within protected areas (Groombridge, 1992). Land outside protected areas, and even within some categories of conservation area, will come under increasing levels of exploitation over the next few decades. As human pressures on wildlands increase, many in the conservation community have cautiously embraced the concept that utilisation may be the best hope for survival of certain species in the face of competing land uses. Indeed wildlife can pay for itself in simple cash terms in some areas. In South America the vicuna has been brought back from the brink of extinction through successful promotion of schemes to ranch animals and harvest their valuable fur. The very successful CAMPFIRE programme in Zimbabwe has demonstrated that cash revenues from wildlife tourism and safari hunting encourage local communities to tolerate wildlife on village lands (Child, 1995). The appropriateness of promoting sustainable use as a survival strategy for any species will, however, depend on multiple factors, including the ecology of the species, the method of exploitation and its regulation and, ultimately, how we value biological resources. The controversy over the elephant ivory trade illustrates only too well that even some of those who most ardently promote sustainable utilisation find it politically unacceptable for certain species.

Biodiversity occurs both within and beyond protected area boundaries. As protected areas increasingly become 'islands' in an agricultural landscape, conservationists are seeking new ways of integrating conservation with local and regional development (MacKinnon et al., 1999). Most integrated conservation and development projects (ICDPs) have been local efforts to relieve pressure on parks and reserves by offering small-scale economic activities to surrounding communities as an alternative livelihood to natural resource exploitation (Wells and Brandon, 1992). Often such initiatives have met with only limited success, satisfying neither the conservation nor rural development agenda (Wells et al., 1999).

Encouraging development around the boundaries of protected areas, however, may not be the most appropriate conservation strategy, especially when these protected areas are in remote forest areas or on poor soils where agricultural opportunities are limited. A better alternative for reducing pressure on valuable biodiversity areas and forests may be to promote development elsewhere (Kramer and van Schaik, 1997). The trade-offs and conflicts between conservation and development can often be ameliorated by wise land use planning, with development concentrated in the most appropriate areas for agriculture or production – those offering good soil, level ground and adequate water supply. Box 19.1 describes the Nicaraguan initiative to protect that country's part of the MesoAmerican Biological Corridor through land management strategies that combine agricultural intensification in the more fertile Pacific region with conservation of biologically rich areas in the Atlantic corridor (World Bank, 1997). The case of the Pacific pocket mouse *Perognathus longimembris pacificus* (Box 19.2) shows the problems that arise when a threatened species occurs within habitat that is of enormous commercial value to humans.

The greatest challenge, however, will be to seek out ways to conserve biodiversity, including key mammal species, in areas outside national parks and reserves but within the production landscape. One way to do this is to resort to land use systems that are as similar as possible to natural

Table 19.1
World Bank Projects (including GEF Projects) in Africa and Asia that support conservation of elephants and tigers

Biodiversity Investment Projects	Species			Protected Areas			Sustainable use			Tools and financing instruments		
	La	Em	Pt	1	2	3	4	5	6	7	8	9
Africa												
Benin National Parks and Conservation Management	x			x	x	x	x	x		x		
Benin Natural Resource Management Project	x				x	x	x	x	x	x		
Burkina Faso/Cote d'Ivoire Community-Based Natural Resource and Wildlife Management	x				x		x	x	x	x	x	
Cameroon Biodiversity Conservation and Management	x			x	x	x	x		x	x		
Congo Wildlands Protection and Management	x			x	x	x	x		x	x		
Kenya: Tana River National Primate Reserve	x				x		x		x	x		
Kenya Wildlife Services Project	x				x		x		x	x		
Malawi SADC Lake Malawi/Nyasa Biodiversity Conservation	x				x	x	x	x	x			x
Mozambique Transfrontier Conservation Areas	x			x	x	x	x		x	x	x	
Uganda: Bwindi Impenetrable Forest and the Mgahinga Gorilla N.P.	x				x		x			x		x
Uganda Protected Areas Management and Sustainable Use	x				x	x	x	x	x	x		
Zimbabwe: Park Rehabilitation and Conservation Project	x				x	x	x	x	x	x		

Asia

Project	1	2	3	4	5	6	7	8	9	La	Em	Pt
Bangladesh Forest Resources Management (III)		x	x	x					x			
Bangladesh Sunderbans Forest Biodiversity Conservation		x	x	x	x	x		x				
Bhutan Trust Fund	x	x	x				x		x			x
China Nature Reserves Management	x	x	x		x	x	x	x				
India Ecodevelopment	x	x	x		x	x	x	x			x	x
Indonesia Kerinci Seblat ICDP	x	x	x	x	x	x	x	x			x	x
Lao PDR Wildlife and Protected Areas Conservation	x	x	x	x	x	x	x	x				
Malaysia Sabah Land Settlement and Environmental Management	x	x	x		x	x	x	x				
Sri Lanka Forest Sector Development	x	x			x	x	x		x			
Vietnam Forest Protection and Rural Development	x	x	x	x	x	x	x	x	x			

Table key: 1: Expand the network; 2: Strengthen existing protected areas/institutions; 3: Provide support to transfrontier parks and ecosystems; 4: Integrate management plans and alternative livelihoods; 5: Natural resource management; 6: Research/conservation awareness; 7: Capacity building; 8: Mobilise the private sector; 9: Innovative financing mechanisms; La: African elephant *Loxodonta africana*; Em: Asian elephant *Elephas maximus*; Pt: Tiger *Panthera tigris*.

regimes, either through wildlife ranching or through simulation of natural grazing systems using domestic livestock or sometimes by mixing livestock and species cropping regimes. Already there are many exciting initiatives underway, especially in southern Africa and Latin America (Hoogesteijn and Chapman, 1997; Stockil, 1997) – see Box 19.3.

Box 19.2. Limited options: a mouse in a millionaire's paradise

The Pacific pocket mouse is a small (8 g) heteromyid rodent, with external fur-lined cheek pouches, which historically occurred along the coast of southern California in sandy coastal sage scrub and alluvial habitats. Although the species was probably uncommon even before European colonisation, the nearly complete conversion of its habitat to urban, suburb and agricultural land uses has reduced its population to about 500 individuals in three distinct populations, two of which occur on about 1–2 ha (P. Brylski, personal communication). Whether these populations will be large enough to be viable in the long term only time will tell. For the moment only the US Endangered Species Act stands between these surviving populations and development of their habitats into beach front estates, for this endemic mouse has the misfortune to live on real estate that can command up to $2.4 million/ha.

A CALL TO ACTION

Management of biological resources is entering a critical phase. In the past, land was often used then allowed to lie fallow; vegetation regenerated, animals returned. Increasingly land use is changing in one direction only, from wildlands to extensively used lands (swidden agriculture, grazing livestock) then to intensively used croplands and even degraded lands. At each step of the cascade the biodiversity is reduced (Terborgh and van Schaik, 1997). As the world's population increases and land use intensifies we can expect to see greater attrition of biodiversity. Protected areas will be critical to stemming this loss. With increasing population and pressure on land, however, it is probably unrealistic to hope that many more large areas will be designated purely for conservation. Moreover many of those areas that are designated lack any sort of infrastructure, staff or resources for effective protection or management. It is ironic that so much time, effort and money is spent on reprioritising conservation needs and proposing additional reserves when so few existing conservation areas have adequate resources or manpower for effective protection.

Box 19.3. Savé conservancy: from cattle to wildlife for profit

The Savé Conservancy includes 25 properties on 342 000 ha in the southeast lowveld of Zimbabwe, an area of unreliable rainfall and low agricultural potential. The properties were ranching cattle until the late 1980s when severe drought and poor grazing led to the need to destock. During this period, one ranch was also harbouring 30 black rhinos moved by the Department of National Parks out of the Zambesi valley where poaching was increasing. The success of the rhino translocation led the landowners to decide that rather than restock with cattle, they would change land use to ranching native wildlife for tourism and safari hunting. There were already populations of smaller ungulates such as impala *Aepyceros melampus* and klipspringer *Oreotragus oreotragus* on the estate but the ranchers bought in additional black rhinos, zebra *Equus burchellii*, kudu *Tragelaphus strepsiceros* and giraffe *Giraffa camelopardalis*. A herd of 600 elephants was moved in, the first attempt at translocating a whole herd together.

These animals are breeding well and building up healthy populations; the landowners are still shopping for more species that are attractive to tourists. Each landowner will utilise the wildlife on his property, either for high value ecotourism or for limited trophy hunting. Population levels of animals are being monitored by the World Wide Fund for Nature (WWF) who are providing advice on stocking and harvesting levels. Although no carnivores were introduced to the properties as part of the restocking programme, predator populations have risen. Now that big cats are no longer exterminated as potential predators on cattle, populations of cheetah, leopard *Panthera pardus* and lion *Panthera leo* are rising. A small population of African hunting dogs *Lycaon pictus*, one of the most endangered mammals in Africa, moved onto the property and has subsequently bred up from 15 to 70 animals, one of the healthiest populations of hunting dogs in Zimbabwe. There were five breeding dens in 1997.

With the removal of cattle the habitat is beginning to recover and perennial grasses are reappearing. More than 200 birds have been recorded, including birds of prey. The conservancy is connected through community lands to the 500 000 ha Gonarezhou National Park, one of a complex of transnational frontier parks extending into Mozambique and South Africa. By providing habitat for native species, the Conservancy is further extending the conservation estate in Zimbabwe, but surrounding villages will also benefit through increased employment opportunities. Under cattle ranching, the properties provided only some 260 local jobs. Already with limited tourism they are providing 600 jobs and as the number of tourist beds increases the number of jobs is estimated to rise to 1200. Local communities are supportive to the initiative and at least one community is discussing the opportunity to include part of their lands within the

Box 19.3 (*continued*)

Conservancy. The landowners have set up a trust fund to benefit local communities. Trust resources will be used to purchase animals for restocking, thereby giving the local communities a stake in the enterprise. Local communities have also begun looking at opportunities to benefit from the influx of visitors, for instance by establishing model villages and manufacturing handicrafts. Individual properties are engaged in good neighbour schemes with adjacent local communities.

The Savé story is interesting because the change to more ecologically sustainable landuse was made on economic grounds, i.e., that ecotourism would be more profitable than cattle ranching. The beneficiaries will be biodiversity (through habitat and species restoration), the landowners and local communities. It seems to be a win-win situation for conservation and sustainable development. This process has involved lengthy consultations, good leadership and partnerships between the landowners, local communities, government agencies, NGOs and commercial players, such as Zimbabwe Sun, a major hotel group. The Conservancy is receiving a small concessional loan from the GEF because of the expected global benefits of this initiative.

Outside protected areas conservationists must look for innovative opportunities for conservation in the production landscape. Production forests can support many mature forest species, including many rainforest mammals and species unable to survive in small isolated reserves (Johns, 1992; K. MacKinnon, 1997). Habitat corridors through agricultural lands and protection of watersheds can all benefit conservation as well as maintain ecosystem services. So too can development decisions that draw farmers away from marginal lands or route roads away from the last unexploited wilderness areas. Slowing agricultural expansion into forests, mountains and other habitats that are marginal for agriculture and rehabilitating degraded lands for sustainable production and to benefit biodiversity should become a priority for the future.

The greatest challenge of all will be to address the root causes of biodiversity loss, the land use strategies, policies, programmes and perverse economic incentives that fail to recognise that biodiversity conservation is key to sustainable development. Conservationists, policy makers, government officers, the scientific community, NGOs and local communities need to work together, and with the private sector, to ensure that biodiversity issues, options and concerns are integrated into sustainable sectoral and regional development, promoting conservation within the production landscape (World Bank, 1996b). Unless we are prepared to tackle this challenge then we will be giving up on many species not just a few. William Blake wrote 'To see a robin in a cage puts all Heaven in a rage'. What might we deserve if in future the only way to see many of today's wild species is behind cage bars or as dusty museum specimens?

20

Practical approaches for including mammals in biodiversity conservation

JEFFREY A. MCNEELY

INTRODUCTION

Arguably the world's first conservation programme was Noah's Ark, which reportedly set sail some 7000 years ago (Mestel, 1997). In most popular depictions of the Ark, long lines of mammals, two by two, are marching on to the ship built by Noah and his three sons. In Genesis 6:11–9:27, he is chosen by God, because of his blameless piety, to perpetuate the human race after his wicked contemporaries had perished in the Great Flood – an early example of the impact of climate change. God instructed Noah to build an Ark and in accordance with God's instruction he took into the Ark male and female specimens of all of the world's species of animals (an interesting biogeographic feat in its own right), from which the stocks might be replenished (though genetic variability might have been rather limited). Noah was allowed to also bring his wife, his three sons and their wives. It is notable that the only species allowed to break the 'two by two' rule was *Homo sapiens*, a species that has perhaps taken unfair advantage of its running start. Interestingly, God renewed his commands given at Creation but with at least one important change for the context of this chapter: man could now kill animals and eat meat.

While Noah's effort may have been successful because he had a high-level Decision Maker on his side, the often ark-like focus of conservation on large mammals in our own time has not proven to be nearly so successful. This lack of success is not due to lack of effort. Thousands of field biologists are working on mammals in all parts of the world, many zoos are working to maintain populations of mammals in captivity and build public support for conservation, important research stations are carrying out studies on mammals in Brazil, China, Costa Rica, India, Malaysia, Nepal, Saudi Arabia, South Africa, and elsewhere, and scientists are attempting to return mammals to their natural habitats in many parts of the world. Mammal conservation efforts can claim several success stories, such as the recovery of many of the great whales, the reintroduction of the Arabian oryx *Oryx leucoryx* into Oman, the stabilisation of rhino populations, the reintroduction of the black-footed ferret *Mustela nigripes*, and many other positive efforts identified in this volume.

But at the same time, the *1996 IUCN Red List of Threatened Animals* (IUCN, 1996) shows that more mammals are threatened than ever before, and the trajectory is such that we must expect the threats to grow (Tilman *et al.*, 1994). The *IUCN Red List* focuses on species, but it is clear that many genetically distinct populations of mammals are likely to be far more threatened than the full species, and some apparently are disappearing with hardly a trace (Hughes *et al.*, 1997). The *1996 Red List of Threatened Animals* showed 1096 species of mammals as Critically Endangered, Endangered or Vulnerable, out of a total of 4327 species (Corbet and Hill, 1991), or 25.6% in some danger of extinction in the fairly near future. Comparing this to the birds, where 1107 species are listed from a species list of 9672 (11.4%; Sibley and Munro, 1990) suggests that mammals as a whole are over twice as threatened as birds. Clearly, as latter-day Noahs, our Ark is pretty leaky. We need to be more successful in our conservation battles, and I will suggest some possible approaches to consider.

CONSERVING MAMMALS: SOME PROGRAMMATIC SHORTCOMINGS

First I must briefly examine where we might be losing the conservation fight, and why. I make this critique above all in admiration of those who are doing the hard work on the front lines of mammal conservation. We all recognise that the quality of work being carried out in the name of conservation of mammals is constantly improving. We are getting better and better at describing the threats that mammals are facing and describing solutions to at least the proximate problems. But I am worried that the actions that we are recommending are only necessary to win a few skirmishes, but not sufficient to win many battles, much less the war. I intentionally am using military terminology here, because we often are talking about violent actions being taken against mammals, and the results may be annihilation of a species.

Let me illustrate what I mean through two of the best and most recent SSC action plans, that for Asian rhinos (Foose and van Strien, 1997) and wild cats (Nowell and Jackson, 1996). These two represent the veritable

Table 20.1
Conservation projects proposed in the IUCN *Wild Cats Action Plan*

Project type	No. of projects	Percentages
Research, surveys	75	71.3
Captive breeding/reintroduction	7	6.7
Habitat management		
(including anti-poaching)	5	4.8
Trade and use	4	3.8
Conflict management	4	3.8
Information management	3	2.9
Miscellaneous	7	6.7
Totals	105	100.0

cutting edge in mammalian conservation at the international level, presenting excellent overviews of current knowledge about distribution and population status, and recommending conservation actions.

The *Wild Cats Action Plan*, a superb summary of present knowledge about all 36 species of cats, was based on 5000 scholar-years of collective effort by the 160 members of IUCN's Cat Specialist Group. They proposed 105 actions, ranging from research to habitat management to trade and use (Table 20.1).

This list of projects shows that the Cat Specialist Group considers the main problem facing wild cats to be lack of knowledge about their status and distribution. While not denying the importance of such information, is this really the biggest problem facing the world's cats? Isn't conflict with humans and their livestock a far more important problem?

I will return to this issue in a moment, but first I would like to take a similar look at the *Asian Rhino Action Plan*, directed at the three species of Asian rhinos, all of which are under very serious threat. Perhaps 2000 Indian rhinos *Rhinoceros unicornis* survive, along with slightly over 300 Sumatran rhinos *Dicerorhinus sumatrensis* and around 75 Javan rhinos *Rhinoceros sondaicus*. Prepared by 48 of the world's leading experts on Asian rhinos, of whom 35 are residents of rhino range states, the actions recommended are included in Table 20.2.

This is a rather more even distribution of effort, with anti-poaching receiving the greatest share, an accurate reflection by scientists from within the region that the symptom of poaching needs urgent attention. But the more fundamental problems facing rhinos may also require that much more attention be given to issues of public awareness, trade and tourism, which are receiving relatively little attention; no activities are being proposed to address the development-related problems that are threatening

Table 20.2
Priority projects recommended by the IUCN *Asian Rhino Action Plan*

Project type	No. of projects	Percentage
Intensive protection/anti-poaching	22	38.6
Habitat management	15	26.3
Research	8	14.0
Reintroduction	4	7.0
Training	3	5.2
Tourism	2	3.5
Trade	1	1.8
Public awareness	1	1.8
Veterinary units	1	1.8
Totals	57	100.0

rhino habitats, nor are any looking at the government policies that may be contradictory to the interests of rhino conservation, for example, agricultural subsidies in rhino habitats.

In the case of both cats and rhinos, the proposed actions are undoubtedly necessary and urgent, and will be carried out by qualified and dedicated biologists. However, they are not sufficient: even if all were implemented to perfection, the species would not be as secure as we would like them to be. It clearly is essential to treat the underlying causes of threats to mammals rather than simply treat the symptoms, though of course the symptoms also need their fair share of attention. I think that attention we are giving to symptoms needs to be significantly augmented by serious attention to fundamental causes.

I make no claim that magic solutions are available; the forces of environmental destruction are formidable. But I believe that we can do much better than we are doing, and that 'biodiversity' offers an entry point for doing so.

BIODIVERSITY CAN PROVIDE A SOLUTION

The problem as indicated by my review of the *Wild Cats* and *Asian Rhino Action Plans* is that most efforts to conserve mammals focus too narrowly on issues of mammalian biology or proximate threats and tend to involve those who are already supportive of our efforts. More effective action, I suggest, will come from involving new partners in our conservation efforts. Biodiversity can help provide an introduction to such partners.

The Convention on Biological Diversity (CBD) entered into force at the end of 1993 and has now been ratified by over 170 countries. It defines biological diversity as the variability among living organisms from all sources including terrestrial, marine and other aquatic ecosystems and the ecological complexes of which they are part; this includes diversity within and between species, and of ecosystems. The CBD has three objectives: the conservation of biological diversity; the sustainable use of biological resources; and the fair and equitable sharing of benefits arising out of the utilisation of genetic resources. The Convention thus covers ecological, economic and social aspects of biodiversity. It provides a mechanism for international cooperation on matters of mutual interest, and seeks to provide new and additional financial resources to enable countries to fully implement the Convention.

This is now all very familiar, and seems to be almost displacement behaviour. But by far the most important contribution made by 'biodiversity' is that it provides a basis for influencing the political process, and encourages those interested in conserving mammals to look much more seriously at the ultimate underlying threats to mammals. For example, land grants, tax incentives, zoning regulations and cheap water rights have all subsidised the conversion of critical habitats for mammals into other uses, often in the name of social progress and economic gain. But under closer examination, much of this economic gain is illusory, because it requires considerable financial subsidies from government, in forms varying from direct cash grants to tax benefits to price supports. A careful look at such subsidies may convince governments that they can conserve mammals by *not* spending money, a popular argument these days with decision makers. So if we are interested in conserving mammals, we need to enter the policy and political arenas where the real war over resources is being waged.

BIODIVERSITY AVOIDS THE QUESTION: ECOSYSTEMS OR SPECIES?

Trying to conserve mammals by definition focuses on the species or population, at a time when ecosystem management is becoming increasingly fashionable (Grumbine, 1994). In many cases, good ecosystem management will be identical to good species-level management. 'Biodiversity' means that human impacts on nature need to be managed on multiple scales, including the ecological system scale of time and space as well as the short-term economic scale which seems to dominate current thinking. While attention to individual species may still be required in some cases, it is clear that managing large-scale systems for one or a few resources can lead to increased brittleness, making them susceptible to collapse or gradual degradation (Holling, 1992). Therefore, management actions need to be based on system-level characteristics and the dynamic processes that they represent. But the traditional focus on individual species has at least four major advantages:

- Because ecosystems are less discrete entities, species provide a more objective means of determining the location, size, connectivity, and spacing of protected areas necessary to conserve biodiversity.
- Population declines in individual species, such as otters, may indicate the presence of stress to an ecosystem before it is obvious throughout the system.
- Individual species are the units of interest to people, as game animals or sources of pleasure (including the simple knowledge that they exist). People make greater emotional investments in real species than in abstract ecosystems.
- Although ecological services are provided by ecosystems, individual species often play pivotal roles in the provision of these services (Eisner et al., 1995).

Thus both species and habitats need to be protected, as neither is a complete substitute for the other. Biodiversity combines ecosystem-based approaches with taxa-based criteria such as species richness, endemism, ecological role, and abundance, along with considerations of the physical environment, ecological processes and disturbance regimes. Such more comprehensive approaches can be a significant improvement on either ecosystem-based or species-based approaches alone. Again this is where biodiversity as a political and economic concept can play a major role. A biodiversity approach will link species conservation with habitat conservation, and will address the real political and economic factors threatening mammals.

BIODIVERSITY ENLISTS USEFUL PARTNERS IN CONSERVING MAMMALS

Biodiversity breaks down barriers between disciplines, enabling those concerned with conserving mammals to identify new and useful partners. The list of these is a long one, but I will mention just a few of special interest.

Economists

Most of those working in conservation of mammals appear to have little familiarity with economists, but decision makers listen to economists, and

Table 20.3
The economic value of ecosystem services

Ecosystem	Area (millions ha)	Value ($/ha/yr)	Global value ($trillions/year)
Open ocean	33 200	252	8.4
Coastal	3102	4052	12.6
Tropical forest	1900	2007	3.8
Other forests	2955	302	0.9
Grasslands	3898	232	0.9
Wetlands	330	14 785	4.9
Lakes and rivers	200	8498	1.7
Cropland	1400	92	0.1
Total worth of the biosphere			$33.3

Source: Costanza et al., 1997.

many human decisions are based on real economic factors. Considerable recent attention has been given to the role of biodiversity in ecosystem functions, with a cash value attached. Costanza et al. (1997), for example, presented a considerable body of evidence that indicated that the value of ecological services, primarily from relatively natural habitats, amount to some US$33 trillion per year, a non-trivial sum (Table 20.3). Is anyone looking at the contribution of mammals to these various ecosystem services? Focusing on ecological services of mammals may offer new opportunities for conserving species such as bats, for example, which play important roles in pollination, insect control, and nutrient cycling.

Economists also tell us that the public is willing to pay for the conservation of mammals. As just one recent example from the UK, White et al. (1997) investigated the relative economic values of the otter *Lutra lutra* and the water vole *Arvicola terrestris*, both of which are threatened by habitat change and fragmentation, and pollution. In a survey, they found that the mean willingness to pay for conservation amounted to £11.91 for the otter, £7.44 for the water vole and £10.92 for both species together. Extended to the population of North Yorkshire, where the survey was conducted, these results indicate that the public would be willing to pay £5.8 million to conserve these species, which is far in excess of the £1.8 million costs of the UK action plans for these two species. They interpret their results as demonstrating strong public support for mammal conservation, especially for the higher profile charismatic species, and suggest that public profile may be as important as rarity or degree of threat in determining the economic value of a species.

Farther afield, Western (1984) calculated that each lion in Kenya's

Amboseli National Park is worth US$27 000 per year in visitor attraction (the same lion would have a direct value of about US$1000 as a skin). A more recent study by Vorhies and Vorhies (1993) showed that the introduction of lions into the Pilanesberg National Park in South Africa would generate around US$9 million per year in real income to the regional economy, far exceeding the costs of introduction. Based on this calculation the private hotel industry agreed to finance the lion introduction programme. Such figures help to convince decision makers of the value of conserving a large predator, even if they need to compensate herders for some losses of livestock. Tigers, on the other hand, have very considerable value to a poacher who can market tiger parts for their medicinal values. While the value of a tiger for tourism may be much higher, the benefits from this use are more widely dispersed. The problem here is one of private individual gain versus more widespread non-financial benefits, a problem that economists can help elucidate. These few examples, among literally hundreds that could be quoted, illustrate that an economic perspective can be useful in support of mammal conservation.

Of course, economics is not a panacea, but economic figures and economic perspectives provide policy makers with ammunition they can use in the kinds of skirmishes they face on political battlefields (Pearce et al., 1990; Pearce and Moran, 1994; Swanson, 1997). But conservation biologists also need to be aware of the danger that placing values on species may open them up to market forces, and some policy makers might conclude that a price tag on a resource means that it is for sale. Even so, those concerned with conservation of mammals would be well advised to give much greater attention to couching their conservation arguments in economic terms. Very few of the papers in this volume consider economic factors such as cost-benefit ratios, market failures, economic valuation, externalities, opportunity costs and other such economic concepts that communicate meaning to politicians and other decision makers.

Rural people

Most of the mammal conservation actions that we promote today are designed by scientists with little consideration given to the local people who have long coexisted with the mammals we are trying to conserve. Seeking to establish 'pristine habitats' where mammals can frolic in peace is a forlorn hope, because such habitats are figments of the imagination, since people have lived virtually everywhere for thousands of years, and such efforts are of doubtful validity on conservation grounds (McNeely, 1994). Work done in southeast Asia has demonstrated that the large terrestrial

Indian rhinoceros, *Rhinoceros unicornis*, India. Photograph: Sybil Sassoon.

mammals of the rain forest tend to be most numerous in areas where shifting cultivation is an important land use. The wild cattle, deer, elephants, wild pigs, and so forth feed in the abandoned swiddens, followed by their suite of predators and scavengers (Wharton, 1966, 1968). The game-ridden savannahs of Africa are maintained by fire, many set by people. Wildlife in Amazonia concentrates around forest clearings made by people (Posey, 1982; Gomez-Pompa and Kaus, 1992).

Many members of the public will embrace the abstract idea of conserving biodiversity or species which live in distant wilderness. But this is very different from the real-world practice of conserving individual sites or species, a disparity that has very little to do with science. In many cases, preserving species such as rhinos, whales, wolves or tigers involves primarily abstract benefits to individual members of the general, largely urban, public, while the people who are expected to make economic sacrifices by restricting their activities in the habitat of the species tend to be large-scale farmers and ranchers, forestry interests or developers who are very effective in conveying their concerns to politicians; or small farmers, fishermen or pastoralists over whom conservation agencies have little influence. So while the general public may agree with conserving mammals in the abstract, the support by rural people and commercial interests for specific action on threatened species of mammals tends to be much weaker because they pay more of the costs and perceive fewer of the benefits. Thus many government conservation programmes, especially if they are designed in the capital cities in response to the more powerful urban interests, face difficulties when they need to be implemented in the countryside, sometimes even causing a backlash as rural people protest about the loss of their historical responsibility as resource managers and about having to pay the opportunity costs for conserving species the world regards as its global heritage (Dang, 1991).

Further, given the role of rural people in determining what happens in the countryside, it is critical that international and national conservation organisations find ways of working with them. This may involve giving them land tenure or other incentives to encourage appropriate conservation behaviour. Once communities understand that they themselves are responsible for finding solutions to conservation problems, they begin to think and behave differently. When communities build coalitions to address problems, they can help to reach mutually agreeable decisions regarding seemingly intractable natural resource issues and to simply get things done on the ground. The support of local people for rhinos and tigers in Chitwan National Park in Nepal is just one of many examples that can be quoted (McNeely, 1999). This is not to romanticise local people, because well-armed local villagers can quickly render a forest empty of large mammals (Redford, 1992). Thus even an intact forest, seemingly undisturbed, may lack the large species which make it so attractive. On the other hand, conservation programmes designed by local or indigenous peoples or in close collaboration with them and which are designed to meet their concerns for sustainable use of biological resources can earn strong support (Western and Wright, 1994).

While tapping into local knowledge and motivation can yield better conservation than the top-down regulatory approach favoured by governments and most conservationists, this does not diminish the importance of national legislation for endangered species or habitat protection. On the contrary, community-based conservation can represent a variety of interests and build on good scientific information to substantially improve society's ability to meet national mandates for conserving biodiversity.

NGOs

We need to be much more effective in mobilising public support, and the broader our reach, the better. But we need to recognise that scientists are seldom the best placed to generate the kinds of public concern that can actually change human behaviour. The campaigning NGOs, which are not so constrained by scientific rigour, can often do a much better job than scientists in changing public perceptions.

Other scientists

We need to enlist other scientists in our efforts, through creating a sort of scientific hybrid vigour. Scientists working on fossils, climate, biotechnology, physics and various life sciences can help us to achieve new breakthroughs in our understanding of mammals and how they might be conserved. For example, BirdLife International has been extraordinarily successful in identifying important bird areas, devising maps that are very effective in focusing attention on areas the bird lobby has identified as being particularly important. Such approaches are extremely useful in mobilising broader support. But while the ornithologists have been successful in answering the scientific question of *where* to work, they often still leave unanswered the more difficult question of *how* to work, and this may require other disciplines.

THE POLITICS OF CONSERVING MAMMALS

In the final analysis, we need to become more politically astute in our efforts to conserve mammals. Biologists may see threats to mammals arising primarily from the relationship between people and the environment. But the problem is perhaps more accurately seen as an outcome of the economic relationships among people that determine how any piece of land or set of resources is to be used. Any given development or conservation activity inevitably will advance the interests of some while prejudicing others, so it is a mistake to assume that conservation objectives may be achieved merely through the combinations of improved scientific information, education and technical remedies that our species-based conservation strategies advocate. We need to take a hard look at the economic dimensions of conservation and the political actions needed to address these dimensions.

Further, we need to mobilise political support to advance our positions. Like Noah, we need the support of higher authority. This requires building the broadest possible constituency for the conservation of mammals. The active participation of many actors in developing public policy on mammal conservation is essential, as the critical assessment of information and how it should be used needs to involve all interests and not merely those with narrowly defined technical expertise. On the other hand, biodiversity issues often can be critically assessed only through knowledge and understanding, rare commodities that often seem to be monopolised by scientists. Thus science remains uniquely authoritative, especially if scientists can marshal their evidence in ways that will be useful to policy makers anxious to ensure better management of biological resources. Public support will be essential to encourage them to do so, so partnership is the key principle.

The reality is that many of the most important decisions affecting mammals, especially on issues of budgets, priorities, information and resource management policies, are taken by politicians and 'non-conservation' sectors of government (ministries of finance, trade, defence, etc.). Perhaps even more important decisions are made by the private sector and rural people. Biologists working on mammals may see ourselves as the gatekeepers to observable evidence, but when we try to apply our science to policy, governments and industries tend to treat us as just another interest group. As a result we are often reduced to being little more than concerned bystanders when policies are formulated to address the problems facing mammals (Tobin, 1990). This is perhaps understandable, as most problems affecting mammals reflect a conflict of interests between alternative ways resources should be used.

Research on mammals generally must continue to be science driven, if biologists are to be true to our training and motivations. But at the same time, at least some biologists need to work more actively to ensure that the findings of our colleagues are applied to the messy political battles over the conservation of mammals. The application of science to management and politics need not necessarily be done by the same scientists who are doing the research. But if present trends of exploitation and destruction of mammalian populations continue unabated, we may not long have the luxury of worrying about whether research should be science- or policy-driven.

Helping find ways to conserve mammals in the political quagmire of modern society is the challenge facing us today. Political forces will decide which mammals are conserved, but biologists are most likely to have our point of view heard when we are able to couch our arguments in terms that bureaucrats and politicians will find convincing, and feel that their constituents will support.

CONCLUSIONS

Biologists need to be much more effective in communicating the problems and the solutions to policy makers, and building the public support that will be necessary for supporting the difficult choices ahead. We need to be more creative in linking the conservation of mammals with other major concerns of society, ranging from climate change to desertification to biodiversity. People finally are beginning to approach conservation problems in a more systematic way, so it is up to us to ensure that mammals remain part of the system, and indeed that we turn the 'biodiversity approach' around so that it will support the mammals we care about so much.

Since the public wants their politicians to deliver benefits, not constraints, those seeking to conserve mammals through advocating appropriate policy changes need to become much more politically and economically astute if we wish to have the impact we desire. The Convention on Biological Diversity provides an excellent opportunity for doing so, giving political legitimacy to issues of conservation, sustainable use and equitable sharing of benefits. It is apparent that public support is crucial to any successful conservation programme. Such support will need to be based on a sound ethical footing, good information and economic benefits. We must build on science to demonstrate the benefits of conserving mammals to farmers, fishermen, ranchers, and foresters, balance the attention given to the loss of mammals with concern for sustainable use of harvestable species, and build a broader constituency among business, the public, and academics. An effective overall strategy for mobilising political and economic support for conserving mammals will:

- give management responsibility and tenure rights to the people most directly involved;
- provide economic incentives to encourage individual behaviour which is in the long term benefit of the larger society and remove incentives which promote overconsumption of resources;
- provide the best available science to support decision making; and
- seek a diversity of local solutions to local problems.

Those seeking to conserve mammals need to contribute to approaches to managing biological resources which are ecologically sound, economically feasible and politically palatable. In short, we need to adopt a biodiversity approach to conserving mammals.

21

Future priorities for mammalian conservation

ABIGAIL C. ENTWISTLE AND NIGEL DUNSTONE

INTRODUCTION

This volume has brought together the perspectives of a wide range of contributors on the current status of mammalian conservation from a global
standpoint and has indicated future priorities in this field. The book addressed three main questions: 'why do we often conserve mammals and
not other taxonomic groups?'; 'what have been our priorities to date?'; and
'what lessons can be learnt from the past for effective conservation
measures for mammals and other taxa?'. The contributors to this book have
generally focused on specific topics, biogeographical regions or individual
species, and in this synthesis we attempt the collation of their sometimes
disparate, but frequently complementary, views. In this we have benefited
from their cumulative experience in order to provide an overview and perspective of the discipline of mammalian conservation at the end of the
twentieth century. We hope that this approach to reviewing the issues will
draw out recurring themes to highlight potential priorities for mammalian
conservation into the future.

WHY CONSERVE MAMMALS?

Although mammals represent a relatively small group of animals, it is clear
that the future maintenance of mammalian diversity, and of particular species, is of concern to many people, ranging from conservationists and academics to schoolchildren and the general public. The preceding chapters
have explored conservation from a number of angles enabling differing
values to be placed upon mammals – aesthetic, scientific and economic.

As scientists we are perhaps most comfortable with defending conservation of mammals from the perspective of their function in maintaining
ecosystem integrity. Recent research has highlighted the complexity of

interactions between mammals and other groups of animals and plants, for example, with regard to mammalian herbivores structuring vegetation in rainforests (Asquith et al., 1997), and desert grasslands (Brown and Heske, 1990). Mammals may have an important role as seed dispersers, demonstrating their potential to dramatically shape forest structure and aid regeneration (Andresen, chapter 2, this volume). Andresen also highlights the potential consequences for the habitat of loss of species and assemblages, and the interdependence of faunal and floristic composition. As well as direct functions, the potential role of mammals as tools for conservationists as bio-indicators and as early warning systems for ecosystem damage is being examined. Mammals play an important role as models for research and management of threatened ecosystems over a broad range of spatial scales (Bright and Morris, chapter 8, this volume). Thus although not unique in these functions, the role of mammals in an ecosystem context is becoming better understood.

Recent analyses have shown that around 25% of all mammal species are threatened, to varying degrees, with extinction (IUCN, 1996). This has provided a strong argument in support of a continued focus on mammals in conservation programmes. This figure is significantly higher than similar estimates for birds, but lower than the, albeit limited, assessments of fish and invertebrates, two groups which receive relatively little conservation attention (Mace and Balmford, chapter 3, this volume). The level of threat for mammals (particularly groups such as primates, insectivores and ungulates), and the likely disappearance of up to a quarter of our mammal diversity over the coming decades, indicates that specific conservation actions may be needed for this group. However, this must also be considered in the light of similar threats to other taxa (IUCN, 1996).

Alongside these more 'scientific' justifications for mammalian conservation, there is a need to consider mammals in a wider context – their use by man, and the interest and emotion associated with the mere existence of many of these species. Thus for most people, justifications for mammal conservation are likely to focus on direct economic returns associated with the maintenance of mammal populations (Bodmer, chapter 15; Goodwin and Leader-Williams, chapter 14, this volume), and also on the intrinsic appeal of particular species (Leader-Williams and Dublin, chapter 4; Goodwin and Leader-Williams, chapter 14, this volume).

The economic value of non-domestic mammals should not be underestimated, ranging from the increasing utilisation of mammals for subsistence and sport hunting and particularly for bushmeat (Wilkie et al., 1998; Bowen-Jones and Pendry, 1999), to their diminishing role in international trade (e.g., for furs and ivory). In comparison, indirect revenue from mammals generated from tourism is obviously substantial according to published estimates (Western, 1984; Vorhies and Vorhies, 1993). Further potential economic gain is associated with the genetic reserves represented by wild relatives of domestic species, providing a source of material for improvements in agricultural efficiency (potential value; Edwards and Abivardi, 1998). Indeed, in many countries the way in which mammals are regarded by local people often reflects their direct value, as well as the degree of risk to crops and human health, or simply the aesthetic appreciation of particular species (Entwistle and Stephenson, chapter 7, this volume). The economic potential of mammals has also been exploited by the conservation movement, through the use of a range of mammalian symbols in fundraising. Mammals, particularly large charismatic species, certainly have an important earning power from the general public in Western nations (Leader-Williams and Dublin, chapter 4, this volume), which is unrivalled by any other taxonomic group. Since so many people obviously care very strongly about the future of mammals, this must in itself be a strong argument for their conservation.

Conservation is not only for decision makers and those who implement policy, but is conducted on behalf of a wider constituency, both within countries encompassing a species range and at an international level. A broad range of society, ranging from local people and governments, to scientists, the international community and individual supporters of conservation, have a stake in the conservation of mammals, and these groups often have different reasons why they believe mammals should be conserved. It would therefore seem important that the different values placed on mammals by different groups are reflected in the conservation approaches and priorities set for mammals, rather than attempting to define a single, 'correct' justification for mammalian conservation. Furthermore, we may need to accept the relatively low priority that may be placed on biodiversity conservation by the majority of society, in relation to other environmental, developmental and economic issues.

The challenge is to find mechanisms by which the value of mammals can be harnessed to fund conservation initiatives that meet the concerns of local people, scientists and conservationists, as well as those of the broader populace. The issue of the appropriateness and effectiveness of a flagship species approach within conservation is discussed further below. However, it is clear that mammals, particularly large and highly charismatic species, are likely to continue to be used as a focus for the conservation movement for the foreseeable future. Since the values placed on mammals by Western donors may differ from those of the local community (Entwistle and Stephenson, chapter 7; Leader-Williams and Dublin, chapter 4, this volume), there is a particular need to ensure that conservation investment can also be used to meet the needs and values of those affected most directly by conservation programmes.

WHAT ARE THE PRIORITIES FOR MAMMALIAN CONSERVATION?

What should we protect? Individuals rank the importance of the various components of mammalian diversity in different ways, and a range of different priorities for mammal conservation have been proposed even among the contributors to this book; including small mammals (Entwistle and Stephenson, chapter 7), rare species (Bright and Morris, chapter 8), threatened species (Mace and Balmford, chapter 3), and species of ecological or economic importance (Andresen, chapter 2; Bodmer, chapter 15). While priorities for conservation are generally perceived to be based upon quantitative or objective assessments, such priorities will also reflect the values placed upon mammals by different groups and the underlying assumptions and beliefs about the goal of conservation, no matter what statistical approach is used to analyse the data. For example, if the goal of conservation is to maximise species diversity rather than to protect a small number of large, endangered species, a totally different series of areas would be selected for protection (Williams et al., chapter 5). It therefore cannot be assumed that the promotion of conservation initiatives for one priority species or taxon will also meet broader conservation goals, and it is apparent that even wide-ranging mammals may not be effective 'umbrella species' for mammalian diversity, unless more information on habitat preferences and distributions is considered.

If we accept the precautionary principle, it would seem that the overall goal of conservation should be the survival of the maximum number and range of species and the protection of ecosystem integrity, while recognising that certain species, with particular value to a wide range of people including local communities, may need specific protection. Within this structure, indicators of relative priority are likely to be varied, and will include the degree of threat to species, their role in ecosystems, economic and social value and the extent of existing protection. In addition, priorities are likely to be affected by the scale at which they are considered (for example, individual populations of a particular species are more likely to have greater priority at a national level than in an international context).

This volume contains various analyses that indicate a need to re-evaluate existing assumptions about relative threat and priority. For example, a number of authors have concluded that body size does not directly affect conservation status, and that smaller species are as threatened as larger ones (Entwistle and Stephenson, chapter 7; Mace and Balmford, chapter 3). Furthermore, such small species appear to be under-represented in conservation programmes (Entwistle and Stephenson, chapter 7), despite their clear potential as flagship species (e.g., dormouse, Bright and Morris, chapter 8). In addition, the technique of captive breeding appears under-utilised for small mammals, despite its potential for success among this group (Balmford, chapter 16). Further analyses of relative threat have revealed higher extinction risks associated with island species, but also, unexpectedly, with old-world taxa compared to neotropical forms (Mace and Balmford, chapter 3). Mace and Balmford also considered 'reversibility of threats' and concluded that primates are likely to suffer the greatest losses over coming years, while insectivores, ungulates and dugongs are also at particular risk.

Such analyses use an assessment of threat based on evidence of population decline and natural rarity. However, using different assumptions to indicate relative threat might lead to a re-evaluation of the level of threat faced by different species. For example, use of absolute abundance relative to predicted populations (based on body size) to determine priority, has led to a re-evaluation of relative conservation status of mammals in the UK (Harris et al., chapter 6). Furthermore, consideration may need to be given to the conservation of the common, as well as the rare (Harris et al., chapter 6). So far, much of the prioritisation discussed has been based upon ecological or 'scientific' criteria and does not consider the values placed on mammals by broader sectors of society – a key factor if conservation is to be participatory and, in the long term, successful. A pragmatic view would thus incorporate a range of different approaches and values when prioritising mammals. To some extent this already occurs within conservation, as a result of the often differing perspectives and goals of organisations and individuals working within the discipline. These multiple solutions to the question of 'what should we protect' ensure a range of species and groups are conserved. However, the need remains to identify those groups and habitats which are not covered by existing activities, to ensure that species and ecosystems do not fall through the net of conservation. Alternatively, we must be prepared to accept that the disappearance of a certain number of species or ecosystems cannot be avoided within a broader conservation framework working within limited resources.

WHICH MECHANISMS ARE MOST EFFECTIVE FOR MAMMALIAN CONSERVATION?

A range of approaches to mammalian conservation have been discussed in the preceding chapters. The outcomes and conclusions from these reviews provide useful insight into the relative success of different management strategies that are applicable not only to mammals but also to other taxa.

Research for conservation

The need for effective and ongoing research, to inform and refine conservation action, has been made clear by a number of authors (Feistner and Mallinson, chapter 17; Lu et al., chapter 18; Racey, chapter 9, this volume). A clear example of the need for appropriate research is apparent in the review of giant panda conservation by Lu et al. Recent research on wild panda populations has revealed previous misconceptions and misunderstandings concerning threats to this species (including reproductive behaviour, dietary limitations and abandonment of young), which had originated from reliance on incomplete data and zoo-based studies. In this case conservation action has been improved as a result of ongoing applied study, conducted in parallel to conservation efforts. The pressures to proceed with conservation with only partial scientific understanding are complex where there is a risk of species becoming extinct in the interim while time-consuming research is completed (Racey, chapter 9, this volume).

The type of research that is undertaken may need to be reconsidered if it is to meet the needs of conservation which appears to require an increasing focus on applied and multidisciplinary studies. A shift is needed from the description of problems to the identification and testing of potential solutions (McNeely, chapter 20, this volume). For example, while continued research helps refine the selection of key sites for conservation, it cannot guide the way that such sites should be managed, especially in the absence of political will to protect them (McNeely, chapter 20; Williams et al., chapter 5, this volume). In addition, where conservation programmes do exist, there is an important opportunity to use them as trials or experiments, and to learn how conservation approaches can be refined to be more effective (for example, by designing reintroductions within an experimental framework; Bright and Morris, chapter 8).

However, research on its own is insufficient to achieve conservation and there is a need for effective dialogue between researchers and policy makers (Racey, chapter 9, this volume). An important model for effective feedback between science and policy development is provided by the study of bat conservation in the UK (Racey, chapter 9), where the outcome of research has successfully been used by policy makers to improve the advice and legislation relating to the management of bat species. Thus researchers need to develop effective mechanisms to communicate with, and lobby, decision makers, if their research is to have wider impacts. This often relies on forming partnerships with conservationists and local people (Bodmer, chapter 15, Racey, chapter 9).

Mammals and protected areas

This volume has brought together viewpoints of a range of individuals and organisations directly involved in the management of protected areas for mammals. The focus here on African parks in particular, reflects both their history, and the long-term interest in studying these systems. Nevertheless, many of the conclusions drawn are likely to be relevant for protected areas elsewhere in the world.

Analysis has proved the relative success of a system of protected areas in eastern Africa in conserving larger mammals, particularly the edible ungulate species favoured by hunters, and associated large carnivore populations, mainly through the effects of anti-poaching activities (Caro et al., chapter 12, this volume). However, it has been questioned how far such parks actually meet contemporary concerns for the protection of biodiversity (Caro et al., chapter 12; Entwistle and Stephenson, chapter 7; Williams et al., chapter 5, this volume), given biases in the habitats represented. Gaps in habitat representation in current protected area networks have also been noted in Asia (MacKinnon, chapter 19, this volume), and these may lead to inadequate habitat protection for some groups of species. Furthermore, even when many species do occur in protected areas, it has been questioned whether management regimes focused on particular mammals can take into account the conservation requirements of a broader range of species (Entwistle and Stephenson, chapter 7), given evidence of species extinctions in parks over time (Newmark, 1995).

In future, protected areas may develop in two separate directions. While attempts are being made to expand park systems in Africa, and elsewhere, to create integrated management for conservation across national frontiers (Transfrontier Conservation Areas; Hanks, chapter 13, this volume), other researchers are looking to create smaller refugia in a mosaic landscape (Entwistle and Stephenson, chapter 7, this volume). The development of community parks, to act as sources for exploitable populations of mammals (Bodmer, chapter 15) has enormous potential to develop into an additional network of smaller reserves. Given likely increasing limitations to the land that can be put aside for protection (MacKinnon, chapter 19, this volume), the need to integrate smaller protected areas within a broader landscape approach to conservation appears inevitable (Macdonald *et al.*, chapter 10; MacKinnon, chapter 19, this volume). Furthermore, predictions based on global warming over the coming 50 years suggest a likely shift in the current distribution of vegetation and animal populations with respect to existing park boundaries (O'Connell *et al.*, submitted), meaning that a traditional approach to protected areas will no longer be applicable. Thus the need for flexibility and consideration of dynamic systems for protected areas, with high levels of interconnectivity, may be considered over coming years. However, some species, such as those inhabiting extreme environments (e.g., Siberian tiger; O'Connell *et al.*, submitted b) including montane species (Peters and Lovejoy, 1992), and those with key resource requirements (Scheel *et al.*, 1996), may be left with nowhere to go should the predicted warming occur.

Mammals in the broader landscape

The constraints and size limitations of a protected areas approach have led to consideration of conservation in the broader landscape, both for mammals and also other forms of wildlife (Macdonald *et al.*, chapter 10; MacKinnon, chapter 19, this volume). In addition, there is still a real need to recognise people as part of the natural environment (McNeely, chapter 20, this volume), and thus to accept that conservation be conducted within a wider cultural as well as topographical landscape, shaped to some extent by human activity, rather than solely in pristine habitat (Macdonald *et al.*, chapter 10, this volume). The challenge is to design appropriate management strategies for mammals beyond protected areas, but within existing cultural and agricultural landscape mosaics. This may rely on enhancing public awareness and participation, as well as requiring specific policy changes and legislation (Racey, chapter 9, this volume).

Innovative approaches will be essential to successfully manage biodiversity at the landscape level. There is the possibility that agricultural lands may become an important habitat for biodiversity in the future, be it in small areas of farmed land in Africa (Entwistle and Stephenson, chapter 7, this volume), or as a result of more fundamental change in agricultural policy in Europe (Macdonald *et al.*, chapter 10; Racey, chapter 9, this volume). There may also be a role for managed forests as reservoirs of biodiversity – including mammals (Macdonald *et al.*, chapter 10; MacKinnon, chapter 19, this volume) although further research and validation of the relative importance of such forests is required. Current proposals for affor-estation and forest protection, linked to carbon offset mechanisms, may also increase habitat provision for mammals if managed appropriately to give added value beyond simply a carbon sink role (Macdonald *et al.*, chapter 10, this volume). However, the role of carbon offset forestry for conser-vation of biodiversity is a contentious issue, with potential linkages and benefits only now being examined.

Sustainable use of mammals

The exploitation of mammal populations is a question that continues to be a focus for controversy and strong opinions (Taylor and Dunstone, 1996). However, it is clear that in many countries the values placed on mammals, and hence on their conservation, are driven by their economic worth. Effec-tive conservation, that is relevant to local communities, generally takes ac-count of the need to use populations effectively, and sustainable use may play a key role in conservation outside protected areas, where it is politically acceptable (MacKinnon, chapter 19, this volume). The challenge is for con-servationists to be able to react to this situation, and to act proactively to provide effective analysis of the extent to which controlled and sustainable off-take can be assessed and enforced. Some authors have questioned the sustainable use approach (Struhsaker, 1998). However, we must accept that the direct use of mammals may be one of the strongest political argu-ments for their conservation, particularly at a local level, and could thus be harnessed for broader biodiversity conservation. The need for effective long-term management of exploited mammal populations, could also pro-vide an important motivation for habitat protection. For example, a mosaic approach to sustainable use has been proposed, with community-based protected areas providing source populations for hunting elsewhere (Bod-mer, chapter 15, this volume).

Other forms of use, including ecotourism, may be indirect. The poten-tial income generation from such tourism has already been mentioned, and is generally welcomed as a means to financially justify, and even fund, conservation. However, the downside of ecotourism is also becoming re-cognised. This may include direct impacts, such as disturbance and dam-age to natural habitats. However, it also possible that ecotourism may result in distortions in the priorities and management policies developed for pro-tected areas, given the particular importance of specific large, charismatic mammal species for such forms of income generation (Goodwin and Leader-Williams, chapter 14, this volume).

Ex situ conservation of mammals

The role of *ex situ* conservation, and its relationship to *in situ* approaches, continues to be discussed within conservation (Olney *et al.*, 1994; Snyder *et al.*, 1996). Zoos and other captive breeding institutions obviously play a key role in public awareness and fundraising for conservation. Much has been made of the potential of zoos to undertake captive breeding for reintroduction, all too frequently as an emergency measure to support species already under severe threat in their natural ecosystems. However, of 39 mammal species in captive breeding programmes that are carried out with a view to subsequent reintroduction, only four have successfully met their primary objective (Beck *et al.*, 1994). Unless captive breeding is focused at achieving successful reintroduction, there is a danger that zoos will have a growing role as repositories for species that are extinct in the wild or have no habitat to which they can be reintroduced.

One of the reasons for the lack of success in reintroduction projects may be the focus on inappropriate species for captive breeding (Balmford, chapter 16, this volume). While charisma and absolute threat are obviously key factors in the decision to undertake captive breeding, the current focus on larger mammals may be inappropriate, given that such species tend to be difficult and expensive to maintain successfully, and may have lower potential for reintroduction (Balmford, chapter 16). Another key factor in the effectiveness of *ex situ* conservation is its clear linkage to *in situ* projects (Feistner and Mallinson, chapter 17, this volume). Without *in situ* conservation, and work focusing on the causes of species decline, reintroduction may never be an option, and opportunities for effective protection of sympatric species through this approach may be lost (MacKinnon, chapter 19, this volume). Furthermore, *ex situ*-based research without reference to behaviour under natural conditions can result in major misconceptions about the biology and conservation requirements of a species (for example, in the case of the giant panda; Lu *et al.*, chapter 18, this volume).

The point has been made that *ex situ* conservation should not divert resources from *in situ* programmes (MacKinnon, chapter 19; McNeely, chapter 20, this volume). However, where different funding sources do exist, harnessing the role of zoos in conservation can increase money available for on-the-ground conservation. Considered pragmatically, the forces acting on zoos are different from those driving biodiversity conservation, and will involve a compromise between the most appropriate approach for effective species breeding and reintroduction and approaches important to maximise zoos' broader contributions to conservation through education and fundraising for *in situ* projects (see also Snyder *et al.*, 1996; Hutchins *et al.*, 1997).

The three Ps – politics, participation and partnerships

As the discipline of conservation evolves, there is a growing awareness of it as a political and public issue, rather than a biological one. It is clear that the motivations for conservation, and the methods of implementation, are far-reaching within society. Thus there is a need for conservationists to deal with all elements of that society – from local stakeholders, to decision makers at national and international levels (Feistner and Mallinson, chapter 17, this volume) – in line with similar changes occurring globally in all sectors.

Many of the recent developments within conservation have been linked directly to the facilitation of broader public participation in conservation planning and implementation (for example through the Convention on Access to Information, Public Participation in Decision Making and Access to Justice in Environmental Matters). Although the people most affected by conservation are generally rural communities, decisions are generally made centrally in urban areas, and thus the challenge is often to develop conservation incentives at an appropriate local level (McNeely, chapter 20, this volume). Novel approaches are being developed by which local communities can plan ahead and make effective land-use decisions, given a stable political environment (Hanks, chapter 13, this volume), and can take control of sustainable management of their own resources, with support and advice from conservationists and scientists (Bodmer, chapter 15, this volume). Awareness is an essential underlying stage in participation (Pretty, 1994), and mammals are certainly an important vehicle for delivering information about conservation in general. Mammals have also had a direct role in promoting active public participation in the conservation movement (Bright and Morris, chapter 8, this volume), and certainly in the case of bats have been a key influence in stimulating a focused voluntary conservation movement in the UK (Racey, chapter 9, this volume). The development of novel and appropriate approaches for gaining full-scale participation in conservation are likely to continue to be important goals.

There also remains an ongoing need to involve decision makers and policy makers in the issue of conservation. High level support and understanding is generally essential for the success of any conservation programme, and since decisions are often taken by non-environmental sectors of government, there is a clear need to be able to convey the case for conservation in appropriate language and using understandable terminology (McNeely, chapter 20, this volume). This generally means an expression of conservation in economic terms, with valuations and benefits of species being made clear. This is also the case for mammals, where an economic justification for their conservation will be most convincing in some sectors (McNeely, chapter 20, this volume). In addition, scientific justifications are often essential to convince decision-makers of the case for conservation (McNeely, chapter 20), again reinforcing the possibilities for partnerships between scientists, lobbyists and policy-makers (Racey, chapter 9, this volume).

In general, the case for partnerships within conservation is growing ever stronger, and there is a need for all sectors to collaborate to meet common aims (MacKinnon, chapter 19, this volume). As the breadth of skills required for effective conservation is recognised, a broader range of disciplines are becoming involved, from management planning to basic scientific assessment. To achieve effective conservation, partnerships are often created between sectors and organisations (ranging from NGOs to governments and businesses), providing new opportunities for collaboration (Feistner and Mallinson, chapter 17, this volume). This frequently involves cooperation between different conservation organisations, often working in a traditionally competitive environment (Feistner and Mallinson, chapter 17, this volume), but with opportunities for mutual institutional gain.

Given the global nature of human impacts, effective conservation also hinges upon cooperation between governments. The need for international information sharing and cooperation has been promoted by the Convention on Biological Diversity (Feistner and Mallinson. chapter 17; Hanks, chapter 13; McNeely, chapter 20, this volume). Similarly, at a regional level, Transfrontier Conservation Areas provide a model for promoting the issue of biodiversity to a range of leaders, while using conservation as a focus for political collaboration (Hanks, chapter 13, this volume).

BIODIVERSITY AND MAMMAL CONSERVATION

Biodiversity conservation has been promoted as a means to focus effort on protecting a broad range of systems, rather than merely reacting to species and areas where the situation has now become critical (McNeely, chapter 20; Williams *et al.*, chapter 5, this volume). It is generally accepted that the umbrella of biodiversity conservation provides a means to protect a wider range of species, including low profile or uncharismatic ones (MacKinnon,

chapter 19, this volume). Biodiversity conservation focuses on the maintenance of intact ecosystems and regulation of habitat loss, which remains
the greatest threat to mammals (Mace and Balmford, chapter 3, this volume), and in this way also provides a means to effectively protect individual
species through implementation at a local level (Racey, chapter 9, this
volume).

However, the concept of 'biodiversity' is not easily communicated or
represented. Although biodiversity can be considered as the extent of genetic diversity or the maintenance of ecosystems, these are conceptual entities that are difficult to explain or monitor. Inevitably, we continue to use
species as the unit representing biodiversity, in terms of species richness,
taxonomic diversity, uniqueness (endemism) or ecosystem function (inter-
relationships of species or assemblages). Species are therefore generally
used as a surrogate for biodiversity, and while intellectually we understand
the need for biodiversity and systems conservation, this still tends to be
applied with species in mind. Thus it is still the case that habitat conservation and protection of biodiversity, are still explained through the effects on,
and relationships between, individual species.

While the likely continued focus on species should not undermine the
need and importance for a broader approach, it will also be important to
recognise the need to interpret biodiversity in relation to comprehensible
units (i.e., most often species). However, it has been argued that focus on
conservation at a species level, and particularly single-species approaches,
have diverted energy and resources away from dealing with the underlying
causes of biodiversity loss (McNeely, chapter 20, this volume). This may be
true for some traditional flagship species, where overexploitation was the
key issue, and conservation has focused on species-orientated research, and
specific anti-poaching and *ex situ* conservation activities (McNeely, chapter
20; Muruthi *et al.*, chapter 11, this volume). However, most contemporary
species-focused projects actually focus on habitat protection and integrated
approaches (for example, Feistner and Mallinson, chapter 17; Lu *et al.*,
chapter 18, this volume). Through habitat conservation, there is a clear
opportunity to extend single-species conservation to meet real biodiversity
goals. Thus the difference between species- and biodiversity-focused projects is still frequently one of interpretation, with both undertaking similar
conservation activities on the ground.

Single-species conservation can be a means of achieving biodiversity
protection, if this ultimate goal is clearly understood. However, there is a
danger that species-focused conservation could continue to dominate, in
the name of biodiversity conservation, without really delivering ecosystem

level benefits. Thus, there may be a need to assess and improve existing species-focused conservation programmes, to ensure that they can provide as much added value for biodiversity in general. This may involve consideration of area selection approaches (Caro *et al.*, chapter 12; Williams *et al.*, chapter 5, this volume), management policies (Entwistle and Stephenson, chapter 7, this volume) and multi-disciplinary approaches to conservation (Feistner and Mallinson, chapter 17, this volume). In addition, there may be opportunities to examine conservation projects focusing on assemblages, relationships between species, and potentially on more common species, as a result of their ecosystem function (such as augmentation of prey populations; Harris *et al.*, chapter 6, this volume).

Biodiversity level and species-focused approaches should be complementary, since both ultimately represent differing interpretations of the growing consensus about the underlying threats to a range of species. These different interpretations may be more effective for different audiences: politicians may be more likely to be persuaded by economic arguments tied to knock-on effects of loss of ecosystem function (McNeely, chapter 20, this volume), whereas illustrations of individual species declines may best succeed in public education about the threats of habitat loss and overexploitation. It is to be hoped that both approaches can lead to increased funding. Furthermore, if we consider the issue pragmatically, it is likely that last ditch stands to maintain species on the edge of extinction will continue to be directed towards saving those species which are most highly valued (MacKinnon, chapter 19, this volume), alongside programmes with a broader aim of biodiversity conservation.

MAMMALIAN 'FLAGSHIPS' AND CONSERVATION

The term 'flagship species' appears to have been loosely applied and overused in contemporary conservation (Leader-Williams and Dublin, chapter 4, this volume). The synonymous use of the terms 'flagship' and 'umbrella' has led to confusion – many flagship species (such as the elephant; Johnsingh and Joshua, 1994) are not necessarily effective umbrella species, although it is often assumed they are. A clarification of the functions of flagships (for fundraising) and of umbrellas (to protect sympatric species) is required. Furthermore, there is a need to discriminate between conservation of flagship species and 'single-species programmes', where the role of flagship species is not just as icons used to raise money for their own conservation, but that they bring added benefit to a wider conservation movement (either through funds or awareness). Where our conservation goal is to achieve or maintain broader biodiversity and habitat protection, then the role of flagships needs to be clarified. Otherwise, there is a danger that a continued focus on flagship species could be counterproductive, in setting priorities away from faunal composition and stability of ecosystems (Harris *et al.*, chapter 6, this volume) and might even direct resources away from biodiversity conservation, through setting a donor driven agenda.

Using a flagship species approach for fundraising can be inappropriate if donors lack understanding of how funds will be used. Raising money on the back of one species, for spending within a broader approach to conservation, could undermine the accountability and credibility of conservation organisations. Therefore, the challenge is to apply such funds in a way that benefits both the focal species, and wider biodiversity. One solution to this would be to focus fundraising on flagship species that are also effective umbrella species, and ensure that habitat protection and other *in situ* mechanisms are applied to provide conservation outcomes for a broad range of species. However, it must also accepted that few species fulfil both functions well. The threat of extinction facing Critically Endangered species makes them high profile. However, maintaining populations of these animals may require intensive *ex situ* or anti-poaching activities, rather than habitat or ecosystem protection (McNeely, chapter 20, this volume). In addition, the areas selected for the protection of large flagship species (such as elephants, rhinos and other large ungulates) may not be most effective for wider biodiversity conservation (Entwistle and Stephenson, chapter 7; Williams *et al.*, chapter 5, this volume), and such species may not be considered effective 'umbrella species' (e.g., black rhinos; Berger, 1997), and may not represent habitat requirements of all species in an area (Lambeck, 1997). As well as home range and size, factors such as habitat selection may need to be considered, in relation to knowledge of distribution of biodiversity hotspots. In the case of mammals it has been suggested that groups such as the primates may perform this function in many parts of Africa as a result of their habitat preferences (forest), which also supports the highest mammalian diversity. Furthermore, this group is highly marketable and is considered to be at particular risk (Mace and Balmford, chapter 3, this volume). However, decisions about effective flagship/umbrella species are likely to be best made on a species-by-species basis, selected once priority areas for the conservation of wider biodiversity have been chosen.

Conservation is likely to continue to focus on a few high profile species (MacKinnon, chapter 19, this volume). However, there is also a need for conservation organisations and others to take an active role in balancing the conservation agenda, and move away from simply using traditional flagship species. If we are to select flagship species on the basis of their broader potential for habitat conservation as well as fundraising, then novel flagships are likely to be used. These might include small mammals (Bright and Morris, chapter 8; Entwistle and Stephenson, chapter 7, this volume), which have previously been used successfully in the UK, where options for larger mammal flagships are currently restricted (Macdonald *et al.*, chapter 10, this volume). The 'earning power' of unusual or novel species currently appears to be underestimated, and rather than returning to the existing, proven flagship species, there is an opportunity to promote new, interesting species, recognising that effective marketing can make almost anything attractive and appealing. In addition, there is an opportunity to be proactive in identifying flagship species that will promote conservation effectively at both an international and a local level.

While flagship species are most generally aimed at Western donors, their targeted local use has proved very successful (Feistner and Mallinson, chapter 17, this volume). This is particularly the case where local values and cultural beliefs about wildlife are incorporated into conservation programmes – for example, the ongoing use of elephants as flagships in Aceh province, Sumatra (E. Bowen-Jones, personal communication) and the use of fruit bats in Pemba Island, Tanzania (Entwistle and Corp, 1997). In selecting flagships, we need to recognise the different values placed on particular species by different cultures – while large carnivores are attractive in countries that do not possess them (e.g., in the UK), they are less likely to be so in their range countries (Entwistle and Stephenson, chapter 7, this volume). The most effective flagship species are those which generate international recognition and appreciation, but are also strong local cultural symbols and generate national pride (for example the giant panda in China; Lu *et al.*, chapter 18, this volume). This would also provide a chance to broaden the role of flagship species by incorporating them into education programmes about conservation in a broader context, by clarifying the strong links between mammals and human culture.

GLOBAL PERSPECTIVES OF UK CONSERVATION

A number of chapters in this volume have dealt specifically with priorities for mammal conservation within the UK. This is not meant to be parochial or to place undue importance on UK conservation, but rather to indicate that national conservation activities should not be considered separately from global perspectives on conservation. The need for countries to share experiences and cooperate in integrated approaches to conservation has been widely recognised, and structures are in place to aid information transfer (such as the clearing house mechanism of the Convention on Biological Diversity). This learning process is two-way, while the UK serves as a model for hands-on conservation, the experience from developing countries is also directly relevant to the British conservation movement. Many of the issues discussed elsewhere in this volume, including the role of mammals as flagships, and the relationship between species-focused programmes and biodiversity conservation are of direct relevance to conservation of mammals in the UK and draw on experiences from across the world.

Having said that, there are some distinctive features of mammal conservation within the UK. Here we are largely considering conservation within a synanthropic landscape, requiring intensive monitoring and interference, including translocation (Bright and Morris, chapter 8, this volume) and potentially reintroduction of nationally extirpated species (Macdonald et al., chapter 10, this volume). Furthermore, in the UK naturalised mammals (e.g., rabbits) represent an important component of mammalian diversity, and provide the prey base for many native carnivores and raptors (Harris et al., chapter 6, this volume). Such situations result in ambitious suggestions for landscape scale approaches which might include designating new and more extensive wildlife parks, and the adoption of farmland for conservation purposes (Macdonald et al., chapter 10, this volume).

Mammalian conservation in the UK has the advantage of providing a relatively simple model, in terms of a depauperate, but relatively well-studied, mammal fauna (Macdonald et al., chapter 10, this volume). In addition, within the UK conservation movement, conservation biology has made an important contribution to the development of government policy for a range of mammals (including bats, badgers and foxes). Biologists are directly involved in government consultations on the development of policies for conservation, and partnerships have been developed for species recovery through the implementation of the Convention on Biological Diversity. However, even in a relatively simple system such as this, the answers from conservation biology may not always be straightforward and easily applied. For example, the reassessment of relative status of mammals indicating the need for conservation action for pine martens and polecats (Harris et al., chapter 6, this volume) must be reconciled with the apparent expansions in distribution of both these species noted over recent years (see Macdonald et al., chapter 10, this volume). Such ambiguities illustrate the need for ongoing research and refinements of conservation priorities, and the benefits of contrasting different views during the development of conservation plans.

FUTURE PRIORITIES FOR THE CONSERVATION OF MAMMALIAN DIVERSITY: CONCLUSIONS

The views expressed by the contributors to this volume suggest that in the future conservation of mammals will be conducted within a landscape approach, taking into account the integrity of systems and other elements of biodiversity. However, protected areas will also continue to have a role as reservoirs of biodiversity, although it is generally accepted that their selection might better be based on overall species diversity rather than the distributions of a few large mammal species. Furthermore, complementarity (selection of sites with different, but complementary, species compositions) is likely to be the most effective means to achieve conservation of maximal mammalian diversity. This may require gap analysis with respect to species, groups or ecosystems currently protected. Thus in the future conservation may need to be focused on less diverse or species-rich areas of the world, in ecosystems currently not well represented in conservation programmes. However, wherever mammals are protected, the potential of climate change over the coming century may have direct impacts on mammalian distributions. Although less vulnerable than some other groups (such as amphibians), some mammals living in areas subject to areas of extreme microclimate, and particularly in montane systems, may be severely affected. Thus relationships between biodiversity and climate change need further investigation, especially given the current discussions about whether carbon offset approaches will realistically increase the areas available for mammalian conservation.

Effective conservation will increasingly depend on international cooperation (perhaps through a range of conventions and international agreements), on increased inter-organisational cooperation and potentially upon the involvement of business. Successful conservation will be supported by targeted research, and there is a need for conservation biology to tackle more applied questions which identify the means, as well as the targets, for conservation. In parallel, there is a need to develop effective multidisciplinary approaches to priority setting, to reconcile political and social factors with purely biological assessments.

Within the conservation movement there is a need to understand the values placed on the natural environment by different sectors of society, and accept the importance of such values, whether or not they are based on truly 'scientific' criteria. Within this framework it will be important not just to recognise economic values of mammals, but also cultural and aesthetic ones, particularly those held by communities most directly affected by conservation activities. It is clear that biodiversity- and species-orientated conservation approaches can be reconciled, and that both have a role within mammalian conservation overall. However, effective conservation will require clarification of realistic goals, and attempts to give added value from single-species programmes. Furthermore, there is a need to use flagship species carefully and appropriately, based on their effectiveness in fundraising for other species and in raising conservation awareness. The effectiveness of flagship species in protecting broader biodiversity would also be improved through selection of appropriate umbrella species for specific target habitats, and a broader range of species could potentially be used as flagships, including novel species and those of cultural value at a local level.

Over the coming years we might expect to see a shift in the balance within mammalian conservation, towards broader programmes aimed at the conservation of assemblages or of 'mammalian diversity', complemented by the use of specific mammalian flagship species, selected on the basis of ecological value and role in protecting other species, as well as cultural value at local and international levels. Conservation of mammals is likely to continue to have a high public profile, and this opportunity should be used to involve the broadest constituency in the conservation movement, including not just the general public, but also governments and other decision makers. It is clear that the panda, as with other charismatic species, has not yet had its day, but is just reinventing its future.

References

Ackery, P. I. and Vane-Wright, R. I. (1984). *Milkweed Butterflies, their Cladistics and Biology being an Account of the Natural History of the Danainae, a Subfamily of the Lepidoptera, Nymphalidae*. Publication No. 893. London: British Museum (Natural History).

Acocks, J. P. H. (1988). Veld types of South Africa. *Memoirs of the Botanical Survey of South Africa*, **57**, 1–146.

Action Comores (1993). *The Final Report of the 1993 Action Comores Expedition to the Comoro Islands*. Compiled by W. J. Trewhella and P. F. Reason. Fauna & Flora International 100% Fund Report.

Action Comores (1994). *The Final Report of the 1994 Action Comores Expedition to the Comoro Islands*. Compiled by W. J. Trewhella and P. F. Reason. Fauna & Flora International 100% Fund Report.

Action Comores (1997). *Action Comores Report 1995–97 Including the 1995 Expedition to the Comoro Islands*. Compiled by K. M. Clark, S. R. T. Garrett and P. F. Reason. Fauna & Flora International 100% Fund Report.

Adams, J. S. and McShane, T. O. (1992). *The Myth of Wild Africa, Conservation Without Illusion*. New York: W. W. Norton and Co.

Adger, W. N. and Brown, K. (1994). *Land Use and the Causes of Global Warming*. Chichester: John Wiley and Sons.

Adger, W. N., Brown, K., Shiel, R. S. and Whitby, M. C. (1994). Carbon dynamics of land use in Britain. *Journal of Environmental Management*, **36**, 117–133.

Adger, W. N., Pettenella, D. and Whitby, M. (eds) (1997a). *Climate Change Mitigation and European Land Use Policies*. Wallingford: CAB International.

Adger, W. N., Pettenella, D. and Whitby, M. (1997b). Land use in Europe and the reduction of greenhouse-gas emissions. In *Climate Change Mitigation and European Land Use Policies*, eds W. N. Adger, D. Pettenella, and M. Whitby, pp. 1–22. Wallingford: CAB International.

AfRSG (African Rhino Specialist Group) (1996). *Numbers of white and black rhino in Africa: 1995*. Unpublished table from the February 1996 Meeting of IUCN's African Rhino Specialist Group. Available from the author.

Aldhous, P. (1993). Tropical deforestation; not just a problem in Amazonia. *Science*, **259**, 1390.

Alvarez, K. (1993). *The Twilight of the Panther*. Florida: Myakka River Publishing.

Amend, S. and Amend, T. (1995). *National Parks Without People? The South American Experience*. Quito: IUCN.

Amengual, B., Whitby, J. E., King, A., Serra Coba, J. and Bourhy, H. (1997). Evolution of European bat lissa viruses. *Journal of General Virology*, **78**, 2319–2328.

Andersen, I. B. F. (1995). *Ecotourists' Attitudes to Nature and Nature Conservation in Hwange National Park, Zimbabwe*. MSc thesis. Canterbury: University of Kent.

Andresen, E. (1999). Seed dispersal by monkeys and the fate of dispersed seeds in Peruvian rainforest. *Biotropica*, **31**, 145–158.

Anon. (1994a). *Biodiversity: The UK Action Plan*. London: Her Majesty's Stationery Office.

Anon. (1994b) *Climate Change: The UK Programme*. London: Her Majesty's Stationery Office.

Anon. (1995a). *Biodiversity: The UK Steering Group Report. Volume 1: Meeting the Rio Challenge*. London: Her Majesty's Stationery Office.

Anon. (1995b). *Biodiversity: The UK Steering Group Report. Volume 2: Action Plans*. London: Her Majesty's Stationery Office.

Anon. (1997). Wild boars clean up at Beecraigs. *The Scotsman*, 17 November 1997.

Anon. (1998a). *Current Status and Potential Impact of Wild Boar* (Sus scrofa) *in the English Countryside: A Risk Assessment*. London: Ministry of Agriculture, Fisheries and Food.

Anon. (1998b). Action against a snake. *Oryx*, **32**, 261.

van Apeldoorn, R. C., Celada, C. and Nieuwenhuizen, W. (1994). Distribution and dynamics of the red squirrel (*Sciurus vulgaris* L.) in a landscape with fragmented habitat. *Landscape Ecology*, **9**, 227–235.

Arcese, P., Hando, J. and Campbell, K. (1995). Historical and present-day anti-poaching efforts in Serengeti. In *Serengeti II: Dynamics, Management, and Conservation of an Ecosystem*, eds A. R. E. Sinclair and P. Arcese, pp. 506–533. Chicago: University of Chicago Press.

Arita, H. T., Robinson, J. G. and Redford, K. (1990). Rarity in Neotropical forest mammals and its ecological correlates. *Conservation Biology*, **4**, 181–192.

Arnold, H. R. (1993). *Atlas of Mammals in Britain*. London: Her Majesty's Stationery Office.

Ashley, C. and Roe, D. (1998). *Enhancing Community Involvement in Wildlife Tourism: Issues and Challenges*. London: International Institute for Environment and Development.

Askins, R. A., Philbrock, M. J. and Sugero, D. S. (1987). Relationship between regional abundance of forest and the composition of forest bird communities. *Biological Conservation*, **39**, 129–152.

Asquith, N. M., Wright, S. J. and Clauss, M. J. (1997). Does mammal community composition control recruitment in Neotropical forests? Evidence from Panama. *Ecology*, **78**, 941–946.

Avery, M. I. (1985). Winter activity of pipistrelle bats. *Journal of Animal Ecology*, **54**, 721–738.

Bainbridge, W. R. and Motsami, B. (1995). *Project Motivation Document. Greater Drakensberg-Maloti Mountain Region: Community Development and Conservation Programme*. Maseru: Lesotho National Environment Secretariat, and Pietermaritzburg: Planning Division, Natal Parks Board.

Baines, M., Johnson, P. J., Smith, H. E., Hambler, C. and Macdonald, D. W. (1998). The effects of arable field margin management on the abundance and species richness of Araneae (spiders). *Ecography*, **21**, 74–86.

Ballou, J. D. and Foose, T. (1996). Demographic and genetic management of captive populations. In *Wild Mammals in Captivity*, eds D. G. Kleiman, M. E. Allen, K. V. Thompson and S. Lumpkin, pp. 263–283. Chicago: University of Chicago Press.

Ballou, J., Lacy, R. C., Kleiman, D., Rylands, K. and Ellis, S. (1998). *Leontopithecus II: The Second Population and Habitat Viability Assessment for Lion Tamarins* (Leontopithecus): *Final Report*. Apple Valley: Conservation Breeding Specialist Group (IUCN/SSC).

Balmford, A. (1996). Extinction filters and current resilience: the significance of past selection pressures for conservation biology. *Trends in Ecology and Evolution*, **11**, 193–196.

Balmford, A. (in press). Separating fact from artefact in analysis of zoo visitor preference. *Conservation Biology*.

Balmford, A., Leader-Williams, N. and Green, M. J. B. (1995). Parks or arks: where to conserve threatened mammals? *Biodiversity and Conservation*, **4**, 595–607.

Balmford, A. and Long, A. (1994). Avian endemism and tropical deforestation. *Nature*, **372**, 623–624.

Balmford, A., Mace, G. M. and Leader-Williams, N. (1996). Designing the ark: setting priorities for captive breeding. *Conservation Biology*, **10**, 719–727.

Balmford, A., Mace, G. M. and Leader-Williams, N. (1997). Priority-setting for *ex situ* conservation. *Conservation Biology*, **11**, 593–594.

Barlow, K. E. and Jones, G. (1996). *Pipistrellus nathusii* (Chiroptera: Vespertilionidae) in Britain in the mating season. *Journal of Zoology*, **24**, 767–773.

Barnes, R. (1994). Case study 3. Sustainable development of African game parks. In *Principles of Conservation Biology*, eds G. K. Meffe and C. R. Caroll, pp. 504–511. Sunderland: Sinauer Associates.

Barnes, R. F. W. and Kapela, E. B. (1991). Changes in the Ruaha elephant population caused by poaching. *African Journal of Ecology*, **29**, 289–294.

Barnett, A. (1992). *Small Mammals: Expedition Field techniques*. London: Expedition Advisory Centre.

Barreto, G. R., Rushton, S., Strachan, R. and Macdonald, D. W. (1998). The habitat of a declining population of water voles in England: a generalised linear model. *Animal Conservation*, **1**, 129–137.

Barzetti, V. (1993). *Parks and Progress*. Cambridge: IUCN.

Batisse, M. (1997). Biosphere reserves: a challenge for biodiversity conservation and regional development. *Environment*, **39**, 7–15, 31–33.

Beck, B. B., Rapaport, L. G., Stanley Price, M. R. and Wilson, A. C. (1994). Reintroduction of captive-born animals. In *Creative Conservation. Interactive Management of Wild and Captive Animals*, eds P. J. S. Olney, G. M. Mace and A. T. C. Feistner, pp. 265–286. London: Chapman and Hall.

Beier, P. (1993). Determining minimum habitat areas and habitat corridors for cougars. *Conservation Biology*, **7**, 94–108.

Bella, L. (1987). *Parks for Profit*. Montreal: Harvest House.

Bellamy, P. E., Hinsley, S. A. and Newton, I. (1996a). Local extinction and recolonisations of passerine bird species in small woods. *Oecologia*, **108**, 64–71.

Bellamy, P.E., Hinsley, S.A. and Newton, I. (1996b). Factors influencing bird species numbers in small woods in South East England. *Journal of Applied Ecology*, **33**, 249–262.

Bennett, E., Nyaoi, A. J. and Sompud, J. (2000). Saving Borneo's bacon: the sustainability of hunting in Sarawak. In *Hunting for Sustainability in Tropical Forests*, eds J. Robinson and E. Bennett, pp. 305–334. New York: Columbia University Press.

Bennett, P. M. and Owens, I. P. F. (1997). Variation in extinction risk among birds: chance or evolutionary predisposition? *Proceedings of the Royal Society of London, Series B*, **264**, 401–408.

Berger, D. (1996). The challenge of integrating Maasai tradition with tourism. In *People and Tourism in Fragile Environments*, ed. M. Price, pp. 175–197. Chichester: John Wiley and Sons.

Berger, J. (1997) Population constraints associated with the use of black rhinos as an umbrella species for desert herbivores. *Conservation Biology*, **11**, 69–78.

Best, L. B., Campa III, H., Kemp, K. E., Robel, R. J., Ryan, M. R., Savidge, J. A., Weeks Jr., H. P. and Winterstein, S. R. (1997). Bird abundance and nesting in CRP fields and cropland in the Midwest: a regional approach. *Wildlife Society Bulletin*, **25**, 864–877.

Bezuidenhout, H. (1997). *Preliminary Report on the Vegetation of the Possible Transfrontier Onseepkans Area*. Unpublished report. Kimberley: National Parks Board's Research and Development Section.

Bibby, C. J., Collar, N. J., Crosby, M. J., Heath, M. F., Imboden, C., Johnson, T. H., Long, A. J., Stattersfield, A. J. and Thirgood, S. J. (1992). *Putting Biodiversity on the Map: Priority Areas for Global Conservation*. Cambridge: International Council for Bird Preservation.

Bibikov, D. I. (1991). The steppe marmot – its past and future. *Oryx*, **25**, 45–49.

Bieber, C. (1998). Population dynamics, sexual activity, and reproduction failure in the fat dormouse *(Myoxus glis)*. *Journal of Zoology*, **244**, 223–229.

Blaustein, A. R. and Wake, D. B. (1990). Declining amphibian populations: a global phenomenon. *Trends in Ecology and Evolution*, **5**, 203–204.

Bloxam, Q. M. C. and Durrell, L. (1985). A note of the Trust's recent work in Madagascar. *Dodo, Journal of the Wildlife Preservation Trusts*, **22**, 18–23.

Bodmer, R. (1991). Strategies of seed dispersal and seed predation in Amazonian ungulates. *Biotropica*, **23**, 255–261.

Bodmer, R. (1994). Managing wildlife with local communities in the Peruvian Amazon: The case of the Reserva Comunal Tamshiyacu–Tahuayo. In *Natural Connections: Perspectives in Community-based Conservation*, eds D. Western and R. M. Wright, pp. 113–134. Washington, DC: Island Press.

Bodmer, R. (1995). Susceptibility of mammals to overhunting in Amazonia. In *Integrating People and Wildlife for a Sustainable Future*, eds J. Bissonette and P. Krausman, pp. 292–295. Bethesda: The Wildlife Society.

Bodmer, R. and Ayres, J. (1991). Sustainable development and species diversity in Amazonian forests. *Species*, **16**, 22–24.

Bodmer, R. E., Eisenberg, J. F. and Redford, K. H. (1997a). Hunting and the likelihood of extinction of Amazonian mammals. *Conservation Biology*, **11**, 460–466.

Bodmer, R., Fang, T., Moya I. L. and Gill, R. (1994). Managing wildlife to conserve Amazonian forests: population biology and economic considerations of game hunting. *Biological Conservation*, **67**, 29–35.

Bodmer, R., Penn, J., Puertas, P., Moya I. L. and Fang, T. (1997b). Linking conservation and local people through sustainable use of natural resources: community-based management in the Peruvian Amazon. In *Harvesting Wild Species. Implications for Biodiversity Conservation*, ed. C. H. Freese, pp. 315–358. London: John Hopkins University Press.

Bodmer, R. and Puertas, P. (in press). Community-based co-management of wildlife in the Peruvian Amazon. In *Evaluating the Sustainability of Hunting in Tropical Forests*, eds J. G. Robinson and E. L. Bennett. New York: Columbia University Press.

de Boer, L. E. M., Brouwer, K. and Smits, S. (eds) (1993). *EEP Yearbook 1992/93 Including the Proceedings of the 10th EEP Conference, Salzburg 28–30 June 1993*. Amsterdam: EAZA/EEP Executive Office.

Boitani, L., Mattei, L., Nonis, D. and Corsi, F. (1994). Spatial and activity patterns of wild boars in Tuscany, Italy. *Journal of Mammalogy*, **75**, 600–612.

Bowen-Jones, E. and Pendry, S. (1999). The threat to primates and other mammals from the bushmeat trade in Africa, and how this could be diminished. *Oryx*, **33**, 233–246.

Boyce, M. S. (1992). Population Viability Analysis. *Annual Review of Ecology and Systematics*, **23**, 481–506.

Boyd, I. L., Myhill, D. G. and Mitchell-Jones, A. J. (1988). Uptake of gamma-HCH by pipistrelle bats and its effects on survival. *Environmental Pollution*, **51**, 95–111.

Branch, W. R. (1988). *South African Red Data Book. Reptiles and Amphibians*. Report No.151. Pretoria: South African National Science Programme.

Breitenmoser, U. and Breitenmoser-Wursten, C. (1993). *SCALP – Status and Conservation of the Alpine Lynx Population*. Seminar on the Management of Small Populations of Threatened Mammals, Sofia, October 1993.

Breitenmoser, U. and Haller, H. (1993). Patterns of predation by reintroduced European lynx in the Swiss Alps. *Journal of Wildlife Management*, **57**, 144–154.

Breitenmoser, U., Kaczensky, P., Dotterer, M., Breitenmoser-Wursten, C., Capt, S., Bernhart, F. and Liberek, M. (1993). Spatial organisation and recruitment of lynx (*Lynx lynx*) in a reintroduced population in the Swiss Jura Mountains. *Journal of Zoology*, **231**, 449–464.

Brett, R. A. (1991). *Kenya Rhino Project*. Annual Report, Kenya Wildlife Service. Nairobi: Kenya Wildlife Service.

Bright, P. W. (1993). Habitat fragmentation – problems and predictions for British mammals. *Mammal Review*, **23**, 101–111.

Bright, P. W. and Harris, S. (1994). *Reintroduction of The Pine Marten: Feasibility Study*. Research Report No. 84. Peterborough: English Nature.

Bright, P. W., Mitchell, P. and Morris, P. A. (1994). Dormouse distribution: survey techniques, insular ecology and selection of sites for conservation. *Journal of Applied Ecology*, **31**, 329–339.

Bright, P. W. and Morris, P. A. (1990). Habitat requirements of the dormouse *Muscardinus avellanarius* in relation to woodland management in south-west England. *Biological Conservation*, **54**, 307–326.

Bright, P. W. and Morris, P. A. (1993). Foraging behaviour of dormice *Muscardinus avellanarius* in two contrasting habitats. *Journal of Zoology*, **230**, 69–85.

Bright, P. W. and Morris, P. A. (1994). Animal translocation for conservation: performance of dormice in relation to release methods, origin and season. *Journal of Applied Ecology*, **31**, 699–708.

Bright, P. W. and Morris, P. A. (1996). Why are dormice rare? A case study in conservation biology. *Mammal Review*, **26**, 157–187.

Bright, P. W., Morris, P. A. and Mitchell-Jones, A. J. (1996). A new survey of the dormouse *Muscardinus avellanarius* in Britain, 1993–4. *Mammal Review*, **26**, 189–195.

Bromley, D. (1994). Economic dimensions of community-based conservation. In *Natural Connections: Perspectives in Community-based Conservation*, eds D. Western and R. M. Wright, pp. 428–447. Washington, DC: Island Press.

Brooks, D. M., Bodmer, R. E. and Matola, S. (eds) (1997). *Tapirs. Status Survey and Conservation Action Plan*. Gland: IUCN.

Brotein, M. D. and Said, M. (1995). Population trends of ungulates in and around Kenya's Masai Mara Reserve. In *Serengeti II: Dynamics, Management, and Conservation of an Ecosystem*, eds A. R. E. Sinclair and P. Arcese, pp. 169–193. Chicago: University of Chicago Press.

Brown Jr., G. M. and Shogren, J. F. (1998). Economics of the Endangered Species Act. *Journal of Economic Perspectives*, **12**, 3–20.

Brown, I. (1998). *Areas of Outstanding Natural Beauty in Wales*. Cardiff: Countryside Council for Wales.

Brown, J. H. and Heske, E. J. (1990). Control of desert-grassland transition by a keystone rodent guild. *Science*, **250**, 1705–1707.

Brown, J.H. and Kodric-Brown, A. (1977). Turnover rates in insular biogeography: effect of immigration on extinction. *Ecology*, **58**, 445–449.

Brown, L. D. (1991). Bridging organizations and sustainable development. *Human Relations* **44**, 807–831.

Brown, L. N. (1985). Elimination of a small feral swine population in an urbanising section of central Florida. *Florida Scientist*, **48**, 120–123.

Brown, S., Cannell, M. G. R., Kauppi, P. E. and Sathaye, J. (1996). Management of forests for mitigation for greenhouse gas emissions. In *Climate Change 95: Impacts, Adaptations and Mitigation of Climate Change: Scientific-technical Analysis*, eds R. T. Watson, M. C. Zinyowera, and R. H. Moss, pp. 773–797. Cambridge: Cambridge University Press.

Bruton, M. N. and Cooper, K. H. (1980). *Studies on the Ecology of Maputaland*. Grahamstown: Rhodes University.

Buckland, S., Anderson, D., Burnham, K. and Laake, J. (1993). *Distance Sampling: Estimating Abundance of Biological Populations*. New York: Chapman and Hall.

Budowski, G. (1976). Tourism and conservation: conflict, co-existence and symbiosis. *Environmental Conservation*, **3**, 27–31.

Bullock, J. M. and Hodder, K. H. (1997). Reintroductions: challenges and lessons for basic ecology. *Trends in Ecology and Evolution*, **12**, 68–69.

Burbridge, A. A. and Mackenzie, N. L. (1989). Patterns in the modern decline of western Australia's vertebrate fauna: causes and conservation implications. *Biological Conservation*, **50**, 143–198.

Burger, J. and Gochfeld, M. (1993). Tourism and short-term behavioural responses of nesting masked, red-footed and blue-footed boobies in the Galapagos. *Environmental Conservation*, **20**, 255–259.

Burland, T. M., Barratt, E. M., Beaumont, M. A. and Racey, P. A. (1999) Population genetic structure and gene flow in a gleaning bat, *Plecotus auritus*. *Proceedings of the Royal Society of London, series B*, **266**, 975–980.

Butler, C. D. (1996). *The Development of Ecotourism in South Luangwa National Park, Zambia*. MSc thesis. Canterbury: University of Kent.

Butynski, T. and Kalina, J. (1993). Three new mountain national parks for Uganda. *Oryx*, **27**, 4.

Caldecott, J. O. (1996). *Designing Conservation Projects*. Cambridge: Cambridge University Press.

Campbell, K. and Borner, M. (1995). Population trends and distribution of Serengeti herbivores: implications for management. In *Serengeti II: Dynamics, Management, and Conservation of an Ecosystem*, eds A. R. E. Sinclair and P. Arcese, pp. 117–145. Chicago: University of Chicago Press.

Cannell, M. G. R. and Dewar, R. C. (1995). The carbon sink provided by plantation forests and their products in Britain. *Forestry*, **68**, 35–48.

Caro, T. M. (1994). *Cheetahs of the Serengeti Plains*. Chicago: Chicago University Press.

Caro, T. M. (1999a). Densities of mammals in partially protected areas: the Katavi ecosystem of western Tanzania. *Journal of Applied Ecology*, **36**, 205–217.

Caro, T. M. (199b). Conservation monitoring: estimating mammal densities in woodland habitats. *Animal Conservation*, **2**, 305–315.

Caro, T. M., Pelkey, N., Borner, M., Campbell, K. L. I., Woodworth, B. L., Farm. B. P., ole Kuwai, J., Huish, S. A. and Severre, E. (1998a). Consequences of different forms of conservation for large mammals in Tanzania: preliminary analyses. *African Journal of Ecology*, **36**, 303–320.

Caro, T. M., Pelkey, N., Borner, M., Severre, E. L. M., Campbell, K. L. I., Huish, S. A., ole Kuwai, J., Farm, B. P. and Woodworth, B. L. (1998b). The impact of tourist hunting on large mammals in Tanzania: an initial assessment. *African Journal of Ecology*, **36**, 321–346.

Carroll, J. B. (1992). *Pteropus livingstonii*. In *Old World Fruit Bats: An Action Plan for their Conservation*, eds S. P. Mickleburgh, A. M. Hutson, and P. A. Racey, pp. 106–107. Gland: IUCN.

Carroll, J. B., Feistner, A. T. C., Racey, P. A., Reason, P. F. and Trewhella, W. J. (1995). *Species Action Plan for Livingstone's Fruit Bat* Pteropus livingstonii. Gland: IUCN.

Carroll, J. B. and Thorpe, I. C. (1991). The conservation of Livingstone's fruit bat *Pteropus livingstonii*: a report on an expedition to the Comores in 1990. *Dodo, Journal of the Wildlife Preservation Trusts* **27**, 26–40.

Carruthers, J. (1992). The Dongola Wildlife Sanctuary: 'psychological blunder, economic folly and political monstrosity' or 'more valuable than rubies and gold'. *Kleio*, **24**, 82–100.

Carruthers, J. (1995). *The Kruger National Park. A Social and Political History*. Pietermaritzburg: University of Natal Press.

Cater, E. (1993). Ecotourism in the Third World: problems for sustainable tourism development. *Tourism Management*, **14**, 85–90.

Caughley, G. (1977). *Analysis of Vertebrate Populations*. Chichester: John Wiley & Sons.

Caughley, G. (1994). Directions in conservation biology. *Journal of Animal Ecology*, **63**, 215–244.

Caughley, G. and Gunn, A. (1993). Dynamics of large herbivores living in deserts: kangaroos and caribou. *Oikos*, **67**, 47–55.

Caughley, G. and Gunn, A. (1996). *Conservation Biology in Theory and Practice.* Oxford: Blackwell Science.

Caughley, G. and Sinclair, A. (1994). *Wildlife Ecology and Management.* Oxford: Blackwell Science.

CBSG (Captive Breeding Specialist Group) (1992). *Ark into the 21st Century.* Apple Valley: Captive Breeding Specialist Group.

CBSG/SSC/IUCN (Conservation Breeding Specialist Group/Species Survival Commission/ IUCN) (1997) Human demographics in the PHVA process. In *Briefing Book,* CBSG Annual Meeting, Section 3. Berlin: Conservation Breeding Specialist Group.

Ceballos, G. and Brown, J. H. (1995). Global patterns of mammalian diversity, endemism, and endangerment. *Conservation Biology,* **9,** 559–568.

Ceballos-Lascurain, H. (1996). *Tourism, Ecotourism and Protected Areas.* Gland: IUCN.

Celada, C., Bogliani, G., Gariboldi, A. and Maracci, A. (1994). Occupancy of isolated woodlots by the red squirrel *Sciurus vulgaris* L. in Italy. *Biological Conservation,* **69,** 177–183.

Chapman, C. A. (1995). Primate seed dispersal: coevolution and conservation implications. *Evolutionary Anthropology,* **4,** 74–82.

Chapman, C. A. and Chapman, L. J. (1995). Survival without dispersers: seedling recruitment under parents. *Conservation Biology,* **9,** 675–678.

Chapman, C. A. and Onderdonk, D. A. (1998). Forest without primates: primate/ plant codependency. *American Journal of Primatology,* **45,** 127–142.

Chapman, J. A. and Flux, J. E. C. (1990). *Rabbits, Hares and Pikas. Status Survey and Conservation Action Plan.* Gland: IUCN.

Chapman, L. J., Chapman, C. A. and Wrangham, R. W. (1992). *Balanites wilsoniana*: elephant dependent dispersal. *Journal of Tropical Ecology,* **8,** 275–283.

Chapman, P. J., Duvergé, P. L. and Morris, C. J. (1997). Research and conservation work on the greater horseshoe bat. In *The Vincent Wildlife Trust Review of 1996.* London: The Vincent Wildlife Trust.

Charles-Dominique, P. (1986). Inter-relations between frugivorous vertebrates and pioneer plants: *Cecropia,* birds and bats in French Guiana. In *Frugivores and Seed Dispersal,* eds A. Estrada and T. H. Fleming, pp. 119–135. Dordrecht: Dr W. Junk Publishers.

Chibnik, M. (1994). *Risky Rivers: The Economics and Politics of Floodplain Farming in Amazonia.* Tuscon: University of Arizona Press.

Child, G. (1995). *Wildlife and People: the Zimbabwean Success. How the Conflict Between Animals and People Became Progress for Both.* New York and Harare: Wisdom Foundation.

Childs, J. (1998). *Bats and the Law ? What to do when the Law is Broken.* Sandy: Royal Society for the Protection of Birds.

Choquentot, D., Lukins, B.S. and Curran, G. (1997). Assessing lamb predation by feral pigs in Australia's semi-arid rangelands. *Journal of Applied Ecology,* **34,** 1445–1454.

Choquentot, D., McIlroy, J. and Korn, T. (1996). *Managing Vertebrate Pests: Feral Pigs.* Canberra: Australian Government Publishing Service.

Church, R. L., Stoms, D. M. and Davis, F. W. (1996). Reserve selection as a maximal covering location problem. *Biological Conservation,* **76,** 105–112.

Clark, D. R., Bagley, F. M. and Waynon Johnson, W. (1988). Northern Alabama colonies of the endangered grey bat *Myotis grisescens*: organochlorine contamination and mortality. *Biological Conservation*, **43**, 213–225.

Clark, K. M., Carroll, J. B., Clark, M., Garrett, S. T., Pinkus, S. and Saw, P. (1997). Capture and survey of Livingstone's fruit bats, *Pteropus livingstonii* in the Comoros Islands: the 1995 expedition. *Dodo, Journal of the Wildlife Preservation Trusts* **33**, 20–35.

Clarke, M. J. F. (1997). *The Promotion of Zambia and its National Parks: a Study of Tour Operators in the United Kingdom*. MSc thesis. Canterbury: University of Kent.

Coe, M. (1982). The bigger they are... *Oryx*, **16**, 225–228.

Coe, M. J., Cumming, D. H. and Phillipson, J. (1976). Biomass and production of large African herbivores in relation to rainfall and primary production. *Oecologia*, **22**, 341–354.

Cole, R. R., Reeder, D. M. and Wilson, D. E. (1994). A synopsis of the conservation patterns and the conservation of mammal species. *Journal of Mammalogy*, **75**, 266–275.

Collar, N. J., Crosby, M. J. and Stattersfield, A. J. (1994). *Birds to Watch 2*. Cambridge: BirdLife International.

Collar, N. J., Wege, D. C. and Long, A. J. (1997). Patterns and causes of endangerment in the New World avifauna. *Ornithological Monographs*, **48**, 237–260.

Conway, W. G. (1986). The practical difficulties and financial implications of endangered species breeding programmes. *International Zoo Yearbook*, **24/25**, 210–219.

Conway, W. G. (1995). The conservation park: a new zoo synthesis for a changed world. In *The Ark Evolving: Zoos and Aquariums in Transition*, ed. C. Wemmer, pp. 259–276. Fort Royal: Conservation Research Center.

Cooke, A. and Farrell, L. (1998). *Chinese Water Deer*. London: The Mammal Society.

Cop, J. (1992). Reintroduction of lynx in Yugoslavia. *Council of Europe Environmental Encounters Series*, **11**, 60–62.

Corbet, G. B. (1978). *The Mammals of the Palaearctic Region: A Taxonomic Review*. London: British Museum (Natural History).

Corbet, G. B. and Harris, S. (eds) (1991). *The Handbook of British Mammals*, 3rd edn. Oxford: Blackwell Scientific Publications.

Corbet, G. B. and Hill, J. E. (1991). *A World List of Mammalian Species*, 3rd edn. London: Natural History Museum Publications and Oxford University Press.

Corlett, R. T. and Lucas, P. W. (1990). Alternative seed-handling strategies in primates: seed-spitting by long-tailed macaques (*Macaca fascicularis*). *Oecologia*, **82**, 166–171.

Costanza, R., d'Arge, R., de Groot, R., Farber, S., Grasso, M., Hannon, B., Limburg, K., Naeem, S., O'Neill, R. V., Paruelo, J., Raskin, R. G., Sutton, P., and van den Belt, M. (1997). The value of the world's ecosystem services and natural capital. *Nature*, **387**, 253–260.

Cravinho, J. G. (1997). Economy of Mozambique. In *Africa South of the Sahara 1997*, pp. 664–670. London: Europa Publications.

Cresswell, P., Harris, S. and Jefferies, D. J. (1990). *The History, Distribution, Status and Habitat Requirements of the Badger in Britain*. Peterborough: Nature Conservancy Council.

Csuti, B., Polasky, S., Williams, P. H., Pressey, R. L., Camm, J. D., Kershaw, M., Kiester, A. R., Downs, B., Hamilton, R., Huso, M. and Sahr, K. (1997). A comparison of reserve selection algorithms using data on terrestrial vertebrates in Oregon. *Biological Conservation*, **80**, 83–97.

Cumming, D. H. M., Fenton, M. B., Rautenbach, I. L., Taylor, J. S., Cumming, G. S., Cumming, M. S., Dunlop, J., Hovorka, M. D., Johnston, D. S., Kalcounis, M. C., Mahlanga, Z. and Portfors, C. V. (1997). Elephant impacts on biodiversity of Miombo woodlands in Zimbabwe. *South African Journal of Science*, **93**, 231–236.

Cumming, D. H. M., du Toit, R. F. and Stuart, S. N. (1990). *African Elephants and Rhinos. Status Survey and Conservation Action Plan*. Gland: IUCN.

Dang, H. (1991). *Human Conflict in Conservation*. New Delhi: Development Alternatives.

Darvill, T. (1996). *Prehistoric Britain*. London: Routledge.

Decher, J. (1997). Conservation, small mammals, and the future of sacred groves in West Africa. *Biodiversity and Conservation*, **6**, 1007–1026.

Dew, L. J. and Wright, P. (1998). Frugivory and seed dispersal by four species of primates in Madagascar's eastern rain forest. *Biotropica*, **30**, 425–437.

Diamond, J. M. (1984a). Historic extinctions: a Rosetta Stone for understanding prehistoric extinctions. In *Quaternary Extinctions*, eds P. S. Martin and R. G. Klein, pp. 824–862. Tucson: University of Arizona Press.

Diamond, J. M. (1984b). 'Normal' extinction patterns of isolated populations. In *Extinctions*, ed. M. H. Nitecki, pp. 193–246. Chicago: University of Chicago Press.

Diamond, J. M.. (1989). Overview of recent extinctions. In *Conservation for the Twenty-first Century*, eds D. Western and M. Pearl, pp. 37–41. New York: Oxford University Press.

Diamond, J. M., Bishop, K. D. and van Balen, S. (1987). Bird survival in an isolated Javan woodland: island or mirror? *Conservation Biology*, **1**, 132–142.

Dierenfeld, E., Hintz, H., Robertson, J., van Soest, P. and Oftedal, O. (1982). Utilization of bamboo by the giant panda. *Journal of Nutrition*, **112**, 636–641.

Dietz, J. M., Dietz, L. A. and Nagagata, E. Y. (1994). The effective use of flagship species for conservation of biodiversity: the example of lion tamarins in Brazil. In *Creative Conservation: Interactive Management of Wild and Captive Animals*, eds P. J. S. Olney, G. M. Mace, and A. T. C. Feistner, pp. 32–49. London: Chapman and Hall.

Dietz, L. A. and Nagagata, E. (1995). Golden lion tamarin conservation program: a community effort for forest conservation, Rio de Janeiro state, Brazil. In *International Education/Communication Approaches*, ed. S. K. Jacobson, pp. 64–86. New York: Columbia University Press.

Dinerstein, E., Olson, D. M., Graham, D. J., Webster, A. L., Primm, S. A., Bookbinder, M. P. and Ledec, G. (1995). *A Conservation Assessment of the Terrestrial Ecoregions of Latin America and the Caribbean*. Washington, DC: WWF and The World Bank.

Dinerstein, E. and Wemmer, C. M. (1988). Fruits *Rhinoceros* eat: dispersal of *Trewia nudiflora* (Euphorbiaceae) in lowland Nepal. *Ecology*, **69**, 1768–1774.

Dinerstein, E., Wikramanayake, E., Robinson, J., Karanth, U., Rabinowitz, A., Olson D., Mathew, T., Hedao, P. and Connor, M. (1997). *A Framework for Identifying High Priority Areas and Actions for the Conservation of Tigers in the Wild*. Washington, DC: WWF-US and Wildlife Conservation Society.

Dirzo, R. and Miranda, A. (1991). Altered patterns of herbivory and diversity in the forest understory: a case study of the possible consequences of contemporary defaunation. In *Plant–Animal Interactions: Evolutionary Ecology in Tropical and Temperate Regions*, eds P. W. Price, T. M. Lewinsohn, G. W. Fernandes and W. W. Benson, pp. 273–287. New York: John Wiley & Sons.

Dixon, J. and Sherman, P. (1990). *Economics of Protected Areas: A New Look at Benefits and Costs*. Washington, DC: Island Press.

Dobson, A. (1996). *Conservation and Biodiversity*. New York: Scientific American.

Dobson, A. P., Rodriguez, J. P., Roberts, W. M. and Wilcove, D. S. (1997). Geographic distribution of endangered species in the United States. *Science*, **275**, 550–553.

Douglas-Hamilton, I. (1987). African elephants: population trends and their causes. *Oryx*, **21**, 11–24.

Downer, C. (1996). The mountain tapir, endangered 'flagship' species of the high Andes. *Oryx*, **30**, 45–58.

Downs, N. C. and Racey, P. A. (1998). Do bats believe in the Wildlife Corridors hypothesis? *Bat Research News*, **39**, 89.

Driver, A. (1997). River and wetland rehabilitation in the Thames catchment. *British Wildlife*, **8**, 362–372.

Dublin, H. T. (1994). In the eye of the beholder: our image of the African elephant. *Endangered Species Technical Bulletin*, **19**, 5–6.

Dublin, H. T. (1996). *North-south Dissonance in Consumptive Use Policies: with Special Reference to Charismatic Megafauna*. Pan-African Symposium on the Sustainable Use of Natural Resources and Community Participation. Harare, Zimbabwe, June 1996.

Dublin, H. T., Sinclair, A. R. E., Boutin, S., Anderson, E., Jago, M. and Arcese, P. (1990). Does competition regulate ungulate populations? Further evidence from Serengeti, Tanzania. *Oecologia*, **82**, 283–288.

Duffey, E. (1974). *Nature Reserves and Wildlife*. London: Heinemann Educational.

Duffey, E. and Watt, A. S. (eds) (1971). *The Scientific Management of Animal and Plant Communities for Conservation*. British Ecological Society Symposium Number 11. London: British Ecological Society.

Duncan, P. (1992). *Zebras, Asses and Horses. An Action Plan for the Conservation of Wild Equids*. Gland: IUCN.

Dunstone, N. and O'Sullivan, J. N. (1996). The Impact of Ecotourism Development on Rainforest Mammals. In *The Exploitation of Mammal Populations*, eds, V. J. Taylor and N. Dunstone, pp. 313–333. London; Chapman & Hall.

Durbin, J. (1999). Lemurs as flagships for conservation in Madagascar. In *New Directions in Lemur Studies*, eds B. Rakotosamimanana, H. Rasamimanana, J. Ganzhorn and S. Goodman, pp. 269–281. New York: Plenum Press.

Durrell, L. (1991). Notes on the Durrell Expedition to Madagascar September–December 1990. *Dodo, Journal of the Wildlife Preservation Trusts*, **27**, 9–18.

Durrell, L. M. and Mallinson, J. J. C. (1987). Reintroduction as a political and educational tool for conservation. *Dodo, Journal of the Wildlife Preservation Trusts*, **24**, 6–19.

Dutton, J. and Haft, J. (1996). Distribution, ecology and status of an endemic shrew, *Crocidura thomensis*, from São Tomé. *Oryx*, **30**, 195–201.

Duvergé, P. L. and Jones, G. (1994). Greater horseshoe bats: activity, foraging behaviour, and habitat use. *British Wildlife*, **6**, 69–77.

Dyczkowski, J. and Yalden, D. W. (1998). An estimate of the impact of predators on the British field vole *Microtus agrestis* population. *Mammal Review*, **28**, 165–184.

East, R. (1984). Rainfall, soil nutrient status and biomass of large African savanna mammals. *African Journal of Ecology*, **22**, 245–270.

East, R. (1988). *Antelopes. Global Survey and Regional Action Plans. Part 1. East and Northeast Africa.* Gland: IUCN.

East, R. (1989). *Antelopes. Global Survey and Regional Action Plans. Part 2. Southern and South-central Africa.* Gland: IUCN.

East, R. (1990). *Antelopes. Global Survey and Regional Action Plans. Part 3. West and Central Africa.* Gland: IUCN.

East R., Mallon D. and Kingswood, S. (1996). Evaluation of antelopes using IUCN Red List categories. *Antelope Survey Update*, **2**, 57–72.

Ebenhard, T. (1995). Conservation breeding as a tool for saving animal species. *Trends in Ecology and Evolution*, **10**, 438–443.

Edwards, P. J. and Abivardi, C. (1998). The value of biodiversity: where ecology and economy blend. *Biological Conservation*, **83**, 239–246.

Eisenberg, J. F. (1989). *The Mammalian Radiations.* Chicago: Athlone Press.

Eisner, T., Lubchenco, J., Wilson, E. O., Wilcove, D. S. and Bean, M. J. (1995). Building a scientifically sound policy for protecting endangered species. *Science*, **268**, 1231–1232.

Ellis, S. and Seal, U. S. (1995). Tools of the trade to aid decision-making for species survival. *Biodiversity and Conservation*, **4**, 553–572.

Elmes, G. W. and Free, A. (1994). *Climate Change and Rare Species in Britain.* Institute of Terrestrial Ecology Research Publication 8. London: Her Majesty's Stationery Office.

Eloff, F. (1984). The Kalahari ecosystem. *Koedoe* supplement, 11–20.

Elton, C. (1942). *Voles, Mice and Lemmings: Problems in Population Dynamics.* Oxford: Clarendon Press.

Eltringham, S. K. (1977). The numbers and distribution of elephant *Loxodonta africana* in the Ruwenzori National Park and Chambura Game Reserve. *East African Wildlife Journal*, **15**, 19–39.

Eltringham, S. K. and Din, N. A. (1977). Estimates of the population size of some ungulate species in the Ruwenzori National Park, Uganda. *East African Wildlife Journal*, **15**, 305–316.

Eltringham, S. K. and Woodford, M. H. (1973). The numbers and distribution of buffalo in the Ruwenzori National Park, Uganda. *East African Wildlife Journal*, **11**, 154–161.

Emslie, R. H. (1996). *A Continental African Rhinoceros Status Summary and Action Plan.* A draft prepared by The IUCN SSC African Rhino Specialist Group.

Entwistle, A. C. and Corp, N. (1997). Status and distribution of the Pemba flying fox *Pteropus voeltzkowi*. *Oryx*, **31**, 135–142.

Entwistle, A. C., Gibson, S., Harris, S., Hutson, A. M., Racey, P. A. and Walsh, A. L. (in press a). *Habitat Management for Bats.* Peterborough: Joint Nature Conservation Committee.

Entwistle, A. C. Racey, P. A. and Speakman, J. R. (1996). Habitat exploitation by a gleaning bat, *Plecotus auritus*. *Philosophical Transaction of the Royal Society of*

London, Series B, 351, 921–931.

Entwistle, A. C. Racey, P. A. and Speakman, J. R. (1997). Roost selection by the brown long-eared bat (Plecotus auritus). Journal of Applied Ecology, 34, 399–408.

Entwistle, A. C. Racey, P. A. and Speakman, J. R. (in press b). Social and population structure of a gleaning bat, Plecotus auritus. Journal of Zoology, London.

Erdelen, W. (1988). Forest ecosystems and nature conservation in Sri Lanka. Biological Conservation, 43, 115–135.

Estes, R. D. (1991). The Behavior Guide to African Mammals. Berkeley: University of California Press.

Estrada, A. and Coates-Estrada, R. (1996). Tropical rain forest fragmentation and wild populations of primates at Los Tuxtlas, Mexico. International Journal of Primatology, 17, 759–783.

Estrada, A., Coates-Estrada, R. and Meritt Jr., D. (1994). Non flying mammals and landscape changes in the tropical rain forest of Los Tuxtlas, Mexico. Ecography, 177, 229–241.

Estrada, A., Coates-Estrada, R., Meritt Jr., D., Montiel, S. and Curiel, D. (1993). Patterns of frugivore species richness and abundance in forest islands and in agricultural habitats at Los Tuxtlas, Mexico. Vegetatio, 107/108, 245–257.

Eudey, A. A. (1987). Action Plan for Asian Primate Conservation: 1987–1991. Gland: IUCN.

Fa, J. E., Juste, J., Perez del Val, J. and Castroviejo, J. (1995). Impact of market hunting on mammal species in Equatorial Guinea. Conservation Biology, 9, 1107–1115.

Feistner, A. T. C. (in press). Conservation of the Alaotran gentle lemur: A multidisciplinary approach. In New Directions in Lemur Studies, eds B. Rakotosamimanana, H. Rasamimanana, J. Ganzhorn and S. Goodman. New York: Plenum Press.

Feistner, A. T. C. and Beattie, J. B. (1998). International Studbook for the Alaotran Gentle Lemur Hapalemur griseus alaotrensis Number Two 1997. Jersey: Jersey Wildlife Preservation Trust.

Feistner, A. T. C. and Rakotoarinosy, M. (1993). Conservation of gentle lemur Hapalemur griseus alaotrensis at Lac Alaotra Madagascar: Local knowledge. Dodo, Journal of the Wildlife Preservation Trusts, 29, 54–65.

Fenchel, T. (1974). Intrinsic rate of natural increase: the relationship with body size. Oecologia, 14, 317–326.

Fenton, M. B. (1997). Science and the conservation of bats. Journal of Mammalogy, 78, 1–14.

Fenton, M. B. and Rautenbach, I. L. (1998) Impacts of ignorance and human and elephant populations on the conservation of bats in African woodlands. In Bat Biology and Conservation, eds T. H. Kunz and P. A. Racey, pp. 261–270. Washington, DC: Smithsonian Institution Press.

Ferrari, S. F. and Diego, V. H. (1995). Habitat fragmentation and primate conservation in the Atlantic forest of eastern Minas Gerais, Brazil. Oryx, 29, 192–196.

Fiedler, P. L. and Jain, S. K. (1992). Conservation Biology: The Theory and Practice of Nature Conservation, Preservation and Management. New York: Chapman and Hall.

Field, C. R. and Laws, R. M. (1970). The distribution of the larger herbivores in the Queen Elizabeth National Park, Uganda. Journal of Applied Ecology, 7, 273–294.

Filgueiras, R. (1997). *The Promotion of India's Protected Areas by UK Tour Operators.* MSc thesis. Canterbury: University of Kent.

Fitter, R. and Scott, P. (1978). *The Penitent Butchers.* London: The Fauna Preservation Society.

Fitzgibbon, C. D. (1994). The distribution and abundance of the golden-rumped elephant shrew *Rhynchcyon chrysopygas* in Kenyan coastal forests. *Biological Conservation,* **67,** 153–160.

FitzGibbon, C. (1998). The management of subsistence harvesting: Behavioral ecology of hunters and their mammalian prey. In *Behavioral Ecology and Conservation Biology,* ed. T. Caro, pp. 449–473. Oxford: Oxford University Press.

Fitzgibbon, C. D., Mogaka, H. and Fanshawe, J. (1995). Subsistence hunting in Arabuko–Sokoke Forest, Kenya, and its effects on mammal populations. *Conservation Biology,* **9,** 1116–1126.

Flannery, T. (1995a). *Mammals of the South-West Pacific and Moluccan Islands.* Chatswood: Reed Books.

Flannery, T. (1995b). *Mammals of New Guinea.* Revised and updated edition. Chatswood: Reed Books.

Fleming, T. H. (1986). Opportunism versus specialization: the evolution of feeding strategies in frugivorous bats. In *Frugivores and Seed Dispersal,* eds A. Estrada and T. H. Fleming, pp. 105–118. Dordrecht: Dr W. Junk Publishers.

Fleming, T. H., Breitwhisch, R. and Whitesides, G. H. (1987). Patterns of tropical vertebrate frugivore diversity. *Annual Review in Ecology and Systematics,* **18,** 91–109.

Fleming, T. H. and Sosa, V. J. (1994). Effects of nectarivorous and frugivorous mammals on reproductive success of plants. *Journal of Mammalogy,* **75,** 845–851.

Foose, T. J. and van Strien, N. (1997). *Asian Rhinos. Status Survey and Conservation Action Plan.* Second edition. Gland: IUCN.

Forget, P.-M. (1990). Seed-dispersal of *Voucapoua americana* (Caesalpiniaceae) by caviomorph rodents in French Guiana. *Journal of Tropical Ecology,* **6,** 459–468.

Forget, P.-M. (1991). Scatterhoarding of *Astrocaryum paramaca* by *Proechimys* in French Guiana: comparison with *Myoprocta exilis. Tropical Ecology,* **32,** 155–157.

Forget, P.-M. (1996). Removal of seeds of *Carapa procera* (Meliaceae) by rodents and their fate in rainforest in French Guiana. *Journal of Tropical Ecology,* **12,** 751–761.

Foster, J. B. and Kearney, D. (1967). Nairobi National Park game census, 1966. *East African Wildlife Journal,* **5,** 112–120.

Foster-Turley, P., Macdonald, S. and Mason, C. (1990). *Otters. An Action Plan for their Conservation.* Gland: IUCN.

Fragoso, J. (1994). *Large Mammals and the Community Dynamics of an Amazonian Rain Forest.* PhD thesis. Gainesville: University of Florida.

Fragoso, J. M. V. (1997). Tapir-generated seed shadows: scale-dependents patchiness in the Amazon rain forest. *Journal of Ecology,* **85,** 519–529.

Freitag, S., Nicholls, A. O. and van Jaarsveld, A. S. (1996). Nature reserve selection in the Transvaal, South Africa: what data should we be using? *Biodiversity and Conservation,* **5,** 685–698.

Fujita, M. (1991). *Flying Fox (Chiroptera: Pteropodidae) Pollination, Seed Dispersal and Economic Importance.* Austin: Bat Conservation International.

Fujita, M. S. and Tuttle, M. D. (1991). Flying foxes (Chiroptera: Pteropodidae): threatened animals of key ecological and economic importance. *Conservation Biology*, **5**, 455–463.

Fuller, T. K. (1989). Population dynamics of wolves in north-central Minnesota. *Wildlife Monographs*, **105**, 1–41.

Gaston, K. J. (1994). *Rarity*. London: Chapman and Hall.

Gaston, K. J. (1996a). *Biodiversity: A Biology of Numbers and Difference*. Oxford: Blackwell Science.

Gaston, K. J. (1996b). Species richness: measure and measurement. In *Biodiversity: A Biology of Numbers and Difference*, ed. K. J. Gaston, pp. 77–113. Oxford: Blackwell Science.

Gaston, K. J. (1996c). Spatial covariance in the species richness of higher taxa. In *Aspects of the Genesis and Maintenance of Biological Diversity*, eds M. E. Hochberg, J. Clobert and R. Barbault, pp. 221–242. Oxford: Oxford University Press.

Gaston, K. J. and Blackburn, T. M. (1995a). Birds, body size and the threat of extinction. *Philosophical Transactions of the Royal Society of London, Series B*, **347**, 205–212.

Gaston, K. J. and Blackburn, T. M. (1995b). Rarity and body size: some cautionary remarks. *Conservation Biology*, **9**, 210–213.

Gaston, K. J. and Blackburn, T. M. (1997). Evolutionary age and risk of extinction in the global avifauna. *Evolutionary Ecology*, **11**, 557–565.

Gaston, K. J. and Kunin, W. E. (1997). Rare-common differences: an overview. In *The Biology of Rarity*, eds W. E. Kunin and K. J. Gaston, pp. 12–29. London: Chapman and Hall.

Gautier-Hion, A., Duplantier, J.-M., Quris, R., Feer, F., Sourd, C., Decoux, J.-P., Dubost, G., Emmons, L., Erard, C., Hecketsweiler, P., Moungazi, A., Roussilhon, C. and Thiollay, J.-M. (1985). Fruit characteristics as a basis of fruit choice and seed dispersal in a tropical forest vertebrate community. *Oecologia*, **65**, 324–337.

Gelderblom, C., van Wilgen, B. W. and Rossouw, N. (1997). *Proposed Transfrontier Conservation Areas. Maps and Preliminary Data Sheets*. Prepared for the Peace Parks Foundation. Stellenbosch: CSIR Division of Water, Environment and Forestry Technology.

Gibbons, D. W., Reid, J. B. and Chapman, R. A. (1993). *The New Atlas of Breeding Birds in Britain and Ireland: 1988–1991*. London: Poyser.

Gilbert, L. E. (1980). Food web organization and conservation of neotropical diversity. In *Conservation Biology*, eds M. E. Soulé and B. A. Wilcox, pp. 11–34. Sunderland: Sinauer Associates.

Gilpin, M. E. and Soulé, M. E. (1986). Minimum viable populations: processes of species extinctions. In *Conservation Biology: The Science of Scarcity and Diversity*, ed. M. E. Soulé, pp. 19–34. Sunderland: Sinauer Associates.

Gimenez-Dixon, M. and Stuart, S. N. (1993). Action plans for species conservation: a review of their effectiveness. *Species*, **20**, 6–10.

Ginsberg, J. R. and Macdonald, D. W. (1990). *Foxes, Wolves, Jackals and Dogs. An Action Plan for the Conservation of Canids*. Gland: IUCN.

Giongo, F., Bosco-Nizeye, J. and Wallace, G. N. (1993). *A Study of Visitor Management in the World's National Parks and Protected Areas*. Report to Colorado State University.

Gittleman, J. L. and Thompson, S. D. (1988). Energy allocation in mammalian reproduction. *American Zoologist*, **28**, 863–875.

Glatson, A. R. (1994). *The Red Panda, Olingos, Coatis, Raccoons and their Relatives. Status Survey and Conservation Action Plan for Procyonids and Ailurids.* Gland: IUCN.

Glowka, L., Burhenne-Guilmin, F.B., Synge, H., McNeely, J.A. and Gundling, L. (1994). *A Guide to the Convention on Biological Diversity.* Gland: IUCN.

Godfray, H. C. J. and Crawley, M. J. (1998). Introductions. In *Conservation Science and Action*, ed. W. J. Sutherland, pp. 39–65. Oxford: Blackwell Science.

Goldspink, C. R., Holland, R. K., Sweet, G. and Stjernsredt, R. (1998). A note on the distribution of the puku, *Kobus vardoni*, in Kasanka National Park, Zambia. *African Journal of Ecology*, **36**, 23–33.

Gomez-Pompa, A. and Kaus, A. (1992). Taming the wilderness myth. *BioScience*, **42**, 271–279.

Goodman, S. M. (1995). *Rattus* on Madagascar and the dilemma of protecting the endemic rodent fauna. *Conservation Biology*, **9**, 450–453.

Goodwin, H. (1996). In pursuit of ecotourism. *Biodiversity and Conservation*, **5**, 227–291.

Goodwin, H., Kent, I., Parker, K. and Walpole, M. (1998). *Tourism, Conservation and Sustainable Development: Case Studies from Asia and Africa.* London: International Institute for Environment and Development.

Gottdenker, N. and Bodmer, R. (1998) Reproduction and productivity of white-lipped and collared peccaries in the Peruvian Amazon. *Journal of Zoology*, **245**, 423–430.

Greeff, L. (1998). *Preliminary Status Report on the Transfrontier Conservation Areas in South Africa for TRANSFORM (Training and Support for Resource Management).* Pretoria: TRANSFORM, Department of Land Affairs.

Green, R. E. (1997). The influence of numbers released on the outcome of attempts to introduce exotic bird species to New Zealand. *Journal of Animal Ecology*, **66**, 25–35.

Greenwood, J. D. (1994). Trust the wildlife volunteers. *Nature*, **368**, 490.

Greenwood, J. J. D., Gregory, R. D., Harris, S., Morris, P. A. and Yalden, D. W. (1996). Relations between abundance, body size and species number in British birds and mammals. *Philosophical Transactions of the Royal Society of London, Series B*, **351**, 265–278.

Gregory, R. D., Bashford, R. I., Beaven, L. P., Wilson, A. M., Marchant, J. H. and Baillie, S. R. (1998). *Breeding Bird Survey Report 1998.* BTO Research Report 203. Thetford: British Trust for Ornithology.

Greyling, T. and Huntley, B. J. (1984). *Directory of Southern African Conservation Areas.* Report No. 98. Pretoria: South African National Science Programme.

Griffith, J. B., Scott, J. M., Carpenter, J. W. and Reed, C. (1989). Translocation as a species conservation tool: status and strategy. *Science*, **245**, 477–480.

Groombridge, B. (ed.) (1992). *Global Biodiversity: Status of the Earth's Living Resources.* London: Chapman and Hall.

de Groot, R. S. (1983). Tourism and conservation in the Galapagos Islands. *Biological Conservation*, **26**, 291–300.

Groves, C. (1992). Beyond endangered species: gap analysis. *Idaho Wildlife*, **1992**, 26–27.

Grumbine, R. E. (1994). What is ecosystem management? *Conservation Biology*, **8**, 27–38.

Hall, S. J. and Raffaelli, D. (1991). Food-web patterns: lessons from a species-rich web. *Journal of Animal Ecology*, **60**, 823–842.

Hallwachs, W. (1986). Agoutis (*Dasyprocta punctata*): the inheritors of guapinol (*Hymenaea courbairl*: Leguminosae). In *Frugivores and Seed Dispersal*, eds A. Estrada and T. H. Fleming, pp. 286–304. Dordrecht: Dr W. Junk Publishers.

Hambler, C. and Speight, M. R. (1995a). Biodiversity conservation in Britain: science replacing tradition. *British Wildlife*, **6**, 137–147.

Hambler, C. and Speight, M. R. (1995b). Seeing the wood for the trees. *Tree News*, **Autumn 1995**, 8–11.

Hambler, C. and Speight, M. R. (1996). Extinction rates in British non-marine invertebrates since 1600. *Conservation Biology*, **10**, 892–896.

Hamilton, L. S., Mackay, J. C., Worboys, G. L., Jones, R. A. and Manson, G. B. (1996). *Transborder Protected Areas Cooperation*. Canberra: Australian Alps Liaison Committee and IUCN.

Hannah, L., Carr, J. L. and Lankerani, A. (1995). Human disturbance and natural habitat: a biome level analysis of a global data set. *Biodiversity and Conservation*, **4**, 128–155.

Hanski, I. (1982). Dynamics of regional distribution: the core and satellite species hypothesis. *Oikos*, **38**, 210–221.

Hanski, I. and Gyllenberg, M. (1993). General metapopulation models and the core-satellite species. *American Naturalist*, **142**, 17–41.

Happold, D. C. D. (1995). The interactions between humans and mammals in Africa in relation to conservation: a review. *Biodiversity and Conservation*, **4**, 395–414.

Happold, D. C. D. and Happold, M. (1997). Conservation of mammals on a tobacco farm on the highlands of Malawi. *Biodiversity and Conservation*, **6**, 837–852.

Harcourt, A. H. (1986). Gorilla conservation: anatomy of a campaign. In *Primates: the Road to Self-sustaining Populations*, ed. K. Benirschke, pp. 31–46. New York: Springer-Verlag.

Harding, P. T. and Rose, F. (1996). *Pasture Woodland in Lowland Britain*. Huntingdon: Institute of Terrestrial Ecology.

Harrington, L. A., Catto, C. M. C. and Hutson, A. M. (1995). *The Status and Distribution of Barbastelle Bat* (Barbastella barbastellus) *and Bechstein's Bat* (Myotis bechsteinii) *in the UK, with Recovery Plans*. London: The Bat Conservation Trust.

Harris, S., Morris, P., Wray, S. and Yalden, D. (1995). *A Review of British Mammals: Population Estimates and Conservation Status of British Mammals other than Cetaceans*. Peterborough: Joint Nature Conservation Committee.

Harrison, S. (1994). Metapopulations and conservation. In *Large Scale Ecology and Conservation Biology*, eds P. J. Edwards, R. M. May and N. R. Webb, pp. 111–128. Oxford: Blackwell Science.

Hemley, G. (ed.) (1994). *International Wildlife Trade: a CITES Sourcebook*. Washington, DC: Island Press.

Henderson, M. T. (1985). Patchy environments and species survival: chipmunks in an agricultural mosaic. *Biological Conservation*, **24**, 115–128.

Henry, W. R. (1980). Patterns of tourist use in Kenya's Amboseli National Park: implications for planning and management. In *Tourism Marketing and Manage-*

ment Issues, eds D. Hawkins, E. Shafer and J. Rovelstad, pp. 43–57. Washington, DC: George Washington University.

Heywood, V. H. (ed.) (1995). *Global Biodiversity Assessment*. Cambridge: Cambridge University Press.

Hill, K. and Padwe, J. (in press). Sustainability of Ache hunting in the Mbaracayu Reserve, Paraguay. In *Evaluating the Sustainability of Hunting in Tropical Forests*, eds J. G. Robinson and E. L. Bennett. New York: Columbia University Press.

Hilland, O. M. and Burtt, B. L. (1987). The botany of the Southern Natal Drakensberg. *Annals of Kirstenbosch Botanical Gardens*, **15**, 1–253.

Hillman, J. C., Cunningham-van Someren, G. R., Gakahu, C. G. and East, R. (1988). Kenya. In *Antelopes. Global Survey and Regional Action Plans, Part 1: East and Northeast Africa*, compiler R. East, pp. 41–53. Gland: IUCN.

Hinsley, S. A., Bellamy, P. E., Newton, I. and Sparks, T. H. (1996a). Influences of population size and wooded area on bird species distributions in small woods. *Oecologia*, **105**, 100–106.

Hinsley, S. A., Pakeman, R., Bellamy, P. E. and Newton, I. (1996b). Influences of habitat fragmentation on bird species distributions and regional population sizes. *Proceedings of the Royal Society of London, Series B*, **263**, 307–313.

Hodgson, J. G. (1986). Commonness and rarity in plants with special reference to the Sheffield flora. Part III. Taxonomic and evolutionary aspects. *Biological Conservation*, **36**, 275–297.

Holler, N. R., Mason, D. W., Dawson, R. M., Simons, T. and Wooten, M. C. (1989). Reestablishment of the Perdido Key beach mouse (*Peromyscus polionoyus trissyllepsis*) on Gulf Islands National Seashore. *Conservation Biology*, **3**, 397–403.

Holling, C. S. (1992). Cross-scale morphology, geometry, and dynamics of ecosystems. *Ecological Monographs*, **62**, 447–502.

Hoogesteijn, R. and Chapman, C. A. (1997). Large ranches as conservation tools in the Venezuelan llanos. *Oryx*, **31**, 274–284.

Hooper, M. E. and Harrison, S. (1998). Metapopulation, source-sink and distribution dynamics. In *Conservation Science and Action*, ed. W. J. Sutherland, pp. 135–151. Oxford: Blackwell Science.

Horwich, R. H. and Lyon, J. (1990). *A Belizian Rain Forest: The Community Baboon Sanctuary*. Gay Mills: Orang-utan Press.

Houghton, J. T. (1997). *Climate Change: The Complete Briefing*. Cambridge: Cambridge University Press.

Howard, P., Davenport, T. and Kigenyi, F. (1997). Planning conservation areas in Uganda's natural forests. *Oryx*, **31**, 253–264.

Howe, H. F. (1980). Monkey dispersal and waste of a neotropical fruit. *Ecology*, **61**, 944–959.

Howe, H. F. (1984). Implications of seed dispersal by animals for tropical reserve management. *Biological Conservation*, **30**, 261–281.

Howe, H. F. (1986). Seed dispersal by fruit-eating birds and mammals. In *Seed Dispersal*, ed. D. R. Murray, pp. 123–189. Australia: Academic Press.

Howe, H. F. and Smallwood, J. (1982). Ecology of seed dispersal. *Annual Review in Ecology and Systematics*, **13**, 201–228.

Hughes, J. B., Daily, G. C. and Erhlich, P. R. (1997). Population diversity: its extent and extinction. *Science*, **278**, 689–692.

Hulbert, I. A. R. (1990). The response of ruddy shelduck (*Tadorna ferruginea*) to tourist activity in the Royal Chitwan National Park of Nepal. *Biological Conservation*, **52**, 113–123.

Hunter, C. and Green, H. (1995). *Tourism and the Environment: a Sustainable Relationship?* London: Routledge.

Hunter, M. L. (1996). *Fundamentals of Conservation Biology*. Oxford: Blackwell Science.

Hunter, M. L. and Yonazon, P. (1993). Altitudinal distribution of birds, mammals, people, forests and parks in Nepal. *Conservation Biology*, **7**, 420–423.

Huston, M. A. (1994). *Biological Diversity: The Co-existence of Species on Changing Landscapes*. Cambridge: Cambridge University Press.

Hutchins, M. R. and Harris, S. (1996). *The Current Status of the Brown Hare* (Lepus europaeus) *in Britain*. Peterborough: Joint Nature Conservation Committee.

Hutchings, M., Wiese, R. J. and Willis, K. (1997). Captive breeding and conservation. *Conservation Biology*, **11**, 3.

Hutchings, M., Willis, K. and Wiese, R. J. (1995). Strategic collection planning: theory and practice. *Zoo Biology*, **14**, 5–25.

Hutchison, G. E. and MacArthur, R. H. (1959). A theoretical ecological model of size distributions among species of animals. *American Naturalist*, **93**, 117–125.

Hutson, A. M., Mickleburgh, S. and Mitchell-Jones, A. J. (1995). *Bats Underground: A Conservation Code*. London: The Bat Conservation Trust.

Hutterer, R., Jenkins, P. and Verheyen, W. N. (1991). A new forest shrew from southern Tanzania. *Oryx*, **25**, 165–168.

Iltis, H. H. (1988). Serendipity in the exploration of biodiversity: what good are weedy tomatoes? In *Biodiversity*, ed. E. O. Wilson, pp. 98–105. Washington, DC: National Academy Press.

ISCBD (Interim Secretariat for the Convention on Biological Diversity) (1994). *Convention on Biological Diversity. Text and Annexes*. Geneva: United Nations Environment Programme.

ISIS (International Species Information System) (1993). *User Manual for SPARKS – the Single Population Analysis and Record-keeping System* v. 2.11. Apple Valley: ISIS.

IUCN (1986). *1986 IUCN Red List of Threatened Animals*. Gland: IUCN.

IUCN (1990a). *1990 IUCN Red List of Threatened Animals*. Gland: IUCN

IUCN (1990b). *1990 United Nations List of National Parks and Protected Areas*. Gland: IUCN.

IUCN (1993a). *1994 IUCN Red List of Threatened Animals*. Gland: IUCN.

IUCN (1993b). *Species Survival Commission Membership Directory*. Gland: IUCN.

IUCN (1993c). *Environmental Synopsis, Comoros*. Gland: IUCN.

IUCN (1994). *IUCN Red List Categories*. Gland: IUCN.

IUCN (1996). *1996 IUCN Red List of Threatened Animals*. Gland: IUCN.

IUCN (1998). *Best Practice for Introductions*. Gland: IUCN.

IUDZG /CBSG (International Union of the Directors of Zoological Gardens – The World Zoo Organisation, Captive Breeding Specialist Group of IUCN's Species Survival Commission) (1993). *The World Zoo Conservation Strategy; the Role of Zoos and Aquaria of the World in Global Conservation*. Brookfield: Chicago Zoological Society.

van Jaarsveld, E. (1991). A preliminary report on the vegetation of the Richtersveld with specific reference to the trees and shrubs of the area. *Trees in South Africa*, **33**, 58–85.

Jacana Education and National Parks Board (1966). *Kruger Park. Visitors Map*. Johannesburg: Jacana Education.

Jachmann, H. and Billiouw, M. (1997). Elephant poaching and law enforcement in the central Luangwa Valley, Zambia. *Journal of Applied Ecology*, **34**, 233–244.

Janzen, D. H. (1982). Seeds in tapir dung in Santa Rosa National Park, Costa Rica. *Brenesia*, **19/20**, 129–135.

Janzen, D. (1986). The eternal external threat. In *Conservation Biology: the Science of Scarcity and Diversity*, ed. M. Soulé, pp. 286–303. Sunderland: Sinauer Associates.

Jardine, C. L. and Owen, D. R. (1998). *Feasibility Study of the Proposed Gariep Transfrontier Conservation Area: Environmental Overview of the South African Section*. Cape Town: Department of Environmental and Geographical Science, University of Cape Town.

Jefferies, D. J. (1972). Organochlorine insecticide residues in British bats and their significance. *Journal of Zoology*, **166**, 245–263.

Jefferies, D. J., Morris, P. A. and Mulleneux, J. E. (1989). An enquiry into the changing status of the water vole *Arvicola terrestris* in Britain. *Mammal Review*, **19**, 111–131.

Jeffries, M. J. (1997). *Biodiversity and Conservation*. London: Routledge.

Jenner, P. and Smith, C. (1992). *The Tourism Industry and the Environment*. Report to *The Economist* Intelligence Unit, London.

Jensen, T. S. and Nielsen, O. F. (1986). Rodents as seed dispersers in a heath–oak wood succession. *Oecologia*, **70**, 214–221.

JNCC (Joint Nature Conservation Committee) (1996). *British Breeding Birds of Conservation Concern*. Peterborough: JNCC.

Johns, A. D. (1992). Species conservation in managed tropical forests. In *Tropical Deforestation and Species Extinction*, eds J. A. Sayer and T. C. Whitmore, pp. 15–53. Gland: IUCN.

Johns, A. D. and Skorupa, J. P. (1987). Responses of rain-forest primates to habitat disturbance: a review. *International Journal of Primatology*, **8**, 157–191.

Johnsingh, A. J. T. and Joshua, J. (1994). Conserving Rajaji and Corbett National Parks – the elephant as a flagship species. *Oryx*, **28**, 135–140.

Johnson, K., Schaller, G. and Hu Jinchu (1988). Responses of giant pandas to a bamboo die-off. *National Geographic Research*, **4**, 161–177.

Johnson, N. (1995). *Biodiversity in the Balance: Approaches to Setting Geographic Conservation Priorities*. Washington, DC: Biodiversity Support Program.

Jones, G. (1987). *The Conservation of Species and Ecosystems*. London: Croom Helm.

Jones, G., Duvergé L. P. and Ransome, R. D. (1995). Conservation biology of an endangered species: field studies of greater horseshoe bats. In *Ecology, Evolution and Behaviour of Bats*, eds P. A. Racey and S. M. Swift, pp. 309–324. Oxford: Clarendon Press.

Julliot, C. (1996). Seed dispersal by red howling monkeys (*Alouatta seniculus*) in the tropical rain forest of French Guiana. *International Journal of Primatology*, **17**, 239–258.

Julliot, C. (1997). Impact of seed dispersal by red howler monkeys *Alouatta seniculus* on the seedling population in the understory of tropical rain forest. *Journal of Ecology*, **85**, 431–440.

Kalpers, J. (1991). *IGCP Phase I Report, June 1991–December 1992*. Unpublished report.

Kalpers, J. and Lanjouw, A. (1997). *Potential for the Creation of a Peace Park for the Virunga Volcano Region*. Paper presented at Peace Parks Conference, Cape Town.

Kangwana, K. F. (1993). *Elephants and Maasai: Conflict and Conservation in Amboseli, Kenya*. PhD Thesis. Cambridge: University of Cambridge.

Kapteyn, K. and Lina, P. H. C. (1994). Eerste vondst van een kraamkolonie van Nathusius dwergvleermuis *Pipistrellus nathusii* in Nederland. *Lutra*, **37**, 106–109.

Karanth, K. U. (1992). Conservation prospects for lion-tailed macaques in Karnataka, India. *Zoo Biology*, **11**, 33–41.

Keith, L. B. (1983). Population dynamics of wolves. *Canadian Wildlife Service Report Series*, **45**, 66–77.

Kennedy, M. (1992). *Australian Marsupials and Monotremes. An Action Plan for their Conservation*. Gland: IUCN.

Kerth, G., Mayer, F. and König, B. (in press). Mitochondrial DNA reveals evidence for benefits of group living in Bechstein's bats. *Proceedings of the Royal Society of London, Series B*.

Khan, L. M., Monon, S. and Bawa, K. S. (1997). Effectiveness of the protected area network in biodiversity conservation: a case study of Meghalaya State. *Biodiversity and Conservation*, **6**, 853–868.

Kierulff, M. C. M. and de Oliveira, P. P. (1996). Reassessing the status and conservation of the golden lion tamarin *Leontopithecus rosalia* in the wild. *Dodo, Journal of the Wildlife Preservation Trusts*, **32**, 98–115.

Kierulff, M. C. M., Stallings, J. R. and Sabio E. L. (1991). A method to capture the bamboo rat (*Kannabateomys amblyonyx*) in bamboo forests. *Mammalia*, **55**, 633–635.

Kingdon, J. (1977). *East African Mammals: An Atlas of Evolution in Africa*. New York: Academic Press.

Kinnaird, M. F. and O'Brien, T. G. (1996). Ecotourism in the Tangkoko Nature Reserve: opening Pandora's box. *Oryx*, **30**, 65–70.

Kirkpatrick, J. B. (1983). An iterative method for establishing priorities for the selection of nature reserves: an example from Tasmania. *Biological Conservation*, **25**, 127–134.

Kituyi, M. (1990). *Becoming Kenyans: Socioeconomic Transformation of the Pastoral Maasai*. Nairobi: ACTS Press.

Kleiman, D. G. (1989). Reintroduction of captive mammals for conservation. *Bioscience*, **39**, 152–161.

Kleiman, D. G., Beck, B. B, Dietz, J. M. and Dietz, L. A. (1991). Costs of a reintroduction and criteria for success: accounting and accountability in the Golden Lion Tamarin Conservation Program. In *Beyond Captive Breeding. Reintroducing Endangered Mammals to the Wild*, ed. J. H. W. Gipps, pp. 125–142. Oxford: Clarendon Press.

Kleiman, D. G., Dietz, J .M., Baker, A. J., French, J., Rambaldi, D., Dietz, L. A. and Montali, D. (1990). Golden lion tamarin working group. In *Population Viability*

Analysis Workshop Report, eds U.S. Seal, J. D. Ballou and C. Valladares-Padua, pp. 17–21. Apple Valley: IUCN Species Survival Commission and Captive Breeding Specialist Group.

Kleiman, D. G. and Mallinson, J. J. C. (1998). Recovery and management committees for lion tamarins: Partnerships in conservation planning and implementation. *Conservation Biology,* 12, 27–38.

Kleiman, D. G., Stanley Price, M. R. and Beck, B. B. (1994). Criteria for reintroductions. In *Creative Conservation: Interactive Management of Wild and Captive Animals,* eds P. J. S. Olney, G. M. Mace and A. T. C. Feistner, pp. 287–303. London: Chapman and Hall.

Koch, E. (1994). *Ecotourism: a Tool for Rural Reconstruction in South Africa.* Geneva: United Nations Research Institute for Social Development.

Kramer, R. A. and van Schaik, C. P. (1997). Preservation paradigms and tropical rain forests. In *Last Stand. Protected Areas and the Defense of Tropical Biodiversity,* eds R. Kramer, C. van Schaik and J. Johnson, pp. 3–14. New York: Oxford University Press.

Kutilek, M. J. (1974). The density and biomass of large mammals in Lake Nakuru National Park. *East African Wildlife Journal,* 12, 201–212.

Lacy, R. (1993). VORTEX: A computer simulation model for population viability analysis. *Wildlife Research,* 20, 45–65.

Lambeck, R. J. (1997). Focal species: a multi-species umbrella for nature conservation. *Conservation Biology,* 11, 849–856.

Laurance, W. F. (1991). Ecological correlates of extinction proneness in Australian tropical rain forest mammals. *Conservation Biology,* 5, 79–89.

Laurance, W. F. (1994). Rainforest fragmentation and the structure of small mammal communities in tropical Queensland. *Biological Conservation,* 69, 23–32.

Laurance, W. F. and Yensen, E. (1990). Predicting the impacts of edge effects in fragmented habitats. *Biological Conservation,* 55, 77–92.

Lavers, C. P., Haines-Young, R. H. and Avery, M. I. (1996). The habitat associations of dunlin (*Calidris alpina*) in the Flow Country of northern Scotland, and an improved model for predicting habitat quality. *Journal of Applied Ecology,* 33, 279–290.

Laws, R. M., Parker I. S. C. and Johnstone R. C. B. (1975). *Elephants and their Habitats. The Ecology of Elephants in Northern Bunyoro, Uganda.* Oxford: Clarendon Press.

Lawton, J. H. (1994). Population dynamic principles. *Philosophical Transactions of the Royal Society of London, Series B,* 344, 61–68.

Lawton, J. H. (1995). Population dynamic principles. In *Extinction Rates,* eds J. H. Lawton and R. M. May, pp. 147–163. Oxford: Oxford University Press.

Lawton, J. H. and May, R. M. (eds) (1995). *Extinction Rates.* Oxford: Oxford University Press.

Leader-Williams, N. (1988). Patterns of depletion in a black rhinoceros population in Luangwa Valley, Zambia. *African Journal of Ecology,* 26, 181–187.

Leader-Williams, N. (1990). Black rhinos and African elephants: lessons for conservation funding. *Oryx,* 24, 23–29.

Leader-Williams, N., Albon, S. D. and Berry, P. S. (1990a). Illegal exploitation of black rhinoceros and elephant populations: patterns of decline, law enforcement, and patrol effort in Luangwa Valley, Zambia. *Journal of Applied Ecology,* 27, 1055–1087.

Leader-Williams, N., Harrison, J. and Green, M. J. B. (1990b). Designing protected areas to conserve natural resources. *Science Progress*, **74**, 189–204.

Leaper, R., Massel, G., Gorman, M. L. and Aspinall, R. (1999). The feasibility of reintroducing wild boar (*Sus scrofa*) to Scotland. *Mammal Review*, **29**, 239–259.

Leighton, M. and Leighton, D. R. (1983). Vertebrate responses to fruiting seasonality within a Bornean rain forest. In *Tropical Rain Forest: Ecology and Management*, eds S. L. Sutton, T. C. Whitmore and A. C. Chadwich, pp. 181–196. Oxford: Blackwell Scientific Publications.

Leuthold, W. and Leuthold, B. M. (1976). Density and biomass of ungulates in Tsavo East National Park, Kenya. *East African Wildlife Journal*, **14**, 49–58.

Lever, C. (1992). *They Dined on Eland – The Story of the Acclimatisation Societies*. London: Quiller Press.

Lidicker, W. Z. (1989). *Rodents. A World Survey of Species of Conservation Concern*. Gland: IUCN.

Liman, P. D. (1996). *Ecotourism Development in Siberut National Park: a Case Study of Ecotourism Potential in Siberut National Park*. MSc thesis. Canterbury: University of Kent.

Lindberg, K. and Hawkins, D. E. (1993). *Ecotourism: a Guide for Planners and Managers*. Vermont: Ecotourism Society.

Lindsay, W. K. (1987). Integrating parks and pastoralists: some lessons from Amboseli. In *Conservation in Africa*, eds D. Anderson and R. Groves, pp. 149–167. Cambridge: Cambridge University Press.

Lombard, A. T. (1995). The problems with multi-species conservation: do hotspots, ideal reserves and existing reserves coincide? *South African Journal of Zoology*, **30**, 145–164.

Lott, D. F. and McCoy, M. (1995). Asian rhinos (*Rhinoceros unicornis*) on the run? Impact of tourists on one population. *Biological Conservation*, **73**, 23–36.

Lovejoy, T., Bierregard, R. O., Rankin, J. and Schubart, H. O. R. (1983). Ecological dynamics of tropical forest fragments. In *Tropical Rain Forest Ecology and Management*, eds S. L. Sutton, T. C. Whitmore and A. C. Chadwick, pp 377–386. Oxford: Blackwell Scientific Publications.

Lovett, J. C. (1993). Eastern arc moist forest flora. In *Biogeography and Ecology of the Rain Forests of Eastern Africa*, eds J. C. Lovett and S. K. Wasser, pp. 33–55. Cambridge: Cambridge University Press.

Lu Zhi (1991). *The Movement Pattern, Population Dynamics and Social Behaviour of the Giant Panda in Qinling*. PhD thesis. Beijing: Peking University (in Chinese).

Lu Zhi (1992). Huzi grow up. *International Wildlife*, **March–April**, 42–50.

Lu Zhi (1993). Newborn panda in the wild. *National Geographic*, **183**, 60–65.

Lu Zhi, Pan Wenshi and Harkness, J. (1994). Mother-cub relationship in the giant panda in Qinling Mountains – comments to rescuing abandoned cubs. *Zoo Biology*, **187**, 157–158.

Lyster, S. (1985). *International Wildlife Law*. Cambridge: Grotius Publications.

MacArthur, R. H. and Wilson, E. O. (1967). *The Theory of Island Biogeography*. Princeton: Princeton University Press.

Macdonald, D. W. and Johnson, P. J. (1998). Monitoring deer; opportunities within a national mammal monitoring network. In *Population Ecology, Management and Welfare of Deer*, eds. C. R. Goldspink, S. King and R. Putman, pp. 8–18. UFAW.

Macdonald, D. W. and Johnson, P. J. (in press). Farmers and the custody of the countryside: trends in habitat destruction. *Journal of Conservation Biology.*

Macdonald, D. W., Mace, G. M. and Barreto, G. R. (1999a). The effects of predators on fragmented prey populations: a case study for the conservation of endangered prey. *Journal of Zoology*, **247**, 487–506.

Macdonald, D. W., Rushton, S. P., Bryce, J. and Johnson, P. J. (1999b). Monitoring squirrels: opportunities within a National Mammal Network. In *3rd NPI Red Alert U.K. Forum for Red Squirrel Conservation*, eds L. M. Collins and M. D. Cooper, pp. 19–43. Forum proceedings. Perth: Scottish Natural Heritage.

Macdonald, D. W., Rushton, S. and Mace, G. (1998a). *Proposals for Future Monitoring of British Mammals.* London: Department of Environment, Transport and the Regions.

Macdonald, D. W., Rushton, S. and Mace, G. (1998b). *Proposals for Future Monitoring of British Mammals: An Overview.* London: Department of Environment, Transport and the Regions.

Macdonald, D. W. and Smith, H. (1991). New perspectives on agro-ecology: between theory and practice in the agricultural ecosystem. In *The Ecology of Temperate Cereal Fields (32nd Symposium of the British Ecological Society)*, eds L. Firbank, N. Carter, J. F. Darbyshire and G. R. Potts, pp. 413–448. Oxford: Blackwell Scientific Publications.

Macdonald, D. W. and Strachan, R. (1999). *The Mink and the Water Vole: Analyses for Conservation.* Oxford: Wildlife Conservation Research Unit.

Macdonald, D. W. and Tattersall, F. H. (1999). Beavers in Britain: planning reintroduction. In *Beaver Utilisation and Management*, ed. P. Busher, pp. 77–102. Oxford: Blackwell Science.

Macdonald, D. W., Tattersall, F. H., Brown, E. D. and Balharry, D. (1995). Reintroducing the European beaver to Britain: nostalgic meddling or restoring biodiversity. *Mammal Review*, **25**, 161–200.

Macdonald, D. W., Tattersall, F., Rushton, S. and Maitland, P. (in press). Reintroducing the beaver (*Castor fiber*) to Scotland: a protocol for identifying and assessing suitable release sites. *Animal Conservation.*

Mace, G. M. (1994). Classifying threatened species: means and ends. *Philosophical Transactions of the Royal Society of London, Series B*, **344**, 91–97.

Mace, G. M. and Lande, R. (1991) Assessing extinction threats: toward a re-evaluation of IUCN threatened species categories. *Conservation Biology*, **5**, 148–157.

Mack, A. L. (1993). The sizes of vertebrate-dispersed fruits: a Neotropical–Paleotropical comparison. *American Naturalist*, **142**, 840–856.

MacKinnon, J. (1997). *Protected Areas Systems Review of the Indomalayan Realm.* Canterbury: Asian Bureau for Conservation, World Conservation Monitoring Centre and The World Bank.

MacKinnon, J. and MacKinnon, K. (1986a). *Review of the Protected Areas System in the Afrotropical Realm.* Cambridge: IUCN/ United Nations Environment Programme.

MacKinnon, J. and MacKinnon, K. (1986b). *Review of the Protected Areas System in the Indo-Malayan Realm.* Cambridge: IUCN/ United Nations Environment Programme.

MacKinnon J., MacKinnon K., Child, G. and Thorsell, J. (1986). *Managing Protected Areas in the Tropics.* Cambridge: IUCN.

MacKinnon, J. and Stuart, S. N. (1989). *The Kouprey. An Action Plan for its Conservation*. Gland: IUCN.

MacKinnon, K. (1978). Competition between red and grey squirrels. *Mammal Review*, **8**, 185–190.

MacKinnon, K. (1997). The ecological foundations of biodiversity protection. In *Last Stand: Protected Areas and the Defense of Tropical Biodiversity*, eds R. Kramer, C. van Schaik and J. Johnson, pp. 36–63. Oxford: Oxford University Press.

MacKinnon, K., Hatta, G., Halim, H. and Mangalik, A. (1996). *The Ecology of Kalimantan*. Singapore: Periplus.

MacKinnon, K. and MacKinnon, J. (1991). Habitat protection and reintroduction programmes. In *Beyond Captive Breeding. Reintroducing Endangered Mammals to the Wild*, ed. J. H. W. Gipps, pp. 173–198. Oxford: Clarendon Press.

MacKinnon, K., Mishra, H. and Mott, J. (1999). Reconciling the needs of conservation and local communities: the GEF approach to tiger conservation in India. In *Riding the Tiger: Tiger Conservation in Human-dominated Landscapes*, eds. J. Seidensticker, P. Jackson and S. Christie, pp. 307–315. Cambridge: Cambridge University Press.

MAFF (Ministry of Agriculture, Fisheries and Food) (1998). *Current Status and Potential Impact of Wild Boar* (Sus scrofa) *in the English Countryside*. London: MAFF.

Mafuru, N. N. (1997). *Evaluating the Promotion of Tanzania's National Parks and Game Reserves in the United Kingdom*. MSc thesis. Canterbury: University of Kent.

Magin, C. (1996). *Hirola Recovery Plan*. IUCN Antelope Specialist Group in collaboration with the Kenya Wildlife Service. Gland: IUCN.

Magin, C. D., Johnson, T. H., Groombridge, B., Jenkins, M. and Smith, H. (1994). Species extinctions, endangerment and captive breeding. In *Creative Conservation: Interactive Management of Wild and Captive Animals*, eds P. J. S. Olney, G. M. Mace and A. T. C. Feistner, pp. 3–31. London: Chapman and Hall.

Main, M. (1987). *Kalahari: Life's Variety in Dune and Delta*. Johannesburg: Southern Book Publishers.

Mallinson, J. J. C. (1971). The pigmy hog *Sus salvanius* (Hodgson) in northern Assam. *Journal of the Bombay Natural History Society*, **68**, 424–433.

Mallinson, J. J. C. (1991). Partnerships for conservation between zoos, local governments and non-governmental organizations. In *Beyond Captive Breeding: Reintroducing Endangered Mammals to the Wild*, ed. J. H. W. Gipps, pp. 59–74. Oxford: Clarendon Press.

Mallinson, J. J. C. (1997). A case study: partnerships and conservation initiatives resulting from a Population Viability Assessment (PVA) Workshop for the genus *Leontopithecus*. *Der Zoologischer Garten* **67**, 6.

Manne, L. L., Brooks, T. M. and Pimm, S. L. (1999). Relative risk of extinction of passerine birds on continents and islands. *Nature*, **388**, 258–261.

Mansour, J., Redford, K. and Ostria, M. (1995). *Parks in Peril Source Book*. Arlington: The Nature Conservancy.

Margules, C. R., Nicholls, A. O. and Pressey, R. L. (1988). Selecting networks of reserves to maximise biological diversity. *Biological Conservation*, **43**, 63–76.

Marsh, J. (1991). *Tourism in Antarctica and its Implications for Conservation*. Report to Fourth World Congress on Parks and Protected Areas.

Marshall, A. G. (1983). Bats, flowering and fruit: evolutionary relationships in the Old World. *Biological Journal of the Linnean Society*, **20**, 115–135.

Martin, P. and Klein, R. G. (eds) (1984). *Quaternary Extinctions: A Prehistoric Revolution*. Tuscon: University of Arizona Press.

May, R. M. (1994). The effects of spatial scale on ecological questions and answers. In *Large-scale Ecology and Conservation Biology*, eds P. J. Edwards, R. M. May and N. R. Webb, pp. 1–17. Oxford: Blackwell Science.

McCullough, D. (1987). The theory and management of *Odocoileus* populations. In *Biology and Management of the Cervidae*, ed. C. Wemmer, pp. 535–549. Washington, DC: Smithsonian Institution Press.

McCullough, D. (1996). Spatially structured populations and harvest theory. *Journal of Wildlife Management*, **60**, 1–9.

McDowall, R. M. (1969). Extinction and endemism in New Zealand land birds. *Tuatara*, **17**, 1–12.

McDowell, D. (1996). *World Conservation Congress Breaks the Silence of Rio*. Press Release. Gland: IUCN.

McEvedy, C. and Jones, R. (1978). *Atlas of World Population History*. London: Allen Lane.

McIvor, C. (1994). *Management of Wildlife, Tourism and Local Communities in Zimbabwe*. Report to United Nations Research Institute for Social Development.

McKinney, M. L. (1998). Branching models predict the loss of many bird and mammal orders within centuries. *Animal Conservation*, **1**, 159–164.

McNaughton, S. J. (1979). Grazing as an optimization process: grass–ungulate relationships in the Serengeti. *American Naturalist*, **113**, 691.

McNeely, J. A. (1988). *Economics and Biological Diversity: Developing and Using Economic Incentives to Conserve Biological Resources*. Gland: IUCN.

McNeely, J. A. (1994). Lessons from the past: forests and biodiversity. *Biodiversity and Conservation*, **3**, 3–20.

McNeely, J. A. (1999). *Mobilizing Broader Support for Asia's Biodiversity: How Civil Society Can Contribute to Protected Area Management*. Manila: Asian Development Bank.

McNeely, J., Harrison, J. and Dingwall, P. (eds) (1994a). *Protecting Nature: Regional Reviews of Protected Areas*. Cambridge: IUCN.

McNeely, J., Harrison, J. and Dingwall, P. (1994b). Protected areas in the modern world. In *Protecting Nature: Regional Reviews of Protected Areas*, eds J. A. McNeely, J. Harrison and P. Dingwall, pp. 5–28. Cambridge: IUCN.

McNeely, J., Miller, K. R., Reid, V. W., Mittermeier, R. A. and Werner, T. B. (1990). *Conserving the World's Biodiversity*. Gland: IUCN.

Mech, L. D. (1970). *The Wolf: The Ecology and Behaviour of an Endangered Species*. New York: Natural History Press.

Mech, L. D. (1966). The wolves of Isle Royale. *Fauna of the National Parks of the United States*, **7**, 1–210.

Meester, J. (1965). The origins of the southern African mammal fauna. *Zoologica Africana*, **1**, 87–95.

Meester, J. and Setzer, H. W. (eds) (1975). *The Mammals of Africa: an Identification Manual*. Washington, DC: Smithsonian Institution Press.

Meffe, G. K. and Carroll, C. R. (1997). *Principles of Conservation Biology*. Sunderland: Sinauer Associates.

Mellon, J. (1975). *African Hunter*. Long Beach: Safari Press.

Mestel, R. (1997). Noah's Flood. *New Scientist*, **156**, 24–27.

Metrick, A. and Weitzman, M. L. (1998). Conflicts and choices in biodiversity conservation. *Journal of Economic Perspectives*, **12**, 21–34.

Mickleburgh, S. (1997). *The 100% Fund 1971–96*. Report to Fauna & Flora International.

Mickleburgh, S. P., Hutson, A. M. and Racey, P. A. (eds) (1992). *Old World Fruit Bats: An Action Plan for their Conservation*. Gland: IUCN.

Miller, M. F. (1995). *Acacia* seed survival, seed germination and seedling growth following pod consumption by large herbivores and seed chewing by rodents. *African Journal of Ecology*, **33**, 194–210.

Mills, L. S. (1995). Edge effects and isolation: red-backed voles on forest remnants. *Conservation Biology*, **9**, 395–403.

Mills, M. G. L. (1991). Conservation management of large carnivores in Africa. *Koedoe*, **34**, 81–92.

Mills, M. G. L., Ellis, S., Woodroffe, R., Maddock, A., Stander, P., Rasmussen, G., Pole, A., Fletcher, P., Bruford, M., Wildt, D., Macdonald, D. W. and Seal, U. (eds) (1998). *Population and Habitat Viability Assessment for the African Wild Dog* (Lycaon pictus) *in Southern Africa*. Final Workshop Report. Apple Valley: IUCN/SSC Conservation Breeding Specialist Group.

Mills, M. G. L. and Haagner, C. (1989). *Guide to the Kalahari Gemsbok National Park*. Johannesburg: Southern Book Publishers.

Milner-Gulland, E. J. and Mace, R. (1998). *Conservation of Biological Resources*. Oxford: Blackwell Science.

Mink, S. (1993). Poverty and the environment. *Finance and Development*, **30**, 8–9.

Miquelle, D. G., Smirnov, E. N., Merrill, T. W., Myslenkov, A. E., Quigley, H. B., Hornocker, M. G. and Schleyer, B. (1999). Hierarchial spatial analysis of Amur tiger relationships to habitat and prey. In *Riding the Tiger: Tiger Conservation in Human-dominated Landscapes*, eds J. Seidensticker, P. Jackson and S. Christie, pp. 71–99. Cambridge: Cambridge University Press.

Mitchell-Jones, A. J. (1990). The distribution of bats in Britain 1982–87 as revealed by enquiries. *Mammal Review*, **20**, 145–157.

Mitchell-Jones, A. J. (1995). The status and conservation of horseshoe bats in Britain. *Myotis*, **32**, 271–284.

Mitchell-Jones, A. J., Cooke, A. S., Boyd, I. L. and Stebbings, R. E. (1989). Bats and remedial timber treatment chemicals – a review. *Mammal Review* **19**, 93–110.

Mitchell-Jones, A. J., Hutson, A. M. and Racey, P. A. (1993). The growth and development of bat conservation in Britain. *Mammal Review*, **23**, 139–148.

Mitchell-Jones, A. J., Jefferies, D. J., Stebbings, R. E. and Arnold, H. R. (1986). Public concern about bats (Chiroptera) in Britain – an analysis of enquiries in 1982–83. *Biological Conservation*, **36**, 315–328.

Mittermeier, R. A. (1986). Primate conservation priorities in the Neotropical region. In *Primates: The Road to Self-sustaining Populations*, ed. K. Benirschke, pp. 221–240. New York: Springer-Verlag.

Mittermeier, R. A. (1988). Primate diversity and the tropical forest. In *Biodiversity*, ed. E. O. Wilson, pp. 145–154. Washington, DC: National Academy Press.

Mittermeier, R. A., Bowles, I. A., Cavalcanti, R. B., Olivieri, S. and da Fonseca, A. B.

(1994a). *A Participatory Approach to Biodiversity Conservation: The Regional Priority Setting Workshop*. Washington, DC: Conservation International.

Mittermeier, R. A., Konstant, W. R., Nicoll, M. E. and Langrand, O. (1993). *Lemurs of Madagascar. An Action Plan for their Conservation*. Gland: IUCN.

Mittermeier, R. A., Myers, N., Thomsen, J. B., da Fonseca, G. A. B. and Olivieri, S. (1998). Global biodiversity hotspots and major tropical wilderness areas. *Conservation Biology*, **12**, 516–520.

Mittermeier, R. A., Tattersall, I., Konstant, W. R., Meyers, D. M. and Mast, R. B. (1994b). *Lemurs of Madagascar*. Washington, DC: Conservation International.

MoF and WWF (Ministry of Forestry for China and World Wildlife Fund) (1989). *The National Management Plan of the Giant Panda and Its Habitat*. China: Ministry of Forestry for China and WWF.

Mooney, H. A., Lubchenco, J., Dirzo, R. and Sala, O. E. (1995). Biodiversity and ecosystem functioning: basic principles. In *Global Biodiversity Assessment*, ed. V. H. Heywood, pp. 327–452. Cambridge: Cambridge University Press.

Morris, D. J. (1960). An analysis of animal popularity. *International Zoo Yearbook*, **2**, 60–61.

Morris, P. A. (1986). An introduction to reintroductions. *Mammal Review*, **16**, 49–52.

Moss, C. (1988). *Elephant Memories. Thirteen Years in the Life of an Elephant Family*. New York: William Morrow and Company.

Moss, C. (1994). Some reproductive parameters in a population of African elephants, *Loxodonta africana*. In *Proceedings of the Second International National Center for Research in Reproduction Conference on 'Advances in Reproductive Research in Man and Animals'*, ed. C. S. Bambra, pp. 284–292. Nairobi: The Institute of Primate Research and National Museums of Kenya.

Mountain, A. (1990). *Paradise Under Pressure: St Lucia, Kosi Bay, Sodwana, Lake Sibaya, Maputaland*. Johannesburg: Southern Book Publishers.

Mulder, J. L. (1990). The stoat *Mustela erminea* in the Dutch dune region, its local extinction, and a possible cause: the arrival of the fox *Vulpes vulpes*. *Lutra*, **33**, 1–21.

Murphy, P. E. (1985). *Tourism: a Community Approach*. New York: Methuen.

Muthee, L. W. (1992). Ecological impacts of tourist use on habitats and pressure-point animal species. In *Tourist Attitudes and Use Impacts in Masai Mara National Reserve*, ed. G. C. Gakahu, pp. 18–38. Nairobi: Wildlife Conservation International.

Mutschler, T. (1997). Field studies of the Alaotran gentle lemur *Hapalemur griseus alaotrensis*: an update. In *International Studbook for the Alaotran Gentle Lemur Hapalemur griseus alaotrensis Number One 1985–1996*, eds A. T. C. Feistner and J. C. Beattie, pp. 12–18. Jersey: Jersey Wildlife Preservation Trust.

Mutschler, T. (1998). *The Alaotran Gentle Lemur* (Hapalemur griseus alaotrensis): *A Study in Behavioural Ecology*. PhD thesis. Zürich: University of Zürich.

Mutschler, T. and Feistner, A. T. C. (1995). Conservation status and distribution of the Alaotran gentle lemur *Hapalemur griseus alaotrensis*. *Oryx*, **29**, 267–274.

Mutschler, T. Feistner, A. T. C. and Nievergelt, C. (1998). Preliminary field data on group size, diet and activity in the Alaotran gentle lemur *Hapalemur griseus alaotrensis*. *Folia Primatologica*, **69**, 325–330.

Mutschler, T., Nievergelt, C. and Feistner, A. T. C. (1995). Human-induced loss of habitat at Lac Alaotra and its effect on the Alaotran gentle lemur. In *Environmental Change in Madagascar*, eds B. D. Patterson, S. M. Goodman and J. L. Sedlock, pp. 35–36. Chicago: The Field Museum.

Mwenya, L. (1996). *Nature Tourism Potential in Kafue National Park, Zambia*. MSc thesis. Canterbury: University of Kent.

Myers, N. (1972). National parks in savannah Africa. *Science*, 178, 1255–1263.

Myers, N. (1987). The extinction spasm impending: synergisms at work. *Conservation Biology*, 1, 14–21.

Myers, N. (1988). Threatened biotas: 'hot spots' in tropical forests. *Environmentalist*, 8, 187–208.

Myers, N. (1990). The biodiversity challenge: expanded hot-spots analysis. *Environmentalist*, 10, 243–256.

Nagy, K. A. (1987). Field metabolic rate and food requirement scaling in mammals and birds. *Ecological Monographs*, 57, 111–128.

NPB (National Parks Board) (1996). *Richtersveld National Park. Proposal/Nomination. A World Heritage Site*. Pretoria: National Parks Board.

NPB (South Africa) and DWNP (Botswana) (National Parks Board (South Africa) and Department of Wildlife and National Parks (Botswana)) (1997). *Kalahari Transfrontier Park Management Plan*. South Africa: National Parks Board and Botswana: Department of Wildlife and National Parks.

Nee, S. and May, R. M. (1997). Extinction and the loss of evolutionary history. *Science*, 278, 692–693.

Neilson, A. L. and Fenton, M. B. (1994). Responses of little brown myotis to exclusion and to bat houses. *Wildlife Society Bulletin*, 22, 8–14.

Nel, M. (1996). Kruger land claim. South Africa's premier national park faces a major challenge. *African Wildlife*, 50, 6–7.

Nelson, B. W., Ferreira, C. A. C., da Silva, M. F. and Kawasaki, M. L. (1990). Endemism centres, refugia and botanical collection density in Brazilian Amazonia. *Nature*, 345, 714–716.

Neves, A. M. S. and Rylands, A. B. (1991). Diet of a group of howling monkeys, *Alouatta seniculus*, in an isolated forest patch in Central Amazonia. In *A Primatologia no Brasil*, eds A. B. Rylands and A. T. Bernades, pp. 263–274. Volume 3. Belo Horizonte: Sociedade Brasileira de Primatologia.

New, T. R., Pyle, R. M., Thomas, J. A., Thomas, C. D. and Hammond, P.C. (1995). Butterfly conservation management. *Annual Review of Entomology*, 40, 57–83.

Newlands, W. (1997). All creatures, great, small and deadly. *The Sunday Times*, 19 January 1997, 1–19.

Newmark, W. D. (1995). Extinction of mammal populations in western North American National Parks. *Conservation Biology*, 9, 512–526.

Newton, I. and Wyllie, I. (1992). Recovery of a sparrowhawk population in relation to declining pesticide contamination. *Journal of Applied Ecology*, 29, 476–484.

Nicoll, M. E., Rakotondraparany, F. and Randrianasolo, V. (1988). Diversité des petits mammifères en forêt tropicale humide de Madagascar: analyse préliminaire. In *L'Equilibre des Ecosystèmes forestiers à Madagascar: actres d'un Séminaire International*, pp. 241–252. Gland: IUCN.

Nicoll, M. E. and Rathbun, G. B. (1990). *African Insectivora and Elephant-shrews. An Action Plan for their Conservation*. Gland: IUCN.

Nievergelt, C., Mutschler, T. and Feistner, A. T. C. (1998). Group encounters and territoriality in wild Alaotran gentle lemurs (*Hapalemur griseus alaotrensis*). *American Journal of Primatology*, **46**, 251–258.

Njiforti, H. L. (1996). Preferences and present demand for bushmeat in north Cameroon: some implications for wildlife conservation. *Environmental Conservation*, **23**, 149–155.

Norberg, U. M. and Rayner, J. M. V. (1987). Ecological morphology and flight in bats (Mammalia; Chiroptera): wing adaption, flight performance, foraging strategies and echolocation. *Philosophical Transactions of the Royal Society of London, Series B*, **316**, 335–427.

Norton, B. G. (1986). *The Preservation of Species*. Princeton: Princeton University Press.

Norton-Griffiths, M. (1978). *Counting Animals*. 2nd edition. Nairobi: Serengeti Ecological Monitoring Programme, African Wildlife Foundation.

Noss, R. F. (1987). Corridors in real landscapes: a reply to Simberloff and Cox. *Conservation Biology*, **1**, 159–164.

Noss, R. and Cooperrider, A. (1994). *Saving Nature's Legacy: Protecting and Restoring Biodiversity*. Washington, DC: Island Press.

Nowak, R. M and Paradiso, J. L. (1983). *Walker's Mammals of the World*. 4th edition. Baltimore: John Hopkins University Press.

Nowell, K. and Jackson, P. (eds) (1996). *Wild Cats. Status Survey and Conservation Action Plan*. Gland: IUCN.

Oates, J. F. (1986). *Action Plan for African Primate Conservation: 1986–1990*. Gland: IUCN.

Oates, J. F. (1996). *African Primates. Status Survey and Conservation Action Plan*. Revised edition. Gland: IUCN.

O'Brien, P. H. (1985). The impact of feral pigs on livestock production and recent developments in control. *Proceedings of the Australian Society of Animal Production*, **16**, 78–82.

O'Callaghan, J. R. (1996). *Land Use. The Interaction of Economics, Ecology and Hydrology*. London: Chapman and Hall.

O'Connell, M. J., Daniell, J. R. G., Dunstone, N. and Huntley, B. (submitted a). The potential impact of global climate change upon forest ecosystems of the Russian Far East. 1. Vegetation changes.

O'Connell, M. J., Daniell, J. R. G., Dunstone, N. and Huntley, B. (submitted b). The potential impact of global climate change upon forest ecosystems of the Russian Far East. 2. Changes in the distribution of the Amur tiger *Panthera tigris altaica*.

Okubo, A., Maini, P. K., Williamson, M. H. and Murray, J. D. (1989). On the spatial spread of the grey squirrel in Britain. *Proceedings of the Royal Society of London, Series B*, **238**, 113–125.

Oliver, W. L. R. (1980). *The Biology and Conservation of the Pigmy Hog Sus (Porcula) salvanius and the Hispid Hare Caprolagus hispidus*. Special Scientific Report No. 1. Jersey: Jersey Wildlife Preservation Trust.

Oliver, W. L. R. (ed.) (1993). *Pigs, Peccaries and Hippos. Status Survey and Conservation Action Plan*. Gland: IUCN.

Oliver, W. L. R. and Narayan, G. (1996). *Pigmy hog (Sus salvanius) Conservation Programme. First Annual Report*. Unpublished report to the Jersey Wildlife Preservation Trust.

Oliver, W. L. R., Narayan, G. and Manideep, R. A. J. (1997). The pigmy hog *Sus salvanius* conservation programme: background description and report on progress to 31st December, 1996. *Dodo, Journal of the Wildlife Preservation Trusts*, **33**, 45–71.

Olney, P. J. S., Mace, G. M. and Feistner, A. T. C. (eds) (1994). *Creative Conservation: Interactive Management of Wild and Captive Animals.* London: Chapman and Hall.

Olson, S. L. and James, H. F. (1982). Prodromus of the fossil avifauna of the Hawaiian islands. *Smithsonian Contributions to Zoology*, **365**, 1–59.

Orams, M. B. (1995). Towards a more desirable form of ecotourism. *Tourism Management*, **16**, 3–8.

Ostrowski, S., Bedin, E., Lenain, D. M. and Abuzinada, A. H. (1998). Ten years of Arabian oryx conservation breeding in Saudi Arabia: achievements and regional perspectives. *Oryx*, **32**, 209–222.

Owen-Smith, N. (1989). Megafaunal extinctions: the conservation message from 11 000 years B.P. *Conservation Biology*, **3**, 405–412.

Ozanne, C. M. P., Foggo, A., Hambler, C. and Speight, M. R. (1997). The significance of edge-effects in the management of forests for invertebrate biodiversity. In *Canopy Arthropods*, eds N. Stork, J. Adis and R. Didham, pp. 534–550. London: Chapman and Hall.

Padoch, C. (1988). People of the floodplain and forest. In *People of the Tropical Rain Forest*, eds J. S. Denslow and C. Padoch, pp. 127–140. Los Angeles: University of California Press.

Paine, R. T. (1995). A conversation on refining the concept of keystone species. *Conservation Biology*, **9**, 962–964.

Pan Wenshi (1995). New hope for China's pandas. *National Geographic*, **187**, 100–115.

Pan Wenshi *et al.* (in press). Ecology and behaviour of the giant pandas in Qinling, with comments to captive panda reintroduction. In *Workshop on Giant Panda Reintroduction*, eds S. Mainka and Lu Zhi. Beijing: China Forestry Press.

Pan Wenshi, Gao Zhengsheng, Lu Zhi, Xia Zhengkai, Zhang Miaodi, Ma Lailing, Meng Guangli, Zhe Xiaoye, Liu Xuzhuo, Cui Haiting and Chen Hengxiang (1988). *The Giant Panda's Natural Refuge in Qinling.* Beijing: Peking University Press. (in Chinese).

PAWN (Planning and Assessment for Wildlife Management) (1995). The structure of Tanzania's tourist hunting industry. In *Tourist Hunting in Tanzania*, eds N. Leader-Williams, J. A. Kayera and G. L. Overton, pp. 19–29. Occasional paper of the IUCN Species Survival Commission No. 14. Gland: IUCN.

Pearce, D. G. (1981). *Tourist Development.* London: Longman.

Pearce, D. G. (1994). Alternative tourism: concepts, classifications and questions. In *Tourism Alternatives: Potentials and Problems in the Development of Tourism*, eds V. S. Smith and W. R. Eadington, pp. 15–30. Chichester: John Wiley & Sons.

Pearce, D., Barbier, E. and Markandya, A. (1990). *Sustainable Development: Economics and Environment in The Third World.* London: Edward Elgar Ltd.

Pearce, D. and Moran, D. (1994). *The Economic Value of Biodiversity.* London: Earthscan and IUCN.

Perlman, D. L. and Adelson, G. (1997). *Biodiversity: Exploring Values and Priorities in Conservation.* Malden: Blackwells.

Peters, P. (1996). Who's local here?: The politics of participation in development. *Cultural Survival Quarterly*, **Fall**, 22–25.

Peters, R. L. and Lovejoy, T. E. (1992) *Global Warming and Biological Diversity*. London: Yale University Press.

Peterson, R. O. and Page, R. E. (1988). The rise and fall of the Isle Royale wolves. *Journal of Mammalogy*, **69**, 89–99.

Petocz, R. and de Fretes, Y. (1983). *Mammals of the Reserves of Irian Jaya*. Jayapura: WWF/IUCN.

Petri, B., Pääbo, S., Von Haeseler, A. and Tautz, D. (1997). Paternity assessment and population subdivision in a natural population of the larger mouse-eared bat *Myotis myotis*. *Molecular Ecology*, **6**, 235–242.

Pidgeon, M. (1996). *An Ecological Survey of Lake Alaotra and Selected Wetlands of Central and Eastern Madagascar in Analysing the Demise of Madagascar Pochard Aythya innotata*. Antananarivo: Missouri Botanical Gardens.

Piernaar, U. de V., van Wyk, P. and Fairall, N. (1966). An aerial census of elephant and buffalo in the Kruger National Park and the implications thereof on the intended management schemes. *Koedoe*, **9**, 40–107.

Pimlott, D. H. (1967). Wolf predation and ungulate populations. *American Zoologist*, **7**, 267–278.

Pimm, S. L. (1998). Extinctions. In *Conservation Science and Action*, ed. W. J. Sutherland, pp. 20–38. Oxford: Blackwell Science.

Pimm, S. L., Jones, H. L. and Diamond, J. (1988). On the risk of extinction. *American Naturalist*, **132**, 757–785.

Pimm, S. L., Russell, G. J., Gittleman, J. L. and Russell, T. M. (1995). The future of biodiversity. *Science*, **269**, 347–350.

Pinnock, D. (1996). Superparks. The impossible dream? *Getaway*, **8**, 88–97.

Pirie, F. (1996). *The Promotion of Zimbabwe's National Parks in the Brochures of UK Tour Operators*. MSc thesis. Canterbury: University of Kent.

Pleumarom, A. (1994). The political economy of tourism. *Ecologist*, **24**, 142–147.

Plowden, C. and Bowles, D. (1997). The illegal trade in tiger parts in northern Sumatra, Indonesia. *Oryx*, **31**, 59–66.

Poduschka, W. and Richard, B. (1986). The Pyrenean desman – an endangered insectivore. *Oryx*, **20**, 230–232.

Pomeroy, D. (1993). Centres of high biodiversity in Africa. *Conservation Biology*, **7**, 901–907.

Poole, J. H. and Thomson, J. B. (1989). Elephants are not beetles: implications of the ivory trade for the survival of the African elephant. *Oryx*, **23**, 188–198.

Posey, D. A. (1982). The keepers of the forest. *Garden*, **6**, 18–24.

Power, M. E. and Mills, L. S. (1995). The keystone cops meet in Hilo. *Trends in Ecology and Evolution*, **10**, 182–184.

Power, M. E., Tilman, D., Estes, J. A., Menge, B. A., Bond, W. J., Mills, L. S., Dally, G., Castilla, J. C., Lubchenco, J. and Paine, R. T. (1996). Challenges in the quest for keystones. *BioScience*, **46**, 609–620.

Powrie, L. W. (1992). How alert are those Richtersveld plants? *Veld and Flora*, **78**, 14–17.

Prance, G. (1997). A partnership agreement to generate innovative and practical responses to the problems of habitat destruction and species extinction. *Dodo, Journal of the Wildlife Preservation Trusts*, **33**, 14–19.

Prendergast, J., Quinn, R. M., Lawton, J. H., Eversham, B. C. and Gibbons, D. W. (1993). Rare species, the coincidence of diversity hotspots and conservation strategies. *Nature*, **365**, 335–337.

Pressey, R. L. (1994). Ad hoc reservations: forward or backward steps in developing representative reserve systems? *Conservation Biology*, **8**, 662–668.

Pressey, R. L., Humphries, C. J., Margules, C. R., Vane-Wright, R. I. and Williams P. H. (1993). Beyond opportunism: key principles for systematic reserve selection. *Trends in Ecology and Evolution*, **8**, 124–128.

Pressey, R. L., Possingham, H. P. and Margules, C. R. (1997). Optimality in reserve selection algorithms: when does it matter and how much? *Biological Conservation*, **76**, 259–267.

Pretty, J. N. (1994) Alternative systems of inquiry for sustainable agriculture. *IDS Bulletin*, **25**, 37–48. Institute of Development Studies, University of Sussex, UK.

Price, M. V. and Endo, P. R. (1989). Estimating the distribution and abundance of a cryptic species, *Dipodomys stephensi* (Rodentia: Heteromyidae), and its implications for management. *Conservation Biology*, **3**, 293–301.

Price, M. V. and Jenkins, S. H. (1986). Rodents as seed consumers and dispersers. In *Seed Dispersal*, ed. D. R. Murray, pp. 191–235. Australia: Academic Press.

Primack, R. B. (1993). *Essentials of Conservation Biology*. Sunderland: Sinauer Associates.

Primack, R. B. (1995). *Primer of Conservation Biology*. Sunderland: Sinauer Associates.

Primack, R. and Drayton, B. (1997). The experimental ecology of reintroduction. *PlantTalk*, **October 1997**, 25–28.

Prins, H. H. T. (1996). *Ecology and Behaviour of the African Buffalo*. London: Chapman and Hall.

Prins, H. H. T., van der Jeugd, H. P. and Beekman, J. H. (1994). Elephant decline in Lake Manyara National Park, Tanzania. *African Journal of Ecology*, **32**, 185–191.

Pulliam, H. R. (1988). Sources, sinks and population regulation. *American Naturalist*, **132**, 652–661.

Punt, A. (1970). Round table discussion on bat conservation – summary. *Bijdragen tot der Dierkunde*, **40**, 3–4.

Rabb, G. B. and Sullivan, T. A. (1995). Coordinating conservation: global networking for species survival. *Biodiversity and Conservation*, **4**, 536–543.

Racey, P. A. and Entwistle, A. C. (in press). Life history and reproductive strategies of bats. In *Biology of Bats IV*, eds P. H. Krutszch and E. Crichton. London: Academic Press.

Racey, P. A. and Stebbings, R. E. (1972). The status of bats in Britain: a report commissioned by The Fauna Preservation Society from the Mammal Society. *Oryx*, **11**, 319–327.

Racey, P. A. and Swift, S. M. (1985). Feeding ecology of *Pipistrellus pipistrellus* (Chiroptera: Vespertilionidae) during pregnancy and lactation. 1. Foraging behaviour. *Journal of Animal Ecology*, **54**, 205–215.

Racey, P. A. and Swift, S. M. (1986). Residual effects of remedial timber treatments on bats. *Biological Conservation*, **35**, 205–214.

Rackham, O. (1986). *The History of the Countryside*. London: Butler and Tanner Ltd.

Rahbek, C. (1993). Captive breeding – a useful tool in the preservation of biodiversity? *Biodiversity and Conservation*, **2**, 426–437.

Rakotoniaina, L. (1998). The role of community-based activities in the conservation of endangered animals in Madagascar. *Dodo, Journal of the Wildlife Preservation Trusts*, **34**, 174–175.

Ransome, R. D. (1996). *The Management of Feeding Areas for Greater Horseshoe Bats*. English Nature Research Report No. 174. Peterborough: English Nature.

Reaka-Kudla, M. L., Wilson, D. E. and Wilson, E. O. (1997). *Biodiversity II*. Washington, DC: Joseph Henry Press.

Reason, P. F. and Trewhella, W. J. (1994). The status of *Pteropus livingstonii* (Gray 1866) in the Comores. *Oryx*, **28**, 107–114.

Rebelo, A. G. (1992). Preservation of biotic diversity. In *The Ecology of Fynbos*, ed. R.M.Cowling, pp. 309–344. Cape Town: Oxford University Press.

Rebelo, A. G. and Siegfried, W. R. (1990). Where should nature reserves be located in the Cape Floristic Region, South Africa? Models for the spatial configuration of a reserve network aimed at maximising the protection of floral diversity. *Conservation Biology*, **6**, 243–252.

Redford, K. H. (1992). The empty forest. *Bioscience*, **4**, 412–422.

Redford, K. H. and Eisenberg, J. F. (1992). *Mammals of the Neotropics: The Southern Cone, Chile, Argentina, Uruguay, Paraguay*. Chicago: University of Chicago Press.

Redford, K. and Mansour, J. (1996). *Traditional Peoples and Biodiversity Conservation in Large Tropical Landscapes*. Arlington: The Nature Conservancy.

Redford, K. H. and Robinson, J. G. (1991). Park size and the conservation of forest mammals in Latin America. In *Latin American Mammalogy. History, Biodiversity and Conservation*, eds M. A. Mares and D. J. Schmidly, pp. 227–234. Oklahoma: Oklahoma Museum of Natural History.

Redmond, I. (1995) The ethics of eating ape. *BBC Wildlife Magazine*, **October 1995**, 72–74.

Reeves, R. R. and Leatherwood, S. (1994) *Dolphins, Porpoises and Whales: 1994–1998. Action Plan for the Conservation of Cetaceans*. Gland: IUCN.

Reijnders, P., Brasseur, S., van der Toorn, J., van der Wolf, P., Boyd, I., Harwood, J., Lavigne, D. and Lowry, L. (1993) *Seals, Fur Seals, Sea Lions, and Walrus. Status Survey and Conservation Action Plan*. Gland: IUCN.

Reynolds, J. C. (1985). Details of the geographic replacement of the red squirrel (*Sciurus vulgaris*) by the grey squirrel (*Sciurus carolinensis*) in eastern England. *Journal of Animal Ecology*, **54**, 149–162.

Risk and Policy Analysts Ltd. (1996). *The Conservation and Development Benefits of the Wildlife Trade*. Report to Wildlife and Countryside Directorate, Department of the Environment, London.

Robinson, G. A. (1992). *Elephant Conservation Plan for South Africa*. Pretoria: National Parks Board.

Robinson, G. A. (1995). *Dongola National Park. Towards Transfrontier Conservation in Southern Africa*. Pretoria: National Parks Board.

Robinson, J. and Bennett, E. (1999). *Hunting for Sustainability in Tropical Forests*. New York: Columbia University Press.

Robinson, J. G. and Redford, K. H. (1988). Body size, diet, and population density of Neotropical forest mammals. *American Naturalist*, **128**, 665–680.

Robinson, J. and Redford, K. (1991). Sustainable harvest of Neotropical forest mammals. In *Neotropical Wildlife Use and Conservation*, eds J. G. Robinson and K. H.

Redford, pp. 415–429. Chicago: University of Chicago Press.

Robinson, J. and Redford, K. (1994a). Community-based approaches to wildlife conservation in Neotropical forests. In *Natural Connections: Perspectives in Community-based Conservation*, eds D. Western and R. M. Wright, pp. 300–319. Washington, DC: Island Press.

Robinson, J. and Redford, K. (1994b). Measuring the sustainability of hunting in tropical forests. *Oryx*, **28**, 249–256.

Robinson, N. (1993). *Agenda 21: Earth's Action Plan*. New York: Oceana Publishers.

Rodgers, W. A. (1996). The miombo woodlands. In *East African Ecosystems and Their Conservation*, eds T. R. McClanahan and T. P. Young, pp. 299–325. New York: Oxford University Press.

Roe, D., Leader-Williams, N. and Dalal-Clayton, D. B. (1997). *Take Only Photographs, Leave Only Footprints: The Environmental Impacts of Wildlife Tourism*. London: International Institute for Environment and Development.

Rogers, M. E., Voysey, B. C., McDonald, K. E., Parnell, R. J. and Tutin, C. E. G. (1998). Lowland gorillas and seed dispersal: the importance of nest sites. *American Journal of Primatology*, **45**, 45–68.

Rohs, W. (1991). *The Environmental Impacts of Tourism in the Northern Selous Game Reserve*. Report to Selous Conservation Programme, Discussion Paper No 9.

Roosevelt, T. and Heller, E. (1922). *Life-histories of African Game Animals*. London: John Murray.

van Roosmalen, M. G. M. (1985). Habitat preferences, diet, feeding strategy and social organization of the black spider monkey (*Ateles paniscus paniscus* Linnaeus 1758) in Surinam. *Acta Amazonica*, **15 (Supplement)**, 1–238.

Roper, T. J. (1994). The European badger *Meles meles*: food specialist or generalist? *Journal of Zoology*, **234**, 437–452.

Rosenwig, M. L. and Lomolino, M. V. (1997). Who gets the short bits of the broken stick? In *The Biology of Rarity*, eds W. E. Kunin and K. J. Gaston, pp. 63–90. London: Chapman and Hall.

Rosenzweig, M. L. (1995). *Species Diversity in Space and Time*. Cambridge: Cambridge University Press.

Ross, I. C., Field, C. R. and Harrington, G. N. (1976). The savanna ecology of Kidepo Valley National Park, Uganda. *East African Wildlife Journal*, **14**, 35–48.

Round, P. D. (1988). *Resident Forest Birds in Thailand: Their Status and Conservation*. ICBP Monograph No. 2. Cambridge: International Council for Bird Preservation.

Rushton, S. P. (1988). The effects of scrub management regimes on the spider fauna of chalk grassland, Castor Hanglands NNR Cambridgeshire UK. *Biological Conservation*, **46**, 169–182.

Rushton, S. P., Barreto, G. R., Cormack, R. M., Macdonald, D. W. and Fuller, R. (submitted) Modelling dynamics of water vole (*Arvicola terrestris*) and the potential impacts of habitat fragmentation and mink (*Mustela vison*) predation on population viability in a GIS-defined landscape. *Journal of Applied Ecology*.

Rushton, S. P., Eyre, M. D. and Luff, M. L. (1990) The effects of scrub management on the ground beetles of oolitic limestone grassland at Castor Hanglands NNR, Cambridgeshire UK. *Biological Conservation*, **51**, 97–111.

Rushton, S. P., Lurz, P. W., Fuller, R. and Garson, P. J. (1997). Modelling the distribution of the red and grey squirrel at the landscape scale: a combined GIS and population dynamics approach. *Journal of Applied Ecology*, **34**, 1137–1154.

Russ, J. M., O'Neill, J. K. and Montgomery, W. I. (1998). Nathusius' pipistrelle bats (*Pipistrellus nathusii*, Keyserling and Blasius 1839) breeding in Ireland. *Journal of Zoology*, **245**, 345–349.

Russell, G. J., Brooks, T. M., McKinney, M. M. and Anderson, C. G (1998). Present and future taxonomic selectivity in bird and mammal extinctions. *Conservation Biology*, **12**, 1365–1377.

Rydell, J. and Swift, S. M. (1995). Observations of Nathusius' pipistrelle *Pipistrellus nathusii* in northeast Scotland. *Scottish Bats*, **3**, 6.

Ryder, O. A. and Feistner, A. T. C. (1995). Research in zoos: a growth area in conservation. *Biodiversity and Conservation*, **4**, 677.

Rylands, A. B. (1993–1994). Population viability analyses and the conservation of the lion tamarins, *Leontopithecus*, of south-east Brazil. *Primate Conservation*, **14–15**, 34–42.

Rylands, A. B., Mittermeier, R. A. and Luna, E. R. (1995). A species list for the new world primates (Platyrrhini): distribution by country, endemism, and conservation status according to the Mace-Lande system. *Neotropical Primates*, **3 (supplement)**, 113–160.

Ryti, R. T. (1992). Effect of the focal taxon on the selection of nature reserves. *Ecological Applications*, **2**, 404–410.

Saberwal, V. K. (1997). Saving the tiger: more money or less power? *Conservation Biology*, **11**, 815–817.

Santiapillai, C., Chambers, M. R. and Ishwaran, N. (1982). The leopard, *Panthera pardus fusca* (Meyer 1794), in the Ruhuna National Park, Sri Lanka, and observations relevant to its conservation. *Biological Conservation*, **23**, 5–14.

Santiapillai, C. and Jackson, P. (1990). *The Asian Elephant. An Action Plan for its Conservation*. Gland: IUCN.

Saunders, G., White, P. C. L., Rayner, J. M. V. and Harris, S. (1993). Urban foxes (*Vulpes vulpes*): food acquisition, time and energy budgeting of a generalised predator. *Symposia of the Zoological Society of London*, **65**, 215–234.

Sayer, J. (1992). A future for Africa's tropical forests. In *The Conservation Atlas of Tropical Forests. Africa*, eds J. A. Sayer, C. S. Harcourt and N. M. Collins, pp. 81–93. London: Macmilllan.

Sayer, J. (1996). A future for neotropical forests. In *The Conservation Atlas of Tropical Forests. The Americas*, eds C. S. Harcourt and J. A. Sayer, pp. 85–91. New York: Simon and Schuster.

Sayer, J. and Collins, M. (1991). A future for tropical forests. In *The Conservation Atlas of Tropical Forests. Asia and the Pacific*, eds N. M. Collins, J. A. Sayer and T. C. Whitmore, pp. 76–81. London: Macmilllan.

Schaller, G. (1972). *The Serengeti Lion: A Study of Predator–Prey Relations*. Chicago: University of Chicago Press.

Schaller, G. (1986). Secrets of the wild panda. *National Geographic*, **169**, 284–309.

Schaller, G. (1993). *The Last Panda*. Chicago: University of Chicago Press.

Schaller, G., Hu Jinchu, Pan Wenshi and Zhu Jing (1985). *The Giant Panda of Wolong*. Chicago: University of Chicago Press.

Schaller, G., Teng Qitao, Johnson, K., Wang Xiaoming, Shen Heming and Hu Jinchu (1989). The feeding ecology of giant panda and Asiatic black bear in the Tangjiahe Reserve, China. In *Carnivore Behavior, Ecology, Evolution*, ed. J. Gittleman, pp. 212–241. Ithaca: Cornell University Press.

Scheel, D., Vincent, T.L.S. and Cameron, G.N. (1996). Global warming and the species richness of bats in Texas. *Conservation Biology*, **10**, 452–464.

Schmidt, C. R., Mallinson, J. J. C. and Weilenman, P. (1978). International co-operation for captive breeding of the pygmy hog *Sus salvanius*. *International Zoo News*, **25**, 28–31.

Schofield, H. W. (1996). *The Ecology and Conservation Biology of* Rhinolophus hipposideros, *the Lesser Horseshoe Bat*. PhD thesis. Aberdeen: University of Aberdeen.

Schofield, H. W. (in press). Roosting, foraging ecology and landscape use of the lesser horseshoe bat, *Rhinolophus hipposideros*, in Britain. *Journal of Applied Ecology*.

Schofield, H. W., Greenaway, F. and Morris, C. J. (1997). Preliminary studies on Bechstein's bat. In *The Vincent Wildlife Trust Review of 1996*, pp. 71–74. London: The Vincent Wildlife Trust.

Scholey, G. (1993). NRA perspectives on and activities relating to otter conservation. In *Proceedings of the National Otter Conference*, ed. P. A. Morris, pp. 34–37. London: The Mammal Society.

Schreiber, A., Wirth, R., Riffel, M., and van Rompeay, H. (1989). *Weasels, Civets, Mongooses and their Relatives. An Action Plan for the Conservation of Mustelids and Viverrids*. Gland: IUCN.

Scott, J. M., Csuti, B., Jacobi, J. D. and Estes, J. E. (1987). Species richness. A geographic approach to protecting future biological diversity. *BioScience*, **37**, 782–788.

Scott, J. M., Davis, F., Csuti, B., Noss, R., Butterfield, B., Groves, C., Anderson, H., Caicco, S., D'Erchia, F., Edwards Jr, T. C., Ulliman, J. and Wright, R. G. (1993). Gap Analysis: a geographic approach to protection of biological diversity. *Wildlife Monographs*, **123**, 1–41.

Seal, U. S., Ballou, J. D. and Valladares-Padua, C. (eds) (1990). *Leontopithecus: Population Viability Analysis Workshop Report*. Apple Valley: Captive Breeding Specialist Group, IUCN Species Survival Commision.

Seal, U. S., Foose, T. J. and Ellis, S. (1994). Conservation Assessment and Management Plans (CAMPs) and Global Captive Action Plans (GCAPs). In *Creative Conservation: Interactive Management of Wild and Captive Animals*, eds P. J. S. Olney, G. M. Mace and A. T. C. Feistner, pp. 312–325. London: Chapman and Hall.

Selous, F. (1908). *African Nature Notes and Reminiscences*. London: Macmillan.

SEMP (Serengeti Ecological Monitoring Programme) (1988a). *Serengeti Ecological Monitoring Programme*. Programme Report March 1988.

SEMP (Serengeti Ecological Monitoring Programme) (1988b). *Serengeti Ecological Monitoring Programme*. Programme Report September 1988.

SEMP (Serengeti Ecological Monitoring Programme) (1989). *Serengeti Ecological Monitoring Programme. Elephant densities within Tanzanian Conservation Areas*. Report.

Servheen, C., Herrero, S. and Peyton, B. (1999). *Bears. Status Survey and Conservation Action Plan*. Gland: IUCN.

Shackleton, D. M. (ed.) (1997). *Wild Sheep and Goats and their Relatives. Status Survey and Conservation Action Plan for Caprinae*. Gland: IUCN.

Shawyer, C. R. (1987). *The Barn Owl in the British Isles – Its Past, Present and Future.* London: The Hawk Trust.

Sheppard, C. (1995). Propagation of endangered birds in US institutions: how much space is there? *Zoo Biology,* **14**, 197–210.

Shirt, D. B. (ed.) (1987). *British Red Data Books 2. Insects.* Peterborough: The Nature Conservancy Council.

Shore, R. F., Finnie, J. K., Horne, J., Rowland, A. P., Turk, A., Walker, L. A., Woods, C. and Wyatt, C. L. (1998). *Validation of the Mouse Oral Uptake (MORUP) and Toxicity Exposure Ratio (TER) Approaches for Predicting the Toxicity of Remedial Timber Treatments to Bats.* Contract report to the Health and Safety Executive. Huntingdon: Institute of Terrestrial Ecology.

Shore, R. F., Myhill, D. G., French, M. C., Leach, D. V. and Stebbings, R. E. (1991). Toxicity and tissue distribution of pentachlorophenol and permethrin in pipistrelle bats experimentally exposed to treated timber. *Environmental Pollution,* **73**, 101–118.

Short, J., Bradshaw, S. D., Giles, J., Prince, R. I. T. and Wilson, G. R. (1992). Reintroduction of macropods (Marsupialia: Macropodoidea) in Australia – a review. *Biological Conservation,* **62**, 189–204.

Sibley, C. G. and Munro, B. L. (1990). *Distribution and Taxonomy of Birds of the World.* New Haven: Yale University Press.

Siegfried, W. R., Benn, G. A. and Gelderblom, C. M. (1998). Regional assessment and conservation implications of landscape characteristics of African national parks. *Biological Conservation,* **84**, 131–140.

Silva, M., Brown, J. H. and Downing, J. A. (1997). Differences in population density and energy use between birds and mammals: a macroecological perspective. *Journal of Animal Ecology,* **66**, 327–340.

Simberloff, D. (1998a). Small and declining populations. In *Conservation Science and Action,* ed. W.J. Sutherland, pp. 116–134. Oxford: Blackwell Science.

Simberloff, D. (1998b). Flagships, umbrellas, and keystones: is single-species management passé in the landscape era? *Biological Conservation,* **83**, 247–257.

Simberloff, D. and Cox, J. (1987). Consequences of conservation corridors. *Conservation Biology,* **1**, 63–67.

Sinclair, I. and Whyte, I. (1991). *Field Guide to the Birds of the Kruger National Park.* Cape Town: Struik.

Sindiyo, D. M. and Pertet, F. N. (1984). Tourism and its impact on wildlife conservation in Kenya. *UNEP Industry and Environment,* **7**, 14–19.

Skinner, J. D. and Smithers, R. H. N. (1990). *The Mammals of the Southern African Subregion.* Pretoria: University of Pretoria.

Smith, A. P. and Quin, D. G. (1996). Patterns and causes of extinction and decline in Australian conilurine rodents. *Biological Conservation,* **77**, 243–267.

Smith, F. H. (1997). Some factors to consider in the conservation of the Drakensberg Water Catchment Area of KwaZulu–Natal. *South African Journal of Environmental Law and Policy,* **4**, 91–111.

Smithers, R. H. N. (1986). *South African Red Data Book – Mammals.* South African National Science Programme Report No. 125. Pretoria: Foundation for Research Development.

Snow, D. W. (1968). Movements and mortality of British kestrels *Falco tinnunculus. Bird Study,* **15**, 65–83.

Snyder, N. F. R., Derrickson, S. R., Beissinger, S. R., Wiley, J. W., Smith, T. B., Toone, W. D. and Miller, B. (1996). Limitations of captive breeding in endangered species recovery. *Conservation Biology*, **10**, 338–348.

Soorae, P. S. (1997). Update on hirola conservation introduction. *Re-introduction News*, **13**, 6–7.

Sotherton, N. W. (1998). Land use changes and the decline of farmland wildlife: an appraisal of the set-aside approach. *Biological Conservation*, **83**, 259–268.

Soulé, M. E. (1985). What is conservation biology? *Bio-Science*, **35**, 727–734.

Soulé, M. E. (ed) (1986). *Conservation Biology: The Science of Scarcity and Diversity.* Sunderland: Sinauer Associates.

Soulé, M. E. (ed.) (1987). *Viable Populations for Conservation.* Cambridge: Cambridge University Press.

Soulé, M. E., Gilpin, M., Conway, W. and Foose, T. (1986). The millennium ark: how long a voyage, how many staterooms, how many passengers? *Zoo Biology*, **5**, 101–113.

South, A. B., Rushton, S. P. and Macdonald, D. W. (in press). Simulating the proposed reintroduction of the European beaver *Castor fiber* to Scotland. *Biological Conservation*.

Speakman, J. R. and Racey, P. A. (1989). Hibernal ecology of the pipistrelle bat: energy expenditure, water requirements and mass loss, implications for survival and the function of winter emergence flights. *Journal of Animal Ecology*, **58**, 797–814.

Speakman, J. R., Racey, P. A., Hutson, A. M., Webb, P. I. and Burnett, A. M. (1991a). Status of Nathusius' pipistrelle (*Pipistrellus nathusii*) in Britain. *Journal of Zoology*, **225**, 685–690.

Speakman, J. R., Racey, P. A., McLean, J. and Entwistle, A. C. (1993). Six new records of Nathusius' pipistrelle *Pipistrellus nathusii* for Scotland. *Scottish Bats*, **2**, 14–16.

Speakman, J. R., Webb, P. I. and Racey, P. A. (1991b). Effects of disturbance on the energy expenditure of hibernating bats. *Journal of Applied Ecology*, **28**, 1087–1104.

Spellerberg, I. F. (1996). *Conservation Biology.* Harlow: Longmans.

Spinage, C. A., Guinness, F. E., Eltringham, S. K. and Woodford, M. H. (1972). Estimation of large mammal numbers in the Akagera National Park, Rwanda. *La Terre et Vie*, **1**, 561–570.

Stanley-Price, M. R. (1989). *Animal Reintroductions: The Arabian Oryx in Oman.* Cambridge: Cambridge University Press.

Stanley-Price, M. (1993). What will it take to save the rhino? In *Rhinoceros Biology and Conservation*, ed. O. Ryder. San Diego: Zoological Society of San Diego.

Stebbings, R. E. (1969). Observer influence on bat behaviour. *Lynx*, **10**, 79–84.

Stebbings, R. E. (1970). A bat new to Britain, *Pipistrellus nathusii* with notes on its identification and distribution in Europe. *Journal of Zoology*, **161**, 282–286.

Stebbings, R. E. (1971). Bats, their life and conservation. *Journal of the Devon Trust for Nature Conservation*, **3**, 29–36.

Stebbings, R. E. (1992). Mouse-eared bat – extinct in Britain? *Bat News*, **26**, 2–3.

Stebbings, R. E. and Arnold, H. R. (1987). Assessment of trends in size and structure of a colony of the greater horseshoe bat. *Symposia of the Zoological Society of London*, **58**, 7–24.

Stebbings, R. E. and Hutson, A. M. (1991). Mouse-eared bat *Myotis myotis*. In *The Handbook of British Mammals*, 3rd edition, eds G. B. Corbet and S. Harris, pp. 107–108. Oxford: Blackwell Scientific Publications.

Stebbings, R. E. and Jefferies, D. J. (1982). *Focus on Bats, their Conservation and the Law*. London: Nature Conservancy Council.

Stephenson, P. J. (1993). The small mammal fauna of Réserve Spéciale d'Analamazaotra, Madagascar: the effects of human disturbance on endemic species diversity. *Biodiversity and Conservation*, 2, 603–615.

Stephenson, P. J. (1994). Deforestation threatens the Tenrecidae of Madagascar. *Species*, 23, 66–67.

Stephenson, P. J. (1995). Small mammal microhabitat use in lowland rainforest of north-east Madagascar. *Acta Theriologica*, 40, 425–438.

Stephenson, P. J. and Racey, P. A. (1995). Reproductive energetics of the Insectivora. *Comparative Biochemistry and Physiology*, 112A, 215–223.

Stockil, C. (1997). *The Savé Conservancy in Zimbabwe: A Creative Approach to Sustainable Use Through a Private Initiative*. Paper presented to STAP Expert Group Meeting on Sustainable Use of Biological Diversity, Malaysia.

Stoms, D. M. (1994). Scale dependence of species richness maps. *Professional Geographer*, 46, 346–358.

Stone, D. (1995). *Eurasian Insectivores and Tree Shrews. Status Survey and Conservation Action Plan*. Gland: IUCN.

Stone, D., Ringwood, K. and Vorhies, F. (1997). *Business and Biodiversity: A Guide for the Private Sector*. Gland: World Business Council for Sustainable Development and IUCN.

Strachan, R. (1999). *A Handbook for Water Vole Conservation*. Oxford: Wildlife Conservation Research Unit.

Strachan, R. and Jeffries, D. J. (1993). *The Water Vole*, Arvicola terrestris, *in Britain 1989–90: Its Distribution and Changing Status*. London: The Vincent Wildlife Trust.

Strachan, R. and Jeffries, D. J. (1996). *A Report on the Decline and Recovery of the Otter in England and on its Distribution, Status and Conservation in 1991–94*. London: The Vincent Wildlife Trust.

Strahan, R. (ed.) (1991). *The Australian Museum Complete Book of Australian Mammals*. North Ryde: Cornstalk Publishing.

Strelkov, P. P. (1969). Migratory and stationary bats (Chiroptera) of the European part of the Soviet Union. *Acta Zoologica Cracoviensia*, 14, 393–440.

Strelkov, P. P. (1997a). Nursing area and its position within the range in migratory bats (Chiroptera: Vespertilionidae) from Eastern Europe and neighbouring regions Part 1. *Russian Journal of Zoology*, 1, 330–339.

Strelkov, P. P. (1997b). Nursing area and its position within the range in migratory bats (Chiroptera: Vespertilionidae) from Eastern Europe and neighbouring regions Part 2. *Russian Journal of Zoology*, 1, 545–553.

Strong, L. (1992). Avermectins: a review of their impact on insects in cattle dung. *Bulletin of Entomological Research*, 82, 265–274.

Struhsaker, T.T. (1998). A biologist's perspective on the role of sustainable harvest in conservation. *Conservation Biology*, 12, 930–932.

Stuart, S. N., Jensen, F. P., Brogger-Jensen, S. and Miller, R. I. (1993). The zoogeography of the montane forest avifauna of eastern Tanzania. In *Biogeography and*

Ecology of the Rain Forests of Eastern Africa, eds J. C. Lovett and S. K. Wasser, pp. 203–228. Cambridge: Cambridge University Press.

Suárez, E., Stallings, J. and Suárez, L. (1995). Small-mammal hunting by two ethnic groups in north-western Ecuador. *Oryx*, **29**, 35–42.

Sumption, K. J. and Flowerdew, J. R. (1985). The ecological effects of the decline in rabbits (*Oryctolagus cuniculus* L.) due to myxomatosis. *Mammal Review*, **15**, 151–186.

Sutherland, W. J. (1998). *Conservation Science in Action*. Oxford: Blackwell Science.

Swanepoel, R. E., Racey, P. A., Shore, R. F. and Speakman, J. R. (1999). Energetic effects of sub-lethal exposure to lindane on pipistrelle bats (*Pipistrellus pipistrellus*). *Environmental Pollution*, **104**, 169–177.

Swanson, T. (1997). *Global Action for Biodiversity*. London: Earthscan and IUCN.

Swift, S. M. (1997). The use of flyways by bats in Scotland. *Scottish Bats*, **4**, 36–37.

Symington, M. M. (1988). Environmental determinants of population densities in *Ateles*. *Primate Conservation*, **9**, 74–79.

Tapper, S. (1992). *Game Heritage – An Ecological Review From Shooting and Gamekeeping Records*. Fordinbridge: Game Conservancy Ltd.

Tattersall, F., Hart, B. J., Manley, W. J., Macdonald, D. W. and Feber, R. E. (1999). Small mammals on set-aside blocks and margins. *Aspects of Applied Biology*, **54**, 131–138.

Taylor, V. J. and Dunstone, N. (eds) (1996). *The Exploitation of Mammal Populations*. London: Chapman and Hall.

Teelen, S. (1996). *Tourism in the Kirindy Forest, Western Madagascar*. MSc thesis. Canterbury: University of Kent.

Temple, S. A. (1977). Plant-animal mutualism: co-evolution with dodo leads to near extinction of plant. *Science*, **197**, 885–886.

Terborgh, J. (1974). Preservation of natural diversity: the problem of extinction prone species. *Bioscience*, **24**, 715–722.

Terborgh, J. (1983). *Five New World Primates. A Study in Comparative Ecology*. New York: Princeton University Press.

Terborgh, J. (1986a). Community aspects of frugivory in tropical forests. In *Frugivores and Seed Dispersal*, eds A. Estrada and T. H. Fleming, pp. 371–384. Dordrecht: Dr W. Junk Publishers.

Terborgh, J. (1986b). Keystone plant resources in the tropical forest. In *Conservation Biology. The Science of Scarcity and Diversity*, ed. M. E. Soulé, pp. 330–344. Sunderland: Sinauer Associates.

Terborgh, J. (1988). The big things that run the world – a sequel to E. O. Wilson. *Conservation Biology*, **2**, 402–403.

Terborgh, J. (1992). *Tropical Deforestation*. Burlington: Carolina Biological Supply.

Terborgh, J. and van Schaik, C. P. (1997). Minimising species loss: the imperative of protection. In *Last Stand: Protected Areas and the Defense of Tropical Biodiversity*, eds R. Kramer, C. van Schaik, and J. Johnson, pp. 15–35. New York: Oxford University Press.

Terborgh, J. and Winter, B. (1980). Some causes of extinction. In *Conservation Biology: An Evolutionary Ecological Perspective*, eds M. E. Soulé and B. A. Wilcox, pp. 119–134. Sunderland: Sinauer Associates.

Terborgh, J. and Winter, B. (1983). A method for siting parks and reserves with special reference to Colombia and Ecuador. *Biological Conservation*, **27**, 45–58.

Thomas, C. D. and Harrison, S. (1992). Spatial dynamics of a patchily distributed butterfly species. *Journal of Animal Ecology*, **61**, 437–446.

Thomas, C. D. and Mallorie, H. C. (1985). Rarity, species richness and conservation: butterflies of the Atlas Mountains in Morocco. *Biological Conservation*, **33**, 95–117.

Thomas, D. (1995). Hibernating bats are sensitive to non tactile human disturbance. *Journal of Mammalogy*, **76**, 940–946.

Thomas, J. A. and Morris, M. G. (1994). Patterns, mechanisms and rates of extinction among invertebrates in the United Kingdom. *Philosophical Transactions of the Royal Society of London, Series B*, **344**, 47–54.

Thomas, W. W. and de Carvalho A. M. (1993). *Estudo fitosociologico de Serra Grand, Urucuca, Bahia*. Resumo vol 1: 224. XLIV Congresso Nacional de Botanica. Sao Luis: Universidade Federal do Maranhao.

Thompson, D. B. A., Macdonald, A. J., Marsden, J. H. and Galbraith, C. A. (1995). Upland heather moorland in Great Britain: a review of international importance, vegetation changes and some objective for nature conservation. *Biological Conservation*, **71**, 163–178.

Thorpe, I. C., Waters, D., Turner, A. T. and Gilby, L. (1988). *University of East Anglia Comoro Islands Expedition 1988*. Unpublished Report.

Thorsell, J. W. (ed.) (1990). *Parks on the Borderline: Experience in Transfrontier Conservation*. Gland: IUCN.

Tiffney, B. H. (1986). Evolution of seed dispersal syndromes according to the fossil record. In *Seed Dispersal*, ed. D. R. Murray, pp. 273–305. Australia: Academic Press.

Tilman, D., May, R. M., Lehman, C. L. and Nowack, M. A. (1994). Habitat destruction and the extinction debt. *Nature*, **371**, 65–66.

Tilson, R. and Nyhus, P. (1998). Keeping problem tigers from becoming a problem species. *Conservation Biology*, **12**, 261–262.

Timmins, R. J., Evans, D., Khounboline, K. and Sisomphone, C. (1998). Status and conservation of the giant muntjac *Megamuntiacus vuquangensis* and notes on other muntjac species in Laos. *Oryx*, **32**, 59–67.

Tinley, K. L. and van Riet, W. F. (1991). *Conceptual Proposals for Kruger/Banhine: A Transfrontier Natural Resource Area*. Prepared for South African Nature Foundation.

Tisdell, C. A. (1982). *Wild Pigs: Environmental Pest or Economic Resource*. Oxford: Pergamon Press.

TNC (The Nature Conservancy) (1997). *Priorities for Conservation: 1997 Annual Report Card for US Plant and Animal Species*. Arlington: The Nature Conservancy.

Tobin, R. (1990). *The Expendable Future: US Politics and the Protection of Biological Diversity*. Durham: Duke University Press.

du Toit, R. (1996). Modern Technology for rhino management. *Pachyderm*, **22**, 18–24.

Tomlinson, D. (1996). Ospreys for the Millennium. *Natural World*, **47**, 22–23.

Towns, D. R. and Williams, M. (1993). Single-species conservation in New Zealand: towards a refined conceptual approach. *Journal of Royal Society of New Zealand*, **23**, 61–78.

Trent, S. (1999). Interpreting current levels of poaching of African elephants. *Oryx*, **33**, 94–95.

Trewhella, W. J., Reason, P. F., Bullock, R. J., Carroll, J. B., Clark, C. C. M., Davies, J. G., Saw, R., Wray, S. and Young, J. (1995). Conservation of *Pteropus livingstonii*: catching fruit bats in the Comoros (western Indian Ocean). *Myotis*, **32–33**, 297–305.

Tudge, C. (1992). *Last Animals at the Zoo. How Mass Extinction Can Be Stopped.* Oxford: Oxford University Press.

Turpie, J. K. and Crowe, T. M. (1994). Patterns of distribution, diversity and endemism of larger African mammals. *South African Journal of Zoology*, **29**, 19–32.

Tyler, P. A. (1996). Endemism in freshwater algae. *Hydrobiologia*, **336**, 127–135.

UK Round Table on Sustainable Development (1998). *Business and Biodiversity*. Oxford: Earthwatch.

Usher, M. B. (1986). *Wildlife Conservation Evaluation*. London: Chapman and Hall.

Vander Wall, S. B. (1993). Cache site selection by chipmunks (*Tamias* spp.) and its influence on the effectiveness of seed dispersal in Jeffrey pine (*Pinus jeffreyi*). *Oecologia*, **96**, 246–252.

Vane-Wright, R. I., Humphries, C. J. and Williams, P. H. (1991). What to protect? Systematics and the agony of choice. *Biological Conservation*, **55**, 235–254.

Veltman, C. J., Nee, S. and Crawley, M. J. (1996). Correlates of introduction success in New Zealand birds. *American Naturalist*, **147**, 542–557.

Verboom, B. and van Apeldoorn, R. (1990). Effects of habitat fragmentation on the red squirrel, *Sciurus vulgaris* L. *Landscape Ecology*, **4**, 171–176.

Verboom, B. and Huitema, H. (1997). The importance of linear landscape elements for the pipistrelle *Pipistrellus pipistrellus* and the serotine bat *Eptesicus serotinus*. *Landscape Ecology*, **12**, 117–125.

Verner, P. H., Hajek, I. and Rejmanek, M. (1984). Uganda kob and other large mammals. In *Ecological Study of Toro Game Reserve with Special Regard to the Uganda Kob*, eds P. H. Verner and J. Jenik, pp. 34–61. Prague: Academia Nakladatelstvi Ceskoslovenske.

de Villiers, N. N. (1994). *The Open Africa Initiative*. Claremont: Open Africa Initiative.

Vorhies, D. and Vorhies, F. (1993). *Introducing Lion into Pilanesberg: An Economic Assessment*. South Africa: National Parks Board.

Voûte, A. M. and Lina, P. H. C. (1986). Management effects on bat hibernacula in the Netherlands. *Biological Conservation*, **38**, 163–177.

Walsh, A. L. and Harris, S. (1996a). Foraging habitat preferences of vespertilionid bats in Britain. *Journal of Applied Ecology*, **33**, 508–518.

Walsh, A. L. and Harris, S. (1996b). Factors determining the abundance of vespertilionid bats in Britain: Geographic, land class, and local habitat relationships. *Journal of Applied Ecology*, **33**, 519–529.

Walsh, A. L., Harris, S. and Hutson, A. M. (1995). Abundance and habitat selection of foraging vespertilionid bats in Britain: a landscape-scale approach. *Symposia of the Zoological Society of London*, **67**, 325–344.

Ward, P. I., Mosberger, N., Kistler, C. and Fischer, O. (1998). The relationship between popularity and body size in zoo animals. *Conservation Biology*, **12**, 1408–1411.

Webb, N. R. (1989). Studies on the invertebrate fauna of fragmented heathland in Dorset, UK, and implications for conservation. *Biological Conservation*, **47**, 153–165.

Wells, M. and Brandon, K. (1992). *People and Parks. Linking Protected Area Management with Local Communities.* Washington, DC: The World Bank.

Wells, M., Guggenheim, S., Khan, A., Wardojo, W. and Jepson, P. (1999). *Investing in Biodiversity: A Review of Indonesia's Integrated Conservation and Development Projects.* Washington, DC: The World Bank.

Weltzin, J. F., Archer, S. and Heitschmidt, R. K. (1997). Small-mammal regulation of vegetation structure in a temperate savanna. *Ecology,* **78**, 751–763.

Wemmer, C. (ed.) (1998). *Deer. Status Survey and Conservation Action Plan.* Gland: IUCN.

Werikhe, S., Mushenzi, N. and Bizimana, J. (1997). *The Impact of War on Protected Areas in Central Africa: Case Study of the Virunga Volcanoes Region.* Paper presented at Peace Parks Conference, Cape Town.

Western, D. (1969). Amboseli. *Africana,* **3**, 17–20.

Western, D. (1973). *The Structure, Dynamics and Changes of the Amboseli Ecosystem.* PhD thesis. Nairobi: University of Nairobi.

Western, D. (1979). Size, life history and ecology in mammals. *African Journal of Ecology.* **17**, 185–204.

Western, D. (1984). Amboseli National Park: human values and the conservation of a savanna ecosystem. In *National Parks, Conservation and Development: The Role of Protected Areas in Sustaining Society,* eds J. A. McNeely and K. R. Miller, pp. 93–100. Washington, DC: Smithsonian Institution Press.

Western, D. (1987). Africa's elephants and rhinos: flagships in crisis. *TREE,* **2**, 343–345.

Western, D. (1991). Climatic change and biodiversity. In *A Change in the Weather: African Perspectives on Climate Change,* eds S. H. Ominde and C. Juma, pp. 87–96. Nairobi: African Centre for Technology Studies Press.

Western, D. (1992). Patterns of depletion in a Kenya rhino population and the conservation implications. *Biological Conservation,* **24**, 147–156.

Western, D. (1994). Ecosystem conservation and rural development: the case of Amboseli. In *Natural Connections: Perspectives in Community-based Conservation,* eds D. Western, R. M. Wright and S. C. Strum, pp. 15–52. Washington, DC: Island Press.

Western, D. and Lindsay, K. (1984). Seasonal herd dynamics of a savanna elephant population. *African Journal of Ecology,* **22**, 229–244.

Western, D. and Pearl, M. (1989). *Conservation for the Twenty-first Century.* New York: Oxford University Press.

Western, D. and Vigne, L. (1985). The deteriorating status of African rhinos. *Oryx,* **19**, 215–220.

Western, D. and Wright, R. M. (eds) (1994). *Natural Connections: Perspectives in Community- based Conservation.* Washington, DC: Island Press.

Westing, A. H. (1992). Protected natural areas and the military. *Environmental Conservation,* **19**, 343–348.

Westing, A. H. (1993). Building confidence with transfrontier reserves: the global potential. In *Transfrontier Reserves for Peace and Nature: A Contribution to Human Security,* ed. A. H. Westing, pp. 1–15. Nairobi: United Nations Environment Programme.

Westley, F. and Vredenburg, H. (1997). Interorganizational collaboration and the preservation of global biodiversity. *Organization Science,* **8**, 381–403.

Wharton, C. (1966). Man, fire, and wild cattle in north Cambodia. *Proceedings of the Annual Tall Timbers Fire Ecology Conference*, 5, 23–65.

Wharton, C. (1968). Man, fire, and wild cattle in Southeast Asia. *Proceedings of the Annual Tall Timbers Fire Ecology Conference*, 8, 107–167.

Wharton, D., Pearl, M. and Koontz, F. (1988). Minutes from a lemur conservation workshop. *Primate Conservation*, 9, 41–48.

Whitbread, A. and Jenman, W. (1995). A natural method of conserving biodiversity in Britain. *British Wildlife*, 7, 84–93.

Whitby, J. E., Johnstone, P., Parsons, G., King, A. A. and Hutson, A. M. (1996). Ten-year survey of British bats for the existence of rabies. *Veterinary Record*, 139, 491–493.

White, P. C. L., Gregory, K. W., Lindley, P. J. and Richards, G. (1997). Economic values of threatened mammals in Britain: a case study of the otter *Lutra lutra* and the water vole *Arvicola terrestris*. *Biological Conservation*, 82, 345–354.

Whitehouse, P., Crane, M., Redshaw, J. and Turner, C. (1996). Aquatic toxicology tests for the control of effluent discharges in the UK – the influence of test precision. *Ecotoxicology*, 5, 155–168.

Whitmore, T. C. (1984). *Tropical Rain Forests of the Far East*, 2nd edition. Oxford: Clarendon.

Whitmore, T. C. and Sayer, J. A. (eds) (1992). *Tropical Deforestation and Species Extinction*. London: Chapman and Hall.

Wiese, R. J., Willis, K., Bowdoin, J. and Hutchins, M. (eds) (1993). *AAZPA Annual Report on Conservation and Science 1992–1993*. Bethesda: American Association of Zoological Parks and Aquaria.

Wijnstekers, W. (1995). *The Evolution of CITES*, 4th edition. Geneva: CITES Secretariat.

Wikramanayake, E. D., Dinerstein, E., Robinson, J. G., Karanth, U. D., Rabinowitz, A., Olson, D., Mathew, T., Hedao, M., Hemley, G. and Bolze, D. (1998). An ecology-based method for defining priorities for large mammal conservation: the tiger as a case study. *Conservation Biology*, 12, 865–878.

Williams, G. (1997). Africa in retrospect and prospect. In *Africa South of the Sahara 1997*, pp. 3–10. London: Europa Publications.

Williams, P. H. (1996). *WORLDMAP 4 WINDOWS: Software and Help Document 4.1*. Distributed privately and from http://www.nhm.ac.uk/science/projects/worldmap, London.

Williams, P. H. (1998). Key sites for conservation: area-selection methods for biodiversity. In *Conservation in a Changing World: Integrating Processes into Priorities for Action*, eds G. M. Mace, A. Balmford and J. R. Ginsberg, pp. 211–249. Cambridge: Cambridge University Press.

Williams, P. and Gaston, K. J. (1994). Measuring more of biodiversity: can higher-taxon richness predict wholesale species richness? *Biological Conservation*, 67, 211–217.

Williams, P. H. and Gaston, K. J. (1998). Biodiversity indicators: graphical techniques, smoothing and searching for what makes relationships work. *Ecography*, 21, 551–560.

Williams, P., Gibbons, D., Margules, C., Rebelo, A., Humphries, C. and Pressey, R. (1996a). A comparison of richness hotspots, rarity hotspots, and complimentary areas for conserving diversity of British birds. *Conservation Biology*, 10, 155–174.

Williams, P. H. and Humphries, C. J. (1994). Biodiversity, taxonomic relatedness and endemism in conservation. In *Systematics and Conservation Evaluation*, eds P. L. Forey, C. J. Humphries and R. I. Vane-Wright, pp. 269–287. Oxford: Oxford University Press.

Williams, P. H., Humphries, C. J. and Gaston, K. J. (1994). Centres of seed plant diversity: the family way. *Proceedings of the Royal Society of London, Series B*, **256**, 67–70.

Williams, P. H., Prance, G. T., Humphries, C. J. and Edwards, K. S. (1996b). Promise and problems in applying quantitative complementary areas for representing the diversity of some Neotropical plants (families Dichapetalaceae, Lecythidaceae, Caryocaraceae, Chrysobalanaceae and Proteaceae). *Biological Journal of the Linnean Society*, **58**, 125–127.

Willis, E. O. (1974). Populations and local extinctions of birds on Barro Colorado Island, Panama. *Ecological Monographs*, **44**, 153–169.

Willson, M. F. (1986). Avian frugivory and seed dispersal in eastern North America. *Current Ornithology*, **3**, 223–279.

Willson, M. F., Irvine, A. K. and Walsh, N. G. (1989). Vertebrate dispersal syndromes in some Australian and New Zealand plant communities, with geographic comparisons. *Biotropica*, **21**, 133–147.

Wilson, A. C., and Stanley Price, M. R. (1994). Reintroduction as a reason for captive breeding. In *Creative Conservation: Interactive Management of Wild and Captive Animals*, eds P. J. S. Olney, G. M. Mace and A. T. C. Feistner, pp. 243–264. London: Chapman and Hall.

Wilson, D., Cole, F., Nichols, J., Rudran, R. and Foster, M. (1996). *Measuring and Monitoring Biological Diversity: Standard Methods for Mammals*. Washington, DC: Smithsonian Institution Press.

Wilson, D. E. and Reeder, D. M. (eds) (1993). *Mammal Species of the World: A Taxonomic and Geographic Reference*. Washington, DC: Smithsonian Institution Press.

Wilson, E. O. (1988). *Biodiversity*. Washington, DC: National Academy Press.

Wilson, E. O. (1992). *The Diversity of Life*. Cambridge: The Belknap Press of Harvard University Press.

Wilson, G., Harris, S. and McLaren, G. (1997). *Changes in the British Badger Population, 1988 to 1997*. London: People's Trust for Endangered Species.

Wolf, C. M., Griffith, B., Reed, C. and Temple, S. A. (1996). Avian and mammalian translocations: update and reanalysis of 1987 survey data. *Conservation Biology*, **10**, 1142–1154.

Woodford, M. H. and Rossiter, P. B. (1993). Disease risks associated with wildlife translocation projects. *Revue Scientifique et Technique Office International des Epizooties*, **12**, 115–135.

Woodroffe, R. and Ginsberg, J. (1998). Edge effects and the extinction of populations inside protected areas. *Science*, **280**, 2126–2128.

Woodroffe, R. B., Ginsberg, J. R. and Macdonald, D. W. (1997). *The African Wild Dog: Status Survey and Conservation Action Plan*. Gland: IUCN.

World Bank, The (1996a). *Mozambique. Transfrontier Conservation Areas Pilot and Institutional Strengthening Project*. Report No.15534–MOZ, Agriculture and Environment Division, Southern Africa Department, The World Bank. Washington, DC: World Bank.

World Bank, The (1996b). *Mainstreaming Biodiversity in Agricultural Development. Toward Good Practice.* Washington, DC: World Bank.

World Bank, The (1997). *Nicaragua Atlantic Biological Corridor Project.* Project document. Washington, DC: World Bank.

WRI (World Resources Institute) (1994). *World Resources 1994–95.* Oxford: Oxford University Press.

Wright, S. (1931). Evolution in Mendelian populations. *Genetics,* **16**, 97–159.

WTO (World Tourism Organisation) (1996). *Compendium of Tourism Statistics 1991–1995.* Madrid: World Tourism Organisation.

WTO (World Tourism Organisation) (1998). *Yearbook of Tourism Statistics: 50th Edition.* Madrid: World Tourism Organisation.

WTO and UNEP (World Tourism Organisation and United Nations Environment Programme) (1992). *Guidelines: Development of National Parks and Protected Areas for Tourism.* Report to World Tourism Organisation, Madrid.

WTTC (World Travel and Tourism Council) (1994). *Travel and Tourism: Progress and Priorities.* London: World Travel and Tourism Council.

WWF (WorldWide Fund for Nature) (1996a). *Forests for Life – The WWF/IUCN Forest Policy Book.* Godalming: WWF-UK.

WWF (1996b). *WWF's Global Conservation Programme 1996/7.* Ed. E. Kemf. Gland: WWF International.

van Wyk, A. E. (1996). Biodiversity of the Maputaland centre. In *The Biodiversity of African Plants,* eds L. J. G. van der Mensen, X. M. van der Burgt and J. M. van Medenbach de Rooy, pp. 198–207. Dordrecht: Kluwer Academic Publishers.

Wynne, G., Avery, A., Campbell, L., Gubbay, S., Hawkswell, S., Juniper, T., King, M., Newberry, P., Smart, J., Steel, C., Stones, T., Stubbs, A., Taylor, J., Tydeman, C. and Wynde, R. (1995). *Biodiversity Challenge,* 2nd edition. Sandy: Royal Society for the Protection of Birds.

Wynne, G., Avery, M., Campbell, L., Juniper, T., King, M., Smart, J., Steel, C., Stones, A., Stubbs, A., Taylor, J., Tydeman, C. and Wynde, R. (1993). *Biodiversity Challenge.* Sandy: Royal Society for the Protection of Birds.

Xie Zhong and Gibbs, J. (1997). *The Giant Panda Studbook.* Beijing: Chinese Association of Zoological Gardens.

Yajima, M. (1991). The insect ecological land at Tama Zoo. *International Zoo Yearbook,* **30**, 7–15.

Yalden, D. W. (1986). Opportunities for reintroducing British mammals. *Mammal Review,* **16**, 53–63.

Yalden, D. W. (1991). History of the Fauna. In *The Handbook of British Mammals,* 3rd edition, eds G. B. Corbet and S. Harris, pp. 7–18. Oxford: Blackwell Science.

Yalden, D. W. (1993). The problems of reintroducing carnivores. In *Mammals as Predators,* eds N. Dunstone and M. L. Gorman, pp. 289–306. Oxford: Clarendon.

Yalden, D. W. (1999). *The History of British Mammals.* London: Poyser.

Young, H. G. and Smith, J. G. (1989). The search for the Madagascar pochard *Aythya innotata*: Survey of Lac Alaotra, Madagascar October–November, 1989. *Dodo, Journal of the Jersey Wildlife Preservation Trusts,* **26**, 17–34.

Young, J. A., Saw, R., Trewhella, W. J. and Cole, C. J. (1993). Establishing a captive breeding programme for the endangered Livingstone's fruit bat *Pteropus livin-*

gstonii: The 1993 capture expedition. *Dodo, Journal of the Wildlife Preservation Trusts,* **29**, 22–33.

Young, T. P. (1994). Natural die-offs of large mammals: implications for conservation. *Conservation Biology,* **8**, 410–418.

Zebu, E. H. and Bush, M. L. (1990). Park-people relationships: an international review. *Landscape and Urban Planning,* **19**, 117–131.

Zhu Xiaojian (1996). *Vocalization Analysis of the Giant Panda Cubs.* MSc Thesis. Beijing: Peking University.

Zimen, E. and Boitani, L. (1979). Status of the wolf in Europe and the possibilities of conservation and reintroduction. In *The Behavior and Ecology of Wolves: Proceedings of the Symposium on the Behavior and Ecology of Wolves held on 23–24 May 1975 at the Annual Meeting of the Animal Behavior Society in Wilmington, North Carolina,* ed. E. Klinghammer, pp. 43–83. New York: STPM Press.

Index